Gatekeepers to the Franchise

Gatekeepers
to the Franchise

Shaping Election Administration in New York

Ronald Hayduk

NORTHERN

ILLINOIS

UNIVERSITY

PRESS

DeKalb

© 2005 by Northern Illinois University Press

Published by the Northern Illinois University Press, DeKalb, Illinois 60115

Manufactured in the United States using acid-free paper

All Rights Reserved

Design by Julia Fauci

Library of Congress Cataloging-in-Publication Data

Hayduk, Ronald, 1958–

Gatekeepers to the franchise : shaping election administration in New York /
Ronald Hayduk.

   p.   cm.

Includes bibliographical references (p.) and index.

ISBN-13: 978-0-87580-341-8 (hardcover : acid-free paper)

ISBN-10: 0-87580-341-5 (hardcover : acid-free paper)

1. Elections—New York (State)—History. 2. Election law—New York (State)—History.
3. Voter registration—New York (State)—History. 4. Elections—New York (State)—
New York—History. 5. Election law—New York (State)—New York—History.
6. Voter registration—New York (State)—New York—History. I. Title.

JK3490.H39 2005

324.6'5'09747—dc22

2005001380

To Susanna

Contents

Acknowledgments

There are many people and organizations I wish to thank who made this study possible: the thousands of voting rights and community-based activists across the United States and in New York who work with incredible determination to realize the promise of democracy, particularly members of the New York Coalition for Voter Participation, Neil Rosenstein, Gene Russianoff, Louise Altman, and Steve Carbo; members of the administration of Mayor David Dinkins, especially J. Philip Thompson; staff of the New York City Council, especially Marc Lapidus; the many good-hearted and hard-working elections officials, including Tom Wilkey, Danny DeFrancisco, Jon Del Giorno, Douglass Kellner, and Jerome Koenig; the staff of the Voter Assistance Commission during my time there, Dirk Slater, Jocelyn Sargent, and Besty Colon-Diaz; financial and research support provided by the Century Foundation, the National Association for the Advancement of Colored People Legal Defense and Education Fund, Demos, and the Borough of Manhattan Community College; research assistance by Josh Klein, Jason Tarricone, and Troy Wass; my teachers who taught me to think critically about politics and elections, including John Mollenkopf, Ned Schneier, Marshall Berman, and Frances Fox Piven, who encouraged me to pursue this line of research; editorial assistance from Daniel Holt, Stephanie Nilva, Melody Herr, and especially Meg Cox, whose skillful copyediting made this a better book; my family and friends who provided invaluable encouragement and myriad support; and most importantly, my beloved wife, Susanna Jones, who provided incalculable emotional and material support—from tirelessly editing several versions of this book which vastly improved it, to giving me needed inspiration to bring this work to life (at the same time she gave birth to our daughter, Rita). Many thanks to you all.

Gatekeepers to the Franchise

Introduction

The 2000 Election

WHY ELECTION ADMINISTRATION MATTERS

On January 20, 2001, George W. Bush was inaugurated under a cloud of suspicion and uncertainty. The hotly disputed 2000 election left the world wondering whether Bush was legitimately elected. The sight of elections officials recounting ballots in Florida, resulting in weekly and even daily changes in vote totals over the thirty-six days of prolonged partisan wrangling and legal hairsplitting, raised serious doubts about whether Bush really won. The integrity of U.S. elections was brought into question, undermining our belief in the authenticity of our entire democratic system. The richest and most technologically advanced nation in the world, which prides itself on fostering democracy around the globe, resembled a poor developing country with dubious election practices that produce questionable results. Florida laid bare America's antiquated voting technologies, poor training and underpayment of poll workers, and partisanship and lack of professionalism among elections officials, who employ widely varying election methods and practices. A spotlight was cast on America's flawed election apparatus, which, whether by design or default, was shown to routinely disenfranchise millions of Americans.

One of the important lessons of the 2000 presidential election is that the manner in which elections are conducted can significantly affect voter participation, political outcomes, and politics. The unexpectedly protracted debacle in Florida evoked doubt about the personnel, practices, and technologies integral to elections and revealed wide variation in rules and procedures between and even within states. Scrutiny of election procedures in Florida and other states brought into focus the ways in which different election rules and practices can disenfranchise eligible voters or, on the other hand, facilitate voting. In either case, they affect electoral outcomes. This is why election administration can become the focus of sharp conflict, especially in close and contested races.

While scholars have debated the degree to which election rules and practices can affect the participation of certain constituencies, politicians apparently believe that the rules of the game can shape the outcome, as evidenced by the pitched battles public officials wage over election law and practice. The 2000 debacle starkly exposed the political motives and special interests of the contenders, who fought bitterly over election procedures, but the machinery—literally and figuratively—that governs elections was the object of partisan conflict well before the terms *hanging chad* and *butterfly ballot* became household words, precisely because these parts of the electoral system have the potential to determine political fortunes. For example, the imposition of various restrictions on the franchise throughout America's history, such as poll taxes and literacy tests, severely constricted voter turnout, especially among poor and minority voters. Conversely, the provision of greater access to voting, such as through election-day registration, produced greater turnout. Because the stakes are high, the struggles over these electoral rules can be quite bitter, and they are almost always partisan.

For students of election administration, Florida was an electoral time bomb waiting to explode. Widespread dissection of election rules and practices during the limbo period revealed to the public not only that election administration matters, but also that what happened in Florida could happen anywhere. It took an extraordinary crisis in which the presidential outcome hung in the balance of election minutiae to make this clear.[1] The revelation that details of election administration could hold implications for national politics was astounding. For instance, the varying criteria that elections officials used in separate counties to determine whether punch cards with dimpled chads would count as valid votes; the debate over whether there should be a recount of ballots statewide or only in specific counties; the question of whether voters in Palm Beach were misled by the design of the butterfly ballot; the possibility that thousands of suspected felons, found to be disproportionately black and therefore likely Gore voters, were wrongfully purged from the voter rolls; the dispute over whether overseas military ballots, likely to be votes for Bush, could be counted if they were postmarked after the official deadline; and many other peculiarities were important to the outcome. All of these issues created chaos in the system and revealed that decisions on these matters, made by partisan elections officials, can determine who wins and who loses. Al Gore's attorneys advocated for the application of a single set of election standards and argued that every vote must be counted, while George W. Bush's team advocated for another set of standards and sought to prevent a statewide recount. This showed that high political stakes are involved in election administration.

Election rules and administration—like other aspects of government—are contested terrain. They are products of contending political actors and interests, and they embody the gains of the victors. To the extent that elections are concerned with the struggle over power—who gets what, when, how—rules and institutions that influence patterns of electoral participation are the results of such struggles. The reason for this is simple. Given their capacity to influence outcomes, electoral arrangements have been especially susceptible to political contestation and manipulation. As Florida 2000 illustrates—and as this case study of New York demonstrates—such dynamics are abundantly evident in election administration.

Dominant political actors—of both major parties—resist outsiders, whether as candidates or new and unpredictable voters, inasmuch as they have incumbency interests and seek to maintain a stable and constricted electorate and party system. Dominant political actors are represented on election boards and are generally served by the practices of those boards. In most places the boards are staffed by political appointees of the two major parties, and in some jurisdictions chief election officers are elected partisans.[2] In both circumstances employees of election boards are closely tied to and dependent upon dominant politicians and political parties. Boards of elections are vestiges of the fabled political machines, and they continue to contribute to a distinct but persistent form of machine politics. In short, election boards—like the corpus of election law they are mandated to implement—essentially function as an extension of the party system.

Because election administration in the United States is decentralized, with effectively little or no federal oversight, state and local election boards have considerable latitude in the implementation of electoral law. Elections officials have wide discretionary authority, and election practices vary greatly from one board to another and from one state to another. Since elections officials are beholden to the dominant politicians and parties, who are empowered to hire and fire them, their practices reflect these concrete political relations. This explains why even the most sacrosanct and seemingly insulated election procedures and agencies can become the focus of sharp partisan conflict, particularly when elections are close and contested.

Since the 2000 presidential election, a spate of reports and studies have surfaced showing that similar election problems exist around the country, suggesting that millions of would-be voters are routinely disenfranchised in nearly every election.[3] As these studies show—and as this book demonstrates in detail about New York—specific election practices and technologies can function to disenfranchise eligible citizens at every stage: before an election, on election day, and during vote tabulation/certification. This is especially true for low-income individuals, minorities, newly naturalized citizens, people with disabilities, and first-time voters—groups that have disproportionately low voter-turnout rates.[4] For years voting rights advocates and some elections experts have been complaining about the disenfranchising consequences of an antiquated electoral system. What has come to light is that elections are susceptible to the impact of both faulty election systems and political manipulation. What occurred in Florida was merely the most intense and highly scrutinized chapter of a larger story, one that is sure to continue to receive attention as state and local governments implement various election reforms.

Contrary to the prevailing view that the 2004 elections ran relatively smoothly, election problems were more abundant than during the 2000 debacle. If the margin of Bush's lead in Ohio had been closer—Bush led

Kerry by more than 136,000 votes out of 5.6 million cast on the evening of the election—the country would have woken up to a protracted version of Florida 2000. Instead, the 2004 election just "exceeded the margin of litigation."[5]

Because the 2004 election was expected to be closely contested and had the potential to produce Florida 2000–like scenarios, scrutiny ran high, and a wide range of voting rights organizations, civic groups, and partisan campaigns mounted massive monitoring operations and documented a host of problems before, during, and after the election.[6] They found that voters faced the same kinds of problems seen in previous elections, including poll sites opening late, voters not receiving absentee ballots, registered voters' names not appearing on registration rolls, voting machine shortages and failures, confusion over poll site changes, understaffed poll sites, long lines, poll workers asking for identification that was not required, organized voter intimidation and vote suppression, and provisional ballot confusion and shortages. With higher turnout in 2004 (59%, up from 51% in 2000), and with new voting technologies and changes in certain election procedures, a larger number of voters faced problems than in previous elections. Hundreds of thousands (perhaps millions) of eligible voters were disenfranchised.[7] Revelations about problems were extensive enough to prompt two federal agencies, the Government Accountability Office (GAO) and the Election Assistance Commission (EAC), to undertake unprecedented nationwide investigations.[8]

Most disturbing is that many of the problems seen in 2004 resulted from partisan maneuvering by elections and campaign officials who shaped election rules and practices, knowing their potential to affect outcomes in this high-stakes contest. "At every step of the way, elections officials in key states threw up unnecessary barriers to voting. Voter registration was made more difficult than ever. Officials misconstrued and abused identification and provisional ballot rules. There were far too few voting machines in some places, leading to unacceptable wait times, and there were suspicious vote machine 'errors.' Moreover, not surprisingly given the atmosphere, there were enormous numbers of allegations of voter intimidation and vote suppression."[9]

Despite all this, election administration problems remain a largely opaque, even mysterious, subject. The last attempt to analyze election administration in the United States, conducted by Joseph P. Harris and published in 1934, was a fairly thorough but flawed treatment of the subject.[10] Harris was a key figure in the political reform movement during the twentieth century. He held important positions in the National Municipal League, a prominent reform organization that successfully advanced critical changes to state and local governments. Harris was not an unbiased player; like the League, he had vested political interests. Together they were key players in successfully establishing model voter registration procedures and bipartisan boards of elections, among other reforms.

There has been no systematic scholarly treatment of the subject of electoral administration since Harris's 1934 study. Although the General Accounting Office did survey election administrators across the country following the 2000 presidential election, producing a useful compendium, it does not assess the impact of particular election practices on different constituencies and political outcomes; nor does it address the politics of election administration.[11] Research on voting behavior and electoral systems is essentially devoid of analysis of election administration. Until the events in Florida in 2000, political scientists did not deem its workings worthy of even passing mention, let alone serious study. Perhaps this is because boards of elections have generally been viewed as irrelevant to issues of voter participation.

No doubt the dominance of pluralist theory contributed to this lack of interest in and inquiry into election administration. Pluralism posits that government is a neutral arbiter among competing and contending interests, and this is the way election administration is usually depicted. Indeed, such a depiction of boards of elections as neutral administrators fits neatly within the narrative of the historical genesis of election administration in the United States during the late nineteenth century, a narrative that Harris and other Progressive era reformers promoted. Boards of elections, when mentioned at all, are usually described as performing the mundane administrative operations of implementing electoral law. They are generally assumed to provide for the integrity of the ballot and to ensure that elections are fair and free of fraud. In reality, allegations that election fraud was rampant, widely heard in the decades around the turn of the twentieth century, were the main stated justification for the inauguration of voter registration procedures and bipartisan boards of elections. The fear of fraud continues to be the primary stated reason against liberalizing electoral law and dispensing with restrictive practices of boards of elections. The bipartisan structure of boards of elections is founded on the notion that each party will check and balance the other, thereby ensuring a fair process. According to most characterizations of election administration, boards of elections have a negligible influence on participation and politics, or are neutral in that regard.[12]

But such a view is flawed, in regard to both the origins and the contemporary operations of election boards. Their legal mandate and stated mission to safeguard the ballot from fraud—accomplished with measures such as restrictive voter registration procedures—is largely a product of the work of elite Progressive era reformers. While certainly some election fraud did occur (and still does), charges about it appear to be wildly overblown.[13] Even so, charges of fraud, whether intentional or not, were the basis for establishing a host of restrictive election procedures that continue to have significant disenfranchising consequences, especially for lower-strata groups. Fraud charges served to justify the creation and institutionalization of restrictive voting practices that mask and perpetuate a more insidious form of fraud: administrative disenfranchisement of eligible voters.

History is a good teacher. There is general agreement among scholars that poll taxes and literacy tests disenfranchised most African Americans and many poor whites between the end of Reconstruction and 1965. The motives and techniques underlying these tactics, particularly as implemented by elections officials in the South, are clear and widely acknowledged. Ironically, similar disenfranchising measures enacted in the North are not as universally recognized for what they were; these include restrictive voter registration procedures and other stringent practices of boards of elections.[14]

There are troublesome tensions inherent in election administration. One is its twin mission: to guard against vote fraud *and* to provide access to the ballot. Procedures designed to safeguard the ballot—such as voter registration—can limit opportunities to vote, or worse, disenfranchise voters. Reform of election procedures that aims to expand voting has often been criticized as opening the door to mischief. In both cases partisan actors usually take sides on reforms, having interests in influencing turnout and electoral outcomes. Generally speaking, Republicans have pressed for greater safeguards against fraud while Democrats have promoted greater access to the ballot. This pattern points to a related tension built into the structure of election administration: in most places, adversarial partisans, rather than independent personnel, preside over elections. The bipartisan structure, based on the well-intentioned rationale that the two parties will watch each other, has more often led to partisan gridlock and political deal making, however. The result is a war to subvert the structure in order to gain partisan advantage.

This may help to explain an apparent conundrum. Over the past several decades, electoral laws and rules such as poll taxes, literacy tests, residency requirements, and restrictive voter registration procedures have been eliminated or liberalized on the premise that they tend to hinder voting, especially by minorities and poor people. Changing the rules, reform advocates thought, would lead to increased participation. Notwithstanding these developments, in most places across the nation voter registration and turnout has remained low, with the important exception of blacks and poor whites in the South. This ineffectiveness of rule liberalization in increasing voter participation has been termed the "puzzle of participation" and has generated a new round of analyses in the political science literature.[15]

Although scholarly investigation of elections has focused on several factors that affect voter turnout, the machinery that administers elections in the United States has been largely ignored. Furthermore, there has been inadequate analysis of the political influences and environments that determine these agencies' procedures and their place in the electoral system.

While several factors contribute to low rates of registration and turnout, part of the solution to this puzzle may lie in election administration, that little-examined and little-understood aspect of our electoral system. For the most part, reform of the laws governing the franchise has not been accompanied by the necessary and concomitant changes in the bureaucratic structures that administer elections. The patterns of implementing reforms, moreover, may have rendered them practically ineffective. Even well-conceived laws and executive directives have been voided by discretionary administrative actions and noncompliance. For example, making voter registration possible by mail does not in itself put registration forms into the hands of voters; neither does mandating that government agencies expand registration opportunities ensure that they will do so.

As the 2000 presidential election in Florida dramatically illustrated, election boards wield more power than is generally known. Just as the patchwork of election law among states contributes to differential levels of registration and turnout, the process of implementing electoral law is a highly variable process—even within states—and it similarly produces distinct outcomes. Elections officials can institute, and in some places progressive administrators have instituted, programs and practices that yield increases in registration and turnout, but such examples have been few and far between. In many jurisdictions, boards of elections instead employ restrictive measures that can lead to the disenfranchisement of eligible voters, as in the case of Florida elections officials incorrectly purging suspected felons.[16] The wide variation in registration and turnout rates among and within states and cities might in part be more properly attributed to variations in the practices of the election boards that implement election laws than to the laws themselves.

To be sure, election administration is but one factor among many that can affect voter participation: voter disaffection and apathy; the nature of particular candidates, campaigns, and election dynamics in any given election; distinctive features of party systems; various election laws; and other factors all combine to contribute to patterns of voter participation and nonparticipation. Nevertheless, election administration plays a unique role in contributing to low turnout and, conversely, in facilitating voting. Though this factor has received short shrift in the literature, it may be easier to remedy problems in election administration than to address low rates of voter participation by educating and motivating voters and reforming party systems and campaigns.

In this volume I take a systematic and in-depth look at the politics of election administration, this crucial but under-studied element of America's electoral system. Focusing on the case of New York, I investigate political conflict over the way elections are conducted—the rules, procedures, and personnel that govern our electoral process—and reveal that election administration is not a neutral, ministerial process but a system that is highly susceptible to politicization and manipulation. Election administration can have a decisive impact on voter participation, electoral outcomes, and politics. Such has been the case in New York.

New York experienced Florida-like election problems well before 2000. Tens of thousands of New Yorkers have been disenfranchised in nearly every election by a range of election problems, and candidates and political parties have fought over various election procedures. In many ways events in New York presaged the debacle in Florida. The kinds of problems made famous in Florida are thus not isolated or unique. They are part of a larger story that stretches back over a century. Similarly, some electoral reforms enacted in New York presage action taken in other states and at the national level. In this volume I take readers behind the scenes to tell this story.

Here I chronicle the historical rise of restrictive election law and practices, especially voter registration and election administration. My main focus, however, is on the present-day period. I examine the political environments within which election administrators operate and the distinct political actors and interests associated with certain electoral rules and practices. I identify patterns of partisanship associated with particular election rules and practices and calculate their impact on electoral participation of affected constituents, as well as on electoral outcomes and politics. I also detail electoral rules and practices that constrict voter participation and lead to the disenfranchisement of eligible voters, especially low-income, minority, and urban citizens, and document rules and procedures that expand access to registration and voting. Finally, I provide new evidence pertinent to the debate in political science about these issues, also contributing relevant information to current public policy discussions about electoral reforms.

Specifically, I focus on electoral rules and practices that limit access to registration opportunities, election information, and voting, as well as on those that enhance such access and information. I identify administrative standards, procedures, and technologies for processing voter registration applications that restrict access or are flawed or prone to human or mechanical error, as well as the process of removing (or purging) voters from the registration rolls, resulting in the disenfranchisement of eligible voters. I describe election-day operations that are slipshod and produce errors, delays, and chaotic and confusing poll-site conditions, and that involve human inadequacies and machine malfunctions that lead to voters being turned away from poll sites and ballots being invalidated. And it looks at election technologies—from voter registration systems to voting equipment—that depress voter participation and affect electoral outcomes.

There are myriad ways election administration affects voter participation. Sometimes eligible voters' names do not appear on the voter registration rolls because elections officials do not process their registration applications properly in time for election day. Frequently applications are not properly transmitted to an election board by another government agency—such as the department of motor vehicles or a social service agency. With disturbing frequency voters' names are improperly removed in a purge of the voter rolls. Furthermore, many would-be voters are discouraged by long lines at the polls caused by insufficient staffing, a scarcity of functioning voting machines, or a lack of necessary voting materials (such as paper ballots). Poll workers sometimes provide voters with incorrect answers and erroneous information, illegally ask for identification, or otherwise intimidate prospective voters. After an election, poll workers might lose ballots or misread voting machine counts. Various voting technologies can have disenfranchising and discriminatory effects, such as when the now-famous Votomatic ballot-counting machines failed to recognize voter intent in a dimpled chad. Conversely, a host of alternative election practices and technologies can provide greater access to registration and voting. I examine such election rules, practices, and technologies; measure their impact on voter-participation patterns of specific groups; and assess their effects on electoral outcomes and public policy. I also identify those who promoted and opposed such election rules and practices.

To fully understand the intricate details of election systems close scrutiny is required. Toward this end, I examine voter registration procedures and the practices of election administration in New York, detailing their impact on voter registration and turnout in two specific periods: from 1870 to 1920, when voter registration procedures and boards of elections came into being, and from 1980 to 2004, when important election reforms were enacted and implemented. I show how tens of thousands of voters in New York have been disenfranchised in nearly every election and how this disenfranchisement has contributed to the victories and defeats of dozens of candidates locked in close contests and, in turn, has affected politics and public policy. I detail how restrictive election practices are the legacy of turn-of-the-twentieth-century changes in election law and arrangements won by Republicans, conservative Democrats, and elite reformers, and are maintained today by a similar set of dominant political actors.

I also examine practices that facilitate voting and that remedy inadequate systems. These include standards, practices, and technologies that ensure accurate processing of voter registration applications as well as timely dissemination of voter notification packets, with critical poll-site locations and identification cards, for example. In addition I show how specific electoral rules and practices can produce smoothly running poll sites staffed by competent election workers who provide timely and needed assistance and facilitate the accuracy of votes cast and counted. Recent improvements to election administration championed by voting rights advocates and liberal Democrats, along with the inauguration of programs designed to expand the franchise—such as the National Voter Registration Act (NVRA), known as "motor voter," and election-day registration—produced important changes in election practices and led to modest but nevertheless important increases in registration and voting.

Research reveals that similar patterns of partisan politics and election practices hold true for most political jurisdictions in the country. To be sure, some states and localities, including New York and Florida, have enacted progressive legislation and implemented programs aimed toward improving the performance of election administration and expanding voter participation, but other jurisdictions have done the reverse. In this book I situate New York in its broader context by providing an overview of election administration in the United States, and also probe several key representative states for purposes of comparison. Although forms of election administration vary from jurisdiction to jurisdiction, every county of every state in the nation has a system to administer elections. Election practices matter virtually everywhere. Thus this systematic, in-depth study of New York has nationwide applicability.

Election reform—a burning issue after the 2000 presidential debacle— has been sidelined by issues of war and peace, economics, and so on. As for elections, not much has changed. Harris wrote in 1934: "There is probably no other phase of public administration in the U. S. that is so badly managed as the conduct of elections. Every investigation or election contest brings to light glaring irregularities, errors, misconduct on the part of precinct officers, disregard for election laws and instructions, slipshod practices, and downright frauds."[17] Although this statement was written over seventy years ago, it describes all too well the current situation. Election administration continues to be the underfunded stepchild of government. Worse still, elections continue to be controlled by dominant partisan officials of both parties who have incumbency interests in maintaining a stable and constricted electorate. In short, the business of elections remains firmly in the hands of insiders who have little incentive or intention to do more than make cosmetic changes.

Nevertheless, the fiasco in Florida gave voting rights advocates an opening to press for change. They seized the moment to advance some electoral reforms, most notably the Help America Vote Act (HAVA), which was signed into law on October 29, 2002. HAVA is the first major federal election reform legislation since 1993's NVRA, or motor voter, and the Voting Rights Act of 1965 before that. HAVA has great potential to improve election administration by bringing sorely needed federal dollars to the upgrading of aging voting machines, the establishment of a more efficient statewide voter registration system to keep voters on the rolls and their information up to date, the improvement of poll-worker performance and other administrative practices, and efforts to increase voter education and effectiveness. In short, HAVA can help modernize and standardize the infrastructure of election administration and voting practices.

But familiar partisan maneuvering has blunted the potential positive impacts of HAVA, both in its design as well as in its implementation. Republicans and conservative Democrats have used, among other things, the specter of fraud to shape important provisions and methods of implementation. Ironically, HAVA has the potential to wreak havoc, particularly in places like New York. For example, HAVA established new identification requirements—successfully promoted by congressional Republicans over objections by Democrats—with the stated intent to safeguard the ballot. The kinds of acceptable identification are few—such as a driver's license, something that many urban dwellers, and particularly low-income and minority residents of places like New York City, do not possess. States, however, have the capacity to expand or limit the kinds of acceptable identification. Limiting the range of acceptable identification will effectively bar hundreds of thousands of voters from registering and casting ballots, while providing a broad range will better ensure access, particularly by low-income, minority, and urban voters. The stakes are high and the potential consequences are clear. Republicans and conservatives in many states have tried to restrict the kinds of qualifying identification to a few, while Democrats and voting-rights advocates have promoted a longer list of possible forms of identification. Similarly, whether provisional ballots cast in the wrong polling place will be counted or invalidated hinges on parallel partisan considerations and varying practices, as evident in the 2004 elections.

Voting is integral to democracy; it is the principal means by which average citizens participate in the political process. Yet at the beginning of the twenty-first century, American democracy appears to be more enfeebled than at nearly any other time in its history. As compared with other democratic nations, voter turnout in the United States is low—ranking nearly at the bottom. While mass voter participation is only one measure of the vitality of a democratic polity, barely half of the eligible electorate votes in presidential elections, and even fewer vote in state and local elections. This lack of participation is most evident in poor, minority, and urban communities that are often slighted by governmental policies. In a political democracy, such disparities raise troubling questions about the legitimacy of public policy and governance.

Numerous factors are involved in producing low voter turnout in the United States; the role of election administration is an integral part of a more complete explanation. The poor state of election administration indicates a lack of political will to invest the necessary resources in the nation's electoral system to make it truly democratic. It also reflects partisan maneuvering. In this book I introduce new evidence that sheds light on scholarly and public policy debates concerning the causes of low levels of electoral participation. I also present best practices and model programs that point toward promising avenues for remedying the flaws in America's electoral system.

Election Administration

A MISSING PIECE OF THE PUZZLE
OF VOTER PARTICIPATION

In politics as in everything else, it makes a great difference whose game we play. The rules of the game determine the requirements for success. —E. E. Schattschneider, *The Semisovereign People*

Voting matters. Voting continues to be a central feature of modern theories of democracy, and elections remain the principal means of political participation by average citizens. Most conceptions of democracy posit that the legitimacy of governments is derived in large measure from electoral mechanisms that are set up for the purpose of selecting representatives who fashion public policy. The electoral system is viewed as a primary institutional link between citizens and the state. The degree of voter turnout is a critical measure with which to evaluate—both empirically and normatively—the extent and character of democratic participation, as well as the extent of popular input into and support for public policies. While the meaning and significance of nonvoting is not universally perceived as cause for alarm, generally it is viewed as problematic for democratic systems.[1]

However, the United States ranks nearly last among all democratic nations in voter turnout. One study of average voter turnout in national elections from 1945 to 1998 ranks the United States 139 out of 172 countries. Moreover, the American electorate is sharply skewed in terms of class and race: minority and working-class constituencies have disproportionately low rates of registration and turnout in elections. Although the rates of participation among minorities have increased since the Civil Rights movement and the passage of the Voting Rights Act of 1965, especially among African Americans—as they have among poor whites in the South—blacks continue to have lower registration and turnout rates than whites. Latinos have even lower rates, and Asians the lowest. Turnout in urban areas has averaged 10 percent lower than in the suburbs and the rural parts of the United States.

Voting in presidential elections has declined about 10 percent since 1960; turnout in urban centers has been 10 to 20 percent lower than the national rates and has declined even faster in many cities—again, it is skewed in class and racial terms. Thus, given voter preferences, some scholars and politicians argue that increased voter registration and turnout benefits Democrats and independent political formations. Others, however, argue that increased turnout would help either party or might help Republicans. Voter turnout is usually measured by using the voting age population (VAP) derived from census data. This method tends to overestimate the pool of eligible voters. If turnout is instead calculated on the basis of the voter eligible population (VEP)—removing people who are legally barred from voting such as noncitizens, felons, and the mentally incompetent—then the overall decline in voter turnout is much less. Rosenstone and Hansen sum the situation up nicely: "The most important, most familiar, most analyzed, and most conjectured trend in recent American political history is the thirty-year decline of voter turnout in national elections."[2]

The other major trend that has been the focus of study is America's precipitous decline in voter turnout from nineteenth-century highs of 75 percent to 80 percent—even in urban and municipal elections—to twenty-first-century lows of 50 percent to 60 percent.[3] Inequalities in voting patterns translate into inequalities in political power. Skewed voter participation corresponds to unequal allocation of public resources and policymaker attention. As V. O. Key states, "The blunt truth is that politicians and officials are under no compulsion to pay much heed to classes and groups of citizens that do not vote." Why should they? Their political fortunes are not dependent on nonvoters. The relationship between patterns of political participation and policy outcomes is evident in nearly every policy arena. Although mass social movements and other forms of political participation can also shape politics and policy, it matters *who* votes.[4]

Although there is little disagreement over the facts regarding who votes and who does not, there is much dispute about how to explain these voter participation patterns in the United States and what to do to change them. Scholars, politicians, and political scientists all argue about the causes and consequences of and remedies for America's uniquely low and class- and race-skewed voter participation. Why did voter turnout plummet at the turn of the last century, particularly for low-income and minority groups? Why, after some revival in the 1930s, did turnout fall again after 1960, even as education levels continued to rise? Why has the class and race skew of the electorate persisted? The answers to these questions are found, in part, in the role of election rules and administration. There are many pieces to the puzzle of participation, and election administration is surely one of the missing pieces.

Debates about voter turnout have centered on several explanations emphasizing different factors.[5] One general approach, the social-psychological model, focuses on the social characteristics of nonvoters—studies show that they are more likely to be from lower socioeconomic groups: minorities, poor people, young people, and those with lower levels of education—and their attendant lack of motivation, party identification, and sense of political efficacy. Taken together, the relationships between these factors produce a composite—often presented as both description and explanation—of who nonvoters are and why they do not vote. This model remains the dominant approach in political science, among policy makers, and in popular culture.[6]

But the social-psychological model does not adequately explain how and why the correlation between particular psychological attitudes and social characteristics initially arose. Where do such attitudes come from? Are they inherent in these individuals and groups? Could they be socially created, and have they developed historically? Why did turnout during the latter part of the nineteenth century reach historically high levels when education levels were significantly lower, and why is precisely the opposite is true today? These anomalies undermine the explanatory power of the social-psychological model. Although social and psychological factors no doubt contribute to low turnout, there are other factors that also appear to be at work.

A second general approach focuses on structural factors that depress turnout. Within this structural approach, one model, the political-behavioral model, addresses the nature of party systems: the relative decline of the parties, the degree of competition between them, the limited number of parties, the narrow range of issues that candidates address, the presence or absence of salient issues or important elections, the prevalence and impact of media and new campaign technologies, and the increased costs of campaigns and the role of money in them. A second model within the structural approach, the legal-institutional model, focuses on legal and administrative factors that inhibit participation: poll taxes, literacy tests, residency requirements, restrictive voter registration procedures, and so on. Similarly, particular practices of election administration can disenfranchise voters or encourage them to vote. Certain election laws and practices have been shown to increase voter turnout, such as mail-in ballots and all-mail elections, election-day registration, compulsory voting, and easing restrictions on absentee voting.[7]

Both structural models point to how political institutions shape voting behavior. Individuals act within a social and political context that delimits their choices. Restrictive procedures constrict the size and composition of the electorate, especially disenfranchising citizens of lower income, education, and age, and voters of minority background. Similarly, stringent ballot access measures tend to limit the number of candidates—especially insurgents—and the range of issues the candidates address, contributing to the production of oligarchic parties and incumbency. Barriers to voting encourage parties and candidates to ignore the interests of nonvoters, affecting the dynamics of party competition and party systems. This, in turn, can affect the attitudes of these constituencies, turning them away from politics and voting. Conversely, easy access to the franchise enhances the likelihood that marginal voters will participate, which may encourage challengers to run and to stimulate competition or launch effective appeals that could further draw voters into the active electorate.

To be sure, each approach explains some aspect of the phenomenon of nonvoting. Studies have produced a wealth of empirical evidence supporting various positions each viewpoint espouses. But taken alone each approach is incomplete. The present study draws upon the work of Frances Fox Piven and Richard Cloward, which emphasizes the structural perspective and attempts to synthesize important elements of each approach into a more complex and comprehensive model. An integrated structural approach shows how electoral rules and party systems have combined to produce historic and contemporary patterns of voter participation. These structural features shape patterns of voter participation, including part of the class and race skew in the electorate that the social-psychological model highlights. The structural approach shifts the blame from nonvoters themselves to the political system. The parties do not effectively mobilize voters or speak to their interests, and they may throw up barriers to voting instead.

There is nothing intrinsic about the nonvoters that make them predisposed not to vote. Contemporary American politics and electoral arrangements provide few incentives for members of lower socioeconomic groups to vote and instead pose greater costs. Nonvoting might be a rational response to political campaigns that are too often devoid of substantial issue content. When campaigns focus on issues, they tend to focus on middle- and upper-class concerns. The attitudes and social characteristics of nonvoters might more properly be viewed as a consequence of the features of the American political system.

No doubt both approaches have merit and are substantiated by empirical studies. Social and psychological factors appear to have an effect on voter participation independent of structural factors, but in this study I neither directly measure social-psychological effects on nonvoting nor claim that such effects are absent.

Instead, in this study I extend the institutional approach to incorporate the role of election administration. I argue that election administration, which implements electoral law and is an extension of party systems, plays a significant role in shaping patterns of voter participation. I highlight the interrelationship of the political origins of electoral rules and party systems, and the impact of the implementation of those rules and systems on specific constituencies and on the political climate over time. I view election administration as a nexus for examining these dynamics, a lens through which to see connections. Indeed, resolution of the dispute about the causes of nonvoting might be furthered by more serious scrutiny of the rules and practices governing elections, for rules and politics intersect in implementation processes.

Historical Genesis of Restrictive Election Practices and the Decline of Voter Turnout

There is a strong correlation between the decline in turnout and changes in the electoral system at the turn of the twentieth century. During the nineteenth century, voter turnout was robust, but in the early twentieth century, when restrictive voter registration procedures and boards of elections came into being, it declined precipitously. Of course, these developments were accompanied by other significant changes, including the establishment of poll taxes, extended-residency requirements, grandfather clauses, and felon voting restrictions, as well as the gradual elimination of noncitizen voting rights. All of these factors, as well as the changing nature of the parties and a reduction of party competition, combined to depress voter turnout.

For example, new requirements that voters register in person shifted the burden of registering away from the state, which had formerly drawn up registration lists, to the individual. Requirements that voters enroll months before an election and that they appear at a central office during working hours disproportionately affected low-income and marginally involved citizens, who found themselves unable to vote because they had not registered. These developments, in turn, affected party competition and electoral outcomes. In short, the new laws changed politics.

In his study of the rise of voter registration procedures, Joseph Harris did not attempt "to enumerate the thousands of steps in the evolution of registration laws in all the states, for this would be unduly tedious and not particularly useful."[8] But empirical analysis shows that the places where registration laws were adopted correlate with areas where turnout declined, suggesting a relationship. Indeed, differentials in turnout between urban and rural areas "fit so astonishingly well with what is known of the spread of registration laws in exactly the same era."[9] For example, Indiana had high rates of turnout until 1911 when voter registration was required, and then saw its participation decline; similarly, Philadelphia's turnout plummeted around 1900 when a stringent personal registration system was introduced.[10] As we shall see, the same holds true for the inauguration of election administration. Examination of the political origins of these election procedures and institutions sheds light on who promoted and opposed these changes, and who stood to benefit from them.

Progressive era reformers successfully enacted measures aimed at cleaning up what they considered corrupt elections, particularly targeting urban political machines. While many reform advocates were well-intentioned and worked for the passage of important measures that expanded democracy, some supported the establishment of electoral rules and mechanisms that posed substantial barriers to voting. The establishment of restrictive voter registration procedures and partisan election boards are examples of the latter. These measures have been subject to political manipulation and continue to disenfranchise millions of eligible voters.

The period from 1860 to 1910, particularly the years after 1890, saw the spread of voter registration laws across the nation. During the early period, registration legislation varied both geographically and procedurally. Over time, certain general features of these new laws and practices became more uniform and were institutionalized, becoming more onerous.

Initially registration systems were weak. Legislation commissioned elections officials to draw up lists of residents eligible to vote within their districts. This was done on the basis of the officials' familiarity with their precincts or on the basis of door-to-door canvassing. To a large extent the burden of registration remained with the state. From 1860 to 1880 northern states enacted registration laws that applied only to their large cities.[11] During the 1890s, stronger types of voter registration systems replaced weaker ones, and they were introduced in some states that previously had had no registration systems. The key feature of these new laws was the introduction of a personal registration requirement, which shifted the burden of establishing eligibility from the state to the individual.[12] Strong systems were also characterized by more frequent, supervised purges of the voter rolls to validate and update them. In addition, these systems required citizens to appear in front of an election board to register to vote some specific amount of time before the election; the time varied from six months in many places in the South to one week elsewhere, in the majority of cases ranging from one to two months. Satisfactory proof of identity and eligibility was required, along with the voter's signature, to be verified on election day. These attempts to prevent fraudulent voting resulted in "exceedingly expensive, cumbersome, and inconvenient" voting systems, particularly in large cities.[13]

Ostensibly, registration procedures were designed to eliminate or reduce the reportedly rampant electoral fraud committed by burgeoning numbers of new immigrants and urban political-machine ward bosses. The literature of the period refers to allegations that unscrupulous individuals had voted multiple times, using fictitious names or names of the dead. There were also reports of officials who were bribed to cast ballots in the names of people who had not turned out to vote.[14]

Some states imposed registration requirements statewide, while others applied one type of requirement to urban places and a less stringent one to nonurban areas. States with these mixed registration systems often amended their statutes to raise or lower the city size limits. A few states pursued a gradualist approach, first requiring personal registration in the largest cities and then extending coverage to smaller-sized cities. In most states, the personal registration requirement put into place near the turn of the nineteenth century was the final stage in the evolution of its system from weak to strong. The more stringent registration requirements replaced either a loosely administered nonpersonal system or the complete absence of registration.[15] A pattern emerged in the development and implementation of voter registration procedures: "from non-personal to personal, from permanent to periodic, and even to annual registration, and from local to centralized administration," which held consequences for political outcomes and also reflected political struggles over rules governing the franchise.[16]

Many examples prove this point. Prior to the twentieth century, and to a lesser extent thereafter, debate over the merits and consequences of voter registration procedures and their implementation occurred at the national and state level. In 1887, Judge George W. McCreary of the U.S. Circuit Court, a former member of the House of Representatives and chairman of the Committee on Elections of that body, observed that voter registration laws were causing quite a bit of contention and were the subject of litigation in the courts. He raised the pointed question: "Is an act which denies the right to vote to all persons not registered on or before a fixed day prior to the day of election and which makes no provision for registration after the time limited, so onerous and unreasonable as to be justly regarded an impairment of the constitutional right to vote?"[17] Similarly, William H. Michael, a prominent lawyer, acknowledged the implications and potential consequences of the new registry laws: "The object of the registration law is to prevent illegal voting by providing in advance of election an authentic list of the qualified electors. Necessarily an efficient system of registration must involve a certain amount of inconvenience to voters, and probably under the best system that could be devised some qualified electors would lose their votes through inability to avail themselves of the opportunities or to comply with the conditions of registration."[18] Clearly, the disenfranchising consequences of these new, more restrictive laws were not lost on the proponents of either side in these debates.

The issue of voter registration stimulated heated political controversy along direct urban-rural and partisan lines. New immigrants and minority groups in the largest urban centers typically used the Democratic Party as a vehicle to challenge registration laws that forced them into elaborate procedures not required of rural dwellers. Republicans, sharply aware of the extent to which their rural voting base might shrink with the extension of registration to the countryside, fought vehemently to preserve their legal advantage. The many switches back and forth in statewide registration laws that occurred in some states simply reflected the momentary ascendancy of one or the other party.[19] We can examine this assertion by looking at the positions of the parties within each state; the case of New York tests—and corroborates—the proposition.

The impetus behind restrictive registration procedures arose from "nativist and corporate-minded hostility to the political machine, the polyglot city, and the immigrant."[20] These new laws were produced by and enhanced a nativistic animus aimed at the new urban immigrants who were tied to party machines. These and other new rule changes—such as requirements that registrants pass a literacy test—redefined voter eligibility. They were intended by elites to exclude opposition voters, and they reshaped the electorate by dampening turnout.[21] Also as part of the campaign to detect and deter allegedly rampant fraud by immigrants and party machines, boards of elections were established in larger cities between 1880 and 1910. Like registration laws, they were instituted by a coalition of Republicans and middle- and upper-class reformers.[22] Importantly, the "demobilization of lower-strata voters occurred at precisely that time in our history when the possibilities of electoral politics had begun to enlarge."[23]

Thus, integral to these legal and procedural reforms is the issue of election fraud. The nature and extent of fraud— in both the past and the present—is important for two reasons. First, fraud was the principal stated justification for the inauguration of voter registration procedures and boards of elections—indeed, it was their raison d'être; second, concern about the increased possibility of fraud continues to be the principal stated reason for the ongoing restrictive practices of boards of elections and for opposition to the reform of election law.[24]

The Specter of Fraud and the Politics of Voter Registration and Election Administration

Some scholars allege that fraud was rampant and that its elimination—by means of boards of elections and restrictive registration procedures—explains why turnout declined around the turn of the twentieth century. That is, vote fraud had artificially inflated turnout rates, and the elimination of fraud produced cleaner elections and what appeared to be lower voter turnout.[25] These legal and procedural changes reduced control over the electoral process by the parties in general and by the organized political machines in particular, and they increased regulation and control by nonpartisan or bipartisan officials and boards of elections. Indeed, the introduction of reforms correlates with the decline in turnout, and variations in registration and voting requirements (such as residency requirements, poll taxes, and closing dates for registration) also correlates with changes in turnout levels from state to state.[26]

This line of analysis takes the charges of fraud at face value and accepts them as evidence. The contention that fraud prompted reforms leading to lower turnout rates rests on certain assumptions: that voter fraud was extensive and pervasive; that the kinds of fraud perpetrated artificially inflated turnout levels; that turn-of-the-century reformers were idealistic and politically disinterested—that is, that they were legitimately concerned with eliminating fraud and that other ramifications, such as disenfranchisement, weakening of the party system, and partisan advantage, were unintended consequences; and finally, that lower turnout is evidence of the elimination of fraudulent ballots.[27]

Although election fraud certainly existed then and still does, the extent of it appears to be overstated. Allegations of fraud are numerous, but only a handful of well-based cases have been cited. Because it is impossible to know the scope of fraud, we will never know the whole truth of the matter, but we should not assume—despite the frequently cited notorious cases—that election fraud was widespread.[28] Moreover, the remedies for fraud had other deleterious effects.

First, deflationary forms of fraud were, and are, as likely as inflationary forms. Many forms of deflationary fraud could be committed independently of reforms—destruction of ballots, alteration of vote counts, payments to potential voters for not voting, intimidation of voters, and so on. Even if fraud was as prevalent as it was alleged to be, it existed in various forms with contradictory effects, so the decline in turnout following the institution of reforms cannot be attributed solely to the elimination of fraud. The rate of turnout decline following reforms was so great that it is implausible to attribute the decline only to the elimination of fraud. Moreover, charges of fraud still continued—albeit to a lesser degree—long after voter turnout rates decreased. The frequency with which such charges were made appears to be associated not with the level of voter turnout, but with particular partisan motives and interests. Such political considerations suggest a different and more complicated relationship between fraud charges and the enactment of reforms, and thus between the nature of electoral changes and the decline in voter turnout during the twentieth century.[29]

Second, the evidence of fraud is suspect. To be sure, we cannot dismiss the charges by appealing to the facts because little documented evidence exists. But much of the so-called corruption attributed to political machines had little to do with vote fraud. What reformers called vote fraud was not universally regarded as corrupt, and by today's standards it would not be considered illegal. For example, vote choices guided by perceptions of economic benefit or habits of party loyalty, rather than by some notion of the public good, were often defined as corruption. The way in which the term *corruption* was often applied provides insight into the values of the reformers and commentators who leveled charges of fraud and criticized the party system—that is, their strong antimajority and antiparty viewpoints—but tells us little about the extent of fraudulent practices. This lends support to those who suggest that the charges of fraud and the advocacy and imposition of restrictive measures in the North were designed to secure partisan advantage and to disenfranchise significant segments of the opposition parties' constituency, especially members of the immigrant working classes, who were organizing politically.[30]

Indeed, the way electoral fraud was defined and the reforms enacted to address it reveal similar motives and interests. Some forms of fraud inflated turnout rates (like repeat voting and voting for the dead), while other forms of fraud deflated turnout (like intimidating voters, destroying ballots, changing vote totals, and paying potential voters not to vote). Indeed, deflationary fraud may have canceled out inflationary fraud. Yet the reforms generally addressed only inflationary fraud.[31]

What is offered as evidence of fraud often reveals strong social and moral values embedded in data and analysis. For example, much of the evidence of fraud cited by reformers (high turnout in machine wards, uniformity in voting, inability to find registered voters at given addresses in postelection surveys, high numbers of newly naturalized citizens, revelations of patronage and bribery, and so on), although consistent with the view that large-scale fraud existed, is inconclusive, and there are plausible alternative explanations for such findings. These include explanations that take into account the fact that city tenement districts had very large immigrant and transient populations who lived in overcrowded housing and were responsive to the mobilizing efforts of local party workers. Some party organizations facilitated the naturalization and registration of immigrants, believing such constituents would likely vote for them. Moreover, it is probable that census data undercounted tenement-district population, which may well have exceeded the official numbers used to calculate the rate of turnout. Turnout that seemed to be excessively high might have been an accurate reflection of reality. The appearance of fraud also may have resulted from the poor operation of election administration. For example, recounts of votes often revealed the "widespread prevalence of errors," and observers noted that "every election contest brings to light slipshod, careless and irregular administration."[32]

The lack of hard evidence and scarcity of systematic studies are not surprising since charges of fraud were to some extent "part of the political campaign of elite groups to regain or retain control of city politics."[33] Subsequent writing on fraud has been done in the context of substantially lower rates of turnout, so it is not surprising that social scientists have attributed the change from high to lower turnout to a reduction in fraud rather than to broader behavioral, legal, and institutional changes that demobilized and effectively barred substantial portions of the eligible electorate.

Another reason for skepticism is that political actors who charge fraud are related to partisan groups, constituents, and geographic centers possessing specific interests. Most allegations originated within Republican Party organizations, dissident Democratic factions, and reform and independent movements that charged dominant or incumbent administrations, generally Democratic, with fraud. The most frequent charges came during the years of heaviest immigration (the 1870s through the 1920s), and much of the writing was "openly condescending, moralistic, and prejudiced toward the new arrivals," including writing in connection to supposed election fraud.[34]

Indeed, many of the charges originated from middle- and upper-class groups and from muckraking magazines such as *The Nation, Harper's Weekly, Outlook, McClure's, Century,* and *Forum.* Most studies of urban politics and fraud were written prior to 1930, when hostility to bosses, machines, immigrants, blacks, radicals, and others ran high. The literature is largely anecdotal and based on accounts by highly motivated observers and participants—native-born, white, Protestant, middle- and upper-class people who were engaged in reform activity. Their perspective has been substantially generalized and incorporated into the literature.[35]

Because the allegations were so often repeated, they took on a material force of their own, so even groups with varying and conflicting interests came to share similar notions and worked together toward a general goal of reform. And while not all reformers were alike, most held a normative view of how the political system ought to work. Turn-of-the-century social justice reformers supported the elimination of fraud and increased efficiency and democracy by means of reform measures much as did very different political actors and interests, but for very different reasons.[36]

The changing economic and political environment in the United States in the decades surrounding the turn of the twentieth century, including rapid industrialization and urbanization, engendered intense class conflict and gave rise to social movements and to challenges from labor and from third parties such as the Populists and the Socialists. These developments led to changes in party systems, most notably to an increasingly oligarchic character of the dominant parties, a sectional realignment in the North and the South, and a concomitant reduction in competition between and within parties. This in turn negatively impacted voter participation and the nature of politics during the twentieth century. Southern and northern elites in both parties acted to restrict electoral participation, especially among groups at the bottom of the social ladder, revealing partisan, class, and racial motivations and interests and affecting the development of the electorate, the party system, and policies. While the disenfranchisement in the South was less veiled and more successful than in the North, there is a growing body of literature documenting politically motivated parallels in the North, particularly in urban centers. The allegations of electoral fraud were part of these developments and therefore cannot be accepted at face value alone. Moreover, the electoral reforms that followed these charges of fraud reflected the motives and special interests of the elites within both political parties who inaugurated and implemented them.[37]

Allegations of fraud, then, were part and parcel of reform-led campaigns that resulted in legal and institutional changes, which, in turn, affected patterns of voter participation and political outcomes. In the North, it was immigrant-stock, working-class voters whose turnout significantly decreased. In the South, it was largely blacks and poor whites. These developments had an impact on the political parties' and candidates' choice of issues with which to mobilize their perceived constituencies. The restrictive registration laws and the bipartisan boards of elections that implemented them had important disenfranchising impacts and helped shape subsequent American political development. Although the political universe and political culture have undergone significant change since the early twentieth century, these developments have had profound significance for present-day politics.

Political parties and boards of elections both shaped legal and institutional arrangements and were shaped by them, ultimately adapting to and benefiting from a more restricted political universe, and they therefore developed a stake in maintaining these new arrangements. Especially in local elections, political organizations have incumbency interests in and patronage reasons for shaping the impact of election reform; they also have the organizational capacity to dominate implementation through their positions on election boards.[38] Early on, as party organizations developed and vied for control of the machinery of government, the parties generally had greater interest in mobilizing constituents—especially in the context of keen competition—in order to win elections and patronage resources. Once political machines had been consolidated, however, they had greater interest in maintaining stable coalitions and restricting the size of the electorate, particularly among constituents linked to rival factions. Indeed, most machines consolidated their power at the time of or after the implementation of these reforms. Many machines dropped their initial resistance to voter registration and election boards and used registration to their advantage in constructing "minimal winning coalitions" to "manage electoral demand."[39]

Important aspects of machine politics have persisted to the present day that are distinct from the fabled political machines. The stakes of local elections remain significantly tied to patronage resources and relationships, such as important municipal agencies, commissions, judgeships, and the like. While not impervious to challenges from reformers, elite political groupings and so-called regular party organizations continue to be adept at dominating or recapturing electoral processes in many urban centers and may very well have survived insurgent efforts through their capacity to limit voting by restricting registration of opposing constituencies and limiting the number and efficiency of polling places. They dominate the boards of elections and the selection of candidates for the bench, and judges, in turn, rule on ballot-access challenges and other election matters.[40]

This approach has particular relevance for electoral systems dominated by a single party, which are prevalent from coast to coast. V. O. Key's seminal work on state politics and one-party systems of the South shows the critical role played by election administration. The dominant faction is in a better position to work the machinery of government and often erects barriers in order to defeat insurgent rivals and inhibits the participation of opponents' constituents. The administration of elections—especially with regard to voter registration and literacy tests—can be significantly biased, in part because of the dominant faction's close links to the presiding election administration and the means by which this administration can exercise discretionary capacity to affect processes and outcomes.[41]

Ostensibly the purpose of voter registration laws and procedures is to compile a list of voters who are eligible to participate in elections. Yet bipartisan boards of elections are also charged with ensuring that only registered individuals vote and that they do so only in their own districts—that is, they are charged with policing the election process. In general, the greater the number of stringent procedures to safeguard the ballot, the greater the likelihood that some eligible voters will be barred from voting. To the extent that boards institute such restrictive procedures, they disenfranchise voters—whether intentionally or not—and such restrictive practices disproportionately affect low-income and minority citizens. This, in turn, reduces the size of the electorate, increases the bias toward middle- and upper-income groups, contributes to decreases in party competition, and produces oligarchic parties.

The inauguration and implementation of electoral reforms and the political consequences of those reforms were mutually reinforcing and have had cumulative effects that have combined to constrict the electoral universe. These rules have had different impacts on various groups over time and may have contributed to the emergence of the twentieth-century phenomenon of low turnout among low socioeconomic status (SES) groups. As registration and other barriers gradually took effect, coupled with the decrease in party competition, the parties' links to working-class and ethnic/immigrant constituents withered, and the electoral calculations of party strategists turned increasingly toward appealing to the better-off—that is, the active voters. Local urban parties gradually dropped their original opposition to registration procedures and bipartisan boards of elections, institutionalizing a more constricted and stable electorate that, in turn, enhanced their incumbency and further reinforced the politics that accompanied the origins of such rules. This shrinking electoral universe may have also helped shape the responses and attitudes of voters and nonvoters as much as it was shaped by them. Indeed, the apathy and lack of motivation associated with nonvoters, primarily among low-SES groups, could be in part a result of their marginalization from electoral politics.[42]

Thus, on the basis of history there is good reason to believe that boards of elections function as gatekeeping institutions and continue to play a significant role in maintaining an increasingly race- and class-skewed electorate, especially through the use of registration procedures and regulations on access to the ballot. The interests of those who historically dominated political struggles and developments are embedded in the institutional residue and trajectory of election law and in agencies such as election boards. In the name of protecting against election fraud and reforming corrupt political machines, elite political interests established an election system—whether by design or default—that perpetrated and perpetuated a more insidious form of fraud: restrictive electoral practices that produce administrative disenfranchisement. The political biases of the past are firmly ensconced in the present-day electoral system through the development of these legal and institutional arrangements.[43]

The thrust of restrictive voter registration procedures and practices of boards of elections continues to operate today. In the context of the decline of traditional vehicles of electoral mobilization such as party organizations, political clubs, unions, and mass social movements over the past thirty years, and coupled with the rise of media-based, cash-intensive, candidate-centered politics, restrictive practices have became increasingly difficult to surmount, especially for lower-strata groups. Restrictions on access to the franchise and the ballot have buttressed and furthered these other developments.

Contemporary Politics: That Was Then, This Is Now, and Not a Whole Lot Has Changed

If the establishment of restrictive electoral arrangements was not accidental, neither is their persistence. Contemporary political actors continue to benefit from restrictive voter registration procedures and practices of boards of elections. Although there have been some important successes in reforming the electoral system, particularly the toppling of the most egregious features of the southern registration system and, more recently, the passage of the National Voter Registration Act (NVRA) and the Help America Vote Act (HAVA), efforts to liberalize election procedures have been repeatedly thwarted and undermined.

Since the 1960s opposition to legislation that would ease restrictions in voter registration and election administration, both at the federal and the state level, has come mainly from Republicans and conservatives, as well as from entrenched incumbents of all political stripes. The fraud bugaboo still serves as the major justification for blocking new reforms.[44] Some contend that serious fraud exists today and is having a "blooming renaissance," and that the liberalization of registration procedures—including eliminating purges of voter rolls for nonvoting, increasing access to absentee ballots, and allowing election-day registration—has increased fraud. If security measures cause inconvenience to voters, the argument goes, this is unfortunate and unintentional.[45]

But the incidence of confirmed or proven contemporary fraud is minimal. More importantly, the fraud identified is primarily perpetrated by elections officials and party operatives. Elizabeth Holzman, former district attorney in Brooklyn, investigated election fraud in that borough during several elections from 1968 to 1982. In those cases several elections officials perpetrated fraud in conjunction with small groups or factions of the Democratic Party. Another example of fraud, this time committed by Republican officials, is the changing of information on overseas voters' ballots in Florida during the 2000 presidential election. Even so, security measures imposed by election law and administration are primarily aimed at average voters, not elections officials.[46] Elected officials and election administrators maintain that safeguards on the ballot are as necessary today as they were in the past. In fact, elections officials often say that a large part of their work activity is related to fraud prevention. They maintain fraud does occur and that it could be significant.[47]

On the other hand, efforts to ease voting procedures have generally been championed by insurgent candidates, liberal Democrats, and voting-rights organizations and other independent political formations. Advocates of reform indict the American political system as undemocratic and insufficiently representative, and they place part of the blame on the unique electoral arrangements in the United States. These reformers aim to increase turnout, especially among minorities and the poor, who have had very low rates of turnout since the turn of the twentieth century, and who generally support Democratic and independent candidates. They contend that an enlarged electorate might lead to the fielding of a wider range of candidates and policies and that it would invigorate the polity. Their reform efforts have often met with defeat.

These defeats usually come at the hands of the reformers' Republican opponents, but dominant politicians in both major parties have opposed reforms. Incumbency interests appear to trump all. For example, President Jimmy Carter attributed the rejection of his proposal for Election Day registration by a Democratically controlled Congress in 1977 to incumbency concerns: "Incumbent members of congress don't want to see additional unpredictable voters registered. . . . The more senior and influential members of the Congress have very safe districts. To have a 25 or 30 percent increase of unpredictable new voters is something they don't relish. . . . I would suggest to you that this is the single most important obstacle to increasing participation on election day."[48]

William Crotty sums up this line of reasoning nicely:

> Election day registration has been opposed out of fear of increasing the likelihood of fraudulent voting. The safeguards against fraud appear as strong as in the more traditional enrollment systems, and the concern does not appear to have merit. . . . The most powerful argument, . . . and the one underlying most of the other objections, is the fear that it might work sufficiently well to bring new and untested voters into the electorate. This is a disturbing prospect for most politicians and one that could, although it is a long-shot possibility, tilt the balance of power in politics.[49]

Nevertheless, more often than not party difference distinguishes supporters of such reform efforts from opponents. Questions about electronic voting machines' vulnerability to fraud are an exception: they have been raised from quarters of all political stripes.

Evidence of the Impact of Election Administration on Voter Participation

What do we know about the politics and operation of election administration? Although few studies directly examine election administration, several have shown that practices of boards of elections vary substantially and produce differing impacts on voter registration and participation. Some provide examples of liberal or progressive elections officials who have taken measures to improve efficiency and increase access to voting. These, however, are few. Election administration instead tends to depress voter registration and participation.

One of the earliest studies shows that "legal and administrative obstacles" contributed to nonvoting in the 1923 mayoral election in Chicago.

This study, which examined information from six thousand voters and three hundred experts, found that the manner in which elections are conducted, including "congestion at the polls" and "poor location of polling" sites, can contribute to nonvoting. Although there were election laws that prescribed specific parameters for election administration, these laws were not always observed, and disregard of them could result in nonvoting. For example, the Illinois election law stated that a voting precinct should contain no more than four hundred voters, but some precincts contained five hundred to six hundred voters. Similarly, the law stated that polling sites should be "the most public and convenient places that can be found in each precinct," but many were located in hard-to-find places.[50]

Moreover, complaints regarding voting facilities occurred largely in "colored," German, Polish, Russian, and poor neighborhoods, which implicates the motives of the dominant Democratic Party organization and its election workers as the underlying reason for such conditions. The greatest number of cases "of intimidation were found in the colored settlement" where the Democratic Party organization "was strongly entrenched and resented the influx of colored Republican voters." Democratic Party workers used "various devices to persuade the Negroes not to vote," including attempting to have "the names of registered Negroes erased" and sending "suspect" Negroes notices that required them to go before the election commissioners in person to answer questions—all of which depressed voter turnout.[51]

More recent studies, conducted from the 1970s to the first years of the new millennium, describe election administration and its impact on voter participation in strikingly similar terms. Two national studies of voter registration procedures and election administration practices were conducted in the early 1970s. The National Municipal League (NML) launched the Elections Systems Project, a two-year study with the goal of producing reform in policy and practice, which culminated in the publication of several monographs and collections of essays. In 1971 the League of Women Voters (LWV) conducted a study that documented the administrative practices of elections officials in 257 communities in 47 states. The LWV's study covered at least one of each of four types of jurisdiction in each state: a large city, a medium-sized or small town, a suburb, and a rural community, encompassing approximately 40 million people, or one-fifth of the total population of the United States at that time. The National Municipal League concluded that "legal expansion of the electorate can be administratively blunted . . . when that is the intention of local administrators," and that this "demonstrates the important relationship between administrative procedures and electoral participation." Similarly, the League of Women Voters found that election administration in the United States was generally "inefficient" and often "obstructive" to efforts to increase participation, and that "millions" were disenfranchised by the practices of boards of elections.[52]

Both studies identified various practices that resulted in disenfranchisement, particularly of minority, poor, uneducated, and elderly voters. For instance more than half of the registration places observed were not clearly identified; nor were prospective voters properly notified of their location. Election boards charged voter registration organizations fees for lists of voters or required authorization to use the lists, which were often inaccurate; they denied the organizations authorization to have their members deputized to register voters; they limited the hours and places for registration; they provided unnecessarily complicated voter registration forms; they employed unhelpful election workers; and bilingual staff were unavailable. Similar kinds of problems were found at polling sites during elections.

The discretionary power of elections officials is a critical factor in producing such outcomes. Many election laws are vague or imprecise in the first place, but even when laws are clear, elections officials can shape their implementation. The real authority for election procedures resides with these local officials, who can increase or decrease access to the polls and availability of public information, and thus increase or decrease participation. Most elections officials do not employ their powers to expand participation either because they are not provided with adequate funding or because they oppose efforts to increase participation.

The LWV framed the reason for such practices starkly, stating that election administration still bore "the mark of forces which originally gave it birth at the turn of the century: fear of . . . fraud at the polls and a desire to control the voting participation of millions of European immigrants who threatened the political status quo." The League contended that the biggest fraud of all was the "fraud perpetrated on the American people by a system which excludes millions of eligible voters from the electoral process in the name of preventing a few dishonestly cast votes."[53]

Today sharp differences between jurisdictions continue to exist, and decision-making power regarding election practices is still located primarily at the local level. The Federal Election Commission (FEC), the Council on State Governments, the Election Center, and the General Accounting Office (GAO) all confirm that such conditions continue to characterize election administration in the United States. Following the 2000 presidential election, numerous studies were produced that examined various aspects of elections. Most focused on the impact of voting technology, and some provided information about various election laws and rules and about the structure of election administration systems in the United States. Most of the studies were technical in nature and format. Although none provided analysis of the political makeup of boards of elections or their political environments, some provided valuable insights and information about how election administration actually works and its impact on registration and voting.[54]

A national survey of election administrators was conducted by the GAO in the aftermath of the 2000 presidential election to obtain information about the operations and challenges associated with each stage of the election process.[55] The report found that states vary widely in their laws, practices, and personnel. Some states' codes and regulations are very specific and others' are very general. Because each state and the District of Columbia sets the requirements for conducting its own elections, there are fifty-one particular approaches, and within many states there is considerable variation in the processes for administering elections. A few states have mandatory statewide election administration guidelines; most others allow local jurisdictions wide discretion. The details of election administration are carried out by counties, townships, cities, and villages, and, of course, voting is done at the local level. For example, Oklahoma standardizes most aspects of local and statewide elections, but in Pennsylvania there are "67 counties and consequently 67 different ways of handling elections." Other states reportedly fall somewhere in between. Virginia mandates local jurisdictions to follow some standardized election procedures but allows localities to implement the procedures. Elections are conducted at the local level by various offices and officers, including election boards, bureaus, and commissions, and county and town clerks and registrars. The different officials may have little experience or training in actually conducting elections.

Elections officials reported a range of problems in conducting elections. Fifty-seven percent of local elections officials surveyed reported shortages of poll workers, in part because of low pay. In addition, there are a shrinking number of accessible and appropriate polling places, ballots are overly complex, voting technology is changing and can be unfamiliar to voters, and funds and resources for voter education are insufficient. In one large jurisdiction, 20 percent of the poll workers assigned to work canceled or did not show up on election day. While some elections officials recruit and train additional poll workers in anticipation of such circumstances, many do not.

Several factors account for the insufficient number and poor performance of poll workers, including long hours, low pay, and insufficient channels for recruitment. A typical report by one election official illustrates the consequences of these conditions: "Inspectors serve seventeen or eighteen hours, creating a very long, tiring day. Because many of our inspectors are senior citizens, between the ages of seventy and eighty-plus years, such conditions are difficult on them physically, as well as creating the potential for errors at the end of election day. Since compensation for this job is only $80 to $135 per day, depending upon the election district, it is not sufficient to attract a younger workforce." In addition, workforce training is insufficient or lacking altogether; political parties do not supply a sufficient number of individuals, and those they do supply sometimes lack the qualities necessary for doing the work well; and poll workers were free to exert a tremendous amount of subjective discretion and autonomy in decision making during election day. Other problems were reported, such as long lines at polling places and a lack of channels of communication between polling places and elections offices.

Perhaps the most thorough examination of election problems following the 2000 presidential election was conducted by the Caltech/MIT Voting Technology Project. Their report found that as many as 6 million votes were lost in the 2000 elections. These "lost votes" were due to "faulty voting equipment, inaccuracies in the voter registration database, long lines at the polling places, and other problems." Of those 6 million votes, an estimated 1.5 to 2 million were lost because of "faulty voting equipment and confusing ballots," 1.5 to 3 million were lost because of "registration mix-ups," and 500,000 to 1.2 million were lost because of problematic polling place operations. An unknown number of votes were lost because of "mishandled" and "controversial" absentee and overseas military ballots. The study notes that polling place problems have been reported to census takers for a long time; according to the U.S. Bureau of the Census, "2.8 percent of the forty million registered voters who did not vote in 2000 stated that they did not vote because of problems with polling place operations such as lines, hours, or locations."[56]

Elections officials, put on the spot after the 2000 elections, also provided assessments and recommendations. The most prominent national group is the Election Center, a nonprofit organization made up of elections officials whose job is to serve elections officials. As is true of most reporting from elections officials in the aftermath of the Florida contest, the Election Center's report on the 2000 elections attempted to tread the line between acknowledging problems and defending practices. It attempted to deflect responsibility for election failures away from elections officials and onto other entities, such as legislatures, and other factors, such as voter error. This is justifiable in part.[57] For example, they argued that problems in the 2000 election reflected "blemishes" of an election system that has been "overlooked and under valued, over tasked and under funded" for decades, and whose "complexities have been under estimated and misunderstood by those for whom the system is designed." Still, they concluded that the election system is "not in crisis." Rather, they contended, given the magnitude of the task at hand, observers should be impressed by how well elections work. To be sure, election administration is a huge operation to coordinate. There are about 1,400,000 poll workers who work the nearly 200,000 polling precincts using different technologies on election day. The vast majority of these poll workers receive little training and work fourteen hours or more for minimum wage or less, with the whole process being supervised by about 20,000 election administrators.

One of the most common reform proposals made after the 2000 election was that methods and equipment for voting be standardized. Two days after the Supreme Court settled the disputed presidential election by stopping the recount of ballots, making George W. Bush president, a

Washington Post–ABC News poll found that 61 percent of Americans supported standardization of election procedures, development of a standard ballot, and adoption of uniform election equipment.[58] Similarly, in a December 2000 CBS News poll 71 percent of respondents endorsed the development of a "uniform method" of voting, and 65 percent said elections require "fundamental changes" or should be "completely rebuilt."[59] Leading elections experts followed suit, as did a host of blue-ribbon commissions that produced national reports that made similar recommendations for sweeping changes. Yet the Election Center responded emphatically: "We, America's elections officials, respectfully disagree." Along with other national associations that represent state and local elections officials, the Election Center has attempted, with a large measure of success, to keep the decentralized structure of election administration intact.[60] Some states passed legislation requiring uniform standards, but most did not. Crafting standards and their implementation still largely rests with state and local elections officials.

Increased funding for new technology will not alone remedy these problems. After the fiasco of the 2000 presidential election, for example, the state of Florida undertook a major overhaul of its election system. Among other things, elections officials in Florida acquired new voting machines. However, the first test of these improved machines and procedures in Florida's September 2002 primary elections revealed was that these technological changes were not matched with improvements in poll-worker training and voter education. The human element proved to be decisive in the breakdown in the election process during the 2002 elections, and it caused voter disenfranchisement. A range of problems beset voters and poll workers alike. For instance, many poll workers did not know how to set up the new voting machines, and there were an insufficient number of outlets. Voters in many counties had not been trained to use the machines. "Stories of malfunctioning machines, incorrect ballots, poll workers not following a host of new rules, and polling places opening in some cases hours late came in from all corners of the state."[61] While these problems were not as numerous or severe as in 2000, the September 2002 primary was far from the model of reform that elections officials and elected officials had anticipated.

Because Florida refused to institute statewide uniform standards and procedures, conditions varied widely from county to county. According to Doug Chapin, director of electionline.org, "Florida's experience on September 10 revealed what happens when each county approaches election administration differently. Some Florida counties trained their poll workers for up to twelve hours on new machines. In Broward County poll workers received only three hours of training. That may have made the difference between success and chaos at the polls."[62]

These kinds of problems, however, were not unanticipated. One official in the Florida Division of Elections noted in 2001 that "human error is the biggest threat to the integrity of any voting system. Even with your crudest systems, if the human does everything they're supposed to, that system will work."[63] To be sure, other factors contributed to election problems, such as power outages, busy telephone lines, and so on. Still, at some level these problems reflect a lack of sufficient planning and forethought about backup procedures. The Florida 2002 experience shows that humans—both poll workers and voters—are vulnerable and are a crucial link to successful election reform. Replacing outmoded technologies is important, but without resources and time to adequately train poll workers and educate voters, such disenfranchising problems will persist.

Thankfully Florida's experience in 2002 was not universal. Georgia also purchased new electronic voting machines following the 2000 elections (to head off a lawsuit that was filed shortly after the debacle in Florida). But Georgia went about the process much differently, and their strategy yielded much better results. For one thing, Georgia purchased a single kind of machine for use statewide. More important, Georgia went to great lengths to educate voters and poll workers alike about how to properly use the new voting machines. It undertook an extensive statewide voter education campaign that permitted voters to practice on the new machines in locations throughout Georgia prior to election day. As a consequence, the 2002 elections ran smoothly. This was a result of two interconnected changes: use of new voting machines *and* education of the people expected to operate them.[64] Some have questioned the reliability of some of Georgia's voting machines' computer programming and security systems, however, raising concerns that some machines' vote totals were not accurate.[65] Similar examples of divergent experiences were manifested in the 2004 elections in many states, pointing to an inescapable conclusion: voting technology by itself will not improve election administration. It can help, particularly where inferior technologies produce disparities in results. But success depends in large measure on how the new technology is used.

The political and management structure of election administration also matters. Even in states in which responsibility for voter registration and election administration falls under a secretary of state, local structures generally are bipartisan boards beholden to local officials, and these boards continue to exercise significant autonomy and discretion.[66] A few states continue to have a bipartisan board of elections at the state level. Six states have such a bipartisan board (Illinois, Maryland, New York, North Carolina, Virginia, and Wisconsin); five states have more than one state entity with overall election management responsibility (Oklahoma, Rhode Island, South Carolina, South Dakota, and Tennessee); the remaining thirty-nine states have a single appointed or elected official in charge. In most states (thirty-four) the secretary of state is the chief election official responsible for maintaining voter registration and administering elections; some secretaries of state are elected, and others are appointed by governors.[67] Yet in all cases partisan actors and dynamics are involved. The same is true for local election boards and officials.

Indeed, the methods used to select personnel at the state and, especially, local level and the manner in which these practices are employed by election administrators raise questions about how independent or nonpartisan they really can be. Whether elected or appointed, secretaries of state and local elections officials are usually active members of political parties and therefore subject to pressures similar to those exerted on other politicians. Given the discretionary capacity of elections officials and their ties to state and local political officials, it is no surprise that election administrators in some jurisdictions are more open to reform than those in other jurisdictions. Most are not open to reform.

The degree to which party leaders and elections officials restrict or promote access to registration and voting depends on several factors, including, but not limited to, the level of interparty and intraparty competition and the dominance of a particular party or faction at a specific time and place; the level of nonparticipation and the social and political characteristics of the nonvoters, which influences the political calculus of parties and candidates about mobilizing or demobilizing these potential voters; and the relations of elected officials and election administrators to other political forces and interest groups, and these groups' capacity to influence officials.[68] According to election experts this is true of virtually all jurisdictions, though nowhere is it more evident than in the historical experience of African Americans in the South. Other classes of citizens also experience disenfranchisement through discriminatory practices of elections officials, including young people and people with disabilities. Discriminatory behavior is not merely a relic of the past; it persists in the present.[69]

In response to reports of discrimination, some have argued for greater professionalism in election administration. For example, Richard Smolka, who runs the Institute of Election Administration and publishes a newsletter for elections officials called *Election Administration Reports,* has argued, "If integrity, accuracy, speed, efficiency and economy are to be achieved, . . . performance standards can ensure that elections officials, political parties, candidates and the public will receive the necessary service for a reasonable price." Performance standards, such as a minimum percentage of registered voters in the voting age population, and service standards, such as convenient polling place locations, availability of printed material, and availability of personnel to answer questions about registration and voting, would go far to improve the operations of election administration.[70] Similarly, election reformers have advocated for national standards and nonpartisan and professional election administration.[71]

Thankfully there have been important improvements in election administration over the past several decades. New legal and policy mandates in some jurisdictions provide greater access to registration and voting, organizations have been established to enhance the performance and professionalization of elections officials, and new technologies have been implemented to increase efficiency and decreased disenfranchisement. For example, the Americans with Disabilities Act and related court cases have forced elections officials in numerous jurisdictions to alter their practices to ensure equal access to people with disabilities. Similarly amendments to the Voting Rights Act and decisions in related cases have compelled elections officials to provide assistance to certain language minorities. The NVRA has forced even the most retrograde elections officials to comply with new proactive registration mandates. Regarding professionalization of election administration, the Election Center, in conjunction with Auburn University, offers training and certificate courses in various areas of elections, and the National Association of Secretaries of State and the National Association of State Election Directors have also made efforts to improve the operation of election administration.[72] Automation and computerization of registration records, as well as new voting and tabulation technologies, while not perfect, provide improvements over paper-intensive and error-prone registration methods and outmoded punch card and lever machine technologies.

HAVA has produced improvements already: from providing states and counties with sorely needed funding to purchase new, more technologically advanced voting equipment and requiring states to offer provisional ballots, to instituting incentives for standardizing procedures and establishing computerized, interactive statewide voter registration databases. But it remains to be seen how elected officials and election administrators will shape HAVA's implementation. The law leaves much to states and localities, including the crafting of enabling legislation, the establishment of standards and procedures, and the appropriation of funds. Given the political dynamics inherent in election administration—and specific provisions such as onerous new voter identification and provisional ballot requirements—HAVA has the potential to be either a boon or a bane to democracy in the United States. As evident in the 2004 elections, HAVA has been both thus far.

Although several factors produce America's low voter participation, restrictive election practices are a key part of the story. And while the extent of fraud is uncertain, one thing is sure: it was concerns about fraud that led to the imposition of restrictions that depress voter registration and turnout, whether intentionally or not. In both historical and contemporary contexts, certain groups have had an interest in alleging fraud and thereby shaping electoral rules and practices in a restrictive direction, and other groups have had an opposite interest. Review of historical and contemporary literature on election practices shows that election administration affects voter participation; thus this line of inquiry has the potential to produce a fuller explanation of voting behavior in the United States. As the following chapters show, political actors in New York have recognized this fact for well over a century. The stakes and prizes of politics are evident in contests over electoral arrangements.

Historical Roots of Election Rules
and Practices in New York

Why were so many Americans, in different places and at different times, denied the right to vote? How could Americans have thought of themselves as democratic while they possessed such a restricted franchise? Most fundamentally, perhaps, how, why and when did the laws governing suffrage change? —**Alexander Keyssar,** *The Right to Vote: The Contested History of Democracy in the United States*

The history and politics of voter registration and election administration is revealing. Examination of when and how particular voter registration procedures and administrative structures came into being, who promoted and opposed them, and what impacts they had on voter participation and electoral politics shows that election administration is far more important in times and places other than the post-Reconstruction South than is generally assumed. The classic case is indeed the South, where electoral rules implemented around the turn of the twentieth century intentionally and systematically disenfranchised most blacks and many poor whites. But similar measures, often more subtle and not as extensive, were also enacted in the North, as the history of New York, both the city and the state, clearly demonstrates.[1]

The genesis of voter registration procedures and the rise of election administration reflect important parallels between the South and the North, and particularly the Northeast. Republicans, reformers, independents, and dissident Democrats promoted changes in election law and practice to address a perception—which they themselves propagated—that "fraud, corruption and violence have marked the operation of our electoral system."[2] Efforts to eliminate big-city party machines' allegedly rampant corrupt practices in local government and electoral politics culminated in a series of reform measures passed by state legislatures at the end of the nineteenth and beginning of the twentieth century. New and increasingly stringent voter registration procedures and bipartisan boards of elections were instituted with the hope of ensuring more fair, honest, and legitimate elections and government.

Instead, the implementation of increasingly restrictive voter registration procedures and the establishment of bipartisan boards of elections coincided with a precipitous decline in voter participation. In New York state participation of eligible voters declined from a high of approximately 90 percent for presidential elections during the 1880s to only 57 percent by 1920; the most significant drop occurred between 1904 and 1912. The sharpest declines occurred in New York City: of all the state's counties, New York County (Manhattan) had the lowest turnout by 1910, having declined from 73.2 percent in 1894 to 59.4 percent in that year; similarly, turnout in Kings County (Brooklyn) declined from 77.6 percent in 1894 to 64.2 percent in 1910. Importantly, during this period only these two counties in all of New York state required 100 percent of voters to register in person. The election law required personal registration only in cities and villages with populations over five thousand, thus allowing large portions of the populations in other counties and unincorporated areas not to be fettered by in-person registration. In 1910 only 39.5 percent of the people of Dutchess County lived in cities or villages with populations of over 5,000 and were thus subject to in-person registration, and the county posted a 73.1 percent turnout rate. While the decline in turnout cannot be entirely attributed to the new rules and procedures, a significant portion of the drop-off appears to be related to these changes.[3]

The consequences of the institution of the new laws and boards of elections in New York and elsewhere provide insight into the political contests that surrounded their genesis. The political struggles and debates around efforts to inaugurate and implement more stringent voter registration procedures and to establish bipartisan boards of elections reveal patterns of partisan, class, and ethnocultural interests.

New York—The City and the State

Representative of a pattern that recurred all over the United States, the developments in New York state provide an excellent opportunity to examine these issues and to test questions empirically. There are many episodes of allegedly fraudulent electoral activity in the nineteenth and twentieth centuries in New York state, especially in its urban centers and particularly in New York City. Moreover, the numerous bills introduced by the state legislature in the last third of the nineteenth century and the first quarter of the twentieth century to guard against electoral fraud and corruption have left a rich historical record. A review of some of these legislative battles— together with a look at investigations by government agencies, private reform group activities, press coverage, and a wealth of secondary source material—provides ample data to assess the politics of fraud.[4]

Allegations of electoral fraud in New York during the 1867–1868 elections and the subsequent congressional inquiries triggered one of the few pre-1950 efforts by the national government to regulate elections. The result was passage in 1870–1871 of federal election laws that applied to both the North and the South. Supporters declared that the laws prevented people from voting repeatedly or under a false name and simultaneously protected them from intimidation and bribery. Opponents, led by Democrats, argued that these laws were intended not to curtail fraud as such but to limit legitimate franchise rights, and they pointed out that the laws were usually implemented by Republicans' appointees, who at that time held a majority at the national level. Both parties noted that New York held strategic importance for national electoral success. These federal election laws were repealed in 1894.[5]

Partisan Conflict, Procedural Restrictions, and the Role of Fraud

Events in New York state exemplify the introduction of voter registration procedures and the rise of election administration, particularly the pattern of initially applying registration to cities and the tendency to make the practices more stringent and restrictive over time. New York also exhibits the typical pattern of partisan wrangling over such measures, especially the use of charges of electoral fraud to justify an imposition. Whereas reform efforts to some extent may have been noble, motivated by moral and nonpartisan impulses in the interest of the public good, their effectiveness as a political strategy with distinct consequences for conflicting interests should not be overlooked. Charges of fraud, even if implicit, served as a powerful partisan weapon. Consequently they should not be taken at face value; they require thorough investigation and analysis.[6]

Republicans sought to impose a more stringent registration law for New York City while maintaining a weak or nonexistent registration law for the rest of the state. Conversely, Democrats sought a less stringent law for New York City or a uniform statewide registration law, the latter primarily to defeat a more restrictive law for New York City because they calculated that Republicans would balk at the imposition of the law on their constituencies upstate. A similar pattern can be found in neighboring New Jersey, where the majority of the numerous election laws passed between 1870 and 1900 were designed specifically to maintain the supremacy of the party currently in power. Obviously, by controlling election boards the party could seize control of the electoral apparatus and thus perpetuate control of the municipality.[7]

Focusing almost exclusively on Democrats in urban centers such as New York City, Albany, and Troy, reformers claimed that the political machines running the electoral mechanisms produced fraud. Yet this same control, reformers claimed, prevented them from collecting the data necessary to verify their allegations. Party machines may indeed have possessed important control over significant patronage resources and some election processes, but they were not all powerful.[8] Charges of fraud and corruption appear to have been used for political purposes.

Did the New York City political system truly deserve its long-standing reputation for corruption? Was it in fact more corrupt than the political systems in other cities? Or is it possible that New York City's corruption has simply been more fully exposed thanks to opponents of its political officials?

Republican organizations in New York City beat Democratic ones primarily by fueling hostility toward the party system, often through the use of state committees for investigating electoral practices. Periods of party-machine control of government alternated with periods of reform control, and the city's self-appointed reformers used exposés and investigations as a central strategy to gain political advantage. Then as now, documentation of incompetence, graft, and under-the-table dealings had potential to undermine the public's trust in the incumbent administration. The reform movements used exposés of corruption to gain power, and in the process they laid claim to their own leaders' right to rule.[9]

In determining the interests and stakes strategic actors had—and still have—in the charges of fraud and the struggles over rule changes regulating the franchise, we need to ask a set of related questions: First, what was the nature of the party system in New York—the state and the city—with reference to the links between parties and voters, particularly between the machines and various constituencies and conflicting group interests? Second, what was the nature of the variegated reform movements, as well as of mass popular mobilizations and third-party challenges? And third, how did the electoral system develop and change over time in the context of the New York political economy and the expansion of the role of urban government?

For example, what was the relationship between political machines and immigrant working-class constituents and interests? Did machines perform positive latent functions and help in the integration, ethnic succession, and social mobility of ethnic minorities, or were machines ultimately inimical to the interests of working-class constituencies? Did machines subversively threaten the interests of traditional elites and their ability to rule, and is that why they were attacked by opponents as criminal and illegal? Or were machines accommodating to elite interests and relatively corruption free?[10]

New York's Electoral History

On April 13, 1855, Governor Myron H. Clark vetoed one of the earliest attempts to establish voter registration in New York. The bill, he claimed, would disenfranchise citizens who, for one reason or another, failed to appear at the registration offices before the election. "However important may be the protection of the elective franchise from abuse," he concluded, "it must be done in such manner as not to restrict the exercise of a constitutional right, or prohibit any individual . . . from exercising the privilege guaranteed to him by the constitution."[11]

In 1857 and 1858 Governor John A. King strongly but unsuccessfully urged the passage of a registration law. In 1859 Governor Edwin D. Morgan made the same recommendation, and the legislature passed a limited registration law providing for the precinct officers in some municipalities to draw up registration lists without the personal application of voters. These were far less restrictive methods than the more stringent procedures called for in 1865 by Governor Reuben E. Fenton, who urged the legislature to apply the law not only to cities and large villages but county wide. According to this proposal, after the first day of registration no more names could be added except by personal application of the voter.[12]

In 1867 a debate between Democrats and Republicans took place that was to be repeated time and time again in New York state. An amendment proposed at the constitutional convention required a statewide compulsory registration law. Democratic delegates from New York City insisted that registration should be uniform throughout the state, while upstate delegates, who were Republicans, stoutly maintained that registration laws should not apply to rural sections. Consequently the proposed amendment was defeated.[13]

In a maneuver apparently intended to obtain a more lenient registration law for New York City, in 1869 Governor John T. Hoffman, a Democrat, advocated a uniform statewide registration law. He believed that in principle any registration law should apply equally to all areas of the state. Yet even he conceded that a law requiring in-person registration was unnecessary in rural districts. "The inconvenience and expense to the electors in such districts, from such a law, are very great, with no adequate good result in compensation." As a result, all registry laws were repealed on April 28, 1870, except those affecting the city and county of New York.[14]

Much of the dispute over these registration laws was a direct result of the allegedly rampant fraudulent electoral activities in New York City under the Tweed administration in 1867–1870. These allegations, made by Republicans and muckraking reformers, also led to local, state, and federal investigations; to the production of the first federal legislation regulating elections; and to intervention by the federal government in election procedures within the states.[15]

The Tweed ring has been regarded as the preeminent symbol of municipal corruption.[16] Allegedly fraudulent electoral activity by the Tammany organization occurred during the 1867 elections, leading Republicans and their supporters to address this issue before the 1868 elections. Taking such measures as invoking the aid of the U.S. Circuit Court to prevent the use of allegedly forged naturalization papers to prove eligibility to vote, Republican supporters secured the indictments of several men and published allegedly fraudulent registry lists. Against such actions John T. Hoffman, at that time the Tammany Democratic mayor, protested: "We are on the eve of an important election. Intense excitement pervades the whole community. Unscrupulous, designing and dangerous men, political partisans, are resorting to extraordinary means to increase it. Gross and unfounded charges of fraud are made by them against those high in authority. Threats are made against naturalized citizens. . . . Let no citizen, however, be deterred by any threats or fears, but let him assert his rights boldly and resolutely, and he will find his perfect protection under the laws and the lawfully constituted authorities of the State." Hoffman offered a reward of one hundred dollars for the arrest and conviction of any person charged with "intimidating, obstructing or defrauding any voter in the exercise of his right as an elector."[17]

These charges and countercharges led to further charges and investigations. In response to a demand by the prestigious Union League Club, the U.S. House of Representatives appointed an investigating committee. The committee's majority report, submitted on February 23, 1869, led to the passage of the federal election laws of 1870–1871. The Republican majority reported that thousands of aliens had been fraudulently naturalized, that thousands of certificates had been counted in the names of fictitious persons, that people had voted from two to forty times, that extensive fraud was committed during the counting of the vote, and that some courts and officials had showed gross neglect and disregard for the law. They concluded that through these methods Hoffman and the Democratic electors had been fraudulently chosen.[18]

The evidence consisted primarily of witnesses' statements and statistics on the rate of naturalization and on the ratio of votes to population. These were compared to corresponding figures from previous elections to show what Republicans contended was a disproportionately large increase in turnout that must have been accomplished fraudulently. For example, the committee's majority observed that the Supreme Court and the superior courts, supposedly controlled by Tweed, naturalized immigrants very quickly, and concluded that therefore they did so fraudulently (they completed naturalizations in thirty to ninety seconds per person, whereas the court of common pleas, which was supposedly controlled not by Tweed but by Republicans, completed them in three to five minutes per person). Moreover, the ratio of votes cast to population in 1868 was almost one to five, whereas from 1856 to 1867 it had been one to eight. The committee concluded that "these frauds were the result of a systematic plan of gigantic proportions, stealthily prearranged and boldly executed, not merely by bands of degraded desperados, but with the direct sanction, approval, or aid of many prominent officials and citizens of New York."[19]

By contrast, the Democratic minority of the House committee issued a report in which they attempted to "systematically address and repudiate" the various charges. They "attributed the whole investigation to partisan motives," noting that the investigation arose initially at the behest of the Republican-leaning Union League Club of New York City. The Democrats' minority report included testimony from witnesses who admitted they were paid to lie regarding fraud—that is, they had testified before the committee that they had committed fraud themselves or had witnessed fraud by others when, in reality, they had not. Moreover, the Democrats pointed to alternative explanations for the increase in naturalization and voting: they contended that immigration patterns in 1867–1868 were different from those during the Civil War, alleged that a census completed in 1865 under Republican auspices was faulty, and argued that the previous naturalization methods of the courts were ineffective and reflected a pattern of discrimination and hostility to immigrants.

The report noted that in 1865 the Republican legislature, "in the hope of reducing the democratic vote, which was fast becoming a majority in the State," had passed a law requiring adopted citizens to exhibit a certificate of naturalization to register to vote, which effectively disenfranchised large numbers of voters who had voted in previous elections but could not produce their papers. "Although this shut out thousands of naturalized voters, it did not reduce the democratic vote in the city as largely as the republican managers had expected. So the next year, 1866, they passed a law . . . by which no person could be registered unless he appeared before the inspectors in person." As a result, individuals who had been naturalized while minors through the citizenship of their fathers and were unable to produce their fathers' certificates had to go through the naturalization process again before they could vote. The Democrats concluded that the "chief desire of the majority in the testimony taken and in their report seems to have been the injury of the democratic party, by showing that the vote in the city of New York was both excessive and fraudulent."[20]

The 1870 electoral campaign in New York City revolved around such charges, countercharges, and legislative maneuvering, with the Tammany and Tweed frauds at the vortex. The level of scrutiny was visible. Congress authorized circuit courts to appoint one person from each party in each election district to oversee registration, the operation of the polls, and the counting of votes.[21]

Immigrants were those most often identified as the instruments of unscrupulous politicians. Yet evidence does not substantiate the claim that illegal voting was done primarily by the foreign born and principally via illegal naturalization and multiple voting. Urban New York counties consistently ranked near the bottom in turnout. The four metropolitan counties of New York City were in the bottom ten, averaging more than 12 percent below the state's median turnout. Moreover, native-born citizens voted at proportionally higher rates than naturalized citizens. "Even while multiple voting may artificially inflate turnout statistics, immigrants did not vote illegally to the extent that has been commonly believed."[22]

In the same way, the legendary image of a thoroughly corrupt Tweed and Tammany in the 1860s and 1870s, which pervades histories of New York, is based upon outdated historiography and a lack of adequate and reliable information. Allegations of Tweed's corruption reached mythic proportions thanks to changes in the political economy and the strong political motives of opponents and reformers, most of whom were drawn from the suburbs and the rural areas of the state. Republicans and Democrats such as Horatio Seymour and Samuel Tilden, and the budding business-backed reform movement, which included such groups as the Committee of Seventy, saw Tweed and Tammany as a symbol of the city and thus a symbol of the threat to their own political and economic dominance. These interest groups joined hands to beat back the city by attacking Tammany Hall.[23]

The charges against Tweed, including those of electoral fraud, were unfounded or at least wildly exaggerated, and the campaign against him staged kangaroo proceedings for partisan ends. Even Samuel Tilden, who later would aid in dethroning Tweed, admitted that the investigation into electoral fraud during the 1868 elections was questionable: "It would have been impossible to credit beforehand that, under these circumstances, at a hotly contested Presidential election, when the Republican party was watchful, and straining itself to the utmost—systematic frauds in voting and canvassing could be perpetrated without the complicity of the leading representatives of the Republican party in the city; nor is it easy now to see how that was possible."[24]

Similarly, critics—primarily Democrats—denounced a commission headed by Tilden that recommended restricting the franchise in municipal elections to taxpayers and rent payers. This was ostensibly to limit the electorate to citizens whose economic interests made them more invested and fit for political participation, but it would have disenfranchised poor voters.[25]

The struggles heated up during the late 1880s and through the 1890s, culminating in the creation of the most restrictive voter registration procedures in New York's history and the institutionalization of bipartisan boards of elections near the century's end. These developments coincided with convulsive economic and social changes, including the rapid expansion of New York's economy and population—particularly in New York City—and labor, progressive, and socialist challenges, most notably the campaign of Henry George, who ran for mayor of New York City in 1886. The eventual imposition of the new registration laws and creation of the boards of elections produced a constricted electorate, particularly among New York City residents and especially working-class constituents within the city, and resulted in important political changes.

Soon after New York City's intensely scrutinized elections under Tweed, there were further attempts to increase the stringency of registration laws and to expand such laws to other cities. The primary new restriction was that voters must register in person yearly at an election office or site, whereas previously election registrars had drawn up lists of registrants. This shifted the burden of registering from government to the individual. The new requirement was introduced ostensibly to reduce the possibility of election fraud, but it proved particularly burdensome for working people who found it difficult to register at the hours and locations available. In 1880 such registration laws were enacted for cities containing 300,000 inhabitants; then, in response to allegations of fraud in parts of the state where personal registration was not required, it was expanded to include cities containing 16,000 people. Governor Alonzo Cornell pushed for and got minor extensions into other jurisdictions as well.

From 1888 to 1892, a reform movement led by such groups as the Commonwealth Club, the Ballot Reform League, and the City Reform Club, with the aid of Republican allies, pushed state legislators to introduce several bills that were ostensibly intended to curtail fraud in the electoral process. The most significant were the Saxton Bill, which proposed the adoption of the Australian ballot (or secret ballot, which allowed voters to cast ballots in private), and several registration bills. The Saxton Bill was introduced in 1888 and 1889, then was finally adopted in a modified form in 1890, and a general registration bill including a personal registration provision for New York City was adopted for all cities in 1890. The electoral fraud issue encouraged discontent with those in power and gave challengers and reformers opportunity to broaden their electoral support, which, in turn, led to electoral rule changes. Apparently, the strategic actors believed the stakes were high.[26]

In March 1889 Governor David B. Hill vetoed a bill that would have required voter registration in Fishkill, Dutchess County, arguing that if there were registration in Fishkill, there should be registration all over Dutchess County, and all over the state for that matter. "I cannot approve a special law for one town, not because a registration law is not required for that town, but because there should be passed a general registration law applicable to all the towns of the state. . . . Frauds would be impossible, or rendered more difficult, by a well-considered general registration act such as now exists in the cities of the state."[27] Hill pushed for a statewide bill, claiming that frauds occur also in rural communities and villages. In 1890 a general registration law was passed that applied throughout the state, except in the cities of New York and Brooklyn and in certain local elections that required personal registration.

Governor Roswell P. Flower, in his annual message to the state legislature during January 1893, attempted to have personal registration extended:

> In 1890 the Ballot Reform act was fitly supplemented by a statute compelling personal annual registration of voters in all the cities of the State—the statute being in this respect merely an extension of the law which had for years applied only to New York and Brooklyn. . . . I recommend its still further extension to the remainder of the State. . . . This is necessary to prevent false registration in villages and country districts. . . . While it imposes hardships and to some extent discourages voting, its advantages are greater than its disadvantages. . . . There is no good reason, however, why the safeguards thus thrown around the ballot in cities should not be extended to the towns and villages of this State. Such laws should, so far as possible, be uniform in their application.[28]

The measure lost by a single vote.

During the mid-1890s Republicans, business groups, and reformers not aligned with the ascendant faction in the Democratic Party campaigned on charges of Democratic electoral fraud. These campaigns played an important part in subsequent electoral defeats of those Democrats, and they led to the passage of significant electoral reform measures, including constitutional changes and statutory legislation that institutionalized much more stringent voter registration procedures and established a system of bipartisan boards of elections.[29]

During the early 1890s the Cleveland faction of the Democratic Party united with a growing independent movement and many Republicans in a campaign to defeat the ascendant Democratic Party faction and its policies, primarily by employing accusations of dishonesty. This coalitional attack was not tightly coordinated and was motivated by various and even conflicting groups and agendas. The first group, dissident Democrats associated with a faction allied to Grover Cleveland, were attempting to prevent the loss of power within their own party. The second group was a revived and rejuvenated independent reform movement led by businessmen and professionals who had faith in nonpartisan government, which they believed would be more efficient. The third group, Republicans, assisted in the revitalization of independent reform by capitalizing on Democratic divisions and mistakes.[30]

One of the main weapons used by this loose coalition—especially by Republicans—was a series of investigations into alleged corruption by the Democratic Party, including electoral fraud, especially within New York City. Negative campaigning via fraud and corruption charges contributed to the defeat of the Democrats. This led to the Republican ascendancy in New York state and reform regimes in the city, as well as significant constitutional and electoral changes, ultimately helping the consolidation of corporate capitalism in New York. In Brooklyn, for example, reform Democrats (such as the German Democratic Club, the Young Men's Democratic Club, and the Citizens Union) broke ranks and endorsed a Republican candidate for mayor. Such rifts produced a snowball effect: the reform antimachine campaign became an effort to prevent allegedly corrupt electoral practices by the Brooklyn Democratic organization. In 1893 such allegations of bossism and corruption led to more setbacks for the Democrats, having an even greater effect than the severe economic depression of that year.[31]

In 1893 allegations of election fraud in Albany led to the formation of the Committee of Fifty, which sought to pass legislation to prevent fraudulent registration and voting. In their efforts to ensure the punishment of those responsible for corruption and to oppose the Democratic machine in municipal elections scheduled for the spring of 1894, the combined force of Republicans, nonpartisans, and independent Democrats ran candidates of the "Honest Election Party" and carried the vote in Albany, also electing a Republican mayor. The Committee of Fifty triumphantly stated: "Earnest work was performed in purging the registry, and on election day at the polls, with the gratifying result of electing the entire city ticket and a controlling representation in the county and city boards. A healthy change in government is already evident both as to efficiency and economy."[32]

The same kinds of dynamics were manifested in Troy. Allegations that the victorious Democratic Party machine had committed fraud in 1893 made honest elections the primary campaign issue of reformers during the following spring. An observer of that time, William Tolman, noted that reform organizations such as the Committee of Public Safety were organized in 1894 in Troy "to investigate and endeavor to bring to the bar of justice all fraud in connection with the liberties of the people, especially crimes against the right of suffrage." These events led to the appointment of a New York state Senate committee to investigate election methods and the alleged fraud; the committee concluded that fraud was committed. But just as in the House committee reports of 1870, the Democratic minority issued a report claiming that the Republican majority report was flawed and politically motivated.[33]

In New York City such scenarios ruled the day. The 1893 victory by the Democrats, which was sizable, spurred reformers and Republicans to charge their opponents with a list of abuses, including fraudulent registration, repeat voting, ballot miscounts, intimidation, and assaults on poll watchers. Reform and Republican-led investigations produced the conviction of thirty-nine Democratic election inspectors on charges of fraud. These scandals produced the sense that Tammany was vulnerable to such allegations and prosecutions, which in turn led to the formation of several new independent and Democratic organizations in late 1893 and early 1894.[34]

For example, the Committee of Seventy, recreated by the Chamber of Commerce to engineer Tammany defeat in 1894, stated that it believed it was continuing in the tradition of its namesake, the committee that had helped to unseat Tweed. A number of these same gentlemen would later put together the Citizens Union in 1897 to again try to oust a Tammany administration, which had won in that year. Their campaign largely revolved around charges of corruption and electoral fraud. The City Reform Club, with the aid of Pinkerton detectives and a score of legal personnel, spent much time and money gathering evidence of alleged electoral corruption and police-connected vice, such as prostitution, gambling, and illegal saloons. Because of debts they turned over their information to Charles Parkhurst, a crusading clergyman, whose activities and sensational revelations led to a highly publicized state investigation by the Lexow Committee.[35]

Largely as a result of these forces and the publicity surrounding the Lexow Committee's investigation of corruption in the New York City police department, including electoral fraud, Tammany met decisive defeat in 1894. Even though both nonpartisans and antimachine Democrats criticized the Republican partisan maneuvering behind the investigations, the exposés resulted in their desired outcome: Democratic defeat. At the time several journals commended the Lexow investigation. *Harper's Weekly* called it "unexpectedly successful," and the anti-Democratic machine *New York Times* said, "Whatever motives actuated the appointment of that Committee, it is . . . incontestable that . . . [it] has performed an enormous public service."[36]

While economic and cultural issues generally dominated the election of 1894 outside of New York City and the other locations discussed here, the main campaign topic of the Republicans and other opponents of the dominant Democratic Party in New York was Democratic corruption, especially in the cities. In the context of the economic depression, the electoral fraud issue appears to have encouraged discontent with those in power and to have given challengers and reformers opportunity to win broad electoral victories in 1894, which, in turn, led to electoral rule changes that helped shape subsequent political developments and corporate consolidation.

Many Republicans—both from upstate and from Brooklyn—were also alarmed at the proposed creation of greater New York City, in which the five boroughs would be unified for the first time. Doubling the city's population had strong political implications. Alarm about the city's political and economic dominance triggered a reaction at the 1894 state constitutional convention, where Republicans passed several provisions to counter the effects of consolidation.[37]

Changes to Electoral Law, Election Administration, and the State Constitution

Among the most significant and lasting changes were those to the state's constitution. The use of fraud allegations played a decisive role in the institutionalization of restrictive voter registration procedures and bipartisan election administration in New York. Once such provisions were placed in the state's constitution, they would be more likely to endure.[38]

The implementation of these new measures was also an important matter.[39] The struggle to establish bipartisan boards of elections to implement registration procedures and conduct elections was integral to the battles among parties and reformers. New York provides a typical and important case. A historical review of the statutory and constitutional provision for New York's election administration is revealing.

In revolutionary-era New York, local officials were appointed, and they or their designees were responsible for the conduct of elections. The administration of elections under New York's first election law (1778) was the duty in rural areas of the town supervisor, clerk, and assessors acting as election inspectors, and in the city of New York of inspectors appointed in each ward by a group that included the mayor, the recorder, aldermen, common councilmen, assessors, and vestrymen. This early model was retained in subsequent law, but the practice was generalized to involve a group of officials, most often the Common Council, acting as the appointing authority for election administrators in the cities.[40]

During the 1830s and 1840s, with the removal of property qualifications and a broadening of participation in local elections, mayors and other local officials came to be elected rather than appointed. In 1840, a New York City law constructed election districts staffed by three election inspectors appointed by the Common Council. Thereafter the law required the election of three commissioners of registry in each ward and three election inspectors in each district. In 1841, a new law divided other cities in the state into election districts, with the explicit provision that one of the initial appointees to each three-member board of election inspectors must belong to a different party from the other two. Thus, following initial appointments the voting system adopted for New York City was used to fill other cities' boards of election inspectors.[41]

The first law that established true bipartisan election administration (1872) was applicable only to New York City. However, a board of elections had not yet been established there. Instead, elections in the city were the responsibility of the Bureau of Elections within the police department. Under the new statute the Police Commission would appoint four election inspectors in each election district to a one-year term, with minority-party police commissioners recommending the minority-party inspectors. New York City was a Democratic town, but this bipartisan system, established by a Republican legislature, ensured Republican patronage.[42] The Police Commission, which headed the police department, included four members who were appointed to six-year terms. There was no statutory requirement that the Police Commission itself be bipartisan until 1894.

For upstate cities and rural areas of the state, by contrast, the law provided for three to five election inspectors in each election district; the posts were filled by a system of election, appointment, or a combination of the two that ensured control for the majority—almost always Republican. Newly created bipartisan police boards were used by Republicans to thwart Democratic control prior to the establishment of separate boards of elections. These police boards were often tailored to fit local conditions to ensure Republican control. For example, the law in Albany was fashioned to shift the power to appoint members to the board from the mayor to the council; the Republicans controlled the council and the Democrats controlled the mayoralty. In New York City, an investigation by the Lexow Committee resulted in the creation of a four-person, bipartisan board in which the party county committees would, in effect, name the members, thus ensuring Republican representation.[43]

In 1880 bipartisan boards had overall supervisory responsibility for elections within a city, rather than responsibility at the actual voting level. These boards first appeared in Brooklyn, where the two major parties each had two members of a city board of elections. The registrars, poll clerks, and inspectors were also of both parties. In 1882 the law was amended to provide for the Police Commission to appoint for every election district three inspectors, two from the majority and one from the minority, for one-year terms. The law also called for appointments to be made by the commission from lists provided by chairs of the party executive committees, and it even established a procedure for determining which recommendations would be used when a political party split into factions. By 1887 New York City had a law requiring that elections officials be appointed, thus involving party leaders in election administration.[44]

In 1892 the Democrats gained control of the state government, and Governor Roswell P. Flower moved to establish their control of the electoral process in New York City, stating: "If boards of inspectors, a majority of whom are Republicans, are safe and economical in Republican strongholds of the state, boards of inspectors, a majority of whom are Democrats, ought to be equally safe and economical in the Democratic strongholds."[45] This was the Democratic measure that lost by one vote. The Democrats planned to adopt a host of such measures at the 1894 constitutional convention. Republicans, however, recaptured control of the state legislature and instead passed a series of countermeasures that transformed New York state's election system; the measures held well into the twentieth century.

Because Governor Flower's term had not yet ended, some compromises were reached following the election of 1894. For example, instead of bipartisan election administration being limited to New York City, it was established throughout the state. In rural areas, two inspectors were to be elected and two appointed to ensure partisan balance. In all of the cities, as in New York, an appointment process would be used that included selection from lists provided by party leaders.[46]

The 1894 constitutional convention offered Republicans the chance to write reforms into law.[47] They sought to secure in perpetuity the prominent role of party leaders in the bipartisan structure created by the provisions of this compromise. The Convention Committee on Suffrage, chaired by Edward Lauterbach, initially drafted a provision requiring equal representation of the major parties on boards of elections, but with no role in their selection for party officials. "Upon submitting the question for debate on the floor of the convention (and after consultation with the Committee on Cities, which was also interested in the question)," however, "Lauterbach immediately added an amendment providing a role in nominating board members for party leaders, similar to the provisions of the 1894 statute. When an objection was raised about the substantial nature of this change by John Cochran, a Brooklyn Democrat and committee member, the matter was laid over so that the committee could meet again. It later reported the provision with the party leader role intact."[48]

Review of the convention documents reveals the partisan nature of the debate on this question. For example, Benjamin Dean, a Republican of Jamestown, observed that the legal change entrenched in the Constitution the power of the state chairmen of the major parties to choose the election officials in every city in the state of New York. John Bowers, a Democrat, offered an amendment to remove party leaders from the process, but it failed in a voice vote.[49] Convention delegate Charles Z. Lincoln pointed out it was not Lauterbach's intent to have the bipartisan requirement apply to "central boards of elections or police boards or commissioners or other officers who might be charged with the duty of appointing local election officers, and that it was intended to apply only to officers in election districts."[50]

Few convention delegates raised general objections to the bipartisan provision. Benjamin Dean, however, argued that partisan deadlock might arise if the parties were divided on a matter before a board with an even number of members. This observation proved to be astute. Nathan Woodward, an upstate Republican from near Buffalo, also questioned the capacity of a bipartisan board with an even number of members to decide controversial matters. Defenders of the provision acknowledged that hypothetically deadlock was possible but argued that experience showed that such deadlocks were rare. Moreover, the annoyance of occasional deadlock between parties was a risk worth taking, said Jesse Johnson of Brooklyn, to "avoid the much greater . . . danger and menace of the majority party having practically the control over the election."[51] The constitutional convention of 1894, strongly influenced by reform elements in the Republican Party, thus quickly developed a plan for bipartisan election administration under which the parties found agreement in the creation of a new source of patronage. Each of the "major parties could reward 18,400 trustworthy adherents with jobs paying at least $5 each on election day," according to one estimate.[52]

Buoyed by their victories at the constitutional convention, Republicans and reformers continued to press for increased "ballot security" measures. In 1898, a law was passed that established state supervision over elections in New York City and nearby towns. It was to be headed by a superintendent of elections and staffed by seven hundred deputies with board powers to investigate election matters and enforce relevant laws. The next year, 1899, another measure was passed that expanded the state's oversight of elections in New York City.[53]

The new election administrative office, the Office of State Superintendent of Elections, created in 1898, was supposed to identify election frauds in New York City and prosecute offenders. Initially the office focused on New York City, but by 1911 it was reorganized and made statewide. The office was abolished in 1921 when it came under bad repute for being dominated by Tammany. The responsibility of election administration in the rest of the state fell to the counties, with the offices of the secretary of state and attorney general sharing responsibility at the state level. A bipartisan state board of elections was not created again until 1974.[54] In New York City, a bipartisan board of elections was created in 1901 when a bipartisan bureau in the police department that had been performing this function was removed and made into a separate agency. These constitutional and statutory changes, which institutionalized bipartisan political control of New York's election administration, established in the late nineteenth century a political structure that has lasted intact to this day.

Post-1900 Investigations into New York City's Election Administration

Several investigations and reports by city agencies conducted during the early twentieth century document the practices and politics of the New

York City Board of Elections. Even though these studies were carried out under different administrations—some reform and some regular—there is a surprising uniformity to their findings. The reports largely described similar conditions and reached the same conclusions, detailing how the board has operated as an appendage of the two major parties, which exercise direct control over its policies and practices.

The reports begin by describing the political composition of the board, which was made up of appointees of Democratic and Republican party county leaders; the two parties were represented equally on the board at all levels. The leadership comprised four commissioners (two each from Manhattan and Brooklyn) until 1973, when the number of commissioners was expanded to ten to represent each of the five boroughs equally. The bipartisan arrangement is replicated at all levels of the board's structure and operation, down to the thousands of poll site workers.

One of the first reports, which were often written in a style reflecting the reform perspective, was presented in 1910 by Commissioner of Accounts Raymond B. Fosdick. It concluded that the board exerted significant discretionary capacity in administering the election law and that it did so in the interests of the Democrat and Republican parties, largely to the detriment of efficiency and economy and, more importantly, to the detriment of voters' interests.[55] The board ignored provisions of the law concerning the location of polling places and failed to keep proper records or conduct examinations for election officers. The same office also conducted a study of the primary election held on March 26, 1912. Fosdick's report concluded that in "many of the election districts no ballots were received at all, while in others they were received too late to be of service. The result was that thousands of voters were effectively disenfranchised. . . . It appears that the greatest inconvenience was felt in Brooklyn."[56]

The accounting office, under a different mayoral administration and Commissioner Leonard Wallerstein, conducted another study of the board in 1917. Wallerstein found similar conditions and disenfranchising practices. His report focused on poll sites: "The Board has abdicated in favor of the two dominant political organizations its function of designating polling places." Moreover, the selection of election officers by the parties led to incompetence and "misconduct." "Party patronage constituted an insuperable obstacle to all Commissioners of Accounts who attempt to reform the Board of Elections."[57]

A two-year study of the board's practices conducted in the late 1930s under Mayor La Guardia produced a scathing indictment of the board. "The Board has operated as an integral part of the spoils system and has abdicated numerous of its functions to the political machines responsible for the appointment of its members. As a result, the administration of the election law in this city has been marked by illegality, inefficiency, laxity and waste."[58] Indeed, the commissioner maintained that even though many of the most glaring defects were at least partially corrected during the investigation, "as long as election law administration remains under the irresponsible dominance of political machines," he had little hope of permanent improvement.

Socialists similarly criticized the practices of the board. They cited a number of "abuses" perpetrated against the citizens of New York by both Republicans and "Tammany Democrats" and Republicans. "How does intimidation work? You live, let us say in a Democratic district where there are reasons for the leader to make a big showing. You are one of the group not definitely lined up already by fear or favor on the boss's side. Your name is checked to show that fact. If English is your native language and you have reasonable self-assurance and a job out of the boss's reach, you usually vote your own way, even if that way is Socialist or Communist. . . . Assuming that you have given the Tammany canvasser no assurances, you run a hostile gauntlet as you stand in line at the polls even though that hostility may not result in immediate violence."[59]

Each of the government reports made a series of recommendations: that civil service exams be required for board employees; that appointment of board commissioners and employees be removed from the control of the county party organizations and given to the mayor and Board of Aldermen (later City Council); that representatives be added from the other boroughs; and so on.

Wallace Sayre and Herbert Kaufman would later report in their exhaustive study of New York City that while "fraud and abuse" had apparently been "all but eliminated," and elections were now more "honest and accurate," similar administrative problems and conditions persisted into the 1950s. "It is the discretionary powers of the Board that are most important—and most controversial—in the contest for the stakes of politics in New York City."[60]

Impact of Law Changes on Voter Participation and Politics

The passage of the election law provisions during the decades around the turn of the twentieth century carried significant consequences. The new voter registration procedures and boards of elections inaugurated increasingly restrictive election practices, which, in turn, contributed to a precipitous decline in voter turnout in New York. By creating obstacles to the polls, the 1890 mandate for personal registration in all cities discouraged voter participation.[61] Whereas 80 to 90 percent of eligible voters cast a vote for president in the 1880s and 1890s, only 55 percent did by 1912. Comparable declines in gubernatorial elections were also posted—turnout rates of 60 to 70 percent in the 1880s and 1890s plummeted to 45 to 49 percent by 1912. The majority of the decline came between 1904 and 1912, when the impact of legal and institutional changes were likely to have been greater, especially with changes in the patterns of implementation by boards of elections. Turnout declined in New York City from 73.2 percent in 1894 to 59.4 percent in 1910, and in Kings County, from 77.6 percent to 64.2 percent in the same years.[62]

Thus restrictive voter registration procedures and election administration practices appear to have constricted the scope of the electorate in the case of New York. They also help account for an increasing class-skewed bias in the electorate. These institutional arrangements persisted well into the twentieth century. For example, Republicans were able to maintain the provision for annual personal registration for downstate and urban New York while upstate counties had been able to use "permanent personal registration" (PPR), which meant a voter needed to register in person only once and could remain registered by voting at least once every two years; thus PPR greatly reduced the burden of registration.

Different voter registration requirements contributed to sharply different rates of voter participation and had different political ramifications. In 1954 a reluctant Republican legislature granted all counties the option to use PPR if they chose; and in 1967 the legislature required counties statewide to do so. The effects of the two systems—permanent versus annual personal registration—are evident in registration rates. In 1950, 88 percent of the voting age population were registered in the twenty-eight counties covered by the more lenient system. By contrast, only 58 percent were registered in the remaining, mostly urban counties, which had the more stringent procedure. Between 1960 and 1967, when more than 90 percent of the state's electorate were free of the annual registration requirement, registration increased 2 percent in presidential election years and more than 10 percent in both gubernatorial and local election years.[63]

Political consequences followed the relaxation of registration requirements. Once PPR was required statewide beginning in 1967, Democrats scored important gains in the legislature. By 1975 they had become the majority party in the Assembly, although Republicans retained their majority in the Senate.

Thus the disparity in registration rates between upstate and downstate voters, which provided the margin of victory for the Republican dominance of New York during much of the twentieth century, not only directly issued from the different registration procedures and election administration practices governing upstate and downstate regions but also contributed to distinct electoral and political outcomes. With a shrinking voter base, particularly in New York City, beginning at the turn of the twentieth century, the partisan split between urban areas and rural and suburban areas became even more pronounced and important politically. Republicans had dominated upstate and rural New York for most of the latter part of the nineteenth century while Democrats dominated the urban centers, and as the twentieth century progressed, the shrinking voter base in New York City gave further advantage to Republicans, who were able to control both houses in the legislature and elect Republican governors (Thomas Dewey, 1943–1954, and Nelson Rockefeller, 1959–1973). While this regional split was never complete, each party possessed an enormous edge in party enrollment and the ability to win legislative races in its respective stronghold.

The Republicans' electoral advantage also translated into distinct policy consequences for the different bases the parties maintained, often in terms of whether policies would benefit New York City or the rest of the state. The parties' control over the legislative branches—with the Republicans dominating the Senate and the Democrats dominating the Assembly after 1975—continues to provide each with an institutional power base. From this base, each party can advocate distinct policy positions, exercise leverage in negotiations over legislation, advance campaign strategies, raise funds, and otherwise work to advance its interests.[64]

Fraud charges and legislative struggles at the turn of the twentieth century led to the imposition of restrictive voter registration procedures and election administrative practices. The actors involved believed the stakes were high, and the consequences for subsequent developments in New York proved significant. As the following chapters make clear, the legacy of these changes in the practice of election administration is significant for politics today.

The Impact of Election Rules and Practices
in New York State, 1984–2004

The electoral arrangements that were forged in the past continue to affect political participation and politics. During most of the twentieth century—in sharp contrast to the previous century—New York, both the state and the city, experienced a long decline in turnout. After New York ranked among the top states in turnout during the nineteenth century, from 1920 to 1956, its turnout declined until it ranked in the bottom third of the thirty-two states outside the South for presidential and gubernatorial races. During recent decades participation in New York has reached new lows. In the 1960s and 1970s only four states outside the South and the border states had lower turnout than New York. By the time of the 1992 presidential election, New York State ranked forty-first in the nation in turnout and forty-seventh in voter registration; in 2000, New York ranked forty-fifth in turnout and forty-sixth in registration. New York's low turnout rates appear to be a result of its increasing noncitizen immigrant population. Nevertheless, calculating voters as a percentage of *citizens* still leaves New York ranking low compared with the rest of the nation: at thirty-sixth in turnout and fortieth in registration in 2000.[1]

It is predominantly low-income and minority people who are unregistered and are the nonvoters. For example, only 49.5 percent of blacks were registered to vote and only 41.3 percent actually voted in the 1988 elections, a high-water mark. Hispanics' rates are considerably worse, with only 32.6 percent of Hispanics of voting age registered and 26.4 percent voting. In contrast, whites have a 63.5 percent registration rate and 57.2 percent turnout rate. In the 2000 elections in the state of New York, whites' registration rate was 63.2 percent, compared to 51 percent for blacks, 35.5 percent for Hispanics, and 23 percent for Asian–Pacific Islanders. Turnout for whites was 55.1 percent compared with 45.7 percent for blacks, 29.4 percent for Hispanics, and 17.3 percent for Asian–Pacific Islanders. Again, the numbers remain highly skewed even after removing noncitizens from the calculation. Registration and voting rates for *citizens* in 2000 were still significantly skewed by race, albeit less so: registration for white citizens was 70.9 percent compared with 63.3 percent for black citizens, 56 percent for Hispanic citizens, and 49.3 percent for Asian–Pacific Islander citizens; voter turnout for white citizens was 62.1 percent compared with 55.6 percent for black citizens, 46.6 percent for Hispanic citizens, and 37 percent for Asian–Pacific Islander citizens.[2]

New York City's turnout rates have been approximately 10 to 15 percent lower than those of the state as a whole. One study showed that out of the twenty-six largest cities in the United States, New York City ranked twenty-third in registration and fifteenth in turnout. Moreover, the city's proportion of the state's electorate dropped from 51 percent in 1940 to 31 percent in 1996. In the 1990s nearly 2 million of the nearly 5 million eligible citizens were unregistered, with only a slight increase in registrations by 2004. As is the case in the state as a whole, low-income and minority citizens in New York City are disproportionately nonvoters.[3]

Some observers have argued that these shifts in voter participation patterns have had important impacts. Low registration and turnout rates for low-income and minority citizens in New York City have contributed to their reduced political power. Since minorities and the poor overwhelmingly register and vote Democratic in New York, the Democratic Party as a whole and particular factions within the party have been weakened at all levels.[4]

New York's skewed voting patterns may also be related to another electoral characteristic of the state: its rates of incumbency are among the highest in the country. According to the National Conference of State Legislatures, between 1979 and 1989 New York's legislature had the lowest rate of turnover of all states. Between 1986 and 1990, both of its houses had a reelection rate of 98 percent or better. From 1980 to 2002, a period in which 2,321 general elections were held for state legislative seats, only thirty incumbents were defeated. In 2002, 98 percent of incumbents in primary and general elections won. Moreover, the margin of victory for incumbents has grown, from 20 percent in 1970 to an average margin of more than 50 percent in 2002. New York's high incumbency rates are also likely to be related to another factor: one-third to one-half of all election law cases in the nation are in New York State; they are primarily legal challenges by the regular county party organizations to get insurgent candidates thrown off the ballot by disqualifying their nominating petitions of registered voters.[5]

To address these developments, a coalition of reform advocates formed in New York during the early 1980s to conduct mass voter registration and to lobby for changes in electoral law and practices. This loose coalition of voting rights advocates operated under several umbrella organizational names—the New York Voter Registration Campaign, the New York State Network on Voter Registration, and subsequently the Statewide Coalition for Voter Participation—and comprised a broad range of over fifty civic groups, including the New York Public Interest Research Group (NYPIRG), Common Cause, the League of Woman Voters, the NAACP, Human SERVE, several unions, and other civil rights and community-based organizations. Together with some allies from the liberal wing of the Democratic Party and from progressive third parties, they contended that New York's comparatively low rates of turnout contribute to a political system that is insufficiently representative and democratic, and they placed part of the blame on what they characterized as New York's restrictive registration system and election administration. They strove to increase turnout, especially among minorities and the poor, and argued that reforming election administration rules and practices would create an enlarged electorate and potentially lead to the selection of different candidates and policies, thus invigorating the polity. They advocated a number of measures, including simplifying registration forms and procedures, making forms more available to most citizens at public agencies, eliminating the purging of registrants for nonvoting, shortening registration deadlines or providing for election-day registration, and upgrading both the human and physical machinery of election administration.

Some of these reform proposals were adopted. Both the state and the city have taken steps during the past dozen years to promote registration and voting. In 1975, for example, the state legislature adopted voter registration by mail, and in 1981 the legislature extended the interval during which a person could fail to vote but still remain registered from two to four years. In 1984 and again in 1990 Governor Mario Cuomo issued an executive order to provide for registration at various state agencies; Mayor Edward Koch did the same for New York City agencies in 1986. In 1988 a revised New York City Charter created the Voter Assistance Commission (VAC), which is mandated to promote voter registration, especially among groups with disproportionately low rates, primarily through agency-based registration. New York's cumbersome voter registration form was simplified in 1993; and some modest improvements in election administration have been implemented.

Yet registration and voting in most of New York continued to stagnate. Why have these reforms been unsuccessful in increasing registration and turnout rates? What can account for the failures of New York's electoral system? While there is surely a complex web of factors involved, the role of New York's election administration may be an integral part of the explanation. Retrograde practices of election administration have contributed, at least in part, to low rates of participation; election administration officials and other state officials have effectively undermined many of the reforms. The partisan struggles around the various reforms and their implementation reveal interests and stakes similar to those evident during earlier periods.

After a review of the political context in which these voter registration groups and reform advocates mobilized, I explore the administrative barriers they encountered and the politics of several election reforms enacted during the past twenty years. Specifically, I examine changes to voter registration procedures and programs—particularly the distribution of voter registration forms through government agencies ("motor voter" programs)—and the role of key political actors, including the state board of elections, in shaping the design and implementation of programs, and I assess the impact of these reforms on voter registration, participation, and politics in New York. These insights into New York's low registration and participation rates should help illuminate what is a general feature of U.S. elections, especially in urban areas and among minority and working-class constituencies.

Political Context, Political Mobilization, and Political Arithmetic

Following Ronald Reagan's election in 1980—for which turnout nationally was the lowest in a presidential election since 1924—a national coalition of reform advocates and liberal Democrats launched a campaign to boost voter registration and participation. Some of these advocates were keenly aware of the political arithmetic: the scale of nonvoting and therefore the political potential of an expanded electorate. In 1980, 163 million Americans were eligible to vote, but only 86.5 million, or 53 percent, actually voted. Only about 100 to 110 million Americans, or 60 percent to 70 percent, were registered. Reagan won with votes from fewer than 27 percent of those eligible to vote, so that nonvoters outnumbered Reagan voters by nearly two to one. Moreover, the sharp skew of the electorate by class and race suggested the significance of the nonvoters for Democrats, progressives, and independents. Thus, voter participation issues became increasingly important points of contention within the dramatically changing political and economic environment of the 1980s.[6]

In the 1982 midterm elections, progressives were encouraged by an upsurge in the number of low-income voters and new voters—blacks, blue-collar workers, and the unemployed—which contributed to Democratic gains in Congress and several state legislatures, and to Democratic gubernatorial wins in New York, Texas, Ohio, and New Mexico. In 1983 the election of a number of black mayors, most notably Harold Washington in Chicago, confirmed their hope. Most importantly, Jesse Jackson's campaign for president in 1984 brought a broad spectrum of progressive activists into electoral work. Together with unions, black churches, and nonpartisan nonprofit organizations, a "rainbow" of progressives mounted mass voter registration drives, many for their first time ever. Primarily targeting low-income groups, this mobilization generated coalitional camaraderie reminiscent of the civil rights and peace movements of the 1960s. While impact varied, the upsurge in electoral activity, especially by blacks, led to increases in voter registration and turnout and to the election of thirty-one black mayors and numerous other local black officials.[7]

Further encouraged by these developments, several advocacy groups lobbied liberal Democrats to expand registration opportunities; one strategy they advocated was offering registration opportunities and forms through government agencies. Beginning in 1984 they succeeded in obtaining gubernatorial executive orders establishing agency-based voter registration programs in six states, including New York. These agency-based registration initiatives provoked political conflict, however, and several programs were rescinded, saddled with stringent limitations, or effectively undermined. Amid charges that agencies were doing partisan voter registration or were steering registrants to vote against Republicans, state Republican Party organizations launched legal challenges, the Reagan administration threatened to cut off grants-in-aid, and social service providers faced political reprisals in Republican-controlled counties, such as those on Long Island. Republican strategists recognized the potential danger of an expanded electorate, but they also saw positive possibilities. In response to Democratic efforts, Republicans constructed a technologically sophisticated and well-financed (with $10 million to $15 million) registration drive targeting upscale voters and Christian fundamentalists. The Republican registration efforts probably equaled or bettered those of the nonprofits and the Democrats, producing close to half of the 7 million new registrants added to the rolls from 1982 to 1984, most of them white, better-off southerners.[8]

Partisans and registration advocates on both sides attribute the mixed results of the 1982–1984 voter mobilization efforts in part to existing legal and institutional barriers that thwarted their registration efforts. Organizers increasingly encountered these barriers and obstructive elections officials, which limited their effectiveness and highlighted election administration as a target for reform. Advocates identified several restrictive practices: elections officials refused to deputize campaign volunteers as registrars in many states, and they limited the number of forms and amount of assistance they made available to organizations, maintained limited working hours, refused to distribute forms at government agencies and other public places, and disqualified many new registrants by using strict standards to process registration forms.

Thus the mobilization to register the new voters generated conflicts over election rules, procedures, and institutions. In response to obstruction by many elections officials, a consortium of legal defense organizations was formed, and it filed lawsuits in more than a dozen states. Most suits, however, failed because judges did not agree that the right to register was constitutionally protected. This left election boards free to continue as before.[9]

Such episodes show that elections officials possess enormous discretionary capacity to implement election law and to act or not act on proposals that could affect voter registration and participation. For example, election boards in New York have exercised broad discretion in determining the eligibility of students, often not allowing students to vote in the jurisdiction where they attend school. Some town boards shifted poll sites away from college campuses when the board was controlled by Republicans and back to campuses when the board was under Democratic control. For example, the Republican majority in the town of Harrison voted in February 1996 "to change electoral district lines and remove a polling place at the State University of New York (SUNY) at Purchase, where the voters are overwhelmingly Democrats. This is a Harrison tradition: when Democrats rule the Town Board, the college gets voting booths, when Republicans rule, the polls are removed."[10] Such episodes have not been limited to the town of Harrison.

Even when state election law requires elections officials to ensure that mailed voter registration forms are "as widely and freely distributed as possible," many county boards choose to interpret such provisions narrowly. For example, in the early to mid-1980s, several counties in New York made forms available only at the election board's offices or in town clerk offices.

NYPIRG reported that Erie, Albany, and New York City limited distribution to board of elections offices; any individual, group, or establishment that wished to obtain or distribute forms had to locate the local board of elections and arrange to pick up materials.[11]

The registration forms themselves can pose obstacles. Prior to 1993, forms were complicated and confusing to many voters, and they required two signatures—one on the front and one on the back of the form. The board of elections in New York City discarded forms that were signed on only one side or that were completed in pencil. In addition, some forms were discarded because they had a discrepancy between the printed name and either signature, such as using Robert and then Bob or a title or initial. These latter types of cases, however, were contrary to election law and probably did not occur as frequently as the former cases.[12]

By contrast, other boards of elections, such as the Monroe County board, instituted programs that provided for wider distribution of voter registration forms at some government agencies and other public places, and they saw modest increases in voter registration and participation. During a public hearing on voter participation in 1983, one advocate noted the relatively higher registration rates in Monroe County, which he attributed to "outstanding cooperation of the election commissioners, both past and present, as well as the super cooperation of the board of election's staff at all levels." Monroe County has been in the forefront of modernization of election administration. It began to replace its aging voting machines and to automate some processes many years before any other county, setting aside funds for this modernization. Thomas Wallace, then executive director of the New York State Board of Elections, confirmed this at a public hearing, stating that "Monroe County . . . probably have the most modern election machines in the State of New York."[13] Jerome Koenig, a former legislative specialist for the Election Law Committee of the state Assembly, corroborated the contention that Monroe County had taken the first and most far-reaching steps in the state to expand access to registration and to move toward modernization. He attributed these initiatives to the liberal Democratic commissioners on the Monroe County board of elections and in the County Executive, who provided funding, as well as to successful lobbying by advocates.[14]

However, elections officials—both within New York state and nationally—have consistently opposed and resisted efforts to increase access to voter registration. Only a minority of elections officials supported passage of the National Voter Registration Act (NVRA), and most opposed it and even lobbied against its passage. One of the few exceptions was Thomas Wilkey, the former executive director of the state board of elections, who supported the NVRA before it passed Congress in 1993. In general, proposals by reformers—such as those for wider distribution of registration forms or less stringent criteria for processing forms—have usually fallen on unsympathetic ears or were adopted only after significant pressure was brought to bear.[15]

Connected to these larger national efforts, dozens of organizations mobilized in New York to conduct mass voter registration during the latter half of 1983 and throughout 1984. The state's coalition of voter registration organizations and voting rights advocates mobilized toward this end, engaging in a variety of nonpartisan activities to increase voter registration and participation throughout the state, with a primary focus on New York City. Coalition members "targeted groups of women, minorities, poorer New Yorkers and students" and claimed to have registered over one hundred thousand voters. While much of this mobilization was related to Jesse Jackson's 1984 campaign, other registration efforts were already under way by black and progressive groups. Several labor unions also mounted voter registration efforts around Jackson's campaign.[16]

Largely as a result of these efforts, New York's registration rate increased significantly. By the end of 1984, registration topped 9 million in New York state for the first time since 1972, increasing 10 percent with 68 percent of its voting age population registered, compared with only 58 percent in 1982.[17] New York City had more than 3 million registered voters in 1984 for the first time since 1972. In New York City alone, 855,000 voter registration applications were submitted to the city board of elections by the registration deadline in October 1984, one of the largest increases ever. (Only 540,000 registrants, however, were found to be new after duplicate registrations, changes of address, deaths, and so on were accounted for.) Registration increased for people of color in particular. J. Phillip Thompson estimates that between 1982 and 1984 black registration increased by 129,000, or 25 percent, while Latino registration increased by 18,000. White registration declined by 22,000. Between 1984 and 1985, black registration increased by 78,700, or 14 percent, and Latino registration increased by 81,800, or 21 percent. John Hull Mollenkopf estimates increases in registration in black and Latino assembly districts between 1982 and 1985 of up to 10,000 per district.[18]

Although the mobilization of voter registration advocates produced significant gains, activist organizations encountered numerous barriers that inhibited their efforts and limited the extent of the voter registration increase. Such administrative obstacles in New York have been highlighted in numerous public forums, including the news media, legislative and public hearings, court cases, and government reports. Participation can be affected by many kinds of action and inaction on the part of boards of elections, including failure to conduct effective outreach; use of slipshod procedures in processing registration applications, which results in applicants not being properly registered; failure to effectively notify voters or misinforming them about registration status, poll site location, voting procedures, and other critical voter information; providing absentee ballots to voters late or not providing them at all; failure to open poll sites on time and to provide them with adequate staffing and sufficient materials; and failure of poll workers to follow provisions intended to ensure that voters correctly cast their ballots, by providing proper instructions on how to use a voting machine or allowing voters to vote by affidavit ballot or emergency ballot, for example. All of these can result in the disenfranchisement of eligible voters.

My research on New York boards of elections—particularly the New York City board—identified numerous kinds of such practices, which can be grouped into three categories: (1) provisions for access to registration opportunities and information, (2) procedures for processing registration applications and certifying registration, and (3) election-day operations and certification of votes. I selected these practices for further examination and analysis on the basis of the following criteria: first, these were the main areas in which voter registration activists found that practices were obstructive and produced disenfranchisement; second, these practices constitute the main activity of boards of elections with regard to voter registration as mandated in state election law; third, boards have discretionary capacities in these areas; and fourth, they are the primary means by which boards can increase or decrease participation. Thus these election practices have relevance to the political actors and interests who have ties to New York's election administration.

Legislative Hearings

Voter registration advocates highlighted these administrative problems during public hearings held by the New York state legislature. One of the first hearings was held during the spring of the 1984 presidential campaign.[19] The general purpose was to receive comment about how to increase voter registration, with a focus on election law reform. Advocates testified about a range of obstacles they experienced in the course of their voter registration activity. Many of those testifying focused on administrative and procedural problems associated with boards of elections and made recommendations for improvement. The nature and scope of the problems highlighted and the recommendations made by advocates during the hearing are numerous, making clear that the administrative problems encountered by voter registration groups were significant and produced disenfranchisement. The advocates' and the media's scrutiny and their criticism of such election practices, and the pressure they were able to bring to bear led directly to changes. Many of the advocates' recommendations were adopted in election law and by the state and local boards, producing important improvements in the boards' operations and modest increases in voter registration.[20]

Registration advocates petitioned key legislators to hold the public hearing in the spring in an attempt to preempt problems they anticipated during the 1984 elections. Following those elections, advocacy organizations continued to lobby for changes. They succeeded in convincing several key Democratic officials to hold four similar public hearings in 1987 and 1988 to address the problems they continued to experience. These efforts did produce some important changes in election law and in boards of elections' administrative practices, particularly in those of the New York City board.[21]

Regarding the first type of disenfranchising practices highlighted during the 1984 public hearing, limited public access to voting information and materials and limited outreach to the public by boards of elections, voter registration advocates complained of a dearth of information that the public needs and is entitled to. In the first place, most people did not know that they need to be registered—and at their current address—to vote; that the board of elections is the agency responsible for running elections, and how to contact the board and register; and where to obtain information about candidates and offices up for election. While there has been some improvement, these claims still largely hold true today.

Advocates recommended that funds be provided for advertising campaigns that contain basic election information for citizens and that more proactive and aggressive steps be taken by elections officials to enlist voter participation. The city and state boards adopted some modest outreach programs in subsequent years. The state and city boards did institute a telephone help line, as voter registration organizations had urged them to do. They also made some progress in advertising election information, and they increased their efforts to distribute registration forms more broadly. For example, Monroe County, which had already begun similar programs in the late 1970s, expanded such efforts, and the New York City board later provided forms to post offices and libraries (although this was done inconsistently and the program was poorly designed and monitored, so it produced only modest increases in registration).

Another problem raised by advocates was that boards of elections treated registration organizations differently from one another. There was a general perception that some groups were treated favorably while other groups had limited access to registration forms, materials, and assistance. Some registration activists reported being treated with "outright disdain" and being "discouraged" from conducting registration. In some cases, organizations that requested registration forms in bulk were given only limited quantities. In other cases, groups were unable to obtain registration forms because of "lack of sufficient supply." There appeared to be a pattern of differential treatment: those clubs and organizations that had good relations with the regular party organizations and elections officials received more favorable treatment than clubs and organizations that had poorer relations. Some groups have thus been disadvantaged in their effectiveness at registering targeted constituencies. Such organizations tended to work primarily with poor and minority groups as opposed to middle-class whites. For example, people from the League of Women Voters, which primarily serves middle-class women, stated they received preferential treatment, while advocates from groups such as ACORN (Association of Community Organizations for Reform Now) and the Community Service Society, which target low-income and minority populations, reported that the board periodically "threw them curve balls of various sorts": they would limit the number of registration forms or delay their availability, there would be problems processing forms with the result that names of registrants would be missing names on election day, and so on. Thomas Wallace, then executive director of the state board of elections, admitted at a public hearing that "there have been problems when groups wish to put on registration drives and wish to obtain registration forms in quantity lots."[22]

The second category of disenfranchising practices, problematic voter registration procedures, can be further broken down into three main types: the design of the voter registration form by the state board of elections, the processing of forms by election boards, and notification to voters of registration status and poll site information.

Election law requires that certain data be provided on a voter registration form, but the state board of elections and local boards have the leeway to require additional information and to design the format. New York's registration form—like that of many other states—has been strongly criticized. For example, until voter registration forms were redesigned in the early 1990s, voters had to sign on the front and the back of the form. Often applicants did not sign both sides, so thousands of applications were invalidated by board clerks. In addition, advocates criticized voter registration forms that contained numerous unnecessary or intimidating items, such as questions regarding employment or citizenship (the question "Were you born in the U.S.?" for example, potentially discriminates against naturalized citizens and those from Puerto Rico, the Virgin Islands, and Guam).

Numerous attempts by advocates to have the state and city boards redesign the form failed. Finally, in 1992–1993, the state moved to adopt several significant changes. The old form was in a cumbersome threefold format, required two signatures, and contained confusing and legalistic language in the instructions; the new form has just one fold, contains fewer items (some of the "intimidating" questions having been removed), has simple and clear instructions, and requires only one signature. To his credit, Thomas Wilkey, then executive director of the state board of elections, consulted with literacy experts and advocates for people with disabilities regarding form design. Advocates hailed these changes as important and universally agreed that their registration work had been greatly simplified. Yet the redesigned form still retained items that advocates contended were unnecessary. For example, the citizenship questions could create problems for some voters, as could the request for a telephone number. The citizenship question should be removed, advocates argued, because registrants were already required to sign an attestation, under penalty of perjury, that they were citizens.

Advocates cited several problems related to the processing of voter registration forms. Boards of elections lost or misfiled applications or rejected them for overly technical reasons. In the former cases, clerical errors were apparently at work, while in the latter instances, board policy and practices were at issue. The problems resulting from board policy and practice—what advocates refer to as disenfranchisement for overly technical reasons—are more serious. Voter registration applications of particular categories of voters, such as students and the homeless, have also been rejected by boards as not meeting residency requirements. Advocates contested rejection on such "technical grounds" as politically motivated. Boards argued that the law required them to reject such applications to guard against potential vote fraud, but advocates were not convinced. They argued that voter disenfranchisement could not be justified, whatever the reason might be.

At a 1984 public hearing, several representatives from civic groups made this point and, more importantly, detailed how voter disenfranchisement was occurring because of such practices. Alan Rothstein, associate director of the Citizens Union, said, "Local boards should be as flexible as possible. Incomplete forms should be accepted and registrants given a chance to complete them, either in person or by mail before an election or, in certain circumstances, at the polls on election day. If one of the two signatures required on the form is omitted, let that be corrected later, too. . . . Some boards do make those adjustments and are that flexible, others are not."

Norman Adler, coordinator of the New York State Network on Voter Registration, provided details of specific administrative practices in the state that resulted in voter disenfranchisement:

> In our experience with processing now upwards of 70,000 forms, when you turn the forms in to many of the boards of elections in the state, regardless of what the law does or does not say, when the clerks at the board of elections process the form, if anything is missing from the form, they do one of three things. In the big boards of elections, they throw the form in the garbage. In the middle-size boards of elections, they try to contact the person by mail. In the small boards of elections, they may actually phone the person and say come in and correct the form. We estimate that we are losing 15 percent of all the people who presently fill out voter registration cards because of the inadequate clerical treatment of the forms. . . . No matter what the law says, that's the way it's treated.

An election expert, Jerome Koenig, then chief of staff for the Assembly Election Law Committee, confirmed at the March 1984 hearing that such disenfranchising practices occur and suggested a possible remedy: "I understand that in some boards of elections if the signature is missing on the back, they photocopy the signature from the front and paste it on the back, and that perhaps should be standard procedure."[23]

If we calculate the potential disenfranchising impact of the 15 percent "clerical error" rate attributed to the New York City boards, of the 70,000 registration applications the Network on Voter Registration claimed to have submitted for processing by March 1984, 10,500 would have been discarded or administratively rejected. Between 1982 and 1985 voter registration increased from 2,544,000 to 3,014,000 (or by 470,000). Thus, at a 15 percent error rate, 70,500 would have been administratively disenfranchised in New York City during this period.

One of the concerns emerging from testimony at the March 1984 public hearing was that procedures should be standardized across the state and across all boards. In New York state, boards of elections have conducted and continue to conduct their operations differently from one another, and employees within a board may also vary in particular procedures. This has a variety of consequences for voter registration and participation. Rothstein noted that the Citizens Union "found that election officials are not always fully informed about proper registration procedures." However, some board officials contended that part of the blame may lie with the registration organizations themselves, arguing that organizations may "lose" applications either inadvertently or purposefully, particularly if they do not like the party the registrant chose to enroll in.

Another problem advocates raised about the processing of forms concerned board personnel's determinations regarding residency requirements. Many boards, advocates contended, discriminated against three discrete classes of citizens: students, the homeless, and the disabled. Arthur Eisenberg, then at the New York Civil Liberties Union, noted that New York had been particularly hostile to college students compared with other states. Testifying before the March 1984 joint committee, Eisenberg stated that a few days after the 1971 ratification of the 26th Amendment, which lowered the voting age to eighteen, New York enacted two laws that would make it more difficult for college students to vote. Lawsuits were immediately filed, including *Ramey* v. *Rockefeller,* in which a federal court said it was too early to know whether local elections officials would use the law to discriminate against college students. Eisenberg noted that after twelve years "it's no longer too early to tell." He had conducted a survey of voting practices in counties that contained large student populations and had found that "students are routinely denied the right to vote by local registrars who believe that college students simply should not vote in their college communities." Some of them were hostile to students who wished to vote from their school addresses, which had "a very significant dampening effect upon the mass registration." Local registrars were able to make this determination because of the "enormous discretion" they possessed.[24]

Another advocate, Hope Geisler, legislative director for the State University of New York (SUNY) Student Association, stated at the same hearing that board officials held powerful discretionary capacity and used it to the detriment of student voters. She explained that the officials required students to complete questionnaires and had "the power to review information which would determine a student's financial independence, income sources, employment and so on, all in an effort to find the student's true residence for voting purposes."

According to a survey conducted by Roman Hedges, professor of political science at SUNY-Albany, the practice of singling out students to complete special questionnaires, oral interviews, and sworn statements regularly occurred in numerous counties, including Chautauqua, Albany, Otsego, Cortland, Erie, Livingston, Oneida, Oswego, Saratoga, and St. Lawrence. Geisler said one of the worst examples of a county election board preventing students from even going through the registration process took place in Otsego County. Students at SUNY-Oneonta tried to register to vote on special registration days that the board holds to enroll new voters, but they were turned away when they identified themselves as students. The county board color coded registration forms that students requested by mail so officials would know they were student forms. Even the college administration cooperated with the county board by sending it lists of all enrolled students so the board could find students' registration applications "to weed them out."[25]

Local elections officials countered that they were only concerned with potential voter fraud, particularly double voting. They would make a determination after reviewing the voter registration application and questionnaire—if a student got that far—about whether to accept or reject the application. According to several advocacy organizations, most such applications were denied. Advocates contended that either local boards were dominated by Republicans, or Republican officials on the boards were more likely to be involved in denying students residency status and, therefore, voting rights. Democratic elections officials, however, were also involved in these places, being members of boards. Eisenberg and representatives from NYPIRG contended that elections officials of both parties were politically motivated. Why? First, students tended to vote Democratic in the 1980s, which Republican officials were aware of. Second, Democratic officials feared that students might vote for insurgents within their own party in primary elections (for example, for Jesse Jackson in 1984).[26]

In response, students took the board to court, and in *Brown v. Maddalone* the judge issued a preliminary injunction compelling the board not only to stop discriminating against students but also to register every student in the county. According to the New York Civil Liberties Union and NYPIRG, in another egregiously bad case in a hotly contested county—Westchester—Republican poll watchers challenged all students attempting to cast ballots, creating "highly intimidating conditions which resulted in many students merely leaving without voting." Advocates estimated that the number of college students affected by such practices in New York state was in the tens of thousands.[27]

Several cases in which homeless persons were denied registration and voting rights also led to litigation that ultimately provided relief. The Coalition for the Homeless won a landmark case, *Pitts v. New York City Board of Elections*, which enjoined boards from rejecting registration applications by homeless persons on the grounds "that they fail to inhabit a home in the traditional sense."[28]

Advocates contended that hundreds of thousands of New Yorkers never were properly notified by mail of their registration status, their poll site, and upcoming election dates as prescribed by law. Alan Rothstein of the Citizens Union argued:

> Boards of elections should inform the applicant promptly as to whether the application has been accepted or rejected. Although boards are required by law to notify the voter in either case, it has been our experience that persons whose applications are not accepted are often not notified. . . . The notice going out from the board of elections as to whether the application is accepted or rejected is crucial. I think if they get a notice that they can vote, with some piece of paper in their hand or some card, that's going to give them much more information than they have now. I think there are hundreds of thousands of people who have no idea whether they are listed or not this year.

Similarly, Hulbert James noted that his organization found numerous examples in which voter notification cards were not properly mailed out to registrants. Moreover, advocates contended there was "an absence of anything from the board of elections" to indicate that it was moving to correct these problems of processing registration applications and mailing notification cards.[29]

Advocates detailed numerous ways people are disenfranchised at poll sites as well. "There is something subtly foreboding about the voting process, from lining up to vote through possible scrutiny by officials and watchers at the polls. . . . Where people turn up at the wrong polling place or are otherwise informed they have no registration on record, how elections officials at the polls handle that situation might determine whether that person will bother to vote at all, ever."[30] This appears to have been an all-too-common problem affecting a large number of people during the early and mid-1980s, and lapses of this sort continue to occur, albeit less frequently. The impact on voting is clear: such problems can lead to disenfranchisement, especially for low-income and minority voters and people with disabilities.

Advocates stressed the need for expanded recruitment and effective training of poll workers, creation of informational materials for the public, and general improvements in the organization of election-day operations. They also pressed for increases in pay and alternative recruitment of workers to remove the staffing of the polls from the patronage system. They recommended that answers to commonly asked questions be made available to voters in written form at poll sites on election day, and they suggested that this informational material could take the form of posters, voting rights flyers, and so on. Advocates continued to press for such legal and administrative changes throughout the rest of the 1980s. Many of their recommendations were adopted and contributed to important improvements in boards' operations. The state board incorporated several recommendations into its materials, training, and oversight work with boards throughout the state, and many of these recommendations were later incorporated into the main goals and achievements of the New York City Elections Project, an agency that was established to assist the city board in automating, computerizing, and generally modernizing its operations.

The issue of poll site selection was also raised, as was accessibility to people with disabilities. Although the state's election law has required a general policy of accessibility since the late 1970s, boards routinely have granted waivers to sites and sidestepped this policy. Following intensive lobbying efforts by disabilities advocates, in 1984 Governor Cuomo presented to the legislature Bill #152, which would limit the circumstances under which waivers could be granted. In New York City, a 1984 lawsuit brought by a group of advocates for people with disabilities (*Hill* v. *Board of Elections*) forced the board to provide accessibility, which was achieved for the entire city by the early 1990s. Boards of elections and several election experts, particularly Jerome Koenig, contend that this requirement has had the detrimental side effect of reducing the overall number of poll sites in the state and city. Outside of New York City, the number of sites declined from 6,644 in 1986 to 5,736 in 1992, with the degree of accessibility increasing from 85 percent in 1986 to 94 percent in 1992. In New York City the number of poll sites declined from 1,359 in 1986 to 1,251 in 1992, with the accessibility rate increasing substantially from only 33 percent in 1986 to 94 percent in 1992. Advocates countered that while surely the number of accessible sites were few and the time to bring these and other sites into compliance has contributed to the decline in the total number of sites, the boards have justified these reductions as cost-saving measures and, perhaps, have used this as an excuse to limit the number of sites for political reasons.[31]

Advocates expressed concern regarding boards of elections being the final arbiter of registration, given their pattern of inefficiency, error, and potential political discrimination. They urged the legislature and boards of elections to adopt a registration form that contained a tear-off receipt or record to indicate that its holder had applied to register. While not legal proof of registration, this would alert elections officials to problems needing follow-up investigation. They also recommended that boards number registration forms given to groups for better accountability. Finally, the recommendation that voter registration records be computerized became one of the cornerstones of efforts to improve and modernize the board's operations. The former two recommendations were not adopted, but New York's boards of elections were computerized at the municipal and county levels during the next two decades, and the federal Help America Vote Act (HAVA) now requires it of all states.

Finally, advocates repeatedly stressed, in the 1984 hearing and in subsequent public hearings and lobbying efforts, that one of their primary recommendations was for the state to establish effective nonpartisan agency-based voter registration programs. Advocates pressed for this as the main solution to the problem of low registration and participation in New York.

Agency-Based Registration Programs in New York

The early attempts to institute agency-based voter registration programs in New York were a gross failure. From 1984 to 1994, Republican legal maneuvering and procedural obstructionism effectively thwarted efforts by voter registration advocates and their liberal Democratic supporters to establish a permanent and effective government-led voter registration system in New York state. The legal and administrative barriers that Republicans erected, combined with the lethargy of conservative Democrats whose incumbency interests may have tempered their support for agency registration, blunted efforts to expand the franchise in New York.

The passage of the National Voter Registration Act (NVRA, popularly known as "motor voter") in 1995 removed most of the legal and procedural obstacles that Republicans had erected. For the most part, motor voter has proven to be an effective system of registering voters, producing the greatest increase in agency-based voter registration in the state's history. Despite late and flawed implementation of the NVRA in New York, compared with many other states and given the potential number of registrants, significant numbers of people have been added to the rolls. During the first year of motor voter—1995, an "off" election year—432,625 people were registered through the NVRA agencies. By comparison, only 8,000 were registered in the state's agency programs in 1994. The executive director of the state board of elections, Thomas Wilkey, stated, "while we have had agency-based registration programs in the past, they have never generated this level of activity" (see table 1).[32] However, Republicans, who captured the state house at the end of 1994, have since undermined fuller and more effective implementation of the NVRA.

In theory, agency-based voter registration enlists government employees, on a daily and year-round basis, to offer nonpartisan voter registration to every member of the public who uses state and local government agencies' services. Such programs have varied widely throughout the states in program design and effectiveness of implementation. In New York most programs initially were passive: agencies placed voter registration forms on a counter or table generally removed from the place where the main business of the agency was conducted. Many agency-based registration programs existed in name only, with many offices lacking forms for extended periods or never implementing registration at all. Such passive systems registered very few agency clients. The active agency-based voter registration programs required by the NVRA, however, have proven to be highly effective at rapidly registering the unregistered.

Indeed, several states and cities that had earlier implemented well-designed active programs—for example, some state motor vehicles agencies amended their agency application forms to include a voter registration form and provided assistance to clients in completion of it—had registered significant numbers of citizens this way.[33] Washington, D.C., for example, had increased voter registration by 9 percent during a four-year period (1990 to 1994) when it lost 10 percent of its voting age population. The program registered a greater number of low-income and minority citizens.[34]

Advocates persuaded Governor Cuomo to issue Executive Order 43, establishing voter registration in state agencies in 1984. According to Frances Fox Piven and Richard A. Cloward, Norman Adler and Victor Gotbaum of AFSCME District Council 37 "were crucial in persuading Governor Cuomo to issue an order, as were . . . political leaders Ruth Messinger, Carl McCall, and Herman Badillo." Reportedly Cuomo and his strategists were keenly aware that their reelection fortunes might depend on turnout of groups that had supported him in 1982. Integral to their calculations was an awareness that increased voter registration and participation of low-income and minority groups would likely benefit Cuomo in his reelection bid in 1986; this strongly figured into his decision to issue Executive Order 43, and in a form that advocates had lobbied for.[35]

Within seventy-two hours of the issuance of Executive Order 43, however, the state Republican Party challenged the program in the state Supreme Court and restrained Cuomo from proceeding. Even though the appellate division and the New York State Court of Appeals (the state's highest court) eventually rejected their arguments, Republicans nevertheless succeeded in severely limiting the scope and effectiveness of Cuomo's program by persuading the courts that state employees should be prohibited from verbally offering voter registration, offering assistance in completing registration forms, or answering questions. Nor could workers collect the forms. Thus, the courts restricted agencies from doing anything more than making forms available in waiting rooms.[36] Moreover, the Republican's court strategy effectively delayed implementation until 1985, long past the 1984 presidential election.

The limitations placed on voter registration in state agencies; other federal restrictions on agencies that received certain federal funds; and lackluster efforts by the then Republican-dominated state board of elections, which did little to enforce the order or to ensure that adequate supplies were maintained in agencies, severely limited the effectiveness of the program. Voter registration forms were available on tables in some offices, and there were no forms in others. This poorly designed passive system, with strong restrictions and weak implementation, coupled with other, existing legal obstacles and disenfranchising procedures—such as the purging of voters for nonvoting, the requirement that voters reregister when they change their address, and the restrictive practices of boards of elections—meant New York's initial attempt to institute agency registration resulted in little net gain of new voters.

After the courts allowed for implementation of Cuomo's executive order, implementation began in nine state agencies with 389 local offices in New York's fifty-six counties. In the first six months 41,533 registration forms

Table 1—Registration in Selected New York Counties, 1994–1995

County	Total Voting-Age Population[a]	Total Registered before NVRA[b]	Total Unregistered before NVRA	New Registrations under NVRA[c]	Percent of Unregistered Now Registered under NVRA
Queens	1,611,134	790,954	820,180	12,579	1.5
Brooklyn	1,791,812	972,205	819,607	18,421	2.2
Bronx	923,857	503,443	420,414	14,023	3.3
New York	1,279,043	773,837	505,206	24,853	4.9
Staten Island	301,429	204,339	97,090	4,739	4.8
Nassau	1,055,219	737,838	317,381	13,142	4.1
Erie	778,863	510,987	267,876	18,777	4.9
Westchester	715,563	458,336	257,227	11,179	4.3
Monroe	564,631	375,228	189,403	15,193	8.0
Albany	239,887	181,919	57,968	6,875	11.0
Orange	235,176	150,550	72,471	7,449	10.3
Oneida	199,700	128,053	71,647	17,242	24.0

Source—New York State Legislative Task Force on Demographic Research and Reapportionment; New York State Board of Elections; U.S. Bureau of the Census, 1990 data.

[a] Voting-age population includes noncitizens.

[b] Registration figures are as of November 1994.

[c] NVRA registration data are for 1995. The number represents only new registrations; it does not include other transactions such as change of address or name.

were submitted through the agencies, mostly from unemployment offices, and 8,763 were submitted from motor vehicles agencies. Subsequently an additional eight agencies with 77 local offices were added to the program. Cuomo claimed that as many as 150,000 were registered in 1986, but this figure is likely exaggerated: on-site surveys by Human SERVE showed that registration was not taking place at many sites. For example, in the fall of 1985, SERVE found that only nine of the fifteen agency sites surveyed had registration forms available, and only seven displayed them conspicuously. In the spring of 1986, SERVE found that only six of twenty-three sites surveyed had forms, and only five had them displayed conspicuously. In the fall of 1986, only eight of twelve had forms, and only seven had them in plain sight.[37]

So poor was the performance of the 1984 program that advocates and liberal Democrats sought several changes in New York's notoriously arcane election law, including the establishment of an effective and permanent agency-based registration program. (Other changes advocates sought included allowing election-day registration or setting the deadline for registration closer to election day.) Republicans, who dominated the state Senate, prevented passage of such legislation.

Frustrated, advocates urged Cuomo to take more vigorous steps to boost New York's anemic registration and participation rates. In November 1987, Cuomo issued Executive Order 104, establishing the blue-ribbon Task Force on Encouraging Electoral Participation, which was charged with identifying "why eligible New Yorkers fail to vote or to register and what steps would tend positively to affect public behavior in those regards."[38] In February 1988 the task force issued its report, making dozens of recommendations. The task force called for, among other measures, introducing election-day registration; reducing the required interval between registration and election day from thirty to fifteen days for general elections and from sixty to fifteen days for primary elections; allowing newly naturalized citizens to register to vote at any time prior to a general election; allowing employees in state and local government agencies to actively assist in registering voters; including registration forms in tax booklets and other standardized mailings to residents; allowing seventeen-year-olds to register to vote; establishing a school-based civics curriculum and a registration program for high school students; registering college students at their school residences and offering voter registration with class registration; instructing state and local boards of elections to take a range of steps to encourage registration; and supporting federal legislation to expand the franchise, such as a law establishing a door-to-door registration canvass by the U.S. Bureau of the Census during its regular survey process. Only a few of the more modest proposals were eventually adopted, and only in certain jurisdictions. For example, registration forms were mailed with tax forms in 1992 and 1993, seventeen-year-olds were permitted to register to vote, and a curriculum and registration program for high school students was established in New York City.

On March 3, 1990, during the gubernatorial election year, advocates persuaded Cuomo to issue another executive order to create an expanded and more effective agency-based system. Executive Order 136 allowed agency personnel to actively assist registrants in completing postage-paid mail registration forms during the intake process at an expanded number of state agencies, while still prohibiting collection by agency personnel because *Clark* v. *Cuomo* was still in effect. It proposed a more proactive, advocate-developed model that had proven effective in other places, such as Michigan, Minnesota, and Washington, D.C. The executive order contained two provisions of importance from the perspective of the advocates: first, a requirement that agency workers be trained to verbally offer the opportunity to register and to offer assistance with completion of the form, and that agencies eventually amend their intake and application forms to include a question asking if clients wished to register to vote; and second, an expanded list of agencies at which registration would occur, including particularly ones that reach unregistered low-income populations. Initially Cuomo asked the legislature for $750,000 to implement the program. The legislature subsequently appropriated $350,000 for the program, eliminating money for postage-paid registration forms.[39]

But again Republicans blocked implementation of the executive order. This time, however, it was the two Republican commissioners of the state board of elections—presumably at the behest of the state Republican Party—who thwarted implementation. They deadlocked the four-member board because they saw potential Democratic gains and Republican losses.

The Structure and Role of the New York State Board of Elections

The New York State Board of Elections was created in 1974 to promote "fair, honest and efficiently administered elections." To accomplish its mission, the board was given the power to adopt regulations concerning election administration, campaign practices, and campaign finance. In addition, it was authorized to encourage voting, study election processes and recommend improvements, oversee local boards, investigate alleged wrongdoing, and compel the production of evidence.[40] Prior to the creation of the state board, many of these functions were vested in the secretary of state, who administered the election laws, and the attorney general, who enforced them. However, this structure was criticized as allowing important matters to "fall through the cracks" between the two offices.[41]

The state board of elections is composed of four commissioners appointed by the governor on the recommendation of the state parties' leaders for two-year terms. Two of these are recommended by the chairs of the state committees of the major parties, and two are recommended by the leaders of the major parties in the legislature. A designee of one of the legislative leaders is named as board chair by the governor, and the other serves as vice chair. Similarly, local commissioners are appointed by county legislatures on the recommendation of the two major parties (in Nassau and Suffolk counties the party chairs make the appointments). In New York City, the City Council appoints the board of elections commissioners on the recommendation of the two major parties. County elections commissioners currently serve for two years, though the term may be extended to four years at local option, and it is now four years in New York City and Schenectady County by state law. There are two commissioners in each county and ten in New York City (two for each county within the city). Additionally, forty-eight counties employ two deputies, each appointed by a commissioner and serving at the commissioner's leisure.[42]

New York boards of elections were historically structured on a bipartisan basis on the thesis that this would prevent either major party from dominating the agency and the electoral process. New York state law requires that state and local boards of elections operate by majority vote. Since boards comprise an even number of members from each of the two largest parties, this means that no decision is possible without the approval of at least three of the appointees, or both of the appointees in the case of a two-member board. Thus, a single board member (on a two-member board) or two members of a party (in the case of the state board or the New York City board) may block any board action on a controversial or contentious matter. Celia Wexler of Common Cause accurately describes the situation: "With a composition of two Democrats and two Republicans, the board is designed for institutional gridlock." Benjamin notes that this potential for political gridlock "may have the effect of driving increased numbers of election disputes into the courts for decision. New York is reputed to have half of the election litigation in the country."[43] Thus reform advocates urged that a fifth commissioner from the advocacy community be added to the state board to overcome these circumstances. Cuomo proposed adding this fifth "public" member to the board to help break ties and to bring an outside, good-government perspective, but that idea did not obtain a sponsor in the legislature, whose leadership and members, of course, have close ties to the party organizations.

The party organizations dominate the process of selecting commissioners. Indeed party officials, even chairs of county party organizations, can also be election commissioners. While election law prohibits commissioners of elections from holding public office, they can hold a party office. Benjamin claims that this dual office holding, which is quite common, is a conflict of interest: "These commissioners preside over the elections in which they themselves run for party office." He compared the list of county election commissioners and deputy commissioners with the list of county party chairs in 2002 and found that eleven individuals (five Democrats and six Republicans) held both jobs. Similarly, he found that twenty-one state party committee members (twelve Republicans and nine Democrats) were also election commissioners or deputy commissioners. He also found that commissioners and party chairs or committee members often had the same last name. "But I stopped [counting]. I figured that in the time I had I could not find all the sisters and cousins and aunts, who no doubt number in the dozens." Moreover, as required by law, these party and elections officials also select the staff for the boards of elections and all the temporary workers, including poll workers. The bipartisan structure of state and local boards can also lead to collusion between the parties; for example, members of one party might promise not to oppose an initiative by the opposing party in exchange for support to squelch insurgents who may challenge the dominant faction of the first party.[44]

In the dispute over Executive Order 136 (1990), the two Republican commissioners of the state board raised questions about whether Governor Cuomo's order interfered with the board's statutory independence, and they also opposed the implementation plan offered by the two Democratic commissioners. The Democrats' plan called for agency employees to receive a two-hour training on verbally encouraging clients to register to vote and offering assistance in completion of the form—this would make it a "staff active" agency-based registration program of the sort that advocates promoted and that has proven effective elsewhere. Republicans insisted that state employees not offer verbal assistance to registrants but instead offer only a written pamphlet with a telephone number for registrants to call if they have questions, saying that workers might give wrong information or might act in a partisan manner and persuade people to register as Democrats. The Democratic commissioners voted to oppose the Republican plan.[45]

The Republican commissioners publicly stated that they were in favor of making registration easier and denied trying to limit registration of potential Democratic voters; they insisted that they were merely complying with the legislature's intent that the board, not the agencies, conduct the program. Legal counsel for the Assembly speaker and the Senate majority leader, however, said that was not the case.[46] Republicans "may feel like, 'Hey what are we doing here, we're registering more Democrats,'" said Evelyn Aquila, one of the two Democratic commissioners of the state board.[47] The other Democratic commissioner, Melvin Barasch, when asked if he thought Republicans feared that most of the new registrants would vote Democratic, said, "I truly believe that's the bottom line." Barasch resigned from the state board in protest on September 18, 1990.[48]

The specific policy disagreement had to do with how to implement the executive order, and it reflected differing perspectives between Democrats and Republicans on the nature of voter registration generally. "If somebody really wants to register, they're not going to object to making a phone call," said Republican board member R. Wells Stout. The other Republican commissioner, Helena Donohue, said in the June meeting of the board that "it's the easiest thing in the world to register to vote."[49]

Liberal Democrats and registration reform advocates countered these arguments by asserting that new immigrant citizens, people who are unfamiliar with or unnerved by bureaucracy, and people who work a lot or are not mobile do not find voter registration easy. Advocates saw current registration procedures as a cumbersome challenge to many potential voters. Travis Plunkett of NYPIRG put it bluntly: "They don't seem to understand the real world—that some people who appear to register are double parked. They seem to think that you should have to sweat a little to register. In fact, helping people become part of the electorate should be a major role of government." Similarly, Susan Schwardt, president of the League of Women Voters, appealed to state board: "Through our years of experience in voter registration, the League has found considerable confusion and anxiety on the part of first time registrants. Despite many revisions, registration forms can easily be invalidated by omission of data or of a signature." For these reasons, Schwardt urged the state board to allow agency workers to be trained to assist registrants in the completion of forms. Indeed, advocates contended that the Republicans' plan to remove the provision for agency workers to ask clients if they want to register and to offer assistance in completion of the form not only was "a clear violation of the executive order" but also "effectively gutted the centerpiece of the order. It looks to us like they're putting partisan interests before the needs of the voting public."[50]

This episode and others show that while Republicans profess a philosophy of access, they typically support measures that have the effect of restricting access in the name of safeguarding the ballot. In addition, Republicans on the state board raised concerns about costs, potential errors by agency workers that might lead to litigation, partisan implementation, and fraud possibilities that they said would result from the Democrats' plan. "We're not saying people in agencies aren't capable. We're saying this is not their normal purview. We just wanted basic security." "We have never been opposed to voter registration drives in this state. Our only hangup was its implementation."[51] But as one editorial board put it, "There's probably more than a little truth" to the Democratic commissioner's charge that the Republicans were trying to discourage expansion of the voter rolls, especially of low-income social service and labor department clients who would likely be Democratic voters. "But the real issue here isn't so much Democrats vs. Republicans as it is the historic tendency of the elections board to bolster the status quo."[52]

After three more months, three more meetings of the state board commissioners, and continued deadlock and inaction, several voting rights organizations brought a lawsuit in the New York State Supreme Court to force the state board to act. "The State Board of Elections has deliberately blocked an innovative and inexpensive program which would register hundreds of thousands of New Yorkers a year to vote," said Travis Plunkett of the New York Public Interest Research Group, one of the groups that brought the suit. "With each passing day, the tens of thousands of New Yorkers who use the services of Motor Vehicle, Labor and Social Service offices are denied the opportunity to register to vote," the suit asserted. NYPIRG further asserted: "We'd expect this kind of obstructionism from a southern registrar in the 1960s, not New York elections officials in the 1990s." Importantly, advocates brought the lawsuit at the same time the national government was debating a motor voter bill in Congress. When the bill was killed in a vote on September 28, 1990 (Republican Senator Alfonse D'Amato voted to kill the bill, and Democratic Senator Patrick Moynihan voted for it), Cuomo's executive order became even more important for advocates.[53]

In October 1990, Judge Irma Santaella of the New York State Supreme Court denied a petition to allow the state board to fill the vacancy left by the departing chair, Melvin Barasch. Both Santaella and the board hoped that his successor might change the deadlocked vote and give the board more time to work out the issue and respond to the court. (The Speaker of the Assembly, who nominates someone to fill the board vacancy, failed to do so until the following year.) But the remaining Democratic board commissioner, Evelyn Aquila, in responding to the court, supported the petitioners in writing on February 22, 1991, "alleging that even if the existing vacancy is filled by a fourth member, there is little likelihood of implementation of the registration program as two board members have been adamantly opposed to it to this date and even with a fourth member the board would remain deadlocked along political lines: two Republicans and two Democrats."[54] Though the board had managed to take other actions during the preceding months, despite the absence of one commissioner, it made no progress on the registration program. The judge noted that neither a commissioner nor any legal counsel had responded to the court in more than four appearance dates and for several months. The *New York Times* summed up the situation: "Voter registration for next month's elections in New York State is over, along with Gov. Mario M. Cuomo's unsuccessful attempt to require state agencies to take an active role in helping register voters. Saturday's deadline also signaled the success of Republican opposition on the State Board of Elections to the Governor's move to enroll more voters."[55]

Finally, Judge Santaella ruled on February 22, 1991, ordering the state board to implement the program as specified in the executive order, with a few modifications. Her judgment scathingly condemned the board:

> It is beyond dispute that millions of New Yorkers engage in transactions at certain state agencies and the subject voter registration program directed by the order would afford hundreds of thousands of voting age citizens who are not registered that opportunity. Yet, not a single citizen has been registered to vote since the inception of Executive Order 136 on March 5, 1990, and the board's paralysis has diluted and abridged the constitutionally protected voting rights of thousands of New Yorkers. . . . Respondents' deadlock abridges the electoral process of the State of New York. The continued inaction by the very agency entrusted by the law with taking all appropriate steps to encourage the broadest voter participation in elections as directed under election law 3-102 (13) is tantamount to invidious discrimination under the 14th amendment equal protective clause and against the public policy of this state. . . . For too long the public interest has been injuriously violated and raped by the arrogance of partisan politics at respondent Board on the subject Executive Order to the detriment of the voting rights of thousands of New Yorkers in contravention to the public interest.[56]

Although the judge's ruling was a decisive victory for the advocates, it soon became evident that it was a hollow one. By the time of the judge's order—almost a year after the executive order was issued—not only had the 1990 gubernatorial election been held but, more importantly, the $375,000 appropriated by the state legislature to implement the program in state agencies was no longer available because the fiscal year had ended. A total of $355,000 was returned to the general fund, leaving only $20,000. Only after the judge ordered the state board to act did the board move to begin implementing the program at the end of March 1991. Therefore, no voters were registered through the executive order's agency program for more than one year. In addition, due to the state's worsening fiscal crisis, Cuomo proposed the allocation of only $125,000 for the fiscal year beginning April 1 to implement the program.

The board continued to compromise the implementation process, even rejecting a donation of postage-paid registration forms from the New York City mayor and board of elections for use in the state's agency-based program. And when the board did begin to implement the program, advocates charged that it limited the number of agency sites participating.[57]

Advocates also documented significant problems at the agency sites. Between April 16, 1991, and May 10, 1991, advocates observed twenty-one sites. In only one site did an agency worker ask clients if they wished to register to vote, as required by the executive order and the court order, and at most agency sites no voter registration materials were visibly displayed or available, and agency workers knew little or nothing about the program.[58]

Then the Senate Republicans cowed the Democratic Assembly into eliminating the proposed $125,000 for postage-paid voter registration forms to implement the executive order for the coming year. Helen Weinstein, the Democratic chair of the Assembly Election Law Committee, said, "I think it's an important program, but it became clear the Senate was no how, no way going to go for it. Sometimes you just have to bite the bullet."[59] Thus Republicans—members of the state board and their counterparts in the state Senate—effectively thwarted another effort by voting rights advocates and liberal Democrats to expand the franchise in New York. What were the policy consequences? For one, an environmental bond act that the governor proposed and supported but that narrowly failed in 1990 probably would have passed with slightly higher turnout.[60]

The Election Reform Act of 1992 and the Changing of the Guard at the New York State Board of Elections

In May 1992 the state legislature passed and the governor signed the Election Reform Act of 1992 (also known as Chapter 79 of the Laws of 1992). Although the Democratic Assembly and the governor had sought a more expansive program—including election-day registration, measures to ease ballot access, and new campaign finance limits—the Republican-dominated state Senate pressed for a watered-down version of the bill, which therefore produced only minor improvements. Indeed, advocacy groups that had helped the Assembly and the governor to draft the initial legislation subsequently criticized the new law as too weak to be effective.

A *New York Times* editorial strongly criticized Republicans, and Cuomo in particular (who, it said, had caved in), for not producing better legislation.[61]

The Chapter 79 legislation charged the state board of elections with the task of implementation. The board's 1992 annual report stated that the new law "dramatically increased the New York State Board of Elections' and county boards of elections' involvement in administering voter registration activities." The state board was given increased responsibilities for training agency staff, producing and distributing supplies (such as coded registration forms, training manuals, and locked receptacles) and promotional materials (such as posters), and monitoring agency registration sites. In addition, several new agencies were added to those originally covered by the governor's executive order, bringing the total to seventeen agencies with 339 state office sites, more than doubling the number of agency sites. In 1992 the program only functioned for the latter half of the year due to the late date of the passage of the legislation. In 1993, the first full year the program functioned, the board made modest efforts to improve its procedures, including producing a training and reference manual for agency workers and increasing monitoring of agency sites (the board made fifty-three site visits), and it adopted rules and regulations for the program. As a result of criticism from advocates, the board also began to work with three additional agencies that serve the disabled.[62]

These small but proactive efforts by the board were a direct result of another significant development in 1992. While the board's bipartisan structure remained intact, a Democrat became its executive director for the first time in its nearly twenty-year history. Republican Tom Wallace, who had been executive director of the state board since its inception in 1974, was replaced by Democrat Tom Wilkey.[63]

Because the administrative staff conducts day-to-day operations, it can strongly shape what does and does not happen at the board. This was amply evident under Republican Wallace's leadership from 1974 to 1992. (Wallace had worked for the New York Department of State beginning in 1959, and in 1965 he was appointed by the Secretary of State to the position of director of the Election Law Bureau. He served in that capacity until 1974, when the state board was created.) Voting rights advocates and liberal Democrats had bitterly complained of Wallace's "backward approach to voter registration."[64] One of the most vocal critics of Wallace has been Deputy Executive Director Michael Losinger, a Democrat. Because of this, advocates favored Losinger over Wilkey for the executive directorship. As the board's deputy executive director, Losinger was the next in line for the position, but he was passed over because Wilkey was a more palatable choice for the board's commissioners, particularly its Republican commissioners, with whom Wilkey had managed to maintain good working relations. Soon after he was passed over for the directorship, Losinger left the board of elections to go to the Department of Motor Vehicles (DMV).

Losinger had served as a commissioner of the Monroe County board of elections from 1977 to 1983 and had pioneered some of the first agency-based registration and voter registration outreach programs in New York state. The state board's 1992 annual report paid tribute to Losinger, stating that "Mike was primarily responsible for moving the Board toward a more aggressive approach in the areas of voter registration and outreach. . . . An avid proponent of the concept of agency based voter registration, Mike was instrumental in the implementation and administration of the agency based registration programs established by Executive Orders 43 and 136 and Chapter 79." An Episcopal seminarian, Losinger considers himself a "peace activist" and "community organizer" engaged in numerous "causes." He believes there were several factors that led to his being passed over for the position, most importantly that he was a "progressive" who alienated Democrats and especially Republicans within the board and the party organizations. For example, Losinger refused to drop an investigation into allegations that Danny DeFrancesco, the Democratic executive director of the New York City Board of Elections until 2003, had allowed violations on petitions for candidates' inclusion on the ballot. "Danny protects Wilkey," Losinger stated. "And Danny has the power to do so—his power base is with the party leadership in the Assembly and Senate which are located in NYC. For those Democrats, not enfranchising more voters—especially Latinos, for example, means threatening them." Advocates characterized Losinger in similar terms. Finally, Losinger particularly "stood up to and alienated" Republicans, and most importantly Helena Donohue, the commissioner who had pushed most for Wilkey's appointment.[65]

The paucity of citizens registered during the three years of the state board's oversight of Chapter 79's operation (1992–1994) clearly shows the weaknesses of design and implementation, bearing in mind the several million clients who pass through the state agencies covered by the law, and considering that there were more than 5 million eligible unregistered potential voters in New York at that time. The performance of all agency programs since 1988 has been abysmal. The number of registration forms distributed in agencies was 65,740 in 1992 (from August to December because the law took effect only in June); 60,718 in 1993; and 46,201 in 1994 (from January to July, the dates for which data are available). By comparison, the number of forms distributed in earlier years ranged from a high of 104,312 in 1991; to 91,000 in 1988; 50,000 in 1989; and zero in 1990.[66] These numbers reflect only the number of voter registration forms distributed. Since no comprehensive mechanisms were established to track the number of actual registrants, it is possible only to estimate how many the programs produced, and that figure is at best approximately one-third of the number of forms distributed.[67]

In 1992 the state board acknowledged that agencies and the board itself had performed poorly: "Based upon the results of our own site monitoring, as well as feedback from the agencies and voter registration groups, the

Board recognizes there is room for improvement in the operation of the agency based program."[68] The board pledged to improve its efforts and to solicit better compliance from agencies and county boards. Advocates had considered bringing additional litigation to force better implementation of the program, but instead they used their leverage to pressure the board to prepare for the advent of the NVRA, which became law on May 20, 1993. The rate of registration in DMV offices did appear to increase somewhat during the last few months before the registration deadline preceding the 1994 election. This is because Cuomo ally and former deputy director of the state board of elections Michael Losinger, now the DMV coordinator for voter registration, had instituted several improvements to the DMV's programs to boost registration, including conducting statewide employee training and providing additional promotional materials.

What little agency registration occurred under Chapter 79 was biased toward better-off New Yorkers. It is also likely that New York City residents fared worse than suburban and rural residents due to the smaller proportion of drivers in the city and higher proportion of public assistance recipients. In 1990 only 51, percent of the voting age population in New York City possessed a driver's license, compared with 91 percent of voting age residents in other parts of the state. (Today, these percentages are roughly the same.) Thus the majority of DMV registrants are likely to be upstate residents. Furthermore, within New York City, women and low-income and minority residents are less likely to have driver's licenses, further skewing the impact of the DMV registrations. In 1990, 59.1 percent of all Latino households included no one with a driver's license, compared with 56.5 percent of all black households, 40.5 percent of Asian households, and only 22.9 percent of all white households.[69]

Such disparate impacts are evident from examination of the number of forms distributed by agencies. In 1992 DMV offices distributed two-thirds of all registration forms distributed by agencies (40,792 of 65,740), while the Department of Social Services (DSS) distributed only 584 forms, the Department of Health distributed 615, and the Department for the Aging distributed only 21. Of the total number of forms distributed during the three-year period during which the program functioned, well over one hundred thousand were distributed through DMV offices, and only about 3,500 through DSS. Thus registration through Chapter 79 perpetuated the existing pattern of disparate registration rates for different income and racial groups.

Employees of the state board of elections claimed that Chapter 79 performed so dismally because the state agencies did not conduct registration as instructed, whether because they perceived voter registration to be outside of their proper purview or as a result of bureaucratic inertia, lack of resources, or fear of alienating dominant politicians to whom they owed their jobs. Advocates, along with several board employees, contended that the state board had neither sufficiently exercised its authority nor used its resources to invigorate these agency programs. For example, instead of merely making telephone calls or sending letters to answer registrants' questions or obtain missing information, though these were admittedly good first steps, the state board could have asked the governor's office to intervene with the agencies, the counsel of the board could have contacted the counsel of the agencies, and so on.

The National Voter Registration Act of 1993

Beginning in January 1995 with the implementation of the NVRA, or motor voter, New York state experienced a dramatic increase in voter registration. Even though the expansion of registration lagged in New York compared with many other states—largely due to obstructionism by Republicans, who now controlled the state house—the results are clear: the NVRA rapidly registers the unregistered. It has already outperformed all previous agency programs in New York combined. Executive director of the state board of elections Thomas Wilkey stated that "while we have had agency-based registration programs in the past, they have never generated this level of activity."[70]

The NVRA began in an off-election year in New York: in 1995 only judges and district attorneys were being elected in New York City, which traditionally generates the lowest registration and turnout of all elections. In some other jurisdictions, counties and municipalities were electing executives and town boards. Yet the number of people registered to vote statewide through all registration methods in 1995 greatly exceeded the number registered in 1994, by 58 percent, even though in 1994 there were races for governor and other statewide offices, the state legislature, and the U.S. Congress. The jump in registration in 1995 was solely due to the implementation of the NVRA. Specifically, the number of individuals registered through agencies rose from an estimated 11,500 in 1994 to over 432,500 in 1995. Similarly, a large number of the 660,000 mail-in registration forms that were processed in 1995 were obtained from agencies, though the exact number is unknown.[71]

Agency registration under the two different programs produced strikingly different results, with many more people registering at agencies under the NVRA than under Chapter 79. While significant problems plagued implementation of the NVRA in New York—particularly in New York City and in the initial stages of the program—during the first four months alone, far more people were registered in DMV offices in New York City (about 24,000) than in the entire year of 1994 (6,500). The state board of elections did not keep records of the number of new registrants by year or by the agency where registration occurred until 1995, when NVRA implementation began. Nevertheless, according to Wilkey, of the approximately 651,000 voters whose forms were processed by all the boards of elections in the state of New York in 1994, about 600,000 registered by mail; 20,000 through forms returned with tax packages; 23,000 through offices of boards of elections; and a mere 8,000 through Chapter 79 agency-based programs. (Recall that only 46,201 registration forms were distributed through Chapter 79 agency programs in 1994.)

Why has the NVRA been so much more successful at registering citizens than previous programs were? The NVRA procedures are specifically designed to actively integrate voter registration with the routine delivery of government services to every agency client on a daily and year-round basis. Voter registration is now an integral part of agencies' intake and application processes when people seek driver's licenses, public assistance, unemployment benefits, and services to people with disabilities. For example, in DMV offices, a computerized system allows for simultaneous voter registration with each DMV transaction, producing the most integrated and effective registration process.

Moreover, the strong federal mandate on states forced removal of most of the legal and procedural barriers that Republicans had erected during the prior decade. For example, now agency employees are not only permitted but are *required* to offer verbal assistance to every client in filling out the registration form, to collect the completed form and rout it to the board of elections, and to offer the same level of assistance as with other agency matters.[72] This critical feature of integration was successfully pushed in New York by a coalition of advocacy organizations and several progressive Democrats over the objections of the Republican-led state Senate. Not only was the process of registration integrated into intake and renewal processes, but registration forms were integrated into agency forms, including applications for public assistance programs and, as of February 1996, unemployment benefits. In addition, the bilingual provisions under the NVRA are clear and strong, which is especially important for New York City. Lastly, the NVRA gave advocates greater leverage to force compliance by allowing for the private right of legal action and for linkage to the Voting Rights Act. Indeed, advocates put all on notice that they intended to closely scrutinize implementation of the NVRA and planned to bring suit against the state for any violations. Thus, the provisions of the NVRA differed significantly from previous programs, which were passive, limited, ad hoc, and irregular. Similar impressive results have been replicated in other states, producing approximately 1 million new registrants and address updates per month in forty-one states since January 1995 when the NVRA went into effect. The NVRA's performance is unprecedented and historic.[73] Many voting rights advocates believe that some of the election problems that began coming to light in 2000 result from a partisan reaction to the success of the NVRA.

The results are even more impressive in light of the fact that the NVRA began in the face of hostile Republican administrations in many states, including New York. Despite the gains, Republicans have prevented what would have been even greater success for the NVRA, undermining more effective implementation of the NVRA legislatively and procedurally. At the beginning of 1995, when the NVRA took effect, Republicans were in control of the state house in New York for the first time in twenty years. They and their allies, who dominate many county and local governments across the state, have been successful at blunting the expansion of registration in New York, particularly for low-income persons and members of minority groups via agencies that serve these constituencies. Some implementation problems have been due to bureaucratic inertia and delays, but the lion's share of the blame rests with Republicans, who succeeded in restricting the NVRA's effectiveness in New York in several ways: Governor George Pataki's administration gutted the unit of the state board that is responsible for implementing and overseeing the NVRA, and state and local Republicans have procedurally undermined the program's effectiveness in agencies— particularly agencies that serve the disabled, the Department of Labor, and DSS, which administers public assistance—and have actively lobbied for the repeal of the NVRA on the national level and have sought to further limit the scope of the legislation's reach in New York. The Pataki administration has sought to roll back the number of agencies mandated to conduct voter registration and to procedurally restrict the level and effectiveness of such activity, and Republicans successfully limited the scope of legislation sought by advocates and Democrats during the planning and legislative sessions prior to 1995.

Governor Pataki's first budget in 1995 sharply cut funds for the state board of elections, which is charged with implementing and monitoring the NVRA. The $306,000 in cuts targeted personnel and resources specifically designated to implement the NVRA, eliminating six new staff hired by the board to oversee the program in public assistance and disabilities agencies.[74] The cut reduced the state board's capacity to effectively oversee all the facets of the law's implementation, including timely identification of agency office sites and subcontractors, adequate training of agency personnel, provision of needed materials, and monitoring of agency progress. The budget cut had its desired effect of weakening the NVRA program especially in New York City, where state agencies serve a greater proportion of low-income and minority voters than elsewhere. The tasks of the staff cut at the state board specifically included site monitoring throughout the state, with an emphasis on New York City. In addition, the state board was unable to identify, supply, and train the subcontractor agencies (such as day care centers and settlement houses) that receive state funds from one of the mandated agencies; a disproportionate number of these subcontractor agencies also are located in New York City. The cut to the state board directly contributed to poorer implementation of the NVRA in New York City than in the rest of the state, producing disparate impacts on registration.

The cut also discouraged the state board from engaging in future activity that might meet with the disapproval of the Pataki administration. For example, Wilkey was asked to testify at congressional hearings into vote fraud during the spring and summer of 1995 but declined, fearing that the Pataki administration might cut more funds to the board or engage in other forms of retaliation. If Wilkey had testified, he would have stated that there is little evidence of registration and vote fraud in New York and that the NVRA would likely reduce such possibilities further rather than increase them as Republicans had charged. Nevertheless, Alphonse D'Amato, U.S. senator from New York, had previously charged in 1993 that 100,000 fraudulent votes were cast in the 1992 election, which he won by a very slim margin. Given that Pataki is a close ally of D'Amato, Wilkey's fear of retaliation may have some validity.

Pataki's spokesman, Robert Bellafiore, stated that the administration would seek to repeal the portion of the NVRA legislation that requires that voter registration forms be attached to applications for public assistance, clearly attempting to undermine the effectiveness of registration efforts in social service agencies. In addition, the administration sought repeal of the NVRA at the national level and indicated that it would attempt to restrict its scope and implementation in New York, claiming the costs of the program were prohibitive. As early as January 1995 Pataki's commissioner for the DMV, Richard E. Jackson, Jr., wrote that the department and the Pataki administration would lobby the federal government for repeal of the NVRA, claiming that it constituted an unfunded mandate. Once this position became public—and it was widely reported in the press and in legislative memos—it confirmed advocates' and liberal Democrats' fear that the Pataki administration would work to undermine the NVRA, and it sent a clear message to state workers that it was acceptable not to implement the law.[75]

The surge in voter registration since the inauguration of the NVRA generated concern among Republicans. Although Pataki voted for the enabling legislation for the NVRA when he was a state senator, "Now in the Governor's mansion, he is quietly trying to thwart the effort, apparently fearful that adding more voters to the rolls will hurt Republicans."[76] Even prior to the advent of the NVRA in 1995, Republicans had prevented Democrats from passing stronger provisions in the proposed enabling legislation during the 1994 legislative session. Democrats—largely prodded and schooled by voting rights advocates—had proposed that New York adopt a more expansive version of the NVRA, including more state agencies to ensure that all segments of the population were reached, particularly low-income and minority residents in New York City. Advocates and liberal Democrats sought the inclusion of agencies such as housing authorities, the Division of Housing and Community Renewal (DHCR), the Department of Labor, the Immigration and Naturalization Service, and the Department Education to reach high school students. Instead, the final, watered-down legislation added only public universities. According to Jerome Koenig, the Democratic chief of staff for the Assembly Election Law Committee, who was intimately involved in negotiations with the

Republican-controlled Senate for passage of New York's enabling legislation for the NVRA, "when the Senate found out where and who were served by DHCR, they wanted it removed. This happened with other agencies too."[77]

In addition, the advocates proposed allowing electronic transfer of data from agencies to the state board of elections, which would have made programs more efficient and effective, and providing voters a more expansive version of the fail-safe provisions of the bill so that citizens who moved within their county could maintain their registration and vote either at a new poll site, their former site, or some central site. Opponents argued that the latter provision would place undue burden on boards of elections and poll workers to print multiple ballots and properly administer them. The proposal for electronic transfer of data was voted down by the Republican-controlled state Senate and rejected by the state board of elections. The plan that was adopted permits people to vote only at their new poll site.

New York did pass legislation that was considered a model by voting rights advocates. It contains several provisions advocates have sought nationally. One is the use of combined forms in public assistance agencies. This was seen as particularly critical for New York, where only 51 percent of the voting-age population in New York City held a driver's license in 1990 compared with 91 percent in the rest of the state.[78] Moreover, 76 percent of the voting-age population was registered to vote upstate, but only 63 percent was registered in New York City. Significant splits between cities and suburban and rural areas exist elsewhere, but the disparity in New York is the most extreme in the country. Thus advocates sought to craft legislation to ensure that this disparity would be overcome.

Another important feature in the New York legislation was the inclusion of a significant number of state agencies and their subcontractors that are not included in the NVRA, most notably the Department of Labor, the Department of Health, the Immigration and Naturalization Service, and the City University of New York and State University of New York—CUNY and SUNY—where the requirement is more modest. New York Republicans' opposition to the inclusion of the U.S. Department of Labor was overcome, in part, when the federal government made funding available to states to implement the NVRA in federal agencies, including by amending their application forms for services to include voter registration. The Clinton administration made federal money available to states when President Clinton's deputy chief of staff, Harold Ickes, was persuaded by the leader of the Park Democrat Club of Manhattan's Upper West Side that such funding would be a means to deflect Republican opposition. Once the money became available, Republican opposition indeed diminished.[79]

New York's relatively good legislation and early preparation to begin implementation were directly due to the work of liberal Democrats, who were prompted by advocates to be comprehensive and who prepared well in advance. Wilkey, the Cuomo administration, and representatives from the legislature were instrumental in laying the groundwork. In particular,

Wilkey had the foresight and support from the governor's office to pull together a thirty-eight-member planning task force made up of election administrators, elected officials, and voting rights advocates.[80] The task force's work was significant because it not only began to prepare for the monumental task of implementation but also produced draft legislation for implementation and established the political fault lines early, which proved useful in subsequent negotiations by legislative leaders.

Wilkey was "one of only a handful of state elections officials who supported the NVRA and worked to support it," stated Louise Altman, associate director of Human SERVE. He has a national reputation and is widely regarded as one of the most informed and effective advocates for the NVRA nationally and in New York state. For example, Wilkey actively promoted early and proactive thinking about the NVRA, establishing the state task force in 1993 to plan for its implementation, and he generally supported more liberal policies and procedures where and when he could, particularly regarding agency-based registration, despite the constraints of his bipartisan board. He led the New York delegation to a conference on the NVRA held by the Federal Election Commission (FEC) and "took a more progressive position than many other states." Advocates' early and clear indications to Wilkey that they were very concerned about New York's implementation—especially given New York City's disparity regarding nondrivers—and their unequivocal indication that he would be sued if implementation was poor no doubt figured into Wilkey's actions. Wilkey was elected vice president of the National Association of State Election Directors (NASED) in late 1994 and also serves as a member of the FEC's advisory panel.

But Republicans effectively blocked portions of the Democrats' proposed provisions and also issued minority reports that were integrated into the task force's report, fueling opposition. Similarly, elections officials across the country, particularly southern elections officials, generally opposed the NVRA and continued to raise concerns. Interestingly, the National Association of Secretaries of State (NASS) and the Election Center—both of which had opposed the NVRA—began to seek foundation funding for the bill's implementation; possibly they saw a way of expanding their influence and organizational resources.

Once the NVRA law took effect on January 1, 1995, there were delays in the initial start-up of the program by some state agencies in New York (most notably DSS and agencies that serve the disabled), and several agencies (the Department of Labor and several disabilities agencies) still had not begun implementation at year's end. Although there was plenty of time to prepare before the January 1 start date, DSS—which serves the largest group of under-registered, low-income, and minority individuals, two-thirds of whom reside in New York City—did not introduce the mandated combined form until April, more than four months after the program was to begin.

When DSS began using the combined form, registration rates doubled, nearly achieving parity with those of DMV offices. Still, even after DSS began to use the forms, significant gaps in implementation remained, significantly limiting the number of registrants through DSS, which, of course, disproportionately negatively impacted low-income and minority groups. DMV offices in New York City were also performing poorly compared with the rest of the state: upstate regions had an advantage of almost 2 to 1 in the percentage of the voting-age population holding a driver's license, but its advantage in actual voter registration at DMV offices was nearly 5 to 1 (only 34,653, or 17%, of all voters registered in DMV offices were registered in New York City, compared with 165,390, or 83%, upstate). Agencies and their subcontractors that serve the disabled population did not begin implementation until late in the year, and once they did begin, implementation proved uneven at best.

The net result was as advocates and liberal Democrats had feared: a smaller proportion of New York City residents were registered under the program compared with upstate New Yorkers. By October 1995, New York City was registering only one person for every three to four people registered upstate, and by the end of the year only 26 percent (110,483) of the people registered to vote by NVRA agencies were registered in New York City compared with 74 percent (322,142) in the rest of the state. Table 1 details the differentials in registration between New York City and selected upstate counties.[81]

The implementation of the NVRA in New York during its first year was uneven, biased in favor of upstate residents and therefore Republicans. Every county outside New York City had a far higher proportion of new registrants than the city did.[82] While New York City had more than 40 percent of the state's eligible unregistered citizens, only 25 percent of new registrations occurred in New York City during 1995. Moreover, in the first three months of 1996, only 25,648 of the 88,380 new NVRA registrants (29%) came from New York City. During this latter period Monroe County, with less than 40 percent of the population of Queens, registered more than 4,000 persons, while Queens registered fewer than 3,500 new voters; Oneida County, with barely one-tenth the population of Brooklyn, registered 5,225 people, whereas Brooklyn registered only 8,158. These data demonstrate biased implementation. While several factors may be at work, Republican control and responsibility for agencies mandated to provide registration under the NVRA suggests Republican-motivated noncompliance.

Advocates mobilized to counter these developments. Having anticipated that the new Pataki administration would attempt to thwart the NVRA, advocates began early to monitor, track, and document implementation. Human SERVE and the NYPIRG rallied other advocates and some liberal Democratic allies, held several press conferences, and obtained some editorial support, including from the *New York Times* and the *Times Union* in

Albany. In addition, they monitored agency compliance with the law, surveying agency sites, gathering data, and producing analyses, and they informed the U.S. Justice Department and U.S. Attorney General's Office of their findings. Eventually they prodded several public officials—including two liberal Democrats—to launch studies of the state's programs.[83] Advocates also filed a series of lawsuits and legal motions to force the state to comply with the law.

The advocates' persistence had important payoffs. In late September 1995, Human SERVE persuaded Mark Green, then public advocate of New York City, to conduct a study of the implementation of the NVRA in Human Resources Administration (HRA), or public assistance, offices. Green's study documented that roughly half of HRA clients interviewed (51% of the 408 clients interviewed at 18 public assistance offices) were not provided with voter registration forms as required by law. Green's study showed that despite the fact that the vast majority of public assistance recipients reside in New York City—two-thirds of the 903,000 statewide— more were registered to vote upstate than in New York City (56%, or 46,967 public assistance recipients, were registered upstate compared with only 44 percent, or 39,498, in New York City).[84]

Similarly, Green noted that 82 percent (11,874) of the people registered at Women, Infants, and Children (WIC) sites were from upstate compared with 18 percent (2,532) in New York City, even though approximately two-thirds of all WIC sites are in New York City. In addition, Green publicized data showing that of the approximately 300,000 people who registered in all NVRA agencies statewide between January and September 1, only one-quarter, or 75,000, were in New York City. Green also noted that even DMV offices in New York City were performing poorly compared with the rest of the state. He concluded that "By not implementing NVRA in New York City, the Mayor and the Governor are both violating the law and allowing the institutions they govern to lose political power to other jurisdictions."

Green and voting-rights advocates held a press conference to make his report public. The resulting *Times* article, the Green report, and continued monitoring and agitating by advocates generated several important developments. The U.S. Department of Justice contacted the HRA and the state board of elections to inquire about the information reported in Green's study, sending both scurrying to improve implementation while attempting to downplay the extent of the poor implementation Green portrayed. Green then scheduled another public hearing in December 1995, keeping the issue alive and the pressure on.[85]

In addition, advocates persuaded State Comptroller Carl McCall to conduct a statewide report on the NVRA. His study began in November 1995 and was completed at the end of February 1996. This report involved a thorough examination of the state board of elections and of every agency and surveys of various agency sites. The study concluded that "participating agency implementation of, and compliance with, NVRA has been inconsistent at best, and that significant improvement is needed in many agencies," particularly "in registering public assistance recipients, and [it] appears to be reaching only a minor portion of eligible disabled persons. . . . New York's overall success in increasing its percentage of registered voters through NVRA is below the national average."[86]

Advocates also worked with Assembly Democrats, who conducted three public hearings during the spring of 1996 on the implementation of the NVRA, one in Albany, one in Buffalo, and one in New York City. The purpose of the hearings was

> to ascertain if and why state and local government agencies are not complying fully with state and federal law. . . . It appears that many state and local government agencies may not be complying in whole or part with the requirements of the National Voter Registration Act of 1993 (NVRA) and Chapter 659 of the Laws of 1994, both of which mandate agency based voter registration in the State of New York. These laws were designed to ease the process of voter registration in this State. The apparent failure of the agencies to implement fully the voter registration programs required by the statutes has frustrated the efforts of many New Yorkers to exercise their franchise and had also generated several lawsuits.[87]

The larger purpose of the hearings was to highlight Republican obstructionism and force improvements in implementation in agencies, particularly in New York City.

Most effective was the use of litigation. Advocates regularly wielded the threat of lawsuits, and in several instances in 1995 and 1996 they took legal action. The Community Service Society (CSS) filed several ninety-day notices against state agencies that were noncompliant or performing poorly. The first was filed against the Department of Labor in the summer of 1995, notifying the department of CSS's intention to sue unless it began to implement. The department had claimed that it had not been given enough state funds to administer the program and that it was barred under federal laws from using federal grant money for those purposes. Apparently realizing that the department would lose the suit and suffer damaging publicity, the Pataki administration negotiated a settlement and began implementation in February 1996. Simultaneously, however, the Pataki administration introduced an Article 7 amendment to state law to eliminate the Department of Labor from the NVRA as part of its budget and legislative package, ostensibly for fiscal reasons. John E. Sweeney, the state labor commissioner under Pataki, stated, "I want my agency staff to focus on job services, and I believe there are state and local agencies that already provide voter registration services." Democrats in the legislature pledged not to allow the Pataki administration's budget maneuver to circumvent the law, and they did not allow the change. However, implementation in the Department of Labor has been slow and poor. Between February and June 1996, only approximately 6 percent of all the clients who visited the Department of Labor registered to vote there.[88]

In 1996, CSS filed ninety-day notices against several other agencies: one against the Department of Health regarding the federal public assistance program WIC; one against DSS in April in relation to Medicaid in hospitals (ACORN also filed one in March against DSS more generally); one against Worker's Compensation; and several against the agencies that serve the disabled (and others), including the Department for the Aging, Office of Mental Health, and Veterans Affairs—all of which produced progress in implementation and increases in the rate of registration.

In March 1996 advocates succeeded in prodding the state board of elections to designate more than seven hundred community-based organizations and private agencies (day care centers, settlement houses, and so on) as official NVRA sites. This was a significant development sought by advocates for well over a year. Advocates and liberal Democrats also added several state agencies to be covered by the NVRA legislation. Under New York law, any state agency that provides services to people with disabilities and any state-funded provider of such services—including private nonprofit groups—must also now offer voter registration to its clients. This was important because the seven state agencies, including the Department of Health, Department for the Aging, Office of Mental Health, and Office of Alcoholism and Substance Abuse Services and their funded nonprofit and private provider organizations offer services to people other than just those with disabilities, and the agencies cannot easily separate these populations to separately administer the programs. Therefore these nonprofit and private organizations—most of which are in New York City and reach hundreds of thousands of people each year—are now being forced to provide voter registration to their clients. The state board is providing registration materials, training staff, and monitoring implementation in these more than seven hundred sites across the state. Advocates also threatened CUNY and SUNY with litigation if they continued to violate the NVRA. CUNY responded by altering its plans for implementation. It incorporated several recommendations made by Human SERVE and NYPIRG and produced improvements in its implementation in 1996.

The amount and rate of registration improved in New York State from 1995 to 1996 and, importantly, improved in New York City. In the first few months of 1996, registration through NVRA agencies statewide climbed to almost half of the amount for the entire year of 1995, with DSS registering half as many as the DMV, compared with only 29.7 percent in 1995. And in New York City in 1996, DSS eclipsed DMV agencies in registration, registering nearly twice as many as the DMV.

The impact of improvements in implementation of the NVRA in New York City can be seen in the number of people registered during 1992–1996: 57,862 in 1992 (a presidential election year); 46,000 in 1993 (municipal elections); 41,000 in 1994 (state elections); rising to 79,273 in

1995 (an off-year election); and to 147,200 in 1996 (a presidential election year).[89] These registration figures are for six-month periods from November through March (so the 1992 figure is for people registered from November 1992 through March 1993, and so on), which is typically the lowest point of registration activity during each year: registration activity associated with an election has peaked, and it is six months before the next election in a cycle. Thus the jump in registration in 1995, an off-election year and the first year of the NVRA, during which significant problems and delays in implementation occurred, and the near doubling again in 1996 clearly illustrate the impact of the NVRA in general, and improvements to agency registration programs from 1995 to 1996 in particular.

In recent years there has been continued improvement in implementation of the NVRA in New York. While some problems persist, the disparities in registration between upstate and downstate regions as well as among agencies have diminished,[90] and overall there has been a significant rise in voter registration in New York due to better implementation. From January 1, 1995, the first month of implementation, to March 31, 2003, nearly 5 million New Yorkers have been registered to vote at government agencies.[91]

New York has more people registered to vote now than it had for many decades: as of March 2004 there were 11,075,460 registered voters out of about 14 million people aged eighteen and older, about 12 million of whom were citizens. Thus, under the persistent watch of advocates and with a greater degree of integration of voter registration procedures into agency activities, the NVRA has contributed to a significant increase in voter registration.

The Help American Vote Act

The fiasco in Florida led to federal reform legislation that is aimed specifically at improving election administration, the Help America Vote Act. HAVA authorizes the allocation of federal dollars to upgrade states' aging voting machines, improve poll-worker performance and other administrative practices, and increase voter education. It requires states to improve access to people with disabilities and to establish a statewide voter registration system that can better keep voters on the rolls and their information up to date. HAVA has the potential to help modernize and standardize the infrastructure of election administration and voting practices in the United States, but it also contains a provision requiring first-time voters whose applications are submitted by mail to present valid identification to an elections official either at the time they fill out the application or when they go to the polls to vote. In New York this was never needed before January 1, 2003, and it has made it more difficult for some people to register and vote, particularly first-time voters, newly naturalized citizens, city residents, people with low income, and members of minority groups. For this reason New York's senators, Charles Schumer and Hillary Clinton, were the only two U.S. senators to vote against HAVA when the final version came up for a vote in Congress in 2002. In short, HAVA holds great promise, but it also contains potential dangers. Like much else regarding election administration, it all depends on how HAVA is crafted and implemented at the state and local levels.[92]

Given the different possible scenarios, it is no surprise to see familiar partisan dynamics playing out in New York and in other states regarding the design and implementation of HAVA. Republicans and Democrats alike have maneuvered to shape the process.[93] In 2003 in New York, Democrat Wilkey quickly established a state task force to draft a plan to submit to the federal government, which is required for funding. The task force included several members of voting rights organizations and civic groups who had long advocated for the kinds of election reform HAVA could facilitate. In addition, Wilkey notified a broad array of other stakeholders that there would be a series of public meetings to receive input regarding the design and implementation of HAVA.[94] But Republican Pataki rebuffed Wilkey. Less than a month after Wilkey's initiative, Pataki appointed the deputy executive director of the state board of elections, Republican Peter Kosinski, to replace Wilkey as the chief state elections official and thus the new head of HAVA (and also now of the NVRA), sidelining Wilkey, other Democrats, and voting rights advocates. Wilkey remained in the position of executive director for several months but was no longer able to exercise the power of the office.

Kosinski took a decidedly different approach: his task force was smaller in size and contained representatives of only two nongovernmental groups (the League of Women Voters and the New York State Independent Living Centers). A majority of the members, fifteen out of twenty, were Republican. In addition, as State assemblyman and chair of the Assembly Election Law Committee Keith Wright (D-Harlem) said, "It's definitely too pale and too male." The task force was also heavily representative of rural and suburban New York, yet Kosinski maintained that it "represents the groups that need to be represented."[95]

There were other controversial aspects of the process. For example, Kosinski stated that New York need not pass legislation to enact HAVA—that the state board of elections alone could write a plan to submit to the federal government to comply with the law. But, as a *New York Times* editorial put it, "in that case, compliance with the federal voting act will be governed by the governor."[96] Some members of the task force and the state legislature, however, disagreed with Kosinski: they argued that changes in New York state election law would be required to implement HAVA. Two task force members who made this point were Keith Wright and Democrat Douglas Kellner, commissioner of the New York City Board Of Elections. In addition, Wright argued that the legislature would be the body appropriating the necessary funding and would thus need to approve the state's plan. Voting rights groups also contended that state enabling legislation was required.

Furthermore, Kosinski insisted that the state report be written by staff of the state board of elections alone, precluding votes on issues by members of the task force, contrary to the wishes of several task force members. Kosinski acknowledged that the task force was "rushed in its deliberations" because it needed to submit a "plan to the federal government in time for New York to qualify for millions of dollars in implementation aid."[97] Democrats and voting rights groups contended that Kosinski had stifled public discussion and kept the process closed. For example, Kosinski invited members of the public to attend task force meetings only after voting rights groups insisted on it. And he refused to distribute to the public position papers on various aspects of HAVA written by voting rights advocates and addressed to members of the task force.

HAVA has potential to modernize New York's election administration and thereby greatly reduce voter disenfranchisement and boost registration and participation; but it also creates potential for mischief. Indeed, depending on how it is designed and implemented, HAVA could wreak havoc. For example, HAVA establishes new identification requirements for first-time voters who register by mail. If the kinds of acceptable identification are few in number and type, these requirements may effectively bar hundreds of thousands of people from registering and voting. Republicans and conservatives may well prevail in restricting the kinds of qualifying identification to as few as possible, while Democrats and voting-rights advocates have promoted a longer list of possible forms of identification. The potential political consequences are clear. Stringent identification requirements would be tantamount to imposing restrictions similar to poll taxes and literacy tests.[98]

At the very least voters and poll workers alike were headed for confusion on election day 2004. Although the state boards of elections had created a list of possible acceptable IDs, local boards were not fully prepared because of the lack of effective guidance and the absence of clear state legislation. A telephone survey conducted by the Brennan Center for Justice shortly after HAVA training for election administrators found that only eighteen of forty-five county election commissioners surveyed responded correctly that only first-time voters who register by mail are subject to the new identification requirements.[99] Shortly thereafter, another study, by the New York Public Research Group, found that only nine of New York's fifty-eight local boards of elections gave substantially complete and correct information about what types of identification would be accepted at the polls.[100] Thus, county boards and poll workers employed an inconsistent set of criteria for what constitutes acceptable identification, contributing to voter disenfranchisement in the 2004 elections.

Another critical issue is what kind of new voting machines New York will acquire, which is also a partisan matter. New York will spend approximately $140 million by 2006 to replace its forty-year-old lever voting machines, a technology singled out by HAVA along with punch cards, because the machines are prone to breakdown and loss of votes. The questions of which company gets the contract and what specifications and capacities the new voting machines will have has taken on partisan dimensions. One leading manufacturer, Sequoia Voting Systems, hired lobbyist Jeff Buley, who has represented Governor Pataki and has served as attorney for many prominent Republicans in New York. According to Lee Daghlian, public information officer for the state board of elections, a company called Election Systems & Software "is the only other competition for Sequoia at the moment."[101] Voting rights organizations—particularly those that represent people with disabilities and members of language minorities—have a stake in the choice of new voting technology: depending on the capabilities of different makes and models, some voters may find it easier or harder to cast their ballots.[102]

HAVA requires states to detail how they plan to implement voting improvements to qualify for federal matching funds, and partisan wrangling jeopardized the matching funds for new voting technology and other HAVA-related expenses in New York. The Democratic-led Assembly and Republican-led Senate passed separate bills, and a conference committee failed to reconcile them. This put $235 million in federal money New York is eligible to receive by 2005 in jeopardy, including $140 million for new voting technology (the rest would cover costs for poll-worker training and voter education). In July 2004 the newly created Federal Election Assistance Commission distributed $861 million to twenty-five states that had submitted such plans; New York was not one of them.

In 2004 HAVA enabling legislation was introduced into the New York state legislature, but its two branches—the Democratically controlled Assembly and the Republican-controlled Senate—passed different versions. A conference committee was established but failed to reach agreement. Finally in August 2004, the state legislature passed a temporary measure that allowed New York to receive some of the federal funding, but this stopgap measure, which expires in July 2005, is "at best a mixed bag," as election watchdog Neal Rosenstein, government reform coordinator for NYPIRG, aptly put it. At worst, the vague legislation could lead to confusion at the polls and voter disenfranchisement. Rosenstein crystallized the problem in terms that reflect the views of many civic groups monitoring New York's election system: "The primary defect in the legislation is its failure to offer clear guidance to local boards of elections over the scope of federally mandated ID checks of certain first-time voters on Election Day. The Legislature could have assisted voters and provided guidance to election officials by including a wide variety of sample IDs that would be acceptable at the polls." Because it failed to do so, local boards of election were "forced to make those decisions themselves." Unfortunately, this led to different types of ID being considered valid in different parts of the state even though, as Rosenstein pointed out, there is no good reason that "voters in Buffalo, Binghamton or the Bronx" should have been subject to different standards at the polls during the 2004 elections.[103]

Advocates also criticized a second provision of the state's stopgap legislation, which deals with the part of the verification process that involves how each board of elections implements the state's database management.

For example, some local boards might consider a missing middle initial or a missing hyphen in a hyphenated last name on one of the records a match for identification purposes and some might not, so the same registration application could be validated or invalidated. In addition, this provision means more voters will face ID checks in jurisdictions that previously considered registration forms complete with a registrant's signature.

There are a host of other HAVA-related issues at stake for partisan groups, including the establishment of a statewide interactive voter registration database, the creation of complaint procedures for voters who believe their rights have been violated, poll-worker training, and voter education—all required by HAVA.[104] In response to the Republicans' consolidation of power, Wilkey finally resigned the post of executive director of the state board of elections at the end of April 2003. Wilkey is widely considered one of the top elections experts in the country. For eight years he was the chair of NASED, he served on several national commissions to study election reform, and he was on the advisory board of the Federal Election Assistance Commission, created by HAVA. The position of executive director was kept vacant for over a year, giving the deputy executive director, Kosinski, whom Pataki appointed acting chief, greater freedom to run the agency. Pataki also waited for eight months to appoint a new Democratic commissioner to the four-person, bipartisan state board of elections.

Democrats have also used tactics to retain control of the position of chair of the board's commissioners. Such political maneuvering results from the structure of New York's election administration in a decidedly political environment. A *New York Times* editorial summed up the state of affairs in raw political terms: "New York's election policies are made by little-known bureaucrats who answer only to the political bosses who put them in place."[105]

Both Republicans and Democrats alike are keenly aware of the political implications involved in shaping election practices, from state-level agency-based voter registration programs, to the NVRA, and to HAVA. Republicans have limited the expansion of the electorate in New York, particularly for low-income, urban, and minority individuals—likely Democratic voters—by undermining effective implementation of these programs. New York's skewed and poorly executed implementation of the NVRA hurt residents of New York City especially. Moreover, New York performed quite badly compared to other states. For example, Texas, which has a voting-age population similar in size to that of New York, registered 30 percent of its unregistered population in 1995, while New York registered only 13 percent of its unregistered population in that year. At the time Texas had a Democratic governor and secretary of state.

Voting rights advocates and liberal Democrats who stood to benefit sought better implementation of the NVRA. Similar dynamics are again evident in the maneuvering to shape the design and implementation of HAVA. Why? Because these programs have the potential to affect electoral outcomes and the political balance of power in each state and in the nation as a whole.

The New York City Board of Elections

Over the past two decades, the New York City Board of Elections has disenfranchised hundreds of thousands of voters, contributing to low rates of voter registration and participation as well as to particular electoral outcomes. Nonetheless, improvements to the board's operations have reduced the scope and extent of disenfranchising election problems. Disenfranchisement is the result of errors, incompetence, bureaucratic inertia, lack of resources, and politics. Improvements are the product of increased funding, computerization, changes to registration procedures, and better election-day operations. Distinct political actors are associated with these differences.

Election administration can be characterized as the stepchild of government agencies—inadequately attended to and poorly funded. Election commissioners and managers, as well as county party leaders, have consistently maintained the view that election administrators are "overworked, vastly underpaid, poorly housed, and starved for resources." Uniformly they hold that employees are "working under extremely difficult circumstances and doing a Herculean task." Similarly, vocal critics of election administrators' operations and political structure also note their plight, sometimes referring to election boards as a "stepchild of government" that is "starved for resources." Such characterizations of the conditions of boards of elections around the country have also been expressed by national experts in election administration.[1]

Election boards are also relics of the past; they are vestiges of the bygone era of machine politics. The New York City's board of elections has been typical of election administration bodies in much of the country. But one observer's description of the board does not paint a quaint or pretty picture: "It was amazing to me to find out how antiquated the Board of Elections was, and to find the extremely gruesome physical setting that they were in. To take just one example, you would find these little old ladies sitting around who would copy all the voter registration buff cards, and then would cut the xeroxes to the right size [to fit into a binder]. And you could tell who was the senior staff because the most senior staff had scissors with two sharp points, and the others had scissors with one point broken off or both points damaged. It was just unbelievable. And these buff cards, three million of them, had to be manually sorted and put in binders that go out to the polls. The system was extremely manually and labor intensive, fraught with error possibilities and extremely stressed. The whole thing was amazingly backwater, and it came pretty close to collapsing in the 1984 election."[2]

Partly because of such conditions and the broad range of problems voters faced during the 1984 elections, significant efforts have been undertaken to improve the operations of the New York City Board of Elections during the last two decades. A mobilization of voter registration organizations and civic groups in the 1980s led to efforts to reform the board and its election practices, and voting rights advocates helped shape reform of the New York City Board of Elections, producing modest increases in registration and participation.[3]

In this chapter I document these developments and measure their impacts on voter participation and politics, focusing on the period from 1980s through the mid-1990s. I identify the political actors and interests associated with such improvements, particularly reform advocates, civic organizations, and key public officials, as well as others who opposed and blunted changes, especially the dominant party organizations of both parties and their representatives on the New York City Board of Elections. I also gauge the impact of election practices on particular constituencies, electoral outcomes, and public policy. We begin with an overview of New York City's political system and the place of the board of elections within it to situate this analysis.

The Board of Elections and New York City's Political Structure

Formal aspects of the political structure can exert influence on how dominant political coalitions form and the parameters within which they operate. Election administration is not only part of the formal political structure, but also a lens that allows examination of other formal and informal elements of the political establishment, particularly the party system and the electorate.

While scholars have explored the ties between New York's political party organizations and elite interests and particular constituencies, they have not explored similar ties to election administration. Yet within New York's machine politics, election administration has figured prominently. Party leaders pick commissioners to the board of elections, who then hire all staff and thereby directly influence policy and practice at the board. Given these relations, the political interests of the party organizations— and of the dominant political establishment more broadly—also come to be reflected in election practices of the board.[4] Such practices have, in turn, served to buttress the power and perpetuate the dominance of party leaders and the political establishment. While much of the fabled political machine is now gone, boards of elections remain as a vestige of a "machine politics" that survives.[5]

Several practices of the New York City Board of Elections were particularly problematic: inadequate information about registration methods and voting procedures, limited access to registration opportunities, flawed processing of registration applications, and poor election-day operations. I selected these election practices for closer scrutiny from a long list of contested issues because, first, these practices were the primary administrative barriers encountered by voter registration activists; second, these practices constitute the main activity of the board of elections with regard to voter registration and election operations, as mandated in state election law; third, the board has discretionary capacities in these areas; fourth, these are the primary means by which the board can cause participation to increase or decrease; and finally, these practices readily reflect the political motivations and interests they arguably serve.

A broad range of election problems resulted from such practices, many of which were highlighted in testimony at public hearings held by the state legislature, the City Council, and the New York City Voter Assistance Commission (VAC), as well as in court cases, investigative journalists' reports, and documents and reports of other government agencies and civic groups. Findings from these materials and from interviews constitute substantial evidence of numerous election and administrative problems, encountered by voter registration groups and voters alike, that led to the disenfranchisement of tens of thousands of voters. The findings also show that scrutiny of these election practices by the media and criticism by voting rights advocates not only illuminated the existence of these barriers, but also cast light on the political actors who perpetuate such practices and resist changing them. Moreover, the findings demonstrate how reformers helped produce significant improvements to the city's board of elections.

Cycles of reform and political incorporation are not new; New York City's "political establishment has confronted the problem of incorporating potentially destabilizing groups for a century and a half."[6] New York's history is dotted with periods when reformers and urban social movements mobilized previously excluded and underserved groups to challenge the political machine or dominant establishment, and the political establishment has simultaneously absorbed or tamed challengers and reconstituted itself in such periods.[7] Even though reform challengers sometimes won mayoral elections, the machine or regular factions sooner or later would return to power, usually by incorporating moderate elements of the insurgent groups. Political establishments have thus been effective at marginalizing radical elements of urban movements and reform challenges. For example, dominant political leaders incorporated only moderate Italians and Jews during the 1940s and 1950s as a precondition for those groups' admittance into the political system, and in the process they marginalized more radical factions.[8] Latinos and Asians would later challenge the dominant Italian and Jewish establishment in Harlem, Brooklyn, and then Queens. In each case particular factions within these insurgent groups would later become part of the dominant political structure. The role of election administration in these developments has been largely obscured and overlooked.

New York City has a weakly organized, highly fragmented, decentralized one-party system. Divided into five boroughs—each with its own separate county party organization—the city has been dominated by Democrats since the early nineteenth century. Today, roughly 65–70 percent of voters are registered Democrats. Even Independents—those who register with a minor party or with no party at all—outnumber Republicans. Similarly, the overwhelming majority of elected officials are Democratic, as are most of the political clubs. The county party organizations have historically drawn their membership and support from among working-class ethnic immigrant groups, first the Irish, Italians, and Jews, successively, and more recently blacks, Latinos, and Asians. Elite interests, however, have also been well represented in and served by the party system.[9]

New York's party system is similar to those of the former one-party states of the South. Such systems are characterized by factions within the dominant party that contend for power. "Coalitions are fluid, personality-oriented, and often based on invidious racial, ethnic, or status distinctions. Issues are blotted out. In such an environment, the regular political clubs, despite losing power at the center of New York City politics, can continue to hold sway at the periphery."[10] The Democratic county organizations have maintained political power through a variety of voter mobilization and demobilization strategies, exercising their influence over patronage resources, redistricting processes, and ballot access, including particular voter registration procedures and election-day operations. Mollenkopf notes:

> The regular Democratic party organizations and the lesser elected officials who make up its leadership lost their ability to determine who would hold the mayoralty after 1960, but they retained their hold on lower offices ranging from the borough presidencies to the city council, state assembly, and judgeships. From these peripheral positions, they extracted concessions from the mayoral center, including appointments to city jobs, influence over the award of contracts, and favorable decisions on matters that affected their jurisdictions. In return for these favors, they could offer some degree of control over the mayor's political environment and consent to the larger policy initiatives the mayor might propose.[11]

Although the power of the party organizations has waxed and waned, they have remained dominant players in New York politics, particularly in New York City; they have recently experienced something of a revival.[12] Democratic Party county organizations have been closely identified with the borough presidents, City Council members, and some mayors. Indeed, the county organizations continue to successfully promote their own candidates by denying others access to the ballot, and they still absorb or co-opt successful insurgents. Similarly, although political clubs have also undergone decline, they remain important players, especially in election administration.[13]

In exchange for support the county organizations and political clubs extracted patronage in the usual forms—jobs, contracts, and favorable decisions for their locales—including patronage from the New York City Board of Elections. Several investigative journalists have documented such relationships. *New York Newsday* conducted a three-month investigation and published a four-part series that extensively detailed the arrangements. The *New York Times* also did a four-part series.[14]

A series of corruption scandals during the middle to late 1980s that played a role in the demise of several Democratic Party leaders amply shows the extent of such arrangements. Bronx County leader Stanley Friedman was involved in a contract awarded to a virtually nonexistent company he partly owned; Queens County leader Donald Manes took kickbacks on parking ticket collections contracts let by Koch officials who had been appointed at Manes's request; and the patronage-hiring operation run out of City Hall under the guise of the Mayor's Talent Bank was headed by Joe DeVincenzo, one of Koch's key advisors on appointments. Ostensibly intended to promote employment of blacks, Latinos, and women in city agencies, the operation instead regularly hired people referred by county party leaders. The new hires were mostly white males, especially from the Staten Island, Bronx, and Queens county organizations. More recently, in 2003, former City Council member Angel Rodriguez began serving time for extortion and bribery.[15] These scandals undermined the party organizations' capacity and credibility during the late 1980s, leading to changes in party leadership and policy. The scandals also led Mayor Koch to distance himself from the party organization, which in turn helps explain Koch's support for electoral reform, including the modernization of the New York City Board of Elections.[16]

How was reform accomplished? In connection with the concurrent national and state political mobilization, a broad-based coalition of dozens of organizations formed in New York City to conduct mass voter registration during the latter half of 1983 and throughout 1984. By the October 1984 registration deadline, 855,000 applications had been submitted to the New York City Board of Elections, representing one of the largest increases in voter registration in the city's history. The number of registered voters reached over 3 million in New York City for the first time since 1972, and coalition members had "targeted groups of women, minorities, poorer New Yorkers and students."[17] As described in chapter 3, much of this mobilization was related to Jesse Jackson's 1984 presidential campaign and to efforts by black and progressive groups to elect an alternative to Koch as mayor in 1985, leading to significant increases in black and Latino voter registration between 1982 and 1985.[18]

These organizations encountered numerous barriers in their voter registration and get-out-the-vote efforts, and the legal requirements and administrative practices that posed significant challenges became targets for reform. The reform efforts contributed to important changes in practices of the city's election administration, which in turn contributed to modest additional increases in voter registration and participation.

Reform advocates and their liberal allies were able to bring pressure to bear on the city and the board that led to a major overhaul of the New York City Board of Elections as well as changes to election law. Advocates succeeded in pressing several Democratic officials to hold public hearings to address the kinds of legal and administrative problems they experienced and also persuaded city officials—particularly Mayor Koch—to institute certain initiatives, including the provision of funds for modernization of the board, that led to improvements in the board's operations. Thus reform advocates not only highlighted barriers, but also played a small but significant role in liberalizing New York's election policy and practices during the middle to late 1980s. A major catalyst for these changes was the severe and extensive election problems voters faced in the 1984 elections.

The influx of new registrants and voters brought on by this political mobilization overwhelmed the New York City Board of Elections. The resulting problems in the administration of the 1984 primary and general presidential elections in New York City led to the disenfranchisement of tens of thousands of voters. The inability of the New York City Board of Elections to adequately process the increased volume of registrations—855,000 new applications—led to a backlog of over 90,000 forms as election day approached. Despite reassurances from the board that all these forms would be processed on time, it is estimated that 62,000 voters were turned away on election day because they were not yet listed on the rolls.[19] In addition, declarations by the board notwithstanding, upwards of 100,000 voters never received mail notification directing them to their poll sites. When the city board of elections ran out of forms before the registration deadline, derailing or delaying some groups' voter registration efforts, a coalition of voter registration organizations helped to arrange for the printing of an additional 80,000 forms.[20]

A range of additional problems were manifested at poll sites: A *New York Times* editorial reported that "groups complained bitterly about confusion at many polling places, missing or misfiled registration forms, incompetent or absent poll workers and absentee ballots that were mailed to voters too late." NYPIRG set up a voter information hotline that received more than 3,500 calls in the few days preceding and including the day of the election. Voters complained that they had not received notification or information about the location of their poll sites, that they had not received absentee ballots or had received them too late, and that they were unable to get through to the city board's phone hotline to obtain needed information.

"Many hundreds of voters who called our hotline on election day had a wide range of complaints. They told us of polling places opening late, voters being given incorrect or out-of-date information leading to their disenfranchisement, and polling inspectors failing to issue paper ballots when machines broke down."[21]

The New York City Board Of Elections "lost the election," claimed the *New York Daily News* editorial board days later. "Consider what happened last Tuesday. Names were misplaced or lost. Tens of thousands of voters had to use paper ballots because their cards couldn't be found. Long lines built up as confused election workers struggled to sort out individual cases. Many angry, impatient people left without voting as a result. And, of course, there were the usual snafus with aging, malfunctioning voting machines."

Calling the 1984 primary election a debacle, a *New York Times* editorial strongly criticized the city board of elections

> For years, the sorry state of the New York City Board of Elections was a dirty little secret shared only by political insiders. The secret erupted into a public scandal when Board incompetence nearly disenfranchised thousands of new voters. Politicians were finally forced to take notice. . . . The mechanical-lever voting machines used by the city are obsolete and costly to maintain. Manual processing of voter forms is drowning the agency in paperwork. Dividing tasks between the central Board and borough offices compounds the chance for errors and weakens accountability. Moreover, as the members of political clubhouses have dwindled, so has the Board's ability to recruit enough qualified inspectors to oversee the polls.[22]

As the general election date drew closer, the relationship between voter registration groups and the board of elections became more adversarial and confrontational. Tom Wathen, executive Director of NYPIRG, said: "Up to now the City Board of Elections has been the Rip Van Winkle of government bureaucracies, with clogged phone lines, shortages of registration forms, and a backlog of new voters a mile long. There's an all too serious possibility that many of these new voters will be disenfranchised by the Board's unjustifiably voiding forms on technicalities or failing to send notices to voters of their polling places." While the city board maintained that the demand for voter registration forms and the volume that needed processing was greater than they anticipated, other observers argued that the board had ample forewarning: "The mobilization to register new voters—by Republicans and Democrats, conservatives and liberals—has been going on steadily for the better part of a year, and in minority neighborhoods for much longer than that. So the Board of Elections has no excuse for not anticipating the demand."[23] Indeed, some of the registration forms waiting to be processed in October had been received by the board in July.

Citing potential disenfranchisement, NYPIRG petitioned the New York City Council to intervene to ensure that the board got all the support it needed to perform its legally mandated duties. In a letter to City Council President Carol Bellamy, NYPIRG and Human SERVE wrote,

> We are concerned that the Board of Elections, despite recent efforts to improve its performance, is still not doing the job it should. . . . The Board of Elections was well aware that this was going to be a year of unusual voter registration activity. Yet, it has acted as if it were business as usual. . . . Polls show the Presidential election in New York State is very close. It would be a tragedy if the race were determined not by the will of the people, but by needless bureaucratic obstacles to voter registration.[24]

Implicit in these challenges was the threat of legal action against the board and the city for violations of state election law and the federal Voting Rights Act. This threat of legal action and public embarrassment pushed city officials to take action, even if only symbolically.

The board's attitude toward the efforts of voter registration organizations was revealing: "This registration drive has gone on [with] too much fanaticism. I'd like everybody to be registered, but not with hysteria," said the executive director of the city board of elections, Bea Dolen. While she acknowledged that the board is "an antiquated agency," she faulted the city for not providing the board with enough money for modernization. However, Alair Townsend, the city's budget director, said the board had not requested any funds for modernization; nor had any funds been cut from the board's budget over the previous few years.[25]

Increased scrutiny of the board's operations by investigative journalists and voter registration advocates brought greater public awareness of the city's election administration. It revealed an archaic institution that "had changed little in decades. Most work is done manually, as it was when the Board was established in the 1880s." Some referred to the board as "Byzantine."[26] In response, Mayor Koch, citing "gross incompetence" at the city board of elections, called for reorganization of the board. He claimed that the board had "nearly put off an election," and he sought to restructure it, giving the mayor's office more control over its operations. Koch said, "its filing systems are antiquated; voting machines need to be replaced; the Board needs a full-time legal counsel and an inspector general." Koch proposed appointing a commissioner to the board who would report to the mayor, who in turn would be responsible for day-to-day operations, and he urged that a full-time counsel and an inspector general be hired to help prevent fraud.[27]

The board attempted to deflect the barrage of criticism, maintaining that the allegations surrounding the elections were unfounded and exaggerated. Declaring that "the elections went well," Bea Dolen claimed that all registration cards had been filed and that all new voters had been notified by mail of where to vote.[28] Subsequently, however, elections officials admitted that there were significant lapses in the board's processes during the 1984 election cycle. Indeed, the board soon began to publicly acknowledge a need to modernize its operations, particularly by means of computerization and acquisition of electronic voting machines. This change occurred only after pressure was exerted by reform advocates, criticism was voiced in the media, and the mayor and state officials had begun to take action; the board acted in response to these developments rather than on its own initiative.

Mayor Koch and Election Reform

Mayor Koch had his own reasons for moving to modernize the board of elections, few of which had to do with expanding voter participation. Foremost was the need to reduce the embarrassing criticism of the city's election system, the problems with which were—not completely rightly— associated with the mayor. In addition, Koch's relations with black and Latino leaders were increasingly strained because they saw the obstacles to mobilizing their constituents as politically motivated. In the context of these mobilizations surrounding the campaign of Jesse Jackson, which gave a shot in the arm to political factions that considered challenging the mayor, such as the Coalition for a Just New York, Koch increasingly felt the need to respond to the new developments, especially given his reform roots. Koch had been drifting rightward politically, and his ties to increasingly scandal-ridden political party organizations also boded ill for his political fortunes. For example, Koch had forged cozy relationships with major real estate developers, and a significant portion of contributions to his 1981 and 1985 campaigns had been made by these interests. In return, Koch had been pursuing business policies favorable to them. But as the number of such scandals grew, Koch put more space between himself and those indicted or implicated, many of whom were Democratic Party county leaders and prominent elected Democrats.[29]

Fueled by the mobilization of voter registration organizations and reform advocates, media coverage of these incidents and political relations was widespread and damning. Some advocates who wielded their capacity to gain access to the media not only criticized the city's election system but also implicated Koch. Moreover, advocates implicitly—and at times explicitly—threatened to bring legal action for violations of state election law and the federal Voting Rights Act. Taken together, these developments posed potential problems for Koch's planned reelection bid in 1985.

Although it was in the mutual incumbency and governing interests of Koch and the party organizations to reduce conflicts with each other and to limit potential challengers, whether as insurgent candidates or as new and unpredictable voters, Koch had to do something concrete and visible to address the mounting criticism and political challenge to his reign. These countervailing pressures led Koch to support certain electoral reform measures. As Martin Shefter observes: "More striking than the support that Ed Koch the *liberal* has received from New York's downtown business community is the alliance that Ed Koch the *reformer* has cultivated with the city's Democratic county machines." He notes that Koch entered New York politics in the 1950s through the Democratic reform movement, but afterward made "peace with the city's Democratic machines" by appointing organization men and backing regular Democratic leaders in the 1980s. Shefter rightly argues that Koch allied with machine politicians "because the county party organizations still commanded an electoral apparatus" capable of affecting electoral and legislative outcomes. Koch also cultivated Republican support, and he won the 1981 GOP primary after receiving the endorsement of four of the five Republican county organizations.[30]

Other local and state Democrats also felt the need to address election problems, at least through symbolic efforts. Democrats in the New York State Assembly held several hearings on the operations of the city board. Two hearings, held in 1988, were titled "Voter Disenfranchisement in New York City" because:

> During the 1984 general election and in the presidential primary held on April 19, 1988, there were accounts of extensive difficulties facing voters throughout New York City. Problems, such as late opening polling sites, malfunctioning voting machines, improper procedures followed by poll inspectors and late mail notifications to potential voters, were reported in all five boroughs. . . . The intent of this particular hearing is to focus specifically on the issues of voter disenfranchisement and structural changes in the management of the City Board of Elections. The Election Law Committee is concerned that, despite sincere efforts to upgrade the operations of the Board, election day performance of the agency shows no marked improvement. This lack of progress results in persistent voter disenfranchisement.[31]

Governor Cuomo also commissioned studies on voter participation and elections to help bring about government reform. For example, Cuomo created the Task Force on Encouraging Electoral Participation, whose report was issued in February 1988. The New York State Commission on Government Integrity issued twenty reports recommending reforms in government ethics and procedures.[32]

These liberal Democrats were also protecting their own election fortunes. Turnout in New York City, where the majority of the state's Democratic voters reside, is critically important for their election victories, especially in statewide elections. Political strategists for Governor Cuomo and members of the Assembly, for example, articulated this view publicly and privately, and it was also made known to Koch. Clearly there was pressure on Koch to respond. At the same time, reform advocates forged effective relations with some key reform-minded Koch administration officials and attained the administration's support for several reforms.[33]

Approaches to Modernization

The nature and scope of modernization, however, was highly contested. Various public officials and political organizations—the New York City Board of Elections, the party organizations, Mayor Koch, the New York City Partnership, the New York City Elections Project Project, the state board of elections, and the advocacy organizations—differed on what modernization of the board would consist of and on how such a process would be carried out and under whose auspices. These differences reflected their conflicting political orientations and interests.

Following the debacle of the 1984 elections, Mayor Koch initially sought to gain direct control over the board and to make it have greater accountability to him. He proposed that he be given power to appoint a commissioner to the board of elections who would be responsible for day-to-day operations. But while the city board of elections is funded entirely from city revenues, the mayor had no legal authority to force such changes: the city board is a bipartisan creature of the state and is under the jurisdiction of the state board of elections; the state board has legislative responsibility and authority to supervise the city board's operations, so the state board is culpable for the failures of the city board. Once it became evident that direct control by the mayor was precluded, Koch took other measures to exert some influence. He commissioned the New York City Partnership, a business group, to conduct a study on how the board operates and to recommend improvements. He also set up the New York City Elections Project (NYCEP), which acted as a city agency and an oversight board, to implement the recommendations made by the Partnership. Because NYCEP was a division of the Department of General Services, its establishment gave Koch direct influence in shaping the process of modernizing the board.

Upon release of the Partnership's report in August 1985, NYCEP began implementing its recommendations for modernizing the board, primarily by automating registration processes and instituting minor administrative changes. Most importantly, he facilitated the expenditure of millions of dollars over the next few years to institute technological and administrative improvements to the board. Lastly, the Koch administration began to give support to advocates who proposed board of elections reform and several other election reform initiatives. For instance, in December 1986 Koch issued Executive Order 101, which established the Voter Assistance Program (VAP), whose mission was to expand voter participation in New York City by mandating voter registration in city government agencies. In 1987, to coincide with the two hundredth anniversary of the U.S. Constitution, Koch helped to coordinate a mass mailing of voter registration forms to all households in New York City through the VAP. As a result of these developments, several important changes to the board's practices were implemented during the late 1980s and early 1990s, producing improvements in the board's operations and contributing to a reduction in the amount of disenfranchisement and a modest increase in voter registration and participation.

The state board of elections moved to contain the political damage to the city's election administration and to itself. Supporting only limited and cosmetic changes, it primarily sought to improve its own and the city board's public image. The state board set up a task force to examine the city board's situation and to institute procedures to ensure better future oversight. The state task force, consisting primarily of Thomas Wilkey, then the state board's liaison to county boards, made several modest criticisms, but attributed the city board's shortcomings mostly to lack of funding. The state board recommended increased funding and procurement of new facilities and equipment.

The city board of elections and the county political organizations also attempted to limit the nature and scope of reform and to repair their damaged public image. They sought to justify the board's structure and procedures and to defend their performance in elections. The board denied the validity of the complaints of election problems highlighted in the media. Instead it attributed responsibility for particular lapses, such as failure to process all registration applications properly and in a timely manner and to mail notifications to all voters, to overzealous voter registration advocates and to certain "partisan" groups—that is, some African American organizations associated with elected officials, several labor unions, and Jesse Jackson supporters—that inundated the board with forms and requests for information within the last months of the election cycle.

Many board of elections officials, as well as the county party organizations and political clubs, opposed most of the proposed reforms, whether the proposals were made by the advocates, the mayor, or the Partnership and NYCEP. The one exception was their support for funding for new facilities, poll workers, and voting machines. Most stridently they sought to retain the political organizational structure of the board, and they did accomplish this goal. Nevertheless, given the extent of the pressure to institute reforms and the political leverage that was brought to bear for change, the board and the party organizations slowly began to take steps toward modernization, albeit with strong resistance and some backpedaling. The board did make efforts to better prepare for the 1985 election—holding more training sessions for poll workers, setting up information tables, and distributing information at some poll sites to voters who had registered but found themselves unlisted, for example. Nevertheless, these efforts were minimal, and many significant problems occurred in the 1985 primary and general elections.[34]

Voter registration advocates urged broader political reform of the board. Not only did they press for full automation of the board's operations and institution of major administrative and organizational changes, they also sought a fundamental reorganization of the board itself, with elimination of political control of the board. Advocates called for "sweeping changes" that would loosen the election administration's ties to political elites.

For example, NYPIRG, which has consistently lobbied for political reform of the state's election administration—at both the city and state board level—proposed several alternative schemes. One proposal called for the creation of a citizens advisory committee for the New York City Board of Elections, modeled on the Permanent Citizens Advisory Committee to the Metropolitan Transit Authority, to "study, investigate, monitor and make recommendations with respect to the operations of the New York City Board of Elections." Along with members of the Statewide Coalition for Voter Participation, NYPIRG also proposed several possible changes to the state board of elections, from adding a fifth "nonpartisan" commissioner to eliminating the entire board. In addition, several public officials also supported broader reform of the political side of the city's election administration.[35]

State senator Franz Leichter, Democrat from Manhattan, introduced legislation in 1988 that would have abolished county and city boards of elections throughout the state and transferred their functions to the state board of elections. He stated that "wholesale change is needed" and that it was "long past time" because the system "doesn't work" and the state "can't just tinker with it. . . . It is time we stop treating elections as a matter that is of particular significance to the political parties and that the political parties have some special right to control the elections. Elections exist for the public and the manner in which we presently run the elections with the role of the political parties ought to be changed." Richard Wade, a professor of history, made similar recommendations at a public hearing of the Voter Assistance Commission in December 1993, and in an article titled "End the Party at the Board of Elections" he called for replacing the existing board with "a nonpartisan one composed of skilled managers, a staff at home with modern high-tech tools and an enterprise dedicated to fair and impartial elections . . . appointed by the administrator of the city's court system."[36]

Advocates contended that political control by the party organizations and elected officials was a primary cause of the poor state of the board of elections. Spurred on by the heightened attention to election problems in the media and embodied in the city's steps toward modernization, advocates pressed for a range of far-reaching reforms that they believed would be more effective at improving the board's performance and increasing access to registration and voting, especially for under-represented groups. They also sought, and generally received, a seat at the table with those charged with the formulation and implementation of reforms—NYCEP and its oversight board, the Koch administration, the City Council, and the board of elections itself. While they did not achieve the full political reform of election administration they sought, voter registration advocates did substantively shape the agenda for reform of the city board of elections for important election law changes, and they saw much of what they proposed successfully implemented in the middle to late 1980s.

Advocates supported the goal of increasing the board's efficiency by means of technological improvements that the Partnership recommended, and they actively worked to see such reforms implemented by NYCEP. Many of the specific recommendations in the Partnership's report and developed by NYCEP actually reflect proposals initially made by advocates over the previous two years.[37] A coalition of voting rights organizations inserted themselves directly into the process of shaping the reform of the board—providing specific proposals for changing board practices, which were incorporated—and played an important part in ensuring effective implementation of the modernization process. They sought the Koch administration's official recognition of the coalition and its previous efforts to monitor the board's performance, and they persuaded the Koch administration to appoint two of their representatives to NYCEP's oversight board, the panel charged with supervising, and in some cases reshaping, the implementation of the Partnership's recommendations. The representatives were Lani Guinier, then at the NAACP Legal Defense Fund, and David Jones, executive director of the Community Service Society. In addition, other advocates were able to attend meetings of the oversight board as observers and to meet with NYCEP at "regular, informal 'kitchen cabinet' sessions."[38]

Advocates also lobbied the governor, state legislature, mayor, City Council, and city and state boards of elections to make far-reaching changes in election law and in the practices of New York's election administration throughout the state. With the problems of the 1984 elections fresh in the public mind and the advent of the 1985 mayoral/municipal election cycle, advocates lobbied for reform of the board of elections and election law with even greater vigor. Indeed, they garnered greater force for their complaints by presenting systematic analysis of affidavit ballots used in the primary election as proof that the board had regularly disenfranchised thousands of eligible voters through mismanagement and poll-worker errors during the 1984 and 1985 elections.

Advocates proposed that voter registration forms be redesigned and that responsibility for design and printing be shifted to the state board to ensure uniformity and adequate supply; that the stringent criteria for determining voter eligibility or removing voters from the rolls be relaxed; that outreach programs to distribute forms be expanded to include the provision of postage-paid forms; that election-day operations be improved by means of an overhaul of poll-worker recruitment, training, and pay; that a voter's rights pamphlet, a voter information pamphlet, and informational signs for poll sites be created; and that an informational telephone hotline be established at the board. Most of these proposals were eventually incorporated into the Partnership's recommendations and NYCEP's modernization initiatives, producing subsequent improvements in the board's operations. Statistics about the performance of the board, including data on increases in voter registration and participation, are evidence of such improvement.

But while these improvements represented an important victory for reformers, the nature and scope of changes to the board's practices were more limited than what most advocates had hoped to achieve. The process of modernizing the board's operations not only was slower than planned but did not fully achieve its stated goals. The Partnership's recommendations were to be implemented in phases by 1988, but each set of recommendations was phased in later than the date initially established, some significantly so, and others have not yet been implemented at all. For example, the Partnership report and NYCEP plans initially projected that electronic voting machines would be procured and ready for use by the time of the 1988 elections. Due to several delays, however, the contract for such machines still has not been finally approved; nor have the aging lever machines been replaced. The plan was eventually scrapped, partly due to concerns about security, but with the advent of HAVA, the forty-year-old lever machines must be replaced by new voting technology by 2006.

Reformers advocated for the creation of an independent election administration insulated from direct political control of the parties and with a more professional staff. They pushed for removal of the board from the political patronage system so that commissioners and staff of the board would no longer be appointed by the two major political parties' leaders. Advocacy organizations petitioned the media and editorial boards to investigate the story of the board and its ties to the party system. The *New York Times* editorial board concurred with advocates that reform of the board of elections more fundamental than the mere installation of capable management was needed to improve its operations: as important as technological improvement would be "the Legislature's political restructuring of the Board to guarantee its long-term ability to function." The *Times* continued that because the board of elections was a state agency whose staff was picked by the party leaders, there was "no accountability to the public," and that leverage from outside the party system was required to produce reform. Koch would have to "try to bring change from the outside." Such "political restructuring" of the board still has not occurred; nor was it ever seriously considered by public officials as part of the modernization of the board. The *Times* maintained that the "Governor and legislative leaders somehow have to be formally involved in the hiring of staff and thus become more accountable." Its position overlooked, however, the fact that the governor and legislative leaders already were involved in appointing elections personnel—particularly at the state board of elections—if indirectly through their representatives and local affiliates.[39]

The New York City Partnership Report

Following the 1984 election debacle, Mayor Koch asked the New York City Partnership, a business organization headed by David Rockefeller, to conduct a "management and efficiency review" of the board. The assessment was to be a "non-partisan review of the Board of Elections operations and procedures," and explicitly "non-political." Frank J. Macchiarola, president and CEO of the Partnership, stated that the "bi-partisan political control" of the board "was not a specific subject of task force review." The Partnership held that "other localities in this state and throughout the country possess a similar electoral administration system and still provide efficient and effective service to all voters. We believe New York City can."[40]

Following a six-month study, the Partnership issued a report in August 1985 titled *Agenda for Reform of the New York City Board of Elections*. The report reflected the Partnership's corporate perspective and the mayor's effort to limit public damage and shape reform. The task force was made up of twenty members and staff, fourteen from large corporate enterprises (including General Electric; New York Telephone Company; and Peat, Marwick, Mitchell & Company), four from academic institutions, and two from the Jewish Community Relations Council. Its report provides a revealing snapshot of the workings of the board during this period. Indeed, few outsiders have ever gotten as close to the workings of the board. As one top board manager put it, "the Board put a wall up, and did not allow people inside. The Board has always been pretty much a closed shop: it didn't publicize what it does, didn't want a lot of press, . . . so no one really knew its operations. But, following the Partnership Report, the Board recognized the fact that it needed to open up its operations."[41]

The findings of the Partnership's task force are significant on three levels. First, the report documented the poor performance of the board and gave legitimacy to complaints, providing an impetus for implementing changes. Second, the task force's recommendations substantively defined the nature and scope of reform. They incorporated many of the proposals put forth by the advocates (or similar proposals), while emphasizing increasing the board's "efficiency" by means of technological improvements and administrative and procedural changes. Third, the report reinforced the political nature of the board, especially through the board's reaction to the report and to efforts to implement reforms.

The report detailed a range of significant problems that pervaded the board's structure and operations. Characterizing the board as "highly inefficient" and "archaic," with procedures that led to "the disenfranchisement of thousands of citizens," the Partnership said "there is a real acute need for massive and immediate in-depth reform." The report stated that the board's "normal processes" produced gross inefficiencies and were prone to errors, and that many procedures "are exactly opposite of what they should be." The Partnership recommended that the board computerize and reorganize its overly cumbersome labor- and paper-intensive procedures for processing registration applications and maintaining registration records. Noting that these cumbersome procedures needlessly produced errors and likely led to disenfranchisement, it outlined how computerization could reduce the registration process from thirty-two steps to seven. "Gross inefficiencies are routine, such as the photocopying of thousands of registration application forms and the trimming of these copies by hand with scissors to permit their proper filing." They recommended "automation and computerization of nearly every aspect of Board operations," including "ballot layout, poll place accessibility, boundary realignment requirements, and activity statistics." The Partnership observed that many of the manual procedures had evolved over years, "usually around the capabilities or interests of individual staff members." While this statement suggests the Partnership believed that the board's disorganized procedures reflected a lack of coherent planning and, instead, organization associated with random and individual staff preferences, some elections officials and election experts have suggested that many cumbersome and illogical board procedures were not random but reflected other factors. These include the desire of the two political parties to check and balance each other by requiring that one or more persons from each party engage in the same operations—a practice that was designed to safeguard the ballot from fraud. As the executive director of NYCEP put it: "The whole organization is designed to prevent people who are not registered from voting, and allowing people who are registered to vote." The Partnership also recommended an overhaul of election-day operations, replacement of voting machines, reorganization of the board's management structure, and establishment of a system to monitor distribution of registration forms.[42]

A comparison of the Partnership's report with proposals for reform by voting rights advocates reveal many common points of criticism and remedy. For example, both emphasized the need for technological improvements and that in-depth reform of voter registration procedures and election-day operations were critical to addressing the board's shortcomings. Moreover, both called for reorganization of the board's management structure and an increase in job standards and qualifications. Importantly, given the broad credibility of the Partnership, its recommendations became what was often referred to as the "blueprint for reform."

The Partnership's recommendations, however, were largely general and nonspecific. They did not address how, in particular, the board's management structure should be reorganized and its processes automated. Nor did they suggest what types of voter outreach programs the board should establish. The Partnership's report only briefly discussed or was silent altogether about specifically what forms action on its recommendations should take; it did not detail a process and structure for the implementation of reforms. The Partnership did, nonetheless, call for the formation of a "blue-ribbon panel to support implementation of its recommendations." It also urged that the recommendations be implemented in several phases to be completed by 1988. These latter two suggestions made in the report apparently reflect the Partnership's perception that the board of elections "lacked internal motivation" to make such changes. Moreover, these provisions would give the appearance of greater independence from the mayor or other political factions.[43]

The New York City Elections Project (NYCEP) and Its Oversight Board

Following the release of the Partnership's report and just before the 1985 elections, Mayor Koch established NYCEP and its oversight board—the blue-ribbon panel the Partnership recommended—to oversee and assist in the implementation of recommendations. The oversight board met quarterly and consisted of sixteen members: several corporate executives from the Partnership's task force (corporate executives from Peat, Marwick, Mitchell & Co.; General Electric; Capital National Bank; and New York Telephone Company); eight heads of mayoral agencies and therefore Koch appointees; the executive director of the New York City Board of Elections, Bea Dolen; and two voting rights advocates, Lani Guinier and David Jones. The role of the oversight board was to "focus on setting policy and strategic direction for the Project. In addition, the Oversight Board is responsible for monitoring the progress of the Project and insuring that a reasonable and acceptable timetable is maintained." This would ostensibly increase accountability and provide continuity over time and administrations.[44]

NYCEP provided technical support to the board of elections to implement the Partnership's recommendations. The role of the project, according to its director, was to "help the Board develop the resources needed to manage the electoral system effectively. Once the new systems and programs were initiated and running effectively, full responsibility was turned over to the Board. The Project's responsibility was to provide the Board with the expertise and resources necessary to undertake the modernization initiative." NYCEP was staffed by Koch appointees and was made part of the Department of General Services, a mayoral agency, giving the mayor substantive influence in shaping the process. Thus, NYCEP and the oversight board not only were given the explicit mission of implementing the Partnership's recommendations, but also largely embodied the same approach and retained many of the same personnel. After much work, NYCEP's staff and mandate were greatly reduced, and its offices were moved into board of elections facilities in 1995. At that point, the sole task of NYCEP was to assist the board in purchasing and installing new electronic voting machines. That task will not be completed until 2006–2007. NYCEP ceased to exist in the late 1990s.[45]

NYCEP developed its strategy with the aim of building momentum for reform of the board and institutionalizing changes while at the same time reassuring the board and the county political organizations that their governance would remain intact. David Moskovitz, the director of NYCEP, noted the project's dilemma:

> A lot of people felt that when we got started, we were not going anywhere. How many times does the government create commissions or a task force that doesn't go anywhere? A lot of people thought this was going to die in thirty days or so. People in the board of elections, political people, and the like.

People told me I shouldn't take the job, that it would be a career ender because the political forces and political infrastructure were resistant to change. And how the election law gave authority to county political leaders and how the board was structured by the law would not allow for the opportunity for this kind of change. We were going up against extremely politically powerful people, so there was built-in resistance to it. Why would these county leaders be inclined to give up political authority and power to the project? I had to figure out how to shape the relationship with the board of elections, which was a very important aspect of the project. No organization likes another organization coming in and looking over its shoulder and evaluating its job. . . . They knew the mayor writes the check for the board, especially prior to the Charter change where the mayor had even stronger authority in determining the board's budget. So they had to let us through the front door. On the surface they were very cordial and responsive, but very concerned and not happy about the situation. There was certainly a lot of resistance on the part of the staff. They were concerned about the nature of the threat: was the mayor trying to take over the board? So there was a lot of tension and feeling each other out.[46]

Stephanie Dawson, who was an organizational systems analyst for NYCEP at that time and later succeeded Moskovitz as director, also noted the extent of the political dilemma facing not only NYCEP but the board and the mayor as well:

In 1984, we had a fiasco of an election. The election system was considered to be in a state of chaos, and that there was a lack of accountability. The press was filled with how machines were breaking down, poll workers not being trained, voters uninformed about where their poll sites were, buff cards missing, the list goes on and on, producing disenfranchisement on a grand scale. Those are observable problems and serious business issues. And we have an agency [the board of elections] that was turning back money or not investing in its infrastructure. They had not a single PC [personal computer] in 1985, and antiquated typewriters! How can you run an agency that was contracting most everything out? The situation dictated that change needed to happen or there was going to be a failed election. Koch seized an opportunity to make change. There was a dynamic happening there. Everything was up in the air about what "reform" would be, and how reform would proceed—whether the mayor would play a bigger role, whether the board would become civil service and nonpartisan, and so on. It was not possible for a mayor not to do anything about the situation.[47]

Thus, much like Florida in the aftermath of the 2000 presidential election debacle, New York City and Mayor Koch were prodded into electoral reform. To begin to defuse the tensions and resolve the problems, NYCEP established ongoing weekly meetings with personnel from the board of elections to examine board practices and to plan how to implement changes.

This process allowed for a lot of venting, and got certain fears out on the table, which helped us move forward to begin to automate the back offices. And what we found—besides vast disorganization and gross inefficiency—was that different borough offices often did things differently. In some cases, these differences apparently produced different impacts. For example, when the board sends out a welcome notice to a new registrant, if it comes back to the board, do you send a second notice or cancel the voter right there? The election law does not specify, and there was some variation in how this and other such things were handled which had an impact on whether a voter stays registered.[48]

Given its mission to implement the Partnership's recommendations, and propelled by public pressure from advocates and the press, NYCEP moved the reform process forward even in the face of resistance from the board. In addition, NYCEP used developments at the state level to give greater legitimacy to its efforts. The Project drew upon "the experiences and expertise of election-related entities in New York State, including the State Board of Elections, the Legislative Task Force on Reapportionment, the New York State Temporary Commission on Voting Machine Equipment and Voter Registration Systems," and several consultants to advance the automation of the board's registration system and to procure electronic voting machines.[49]

NYCEP's documentation over time of the board's deficiencies gave greater credence to critics' claims and further propelled reform of the board's operations. For example, NYCEP helped to counter the board's denials that significant problems pervaded election-day operations: "A majority of the evidence supporting this perception to date has been anecdotal. Yet recent documentation, including the New York City Partnership report and surveys of election chairpersons and police officers who worked at the 1985 primary and general elections, verifies the existence of serious problems with the Board of Elections' management of election day operations." NYCEP documented "systematic problems" that while "not adversely affecting every polling site throughout the city, have caused enough frustrations for voters and inspectors to result in . . . inconveniences, delays, and disenfranchisement." Their list of poll-site "problems areas" included: (1) insufficient staffing of poll sites, (2) lack of training and poor training of workers, (3) misinformation and lack of needed information for voters, (4) shortages of tools and supplies for poll inspectors, and (5) poor poll-site facilities and conditions.[50]

NYCEP used a top-down process as a means to drive the reform process forward, even in the face of resistance and opposition by the board. The process was intended to "define the functional requirements of a system to be developed," and it was "designed to ensure that the users of the system (the Board of Elections) define how the system 'should' operate." First, NYCEP documented "the Board of Election's problems, management objectives, functions, users and data requirements. The user specifications form the basis by which to evaluate alternative system development approaches." NYCEP then refined the user specifications to develop technical requirements for the system. This top-down process allowed NYCEP to forge ahead by establishing guidelines and parameters that "drove the way the Board incorporated reforms."[51]

For example, in establishing several technical positions for computer programmers, imaging systems technicians, and financial auditors, NYCEP set standardized qualifications and job descriptions for each of these new personnel, so even if such staff were hired through the usual channels of the political party system, they would be required to have credentials or experience demonstrating a level of skill to would enable them to be proficient in these newly created positions. Moreover, NYCEP sought to "establish an independent screening mechanism" to "ensure that individuals are hired who can meet the necessary qualifications for the job."[52]

Despite the board's—and in particular the county political organizations'—initial resistance to adoption of these proposed changes, NYCEP did establish standards for the new technical positions. Executive Director David Moscovitz explained:

> One of the most fundamental changes that we made at the board was to require that the board open up the hiring process outside the county political leadership, and to place a greater emphasis on merit, especially in technical areas. We said we want to set up this technical process and it will require particular skilled staff, and we set up a third party [Peat, Marwick, Mitchell & Company] to review the candidates to be hired. In the past, county leaders recommended staff for each position. This now was more specialized. And we negotiated this with the board. We agreed on certain job specifications, salary, etc. This was not their preference. Some members of the board recognized that the board needed to change and were more progressive in accepting this change, where others were very opposed to it. The Democrats were a little more supportive of this than the Republicans, because the Democrats feared the mayor's takeover of the board less than the Republicans did. And they all realized that the mayor wasn't going to put the money up and they couldn't publicly defend having people in there that couldn't do the job. The board wanted the option to continue to recommend candidates for these positions, and we had no problem with this so long as the person had the skill requirements. The commissioners still ultimately make decisions about hiring and firing, per the election law. So we were shaping it in a way that was sellable to the county leadership and the board. It was a protracted negotiating process, getting ten county leaders to agree. And then the hiring was another protracted and contentious process. Now the board advertises for positions in the *New York Times,* where it never did that before.[53]

NYCEP also employed this top-down methodology to develop standards and guidelines for the board regarding various procedures, such as how registration applications would be processed, stored, and maintained; how poll lists would be selected and organized; and what minimal criteria would be used to select electronic voting machines. By using "technological methods and professional standards to drive design," NYCEP propelled the board forward toward implementing reforms and modernizing. NYCEP also set up joint project teams made up of board and NYCEP staff to implement particular reforms, such as computerization of registration and other processes, development of signature digitization systems (SCRIBE), and procurement of electronic voting machines.

Resistance to Reform

Initially the board had reacted incredulously and defensively to criticisms leveled by advocates, the media, and the mayor, maintaining that criticism surrounding the 1984 election was unfounded and exaggerated, and declaring that the elections had gone well. Board staff had maintained that the "accusations and criticisms of the Board are more often than not untrue." Indeed, advocates noted that board staff had reacted to their criticisms and recommendations "incredulously" and that they were "surprised, hurt and resentful, feeling instead that they are doing all they can or is necessary."[54] Similarly, the party organizations—like most of the board's personnel—reacted negatively to claims by advocates, the Partnership's findings and recommendations, and NYCEP's initiatives. Initially most of the board's personnel and party leaders did not perceive that there were significant problems in the board's operations or that significant change was needed.[55]

When the Partnership's report was released, however, the leadership of the board publicly gave tepid support to some of the recommendations, such as acquisition of electronic voting machines and increased compensation of election inspectors. The board began, slowly and incrementally, to acknowledge various problems highlighted by advocates, the Partnership, and NYCEP, and allowed the implementation of some of the changes recommended. Faced with the real threat of lawsuits against the board brought by advocates and increased control and oversight by the city—and, more importantly, loss of funding—the board gave in under pressure and moved to implement modernizing initiatives, even as it sought to shape the reform agenda for its own purposes.

Many board personnel reported a perception pervading the agency that the Partnership's task force, NYCEP, and especially the advocates were "outsiders or intruders," whose "meddling" "forced" the board to undertake what it perceived as significant and often "unreasonable" changes. Ferdinand Marchi, who became president of the New York City Board of Elections, acknowledged that "initially there was resentment because you have outside agencies coming in and telling you what to do." He reported that board personnel viewed these agencies "in a suspicious manner, that they are trying to take over the operation and everything else." Board employees also feared the intervention of the outside agencies. Richard Wagner, of CWA Local 1183, the union representing board personnel, stated that there was "too much interference in the Board's operations by Koch and NYCEP." NYCEP staff assigned to begin working with the board on modernization also reported this fear and resentment on the part of board staff.[56]

Some task force members and NYCEP personnel also reported that the board at times strongly resisted the task force's efforts to complete its study and obstructed NYCEP initiatives to implement recommendations. Board personnel expressed a measure of natural anxiety about restructuring and potential job loss. "One of the primary concerns of the staff of the Board is the impact the modernization program will have on their jobs. Many Board workers fear that automation will lead to elimination of positions." Their union shared these concerns. Security issues and concerns regarding possible election fraud, as well as health and safety concerns about video display terminals, were also raised by board staff. The party organizations feared the loss of their influence over the board and of one of their last bastions of patronage.[57]

The board and party leaders tended to see the board's biggest problem—which they contended produced deficiencies—as insufficient funding. "We are locked into an antiquated system. We want to be automated. It is only a question of money," said Robert S. Black, president of the board of elections. The "problem was not management," Black explained, "but a lack of support for an agency that is forgotten all but a few days a year." But according to the *New York Times*, the New York City Board of Elections had not made concerted efforts to petition the city for increased funds for such automation.[58]

It is true that election administration is underfunded. Indeed, boards of elections make convenient whipping boys for elected officials and critics of election processes. As the director of the New York City Board of Elections at the time, Danny DeFrancesco, put it:

> Machine breakdowns, late openings of polls, election worker shortages, missing buffs, late processing of voter registrations and the lack of documentation by the Board were highlighted. To some degree many of these problems existed. To many of us, these are not unfamiliar problems or concerns. However, it must be noted that for too many years the state would mandate increased responsibilities without mention of increased funding. In New York, the city's severe fiscal crisis drastically cut personnel and other personal service dollars. Little or no guidance was offered by the State Board, however, on how to meet all of our responsibilities with existing funds. We must not forget that at the same time politics itself was changing, causing inspector shortages, increased petition challenges and lawsuits. 1984 forced both the Board of Elections and the City of New York to focus on the resources necessary to conduct elections properly and fairly.[59]

Pay for election-day workers, for example, has been extremely low, providing little incentive to more competent workers and making it difficult to fill all positions. "A lack of resources prohibits the Board from providing proper training materials or utilizing equipment integral to a successful training session." Regarding the training of such workers, the board provided only limited times for training: sessions occurred during working hours, not in the evening or on weekends, and the five-dollar stipend for attending a training session was "insufficient to attract" workers to classes. With increased efforts to address the board's deficiencies, funding for board improvements in this and other areas was put into place by the Koch administration beginning in 1986.[60]

The board and party leaders also contended that New York's election law limited what the board could do and contributed to the board's problems. For example, the election law requires that the board fill poll-worker positions from lists provided by the county party organizations and that the workers be equally divided between the two major political parities. Thus, the board argued, it could go outside the party system only once it had exhausted the party lists, and even then it could use only Democrats and Republicans (not independents or members of other parties). Legal opinion of the New York City Law Department seemed to corroborate this interpretation of the election law.[61] However, according to other election law experts, the board may go outside of the party organizations to fill positions. Moreover, the law does not say the party organizations must nominate only individuals registered in one of the two major parties or that they be in any party at all. Thus even within the parameters set out by the law the board could—though it did not at the time—expand its avenues to recruit workers.[62] Advocates urged the board to recruit workers on college campuses and through a variety of media outlets; this practice began on a modest level in 2001.

The board and county political leaders consistently argued that the existing political process and structure of the board provided the best system to run elections. They contended that board employees and election-day workers recruited through the political club system are among the most dedicated, hardworking, and capable workers in any government agency. With little exception, party leaders and the leadership of the city and state boards consistently maintained this high regard for their staffs. Robert Black, for example, claimed that board employees are better than civil service workers, that they are loyal and hardworking, "which you couldn't expect from civil service workers." Similarly, George Friedman said, "I view them amongst the hardest working people in society." The boards maintained that even workers who are fired or are not rehired as temporary or election-day workers—a rare occurrence—are exceptions to the rule and merely "bad eggs." They did, however, admit that the decline of the party and club system had hurt boards' capacity to recruit workers and fill all positions. The nature of the county party organizations was reflected in most aspects of the city board's operations, including the makeup of the board's personnel: the board had a similar demography (mostly middle and working class and of Italian and Jewish ethnic background) to that of the political clubs.[63] Further, the board and party leaders argued that bipartisan control of election administration provides incentives for each side to perform well under the other's scrutiny and that bipartisan composition is needed to safeguard the election process from fraud: that the checks and balances that bipartisan control provides are the best mechanism for ensuring fair elections.

Nevertheless, once modernization of the board was recognized to be a fate accompli, attention turned toward implementation of reforms. Indeed, even the leadership of the board would proclaim that "a new Board of Elections has been established" that now "embraces reform" and is working to implement changes. Similarly, Danny DeFrancesco, the administrative manager who replaced Bea Dolen in 1988 as executive director, and Jon Del Giorno, who became administrative manager, presented the board as a "new Board that does not do things the old way any more." The next in line and the most recent in the post, John Ravitz, appointed executive director in February 2003, also pledged to improve the board's performance in a number of areas.[64]

Such proclamations rang hollow. In many respects, the board merely paid lip service to modernization and only partially implemented particular recommended reforms. More insidiously, it threw up roadblocks that overtly sabotaged change. In 1988, most observers maintained that the board remained in disrepair and needed serious upgrading:

> Massive disenfranchisement in New York City is well documented. In the 1984 and 1988 elections, tens of thousands of people were turned away from the polls because of administrative errors, broken machines, untrained inspectors, faulty procedures, incorrectly processed registration forms and misleading voter poll information cards. The reasons for the ongoing administrative breakdown of the board are also well documented and well known. The Partnership's findings still hold true today. The board still has no written procedures, still conducts elections with voting machines which are hopelessly out of date and worn out, and still does not have a computer facilitated operation for processing the millions of registration forms it receives each year.[65]

Other advocates concurred. Alan Rothstein said: "The Board hides behind the law. It could do much more regarding expanding voter registration opportunities, implementing reforms, and improving its operations if it wanted to. . . . It is like moving a mountain. We had to go back to them again and again with what we thought were modest proposals, such as placing a Board employee at poll sites as an information person." Similarly, Gene Russianoff argued: "Why the poor performance of the Board? In 1984, the problem was inadequate resources and poor management. Since then the city has devoted major new resources to the Board's work. But today the heart of the problem remains the Board's inadequate management."[66]

This was so in part because the board had exercised its capacity to shape the reform process. Board personnel, for example, limited access to information about its operations and restricted task force members, advocates, and the media to interaction with only particular staff. Although over time relations between the board and the "outsiders" grew more cooperative and produced important improvements in the board's operations, when public scrutiny and pressure ebbed, implementation of reforms was often delayed or thwarted. In 1986, for example, the board reluctantly agreed to hire thirteen new technical staff to implement automated processes, but over a year and a half later only six had been hired; implementation of these changes was therefore delayed. In 1990 the board attempted unsuccessfully to persuade the mayor's office and City Council to defund NYCEP and reallocate its appropriations to hire employees for the board. Moreover, the modernization process was compromised by the coincidence of similar political interests that were represented on the board and in the reform agencies, and in some cases overlapping of personnel, especially given that Koch and the county political organizations had accommodated each other somewhat. This had the consequence of limiting the nature and scope of reform.[67]

Moreover, the explicit mission of NYCEP was merely to initiate implementation of the Partnership's recommendations and then turn over to the board control and responsibility for each activity. Indeed, as implementation of reforms proceeded, NYCEP and the board increasingly accommodated itself to the other's concerns and orientations. For example, NYCEP increasingly worked to repair negative public perception as much as or more than it attempted to improve the board's operations: "Our project is seeking to reverse the negative public perception of the Board and to enhance the Board's ability to manage election day operations and service voters in the future."[68]

Nevertheless, driven by its mission to implement the Partnership's recommended reforms—even in the face of resistance from the board—NYCEP did institute substantial reforms, and significant improvements in the board's operations ensued. Registration files were computerized; postage-paid voter registration forms were introduced; improvements were made in management and staffing; outreach to registration organizations and the public was expanded, with forms being made available in post offices, libraries, and high schools; provision of election information to the public was improved, with expansion of telephone services and public information advertising; and election-day operations were reformed: a model poll-site program was established that augmented the training and testing of workers, recruitment of inspectors was expanded and their pay was increased, poll sites were better organized, election-day procedures were clarified, and useful information was made available to the public in voter-friendly form.

The leverage that was brought to bear on the board from several arenas thus proved decisive in moving the board to modernize. The intense public criticism in the media and by advocates, coupled with continued public scrutiny by investigative journalists and the threat of law suits by advocates, was critical, especially in prodding the Koch administration to take action to improve the board's performance and public image, which in turn brought pressure on the City Council, the political organizations, and the state board of elections to support reform, at least publicly. In addition, critics helped prod the governor's office and liberal Democrats in the Assembly and Senate to support the legislation necessary to move the board forward toward modernization. Changes were made in election law to require boards to prepare outreach plans for voter registration, to allow the purchase of electronic voting machines, and to prompt computerization of voter registration records and the digitization of signatures. Thus important modernization changes were implemented, albeit in fits and starts and with resistance all along the way.

Management reform was one of the most contentious issues of the modernization process. An exemplary case was the replacement of the departing executive director of the board of elections, Bea Dolen.[69] When Dolen, who had been director for twenty-five years, announced on August 16, 1988, that she was retiring (her retirement would be effective on December 31, 1988), extensive political maneuvering began. The commissioners of the board possess the statutory authority to hire the executive director and all staff. Given the commissioners' ties to the county political leaders, however, it was clear that there would be struggle around the selection of the winner of this most prized of the board's patronage plums (a $72,000-a-year position in 1988), not to mention the most powerful position on the board's staff.

Moreover, following the presidential primary election in April 1988, which was characterized by widespread charges of board incompetence and racially motivated mass disenfranchisement, there was renewed public scrutiny by voting rights groups and progressives, especially African American organizations. On May 19, 1988, a class action lawsuit was filed by the Center for Law and Social Justice, a civil rights advocacy group affiliated with CUNY's Medgar Evers College. The suit charged the board, Betty (Bea) Dolen, NYCEP, the governor, and the secretary of state with disenfranchising voters in the primary election. Immediately following the primary, Jackson supporters, U.S. Representative Major Owens, the New York Civil Liberties Union, and the Center for Constitutional Rights sharply criticized the board, and Representative Owens called for Dolen's resignation. The board countered that the charges were "grossly exaggerated."[70] Mayor Koch also jumped into the fray, initially calling on the board to "conduct a search that goes as far and wide as is necessary to find someone with the talent and commitment" to do this immense job.[71]

Advocacy organizations called on the board to "conduct a nation-wide search for a first-class replacement for Betty Dolen" and contended that her resignation provided the board with "a unique opportunity to improve its performance."[72] Manhattan Democratic Leader Herman (Denny) Farrell recommended Hulbert James, the director of Jesse Jackson's primary campaign and former executive director of Human SERVE, for the position;[73] Queens Democratic Leader Thomas Manton promoted Gloria D'Amico, who was then the head of the Queens Board of Elections and was a longtime district leader; and Brooklyn Democratic Leader Howard Golden said he was "wide open on this thing."[74]

An odd coalition of political heavyweights—Governor Cuomo, Mayor Koch, and the Reverend Jesse Jackson—met at the governor's office the week before the board selected a candidate and secretly drafted a letter to the commissioners of the board, urging them to conduct a national search using "an independent merit selection committee for the identification, consideration and recommendation of [three] candidates for executive director." They contended that "the choice of a highly qualified candidate for the post of Executive Director is critical to the long-term success of the modernization of the Board of Elections." The *New York Times* reported that "the agreement arose out of dissatisfaction with the Board's performance in voter registration and election day operations," particularly surrounding the April presidential primary, in which Jackson had run. The Jackson campaign "contended that the Board's inefficiency made it more difficult for many black and Hispanic voters to cast their ballots" in the primary.[75]

The commissioners of the board, however, moved quickly to name Danny DeFrancesco executive director. Six of the ten commissioners voted for his appointment, including Alice Sachs, Democrat from Manhattan, who had been appointed to the board by Denny Farrell, the Democratic leader who had recommended Hulbert James for the position of director. One commissioner, James Bass, Democrat from Brooklyn, abstained; another commissioner was absent; and two Republican seats were vacant. Board officials "acknowledged that they had quickly and quietly selected Mr. DeFrancesco to head off any move for Mr. James." Indeed, the board's press release stated that "the decision by the Commissioners was made after taking into consideration the suggestions by certain groups, to conduct an outside search for a qualified candidate. After careful review, their vote was based on the fact that within the Board's management team there already existed a fully qualified individual who knows the inner workings of the Board of Elections."[76] Apparently the commissioners did not know about the Jackson-Koch-Cuomo agreement.

The commissioners' decision to name DeFrancesco sparked further controversy and conflict. Mayor Koch reacted angrily at the appointment and urged the board to reconsider its decision. An editorial by the *New York Times* stated, "Whatever Mr. DeFrancesco's qualifications, the failure to consider any outsiders is inexcusable. The cronyism looks especially offensive at a time when the Board is under attack by minority voters for its perennial inefficiency." Farrell threatened to remove Alice Sachs, and Sachs was later replaced by Douglass Kellner. Jesse Jackson and others attended the next commissioners' meeting and implied that there would be "riots in the streets." But the board refused to reconsider its appointment of DeFrancesco. Commissioner Bass, who is black and who initially abstained, made a motion to reconsider the appointment, but no one seconded it, and the vote became final.

The board expressed anger over the involvement of Governor Cuomo and Jesse Jackson. Indeed, commissioners who were initially cool to the DeFrancesco appointment were more angered by Cuomo and Jackson's involvement. "I can't understand how a Presidential candidate, the Mayor and the Governor would make an agreement about a Board in which they don't have input," said George Friedman, the Bronx Democratic chair. "It was wrong of them." Similarly, Nicholas LaPorte, the Staten Island Democratic leader, asked about Jackson, "Where does he get off?"[77]

The New York City board has remained dominated by the established party organizations and continues to engage in old-style political patronage, as evidenced by patterns of personnel appointments and the dispensing to political allies of contracts for the provision of goods and services such as the printing of ballots and the purchase, service, storage, and transportation of voting machines.[78] The city board "is the last unrepentant bastion of county machine patronage in the city," Martin Gottlieb and Dean Baquet concluded in 1990. Their examination of contracts for trucking, ballot printing, and the purchase, storage, and maintenance of voting machines showed how "New York's Republican and Democratic Parties, placed at the helm of the agency that runs the city's elections, have shaped it into a powerful patronage tool for dispensing lucrative contracts. . . . With scant monitoring from the city or state, the board has tailored bid specifications to favor specific companies, has ignored lower bids in favor of longstanding and high-priced contractors and has been accused of thwarting new companies forced upon them by the city." Companies that receive business make contributions to the political parties and elected officials who steer contracts their way. "You know, there's big bucks involved," said Lillian Bachman, the cochair of the Queens Republican Party, regarding trucking contracts. The Republican board of elections commissioner from Queens, Joseph Previte, "was removed by the party in 1985 because he was too timid in getting trucking companies to buy tickets for fund-raising events."[79]

One company, R. F. Shoup of Bryn Mawr, Pennsylvania, continuously held contracts for the purchase and maintenance of voting machines for nearly thirty years until recently. The Shoup family has "long, close relationships with New York's political parties," according to Bea Dolen and several commissioners. In fact, Shoup donated money to various political groups over the course of its years of negotiating contracts, and Shoup family members are part of "an informal eating club called the 'Schleppers,' whose members include Dolen, Danny DeFrancesco, and the former Tammany Hall chief, Frank Rossetti, and even more fabled predecessor, Carmine DeSapio," and Lawrence Mandelker, an election lawyer who is close to board commissioners and was the finance chair for Mayor Koch's 1989 campaign. "Records going back ten years indicate the board has bent over backward to ensure that Shoup keeps its contract. . . . The Board has also resisted efforts to end the 25 year near-monopoly that two companies hold over the roughly $3 million in contracts for printing election ballots."[80]

With the support of several legislators, the board and Shoup nearly engineered the steering of the most lucrative contract, the $50 million package for electronic voting machines to replace the existing Shoup machines, to Shoup, but they were thwarted by investigative journalists and government inquiries. Several earlier investigations of the city board of elections conducted by state and city agencies had found substantial corruption and other violations in the board's contracting practices and had revealed political patronage relationships. For example, in 1985 the Department of General Services, at the request of City Council President Carol Bellamy and the Communications Workers of America, the union that represents board employees, conducted an investigation, led by Kenneth Litwack, into the board's procedures of dispensing contracts; they cited numerous problems in board practices, including conflicts of interest. In November 1984 the Corruption Prevention and Management Review Bureau of the city's Department of Investigation conducted an analysis of the contracting and administrative procedures of the New York City board from 1979 to 1984 and cited substantial problems and violations. Thus the board's patronage relationships reveal its ties to politically dominant groups and suggest possible motivations for maintaining policies and practices that constrict voter participation. Such patronage relationships continue to this day.

In early 1990 the City Council introduced a proposal to eliminate the $950,000 budget of NYCEP and move five of its twenty staff members to the board. City Council members have strong ties to the county party organizations, and until term limits began in 2001 they also had strong incumbency interests. Danny DeFrancesco, executive director of the board, testified before the City Council that he needed only five more staffers to do the election project's work. This proposal provoked broad and swift opposition from voting rights advocates and the Dinkins administration: "The Dinkins Administration, which has been pushing the Board to modernize, . . . is furious at the proposal. 'Putting it into the budget environment,' says Deputy Mayor Norman Steisel, 'is the straw that broke the camel's back.'" Noting that "since its creation, NYCEP has had an uneasy relationship with the Board of Elections," Maria Laurino of the *Village Voice* contended that "the project's younger staff is a far cry from the patronage players at the Board of Elections, who are selected by the City Council on the recommendations of the county party leaders. . . . 'They are competent high-level technocrats who do excellent work', said Gene Russianoff of NYPIRG."[81]

The Partnership's Status Reports

In October 1986, almost two years after the 1984 election fiasco, the Partnership released a report outlining the progress NYCEP had made in implementing recommended reforms. The report provided a snapshot of what had been accomplished by that date and what remained to be done. Four years later, in 1990, shortly after the transition from the Koch to the Dinkins administration, the Partnership released another status report. Together, these two reports documented important accomplishments but also serious shortcomings of reform efforts. The 1990 status report was issued to the public by the Partnership and the NYCEP oversight board. Quarterly status reports were also produced by NYCEP, primarily for members of the oversight board, but voting rights advocates and other interested parties requested and obtained copies, so advocates were able to monitor the board's progress in modernizing and were able to intervene at particular junctures.[82]

Although the Partnership had called for its recommendations to be implemented by 1988, only two had been completed by 1990: necessary changes to state election law had been made and the poll-worker stipend had been increased. According to the oversight board, this left several important tasks remaining: (1) replacing mechanical voting machines, (2) implementing signature digitization systems citywide, (3) developing and implementing "a comprehensive organizational structure that provides clear lines of accountability and ensures consistent quality and policies across all five boroughs," (4) developing a "meaningful 'scorecard' system" to effectively monitor the quality of election services provided by the Board of Elections,"[83] and (5) enhancing recruitment of poll workers to achieve full coverage in all positions (inspectors, information clerks, poll-site coordinators, and language interpreters).

Although NYCEP expected that the city would be able to obtain its first machines by the time of the 1988 election, it did not use the first machines until 1993, and then only to test them in the 75th Assembly District in the Bronx. Ultimately, this program was scrapped because opposition stalled the procurement process. The city and state are now slated to obtain new voting machines in 2006 with federal HAVA money. Automation of registration records and other operations was implemented in phases. The new Election Administration System (EASY) became operational in 1988 but was not fully implemented until 1992. The new system could process fifteen to twenty thousand registration applications per day, a significantly higher rate than previously. Subsequent computer updates were implemented that further increased the board's capacity to process registration forms.[84]

NYCEP's "Model Polling Sites" plan included the employment of a poll-site coordinator who would be specially trained to manage large poll sites and to handle problem situations and expedite their resolution; an overhaul of the board's training program, including establishment of a unit in the board responsible for year-round recruitment and training of poll workers; and creation of new instructional materials for poll inspectors. With the assistance of the state and city boards of elections, NYCEP developed a standardized curriculum and a certification process. However, the number of workers who received this new training was very limited at that point in time. Finally, the Model Polling Sites plan called for the establishment of information centers within poll sites that would be staffed by information clerks to ensure that voters could get to their proper election districts, and for the creation of new signs, posters, and other informational materials for voters.[85] Some of these changes were implemented by 1992, and further improvement ensued in subsequent years.

In 1987, the stipend paid to poll workers was raised from $65 to $85 for a sixteen-hour day, in order to provide greater incentive to workers and make it more possible to recruit them. The pay had been raised from $50 to $65 in 1984; the previous raise had been from $37 to $50. According to Bea Dolen, the raise from $37 to $50 attracted more inspectors, but the raise from $50 to $65 did not have that effect. The 1987 raise to $85 helped some, but subsequent raises had a greater impact: to $125 in the late 1990s and then to $200 in 2001. However, split shifts—a reform advocates wanted—have not been instituted.[86]

Moreover, the newly implemented automated system (EASY) now provides a tool to efficiently manage poll workers, and a full-time person was hired by the board to coordinate poll-worker activities citywide. The percentage of inspectors who were trained rose from well below 50 percent in the mid-1980s to 83 percent by 1994. As a result, the board has experienced a decrease in the number of problematic affidavit ballots, fewer complaints, and, most importantly, a lower number of voters turned away at the polls. To provide important election information to the public, the board increased its number of phone lines from two to six in 1986; then in 1988 the phone bank was expanded to thirty lines with terminals to the EASY system. The board's mailings to voters were simplified and sent more regularly, and election-day materials such as posters were revamped.[87]

After county political leaders and the elections commissioners blocked the filling of seven of the thirteen positions that had been created to support the modernization initiatives, NYCEP, the county leaders, and the board engaged in lengthy negotiations. They reached "a compromise solution regarding the hiring of personnel to fill new positions at the Board,"[88] but, as one election expert noted, the "few good competent workers that were hired left and their successors have been chosen the same old way; in other words, once the pressure is off, the party leaders resume their pressure and presence."[89] Indeed, in 1990, the NYCEP oversight board noted that "personnel and organizational changes at the Board are political matters, and progress in this area has been extremely slow."[90]

Lastly, following the recommendation of advocates, the NYCEP oversight board sought to strengthen existing accountability mechanisms and suggested additional ones to provide public accountability and promote effective performance. The city board is formally accountable to the state board of elections and the New York City Council and is required to provide an annual report to the state board covering the its "affairs and proceedings." The oversight board, however, contended that "whether or not the accountability requirements were sufficient . . . they are not sufficient now," given the technological changes to the board. Furthermore, the city board did not produce an annual report from 1970 to 1988, because, according to the board, funds were insufficient to do so. The other existing accountability mechanism is through the City Council. The Council appoints the commissioners of the board on the basis of recommendations from the county political leaders, and because the city funds it, the board is subject to the city's budgetary hearing process, which at the time was carried out by the Council and the Board of Estimate and is now handled by the Council, the mayor, and the Office of Management and Budget.[91]

The NYCEP oversight board said results of direct measures of the board's performance could be regularly reported in its annual report, but to institutionalize better public accountability and to enable more effective monitoring of the board of elections, the oversight board also embraced the advocates' notion of establishing a scorecard system and widely distributing these performance measures. Gene Russianoff of NYPIRG summed it up: "Performance measures are objective criteria to measure the board's operations and progress over time."[92] Essentially, performance statistics are a means to measure how well the board provides services to voters. Such measures were already used to monitor the provision of other government services, such as street cleaning and subway maintenance. NYCEP suggested that this kind of system of accountability could tie the board's performance to self-correcting means of promoting a responsive, service-oriented electoral system. The oversight board's Larry Horner explained:

> There is a direct, ultimate measure of its success: rate of participation by citizens eligible to vote (both registered and unregistered); percentage of eligible citizens registered to vote; percentage of registered voters actually voting; proportion of new inhabitants circularized with mail registration applications; "availability" of voting machines (defined as the total number of hours machines are open, staffed and functional); proportion of polling sites conveniently and safely located and perceived to be convenient and safe by the voters.

The oversight board suggested supplementing these processes with four "structural accountability controls": (1) an elected commissioner of elections so "voters could remove a Commissioner who did not perform adequately," (2) budgetary controls that would make it possible to reward good performance and punish poor performance, (3) audits modeled on General Accounting Office (GAO) standards, and (4) periodic public hearings to generate public pressure on agencies to perform properly.[93] No formal scorecard system was established by NYCEP or the board of elections, but data supplied to advocates by the board—and other data collected by advocates, the police department, NYCEP, and the Voter Assistance Commission —provided a means to evaluate the board's performance over time.

Performance Measures of Board Practices

What were the impacts of these changes? NYPIRG has requested, and has generally received, data from the board following each election to assess the board's progress. It also has advocated passage of legislation mandating that the New York City Board of Elections publish yearly reports containing details of the board's performance on a set of specific measures. On March 29, 1994, state representatives Peter Grannis and Scott Stringer introduced a bill (A-10503) to amend the election law to require the board to produce data on results of specific performance measures each year. Requiring the publication of a report modeled on the Mayor's Management Report, which "is considered a very useful management tool and is the subject of mandatory oversight hearings in the City Council, . . . this bill would foster good management at the Board and efficient running of elections." The bill, however, was withdrawn from the Assembly without being voted on. Some other election experts and academics have attempted to establish and use specific performance standards to assess election administration.[94]

Data on results of these performance measures demonstrate that board practices continued to disenfranchise thousands of voters in each election. Moreover, in several elections—most notably those of 1988 and 1993— there was a pattern of racial and class disenfranchisement: a disproportionate number of low-income and minority voters were adversely affected by the board's practices. Nevertheless, the board's performance has improved since 1985, when the modernization process began, and markedly so in the case of some practices, such as the processing of voter registration applications and, to some extent, poll-site operations. These improvements have in turn reduced the rate of disenfranchisement and contributed to increases in registration and voting in New York City. Of course, other factors also helped to boost voter registration and participation, including voter mobilization by unions and civic groups and the historic campaigns of Jesse Jackson in 1988 and David Dinkins in 1989.

To be sure, some people are prevented from voting by the paucity of critical voter information and by the provisions of the election law itself— such as the deadline to register to vote. But certain specific practices of the New York City Board of Elections also disenfranchise eligible voters. There are three critical measures that indicate how well the board functions: the number of affidavit ballots used, the rate of error in processing voter registration applications, and the number of poll-worker and poll-site problems.

Affidavit Ballots

If a voter's name does not appear on the roles at the poll site, the voter has the opportunity to complete an affidavit, or provisional, ballot. Later, the board checks to determine whether the information the voter has written on the affidavit ballot (name, address, signature, and so on) matches the board's registration records. This is to prevent the fraudulent casting of affidavit ballots. If no registration is found or if the information on the affidavit ballot does not match the registration record at the board, the affidavit is invalidated and not counted. Conversely, if the voter's registration record is located and the information on the affidavit ballot matches the board's registration record, the vote is counted.

NYCEP and the board of elections claimed that the large number of affidavit ballots regularly cast in each election

> does not necessarily indicate an equally large number of errors on the board's part. Board errors are represented only by those affidavit ballots which are found to be valid. A valid affidavit ballot is cast by a voter whose buff card has been either misfiled by the Board or overlooked by the inspector at the polling site. . . . An invalid affidavit ballot is cast by a voter who is not qualified to vote in the election either because he or she was not registered, registered too late, or was not enrolled in a party [for primary elections]. This is indicative of a public awareness problem which can be addressed through voter education programs.[95]

This view is still held by most board officials.

While it is true that the large number of affidavit ballots cast "does not necessarily indicate an equally large number of errors on the Board's part," certain actions and inactions by the board may cause legitimate affidavit ballots to be invalidated. Voting rights advocates and others have demonstrated that the board regularly invalidates numerous valid affidavit ballots. Moreover, when an affidavit is validated, the law requires the board to rectify the problem that caused the voter to need an affidavit ballot in the first place; the board often fails to do this.

At several junctures board personnel may inadvertently or intentionally disenfranchise voters who have cast affidavit ballots. Sometimes a polling site has ballots for several election districts. Before 1994 if an inspector allowed a voter to cast an affidavit ballot for the wrong election district, election law required that the ballot be invalidated, even if it was cast at the correct polling site. Even though inspectors have resources, such as printed street finders, to determine the correct election district, they do not always use them. In other cases, legitimate registrants are not informed by poll inspectors that they have a right to cast an affidavit ballot when no record of their registration can be found at the site. These people—unless they already know their rights and assert them—often leave without voting.

No comprehensive records of such occurrences are kept—indeed, there are no mechanisms to obtain such information—so the precise number of individuals who are thus disenfranchised is unknown. Numerous incidents documented in public hearings and reports reveal, however, that significant numbers of voters continue to be disenfranchised in such a manner.

To examine the extent of such problems, Human SERVE conducted a study of affidavit ballots cast in the 1985 mayoral primary election. They found that approximately 22 percent of the affidavit ballots invalidated by the board had been cast by properly registered citizens at the correct polling place but at the wrong table—that is, for the wrong election district. The voters either had not been directed to the proper table or were misdirected by board personnel, a problem that could be corrected if inspectors routinely and correctly used their street finders. On the basis of this finding, SERVE estimated the number of legitimate voters who are likely to be disenfranchised in this manner in various elections, and their results suggest that the potential number is large and politically significant. In presidential elections where up to 100,000 affidavit ballots are cast, the group conservatively estimated, as many as 15,000 to 20,000 voters might be deprived of their vote. In off-year elections, where 25,000 to 30,000 affidavits are cast, the number of disenfranchised would be 4,000 to 5,000 voters. The study used a sample of 1,105 affidavit ballots from all five boroughs in New York City, and drew from assembly districts with low-income and minority populations as well as those with middle-income and affluent, predominantly white populations.[96]

These figures do not reflect the disenfranchisement that results from other practices by poll inspectors; sometimes inspectors mistakenly overlook a voter's registration record and do not offer an affidavit ballot, and sometimes voters are actively discouraged from casting affidavit ballots. Nor do these figures identify errors committed by personnel in the borough offices of the board of elections during the original processing of registration applications or in the verification process. An investigation by a board commissioner into the verification process showed that errors occurred in 1993 because clerks do not always "look hard enough to verify a registration, or merely make mistakes." Such errors, he said, probably regularly occur in every election.[97]

The New York State Assembly Election Law Committee conducted a study of the affidavit ballots cast in the 1988 Democratic presidential primary. The study found that out of the 38,131 affidavit ballots cast, 30,948 were invalidated, and of those 3,808, or 12.3 percent, were invalidated because election inspectors did not facilitate the casting of the ballots in the proper election district. The board's own records reveal that the disenfranchisement of a significant number of affidavit voters is a regular occurrence. In the 1992 elections, for example, 8,853, or 13.5 percent, of invalidated ballots were rejected because duly registered voters had cast votes for candidates in the wrong election district; sometimes the ballots were cast at an incorrect poll site, but sometimes they were cast at the correct site.[98]

The decline in rate of this error—from 22 percent in 1985 as documented by the Human SERVE study to 12.3 percent in the 1988 Assembly study—reflects improvements in the board's operations, including poll-worker recruitment and training and the provision of instructional materials, and particularly in its election-day operations and computerization. With the full and effective implementation of EASY and SCRIBE, the error rate declined even further, and with it, the rate of disenfranchisement. The slightly higher 1992 rate of 13.5 percent probably reflects several factors that militated against these improvements, including late reapportionment and the fact that SCRIBE had been implemented in only three boroughs at that point—the Bronx, Brooklyn, and Staten Island. (Manhattan and Queens introduced SCRIBE in 1993 and were certified to use it by the state board of elections in 1994.)

Partly due to advocates' lobbying efforts, the New York City Board of Elections changed its practice of invalidating affidavit ballots cast in the wrong election district (that is, at the wrong table). Instead, the board began to treat affidavits as valid if they were cast at the correct polling place, even if they were cast in the wrong election district. The change led to a decline in the proportion of affidavit ballots that were improperly invalidated. The rate at which the ballots were improperly rejected for all reasons dropped to 5 percent in the 1990s; today it is approximately 1–2 percent.[99]

The number of affidavit ballots cast has declined over time, as well as the rate of clerical errors, indicating greater efficiency by the board and thus a reduced incidence of disenfranchisement of voters. The board attributed a steep decrease of valid affidavit ballots cast from 1992 to 1993 to the institution of the SCRIBE poll-list system. While the total number of valid affidavits did decrease by almost half, the figure for valid affidavit ballots as a percentage of affidavits cast was nearly identical for those years. The number invalidated in each election exceeds the number validated by the board, indicating that tens of thousands of voters continue to be disenfranchised by registration deadlines and election law mandates.[100]

Similarly, administrative error regarding the completion of emergency ballots, which are cast when a voting machine breaks down, also negatively impacts on vote counts. In 1993, for example, 2,482 emergency ballots either initially were not counted properly or were not counted at all.[101] In 1994 there were 6,880 emergency ballots out of a total of 1.5 million votes cast. Improvements in the board's processing of emergency ballots and, more importantly, the full and effective use of electronic voting machines, now due in 2006, will likely further improve election-day operations.

Analysis of affidavit ballot procedures highlights two aspects of the board's general procedures that tended to produce administrative disenfranchisement: first, the greater the manual labor– and paper-intensive nature of such procedures, the higher the potential for error. In short, inefficiencies produce disenfranchisement. Thus, with the inauguration of the computerization of registration records in 1988–1992 (EASY) and the digitization of those records in 1992–1993 (SCRIBE), administrative errors were reduced, and with them, the associated disenfranchisement. Second, the more procedures are instituted to secure the vote against fraud, the more voters will likely be disenfranchised. Conversely, when the board reorganized and streamlined its procedures and, just as importantly, relaxed its strict compliance standards in processing registrations and ballots, significantly fewer voters were administratively disenfranchised by these board practices.

Processing of Registration Applications

Other voters—at least several thousand—were disenfranchised before each election because of shoddy procedures in processing registration applications. As the Partnership report outlined, prior to 1987 the board used highly cumbersome manual labor– and paper-intensive procedures to process voter registration applications. The board used thirty-two steps to process each application, including receiving voter registration applications at the central office; manually checking each form; copying, cutting, and transporting forms; and putting the forms into binders in each of the borough offices. This process could be chaotic and lent itself to administrative errors, especially during periods closer to registration deadlines, when voter interest was greater and registration organizations deposited large quantities of forms. Moreover, to handle this increased volume, the board generally hired temporary workers, many of whom had low skill levels and were unfamiliar with board procedures. Indeed, at times a severe backlog would occur, which compounded the whole problem: forms were damaged, misfiled, or "lost"; and voter identification cards and poll-site notices were sometimes mailed out late or were not mailed out at all. Given these conditions, it should not be surprising that significant numbers of errors were committed by board personnel at this stage in the process.

In order to reduce the rate of errors endemic to this paper-intensive system—especially during crunch periods close to registration deadlines, when large numbers of registration applications are turned in for processing—NYCEP assisted the board in instituting several important changes. The major change was the introduction of the Election Administration System, which computerized all registration files. When EASY became fully operational citywide, the board was able to process nearly 700,000 applications per year (332,930 during the peak period from September 1 to October 31). Clerks could keypunch information from voter registration applications into EASY, vastly simplifying the process. The introduction of SCRIBE permitted works to scan applications into board's computer system.

However, both EASY and SCRIBE still require manual input, which continues to make human error a factor. And while there is a quality control person who checks the information keyed into the board's registration system against the actual registration forms, errors still occur. According to several elections officials and experts there remains a 1–2 percent error rate.

Jerome Koenig, former chief of staff of the Assembly Election Law Committee, said election clerks still "make a lot of data entry errors." For example, he found that data entry clerks had keyed in the following incorrect information: 316 E. 97th Street instead of 316 W. 97th Street; 666 5th Avenue instead of 666 Greenwich Avenue; 289 Delancey Street instead of 288 Delancey Street; and 139 W. 42nd Street instead of 139 W. 142nd Street. In each case the latter address was subsequently determined to be the correct address. Koenig reported he found many other such errors, and there were likely to be many more that he did not find.[102] Thirty percent of all registration forms required some kind of follow-up by board personnel for the registration to be completed validly. The system has been upgraded since.[103]

As late as the middle to late 1980s, the New York City board routinely discarded registration applications that, for example, contained only one signature instead of the two technically required, had missing or incomplete data, or had other similar technical errors. Thus a greater proportion of registration applicants were likely to be disenfranchised by the board during this period. Because of such practices, the rate of error in processing voter registration applications at that time was estimated to be approximately 15 percent, according to registration advocates and some elections officials.[104] This 15 percent "clerical error" rate meant tens of thousands of voters were disenfranchised. For example, of the over 700,000 voter registration forms processed by the New York City Board of Elections in 1984, about 105,000 would have been discarded and the applicants administratively disenfranchised during this period. Thankfully, with the automation and improvements described above the board's error rate dropped.

The error rate apparently fluctuated over time and between borough offices, particularly before the introduction of EASY in 1988–1989. In 1993 the board calculated that its error rate was only 1–2 percent in each of the borough offices except Manhattan, which had an 11 percent error rate as recently as 1992–1993.[105] Even with a 2 percent error rate, however, given the volume of registration applications processed by the board offices, the number of inaccurately recorded applications remains significant, and even after automation thousands of voters continue to be disenfranchised by such errors. In the mayoral election year of 1993 about four to five thousand voters were disenfranchised, and over ten thousand were disenfranchised in the presidential election year of 1992.

Thus even with improvements the board disenfranchised tens of thousands of voters over the ten-year period of modernization, and some board personnel have suggested that the real rate of error may actually be much higher than officially acknowledged, especially during peak periods when the board hires temporary workers. Partly because such problems were widely perceived to be pervasive, voter registration organizations began to make photocopies of voter registration forms prior to submitting them to the board.[106] However, in practice the board is the final arbiter: it is the keeper of the official records regarding an individual's registration status, and if board personnel cannot locate an individual's registration record, that person is not officially registered. Indeed, except in the case of an effective legal challenge—which rarely occurs—the board's ruling stands, and the individual is prevented from casting a ballot or from having an affidavit ballot validated. Any attempt to assert that a registration application was submitted or to match an affidavit ballot to a registration record at the board that does not exist because of an initial administrative error by board personnel will inevitably result in that voter being disenfranchised.

Thus in any registration dispute the bias favors the board, and the responsibility for board mismanagement is shifted onto individual voters. Although the number of voters who are disenfranchised is relatively small in proportion to the total number of registrants and voters, the board is nonetheless responsible for this disenfranchisement. In addition to the disenfranchisement that occurs because of the requirements of registration law, such as the twenty-five-day registration deadline, significant numbers of legitimate voters are routinely disenfranchised by the board itself.

Poll-Worker and Poll-Site Problems

A primary cause of administrative disenfranchisement that occurs at poll sites is error on the part of the board's poll workers. Although there have been important substantive improvements in the performance of poll workers over time, significant election-day problems continue to occur in each election. Approximately 20 percent of inspectors who work the polls every election—the line staff of the board with whom voters interact—did not in the past and still do not receive training. Moreover, the caliber of the training itself remains wanting, even though the methods and materials the board uses have improved. Potential poll workers who fail a test at the end of training, thus displaying incompetence in the performance of necessary tasks, can still serve as inspectors on election day. In addition, though the pay for a workday of over sixteen hours has increased substantially (from $65 in 1996 to $200 in 2001), it still does not provide sufficient monetary incentive to attract more competent workers.

Changes in the board's recruitment and training programs have markedly increased the proportion of poll workers who receive training over time—the figure rose from 67 percent in 1988 to 88 percent in 1994, according to board data. Rates varied, however, among the five boroughs: Manhattan had the lowest rates of training (69% in 1992 and 76% in 1994) while Staten Island had the highest (90% in 1992 and 94% in 1994). However, the overwhelming majority of inspectors remain patronage employees. The party organizations, through the district leaders and political clubs, continue to be the main source of inspectors, even though the board has expanded recruitment to outside sources. The parties present to the board the names of individuals they have recruited who are available to work on election day as inspectors, and the board fills slots with outside workers only after the political parties fail to fill them all, which often occurs very late in the election cycle. Board personnel have reported that party officials continue to complain when the board uses or attempts to use inspectors from "outside" sources, such as colleges or recruitment via voter registration applications.

Thus while we can acknowledge that the board of elections whose jurisdiction is the second largest in the country faces an enormous task, its election-day workforce—which numbers over 30,000—includes not only many workers who are highly incompetent, but also many who behave in a politically motivated fashion, the combination of which can lead to significant problems on election day and result in the disenfranchisement of eligible voters. In addition, the board's administrative structure and the aging fleet of voting machines are responsible for a host of other election-day problems. It must be stated, however, that many of the board's personnel—whether poll workers or data clerks or administrators—are dedicated, hardworking, and highly competent, and consistently facilitate access to the franchise.

There have also been problems with poll sites themselves. Sites have been moved without proper notification to the voters, have opened late, have been inadequately staffed, and have lacked sufficient supplies, and voting machines have broken down. All of this can lead to confusion, delays, and disenfranchisement. The reports and testimony I analyzed reveal thousands of examples of these phenomena, albeit fewer in the period after 1985 than before. Indeed, while the board has demonstrated marked improvement, its own records reveal that such occurrences have been frequent.

The board's data demonstrate improvements in several areas. Most notably, poll sites have become more accessible to people with disabilities, and poll-worker vacancies, complaints, and voting machine problems have all been reduced. The board attributed the decrease in machine breakdowns to their preventative maintenance program and to the use of stationary curtains on the voting machines, practices instituted by the board in early 1990 after it received numerous complaints and substantial pressure from advocacy groups following the 1988 and 1989 elections. The board also improved its capacity to field telephone inquiries: 20,467 calls to VOTE-NYC were handled from October 31 to November 2, 1993, and over 20,000 were fielded during the same period in 1992 (60,728 for the year).[107]

The location of poll sites can negatively or positively affect turnout because sites may be long or short distances from people's homes. Site selection is therefore subject to contestation by the political parties and leaders, and any change of poll sites must be approved by both county party leaders. Poll sites are ostensibly selected on the basis of several official criteria, including the number of residents in an area, proximity to other poll sites, whether the site is accessible to people with physical disabilities, and the cost of renting the site if rent is charged to the board. Some board personnel have reported, however, that locations of poll sites have long been the subject of political conflict within the board and between parties, and that periodically poll sites have been changed for "blatantly political" reasons.

In one episode in 1993, for example, a Democratic Party leader persuaded the board to move a poll site from a nursing home, whose the residents were perceived to be likely Giuliani voters, to a site ten blocks away, making the task of voting much more difficult for many of these elderly residents. Similar kinds of interventions reportedly also have been made by Republicans. Such manipulations are not always successful, and they may now be more rare. Nevertheless, the board reduced the total number of poll sites citywide from 1,359 in 1986 to 1,251 in 1992. The board contends that a 1984 court injunction (in *Hill* vs. *Board of Elections*) requiring that poll sites be accessible to people with disabilities necessitated many of the poll-site changes and reductions, that good sites are hard to find, and that nonpublic sites are expensive. Advocates have countered that although the number of available accessible sites was limited in the past, today there are many more because of the Americans with Disabilities Act. While the board may have a financial interest in reducing the number of poll sites, advocates contend that this concern functions as a convenient excuse for both the board and elected city officials not to expand the number of accessible sites.

Varying Validation Standards and Practices

Although the election law clearly prescribes what is required in the casting of affidavit ballots and in the processing of voter registration applications, practice varies considerably between the different borough offices within New York City and among board clerks and poll workers. Differences in how affidavit ballots are handled by poll workers may be due to their different levels of training and experience, to the workers' temperaments, and to the political affiliation of the poll inspectors or poll-site coordinators.[108] More importantly, board policies have changed over time, and these changes appear to contribute to variations in the administration of election processes, including the processing of voter registration applications and affidavit ballots.

When "strict" compliance standards are applied, affidavit ballots and voter registration applications must contain all information that is required by election law and board policy. For example, until 1994, when the forms were redesigned, all applications had to be signed on both the front and the back, and they had to be signed exactly as the name of the applicant was printed (for example, Daniel W. E. Holt had to be signed as such in script and with the middle initials). Under strict compliance standards all voter information on an affidavit ballot has to match a voter's registration record exactly in order for the ballot to be validated. If, for example, a voter's name appears on the registration record as "Daniel" and he wrote "Danny" on his affidavit ballot, strict compliance standards would invalidate his affidavit. While the objective of strict compliance standards is to prevent the casting of any fraudulent ballots, inevitably strict standards applied to affidavit ballots and voter registration applications disenfranchise more voters. In a sense, when strict compliance standards are applied, the new registrant or affidavit voter is presumed guilty of fraud unless the perfect execution of his application or affidavit proves him innocent. In contrast, in some other jurisdictions, such as Alabama, affidavit ballots are all counted on election day on the assumption that the voter is registered, and they are only verified if the election results are challenged.

"Substantial" compliance standards allow a greater number of affidavits and registration applications to be counted and processed. Registrations and affidavits are accepted as valid as long as they provide the main information required. So if someone fails to include a middle initial or to sign a form twice, the board will still accept the document and adjudicate it accordingly. In this case, a registrant or affidavit voter is presumed innocent.

Variations in board practices associated with changes in board policies or standards often reveal the influence of distinct political and partisan interests. Republicans generally—though not universally—tend to use or advocate the use of strict compliance standards, while Democrats, particularly members of certain liberal factions, tend to use or advocate the use of substantial compliance standards. According to New York state law, however, registration forms and ballots (affidavit, absentee, and emergency) are presumptively valid. This is the standard applied in contested elections, in which lawyers for candidates spar over ballots.[109]

Strict compliance standards were generally used by the board prior to the mid-1980s, and the board—or its particular borough offices—has periodically emphasized or reinforced such standards. This has especially been true during particularly close races and contested elections, when scrutiny of ballots and registrations is intense. Furthermore, particular board clerks and poll workers tend to apply compliance standards more assiduously than others. Even before the mid-1980s, when substantial compliance standards were more generally applied because the board was liberalizing its policies and procedures as pressure from advocacy organizations mounted and as modernization proceeded, particular board personnel exercised their capacity to apply these more relaxed standards. According to board personnel and several election lawyers, such employees did so because of "personal temperament" or because it was in the perceived partisan or party factional interest of the board employee who adjudicated such matters, whether Republican or Democrat.

In 1993 pressure from Republicans to guard against alleged registration and vote fraud led the board to reverse its liberalizing trend and to adopt more restrictive measures, likely increasing disenfranchisement. These kinds of variations in board policies and procedures are also evident in other board practices. In 1993 Republican officials also planned to extensively use a "challenge" process, which is permitted by law: a poll worker or a candidate's or a party's poll watcher could challenge the legitimacy of a voter's registration, and the voter would then have to cast an affidavit ballot instead of voting on a voting machine.[110] This policy was used only partially, in part due to opposition by Dinkins campaign lawyers and voting rights advocates, who, arguing that it targeted minorities, threatened to request the intervention of the U.S. Department of Justice.

Undocumented and Politically Motivated Disenfranchisement

While some disenfranchising impacts can be documented, others cannot. Some people do not even know they have been disenfranchised. The applications of some eligible voters are administratively invalidated, sometimes incorrectly; some valid registrants are not properly notified about the status of their application or the location of their poll site, a result not of their own error but of various procedures or mismanagement at the board of elections; some eligible voters are never afforded the opportunity to cast an absentee ballot; others never get to their correct poll site or to the correct election-district table at the correct poll site, and therefore they either do not vote or their vote is not counted; and some leave the poll site after some delay or problem, and no report of the occurrence is made. On the basis of testimony by representatives of a broad range of community-based organizations, we can safely say that an undetermined additional number of eligible voters have also been disenfranchised.

In addition, many others—especially first-time voters—may well become discouraged. The unpleasant experience of being subjected to such ineptitude can reinforce some voters' skepticism or sense of alienation from the political system, leading them to conclude that the costs of electoral participation may outweigh the benefits. Indeed, registration groups attest that some voters have cited such reasons for subsequent nonvoting.[111]

One recent positive change in the board's practices has the capacity to rectify some of these problems. Partly as a result of redistricting, which led to a large number of poll-site changes in 2002, Commissioner Mark Herman persuaded his fellow commissioners to begin sending, in addition to the regular notice to vote, a second, specific notice that reads: "Your polling place has been changed. You now vote at . . ."[112] Although election law requires the board to do this on a regular and widespread basis, the board had not done so as a matter of practice, partly to avoid the expense.[113]

Board employees may also disenfranchise prospective voters intentionally, whether at board offices or at poll sites. While it appears that most voter disenfranchisement results from unintentional errors due to incompetence or flawed procedures, board employees also have political motives and possess the administrative capacity to vitiate an individual's right to vote. As the most local-level and face-to-face representatives of the board of elections to the public, inspectors possess administrative authority and discretionary capacity to shape interactions with voters in important ways. And election inspectors are patronage appointees with political affiliations and interests.

Poll workers are always only Democrats and Republicans, by law, so voters who are registered in one of the other legally constituted minor political parties, as well as members of that 25 percent of the electorate that is not enrolled in any party at all, may be treated in a discriminatory or politically motivated manner by board personnel. The same can be true of voters whose racial or ethnic background is different from that of the inspectors. Some evidence suggests such biased treatment does occur. Testimony of voters and elections personnel in interviews and public hearings, such as VAC and City Council hearings, reveals that cases of such biased treatment of voters, apparently on the basis of party enrollment, race, ethnicity, and class, has occurred.

Consequences of Disenfranchisement

Does disenfranchisement matter? Emphatically yes. Aside from affecting the attitudes of the irate voters who are turned away at the polls, disenfranchising practices can affect the fortunes of candidates and parties, particularly in close races where margins between the winners and losers are small. The extent to which a disproportionate number of low-income and minority voters are disenfranchised affects the degree to which these election practices have partisan and policy consequences. Finally, in several of these episodes partisan actors intervened and pressed for changes in elections practices that produced such outcomes, showing the impact of election administrators' susceptibility to political manipulation.

At the state level, for example, in 1992 Alphonse D'Amato (R) defeated Robert Abrams (D) by only 124,838 votes out of over 4 million in the race for U.S. Senate. In 1994 George Pataki (R) defeated Mario Cuomo (D) for governor by a mere 173,798 votes out of more than 5 million. In 1998 Attorney General Eliot Spitzer (D) defeated Dennis Vaco (R) by a few hundred votes out of over 2 million cast. These elections were determined by a few percentage points or less. Similarly, there are many examples of county and municipal races across the state in which the winner beat the loser by a small margin. Some races were settled by a few votes out of several hundred or thousand cast, and others by a few hundred votes out of tens of thousands cast.[114]

In New York City there have been many close races as well. In 1977 Mayor Koch won in a crowded field of candidates in the Democratic primary election by fewer than 10,000 votes out of 909,774 cast.[115] In the 1989 primary David Dinkins (D) defeated Koch by the smallest margin in a New York City mayoral race since 1905.[116] In the general election of that year Dinkins defeated Rudolph Giuliani (R) by fewer than 50,000 votes out of nearly 2 million cast (a 2–3% margin), then lost to Giuliani by just over 50,000 votes in 1993. In 1997 Ruth Messinger defeated Al Sharpton in the Democratic primary election by 33,529 votes out of 411,459 in a five-way race. The margins were also small in the elections of 2001: in the

Democratic primary Mark Green defeated Fernando Ferrer by about 15,000 votes out of 787,000 votes cast (1.9%), and in the general election Michael Bloomberg defeated Mark Green by about 40,000 votes out of almost 1.5 million votes cast (2.7%). The margins of victory were even smaller in several other races in 2001, such as those for public advocate and City Council. Similarly small margins can be found in dozens of elections for other offices over the past decades.

By all indications, a majority of those disenfranchised are likely supporters of Democratic candidates in statewide and citywide races, and of particular Democratic factions in some races in New York City. Democratic losses and Republican gains have policy implications. The major parties have different race and class bases of support both statewide and within New York City, just as they do nationally: lower-income individuals and minorities tend to identify and vote Democratic, while higher-income people tend to vote Republican. The parties, in turn, tend to promote policies favored by their constituencies. For example, Democrats seek to restrain tuition increases at public universities, to increase social service spending, and to make the tax structure more progressive. Republicans tend to advocate for lower taxes and fewer regulations for businesses and to urge reduction in spending on social programs.[117]

The registration procedures and election-day operations that disenfranchise eligible voters in New York City reflect both the legacy of turn-of-the-twentieth-century reforms, which gradually institutionalized such restrictive practices, and the continued influence of dominant political actors who are represented on the board of elections and have incumbency interests in maintaining a constricted electorate. While much of the political science literature ignores or downplays the role that election administration can play in producing low voter turnout, the practices of boards of elections do affect voter participation.

The rate of disenfranchisement by the New York City board declined from 1984 to 1994 as a result of reforms instituted during this period. The mobilization of and lobbying by registration-reform advocates, the negative media attention generated by the board's poor performance in the 1984 and 1988 elections, and the spate of scandals that enveloped dominant Democratic officials prodded Mayor Koch to support a host of legal and procedural changes to the board's practices, which decreased disenfranchisement by improving the board's operations. These improvements, along with other initiatives, such as registration drives by civic groups and the creation of the Voter Assistance Commission, increased registration and voting rates and certainly contributed to the election of David Dinkins in 1989. Some of these gains were reversed or undermined, however, by a Republican countermobilization in 1993 that increased disenfranchisement in that election and may have contributed to the defeat of David Dinkins and the election of Rudolph Giuliani.

The Specter of Vote Fraud

HOW RESTRICTIVE PRACTICES HELPED
ELECT MAYOR GIULIANI

During the 1993 elections, the previous decade's improvements to the New York City Board of Elections were partially reversed. Republican Party officials coordinated a campaign against election fraud and pressured the New York City Board of Elections to step up security measures to safeguard the ballot. These efforts intensified the board's restrictive administrative procedures and, coupled with a separate Republican ballot-security operation, led to the disenfranchisement of thousands of eligible voters. The voters affected were primarily low-income individuals and people of color, so the efforts contributed to lower turnout and perhaps led to the defeat of David Dinkins, a Democrat and New York's first African American mayor. The victor, Republican Rudolph Giuliani, subsequently made sharp budget and staff cuts to the city board of elections, which further undermined its operations and depressed voter registration and turnout.

Republican and Democratic Concerns: Security versus Voter Access

As the campaign for the 1993 municipal elections began, so too did allegations and expressions of concern regarding potential registration and vote fraud. Charges of fraud were raised by state and local Republican officials, particularly from the Giuliani campaign, and by leaders of the Liberal Party, a minor party that endorsed Giuliani. In addition, Republican operatives from within the New York City Board of Elections provided information to local journalists for many fraud-related news reports that brought pressure to change election practices.

Such tactics were not new. During the 1989 elections, state and local Republican Party officials charged Democratic operatives and Dinkins supporters with registration and vote fraud and claimed that fraud had cost Giuliani votes and perhaps had contributed to his defeat. David Garth, Giuliani's media advisor and a former campaign consultant to Mayor Ed Koch, made similar allegations concerning the 1989 primary elections, principally in regard to Latino voting districts where Koch may have lost crucial votes in the race against Dinkins. These accusations and appeals to fear were echoed throughout the 1993 race with great frequency and force, particularly by Giuliani and several of his campaign staff, especially by

Peter Powers, Giuliani's campaign manager, who became first deputy mayor and then advisor to Giuliani, and by Richard Schwartz, Giuliani's deputy campaign manager and then chief of staff and advisor.

Republicans at the national and state level also alleged fraud. The Republican National Committee alleged that several thousand people were brought in from the South to vote illegally for Dinkins. In 1988 the New York State Republican Party's Victory 88 campaign conducted a "ballot-security operation" in New York City, and the Giuliani campaign also had a ballot-security operation in 1989.[1] In March 1993, during the U.S. Senate's deliberations on the National Voter Registration Act of 1993 (NVRA), Senator Alphonse D'Amato (R) alleged that vote fraud had occurred in New York in the 1992 elections:

> Mr. President, let me tell you that in my election that just took place this past November, they had well over 100,000 paper ballots that were thrown out. The largest percentage was people who were not eligible to even vote. . . . To open the floodgates and doors to those who are not citizens of the United States to be determining who shall be elected and who will not, that is just wrong. . . . There are those who will absolutely go and line them all up and have them all register, no matter who, so that they can determine the outcome of elections. . . . So I . . . hope we do not want to encourage voter fraud.

The senator's comments were made in the context of an argument that the bill should not include a requirement that registration opportunities be made available at social service agencies.[2] Although no evidence of illegal noncitizen voting has been produced, despite requests made to the senator and other Republican officials, these allegations were made repeatedly throughout the 1993 election season. The kinds of illegal activity alleged included false and duplicate registrations, noncitizen registration and voting, repeat voting, and voting in the name of the deceased—all of which ostensibly would have had the effect of inflating turnout for Dinkins.

Early in the spring of 1993 the first in dozens of reports appeared in major New York City newspapers and on radio and television broadcasts raising the issue of possible registration and vote fraud and the threat these posed to the outcome of the upcoming 1993 elections. *New York Newsday* and the *New York Post* assigned investigative staff and other resources to the story. Not since Tammany's heyday had so many news reports raising concerns about fraud appeared prior to an election.

Reminiscent of campaigns led by Republicans and reformers at the turn of the twentieth century, a state committee was brought in to investigate the charges of registration and vote fraud in New York City. The Republican-led Senate Election Law Committee focused largely on the operations of the New York City Board of Elections. The stated purpose was to investigate reports of fraud raised in the news and to take appropriate action. While the investigation turned up no significant evidence of fraud, it did expose slipshod registration procedures and mismanagement at the board of elections. This Republican-led inquest, coupled with efforts to change particular administrative practices of the board, was used as a basis on which to oppose particular legislative reform measures sponsored by Democrats and voting rights advocates. Voting rights groups contend that this Republican maneuvering was done with an eye toward preventing the passage of the NVRA, which was being hotly debated at the national level, and then shaping its design and implementation, as well as toward influencing the outcomes of the 1994 gubernatorial and congressional races and the 1996 presidential race.

Republicans used the investigation to suggest that further "liberalization" of the election law and administrative practices would promote vote fraud. For example, at a public hearing held in conjunction with the investigation, they opposed pending legislation that would have further simplified the New York state voter registration form, particularly the section of the form that deals with citizenship, a change that Democrats had sponsored and voting rights advocates supported. In the context of the recent passage of the NVRA, which Republicans had opposed, the hearings provided a springboard for opposition to early passage of needed enabling legislation and of provisions ensuring effective implementation. Michael Nozzolio (R), chair of the Republican-dominated Senate Election Law Committee, stated "the need to ensure that the integrity of the electoral process is maintained is paramount. Opponents of the federal law have brought to light the possibility of fraud in the Motor Voter system. This possibility will be a topic upon which the efforts of my fellow Committee members and I will be especially focused."[3]

These Republican tactics eventually disenfranchised thousands of voters on election day in 1993, as well as in subsequent elections. Their efforts triggered changes in the way the 1993 elections were conducted, which had a negative effect on voter participation, especially among minorities and the poor. Specifically, Republican-led efforts brought pressure to bear on the city and state boards of elections to step up security measures. By forcing the city board to introduce additional restrictive administrative procedures and apply routine measures in a more stringent manner, Republicans increased the likelihood that greater numbers of eligible voters would be barred from exercising their voting rights. In addition, because the focus of the board's activity shifted toward security-related concerns, there were fewer resources for activities that increase access to the franchise. The city board of elections contributed to the disenfranchisement of eligible voters by instituting restrictive measures, ostensibly to guard against the kinds of fraud alleged during the months before the election; by reinforcing particular routine administrative practices to ensure the integrity of the ballot; and by failing to follow procedures, curb mismanagement, and address the kinds of errors by board personnel that have marred other elections. Some disenfranchisement is also attributable to a separate but related Republican ballot-security operation involving the use of hundreds of poll watchers.

A different set of concerns were raised by the liberal wing of the highly fractionalized New York City Democratic Party—that is, Democrats allied with the Dinkins campaign and those cast in the reform mold of the 1960s—and its supporters, a broad range of private and nonprofit organizations that were allied with or sympathetic to the Dinkins administration, as well as voting rights advocates and good-government organizations. These Democrats expressed worry not about fraud but about the ballot-security operation the Republicans were planning and about particular practices the board of elections had instituted in response to news reports and to the state committee's investigation. In particular, some Democrats and advocacy organizations were concerned that ballot-security measures would have the effect of decreasing turnout of legitimate voters by creating intimidating conditions, cumbersome procedures, and administrative delays and failures. These Democrats and voting rights groups were successful at preventing the implementation of additional restrictive measures, and their efforts thus decreased the probability of even greater disenfranchisement.

While the Republicans' charges of registration and vote fraud were largely unsubstantiated, evidence exists that another form of bureaucratic fraud was perpetrated in the form of restrictive practices that had the effect of decreasing turnout, particularly of minority and working-class voters. These disenfranchising impacts contributed to the defeat of Mayor Dinkins and helped in the election of Mayor Giuliani. To inform this discussion, we begin with a brief review of several important features of that election, which form the context for these events.

From the outset the 1993 mayoral race was projected to be very close, as the race in 1989 had been. Moreover, it was clear that the movement of very small numbers of racially polarized voters in either direction could make the difference between the winner and the loser. Thus measures that might have the effect of increasing or decreasing turnout of particular groups carried special weight for the contestants. Most observers maintained that the Democrats and Dinkins would benefit from an expansion of the electorate, given that there were over 1.5 million eligible but unregistered potential voters, mostly minorities and people with low incomes who were likely to be Dinkins voters, considering the composition of his 1989 electoral coalition.

In this context, any activity that would have the impact of increasing registration and voting of eligible potential voters who were not yet registered, including fraudulent activity, would likely benefit Dinkins and his supporters. Conversely, practices that might restrict or suppress registration and turnout, especially of low-income and minority voters, coupled with strategies that would increase the turnout of groups identified as likely Giuliani or "fusion" voters, would likely benefit the Republicans, Giuliani, and other fusion candidates.

Republicans have long accurately perceived the New York City Board of Elections as being dominated by the regular Democratic Party. Even though the board is bipartisan in composition, Democrats have held many of the most senior administrative positions. At first glance it would appear to be in the political interests of the Democrats on the board to increase voter registration and participation. As in the Democratic Party as a whole, however, distinct factions exist among Democrats on the board. Generally the Democratic faction ascendant within the board was not closely aligned with the liberal or pro-Dinkins elements and was occasionally at odds with the Dinkins administration and progressive factions of the party. Ironically, the Dinkins administration itself was erratic regarding taking measures to expand the franchise. For example, for over a year the Dinkins administration defunded the Voter Assistance Commission (VAC), a nonpartisan agency mandated to facilitate voter participation of under-represented groups, and the Dinkins campaign conducted little registration itself.

Election law assigns twin mandates to boards of elections: ensuring the integrity of elections and enhancing voter registration. As was evident in earlier periods—at the turn of the twentieth century and during the 1980s and 1990s—both parties and many voting rights advocates recognized that the board could affect participation by emphasizing or deemphasizing particular practices that are aimed at achieving one or the other of its mandates. Indeed, some election experts have noted that the various practices boards employ to achieve these mandates often work at cross-purposes.[4] Measures designed to maximize access to voter registration have been perceived as compromising the integrity of the ballot and opening the door to fraudulent activity. In general, Republican officials have tended to emphasize measures designed to ensure the integrity of the ballot, while Democrats have tended to promote efforts to increase voter registration. Thus boards' mandates potentially serve conflicting partisan interests, and emphasizing one over the other might also influence the outcome of elections. Election administrators have often noted the difficulty in striking a workable balance acceptable to both parties and to factions of those parties. It was inevitable that the New York City board's practices soon became a site of struggle between the contending parties. Given that its operations had been roundly criticized over the previous decade, the revelation of new examples of the board's mismanagement in the media and by the state investigation fueled Republican concerns that there would be greater opportunities for registration and vote fraud, and served to justify renewed scrutiny of board practices and provided a reason to press for additional safeguards.

Role of the Media

Numerous news reports appeared during the 1993 elections that cast doubt on the integrity of the election process by raising concerns about possible registration and voting fraud. Most of these reports originated in

New York Newsday, principally in articles written by Joe Calderone, whose ties to the Giuliani campaign apparently played a role in his production of the articles. The *New York Post,* the *Daily News,* and the *New York Times* each ran its own series of articles, often following stories first reported in *Newsday.* The Calderone articles in particular presented registration data and information on election practices, especially the practices of the New York City Board of Elections, with a focus on its Manhattan office.

The reports suggested—sometimes explicitly, sometimes implicitly—that Democrats and the Dinkins campaign would be the beneficiaries of the circumstances highlighted in the articles, or, even worse, that they were involved themselves. The reports cast suspicion on the Dinkins campaign's registration activity, both previous and current, and raised concerns about its links to the board of elections and the board's "lax" practices. The articles served to buttress Republican efforts to change particular practices of the board of elections, to institute restrictive registration and voting procedures for the 1993 elections, and to forestall related election law changes.

Republican and Giuliani operatives and supporters reportedly provided the impetus for some initial articles and were among the journalists' sources of information. According to top administrators in the New York City Board of Elections, several Republican employees of the board supplied information to journalists, including Joe Calderone of *Newsday* and David Seifman of the *New York Post,* both well-known Republicans and Giuliani supporters. In addition, Jerome Koenig, chief of staff of the Assembly Election Law Committee, and Gene Russianoff, senior counsel for the New York Public Interest Research Group (NYPIRG, a nonpartisan, student-led organization), claim to know of particular Republican officials, including Richard Schwartz and Peter Powers, who may have supplied data and information to reporters. Thus, even though many of these stories were researched by the "*New York Newsday* Investigations Team" throughout the campaign cycle thus appeared to be internally generated, and though they did help to expose and document problems at the board of elections and related elections issues, much of the information seems to have emanated from Republican sources and to have served their purposes. Interestingly, a top-ranking board official revealed that campaign finance filings show that the Giuliani campaign had paid an individual named Calderone, and after the election Calderone was offered the position of director of communications in the Giuliani administration, an offer that was subsequently withdrawn.[5]

Notably, alternative perspectives on the fraud concerns were lacking in these articles. Alternative proposals for addressing the concerns raised in the articles were similarly excluded. None of the articles reported the responses of voting rights advocates and reformers who had provided information that countered the reported evidence of fraud and who advocated a set of distinctly different methods to address the concerns raised. Advocates argued, for example, that effective implementation of agency-based voter registration would help eliminate deadwood and produce cleaner rolls, thus reducing the possibility for fraud; that further modernization and political reform of election administration—not merely managerial reform—would produce a more efficient and effective system; and that greater public outreach and voter education would eliminate many of the errors registrants and voters make that might look like fraud. The articles also avoided discussion of other problems related to New York's cumbersome election law and the restrictive administrative procedures that often lead to disenfranchisement.

An initial *New York Newsday* article expressly illustrates these problems. The article proved to be significant in that it generated further concerns regarding registration and vote fraud as well as increased scrutiny and activity to address these concerns, as manifested in subsequent news reports and the Republican-led investigation by the state's Senate Election Law Committee. Written by Joe Calderone and Tom Curran, the story reported that 1,247 Manhattan registrants had listed the address of the main post office at 390 9th Avenue in Midtown as their residence, as opposed to their own mailing address, which violated state election law. The journalists noted that many of the registrations may have been welfare recipients and homeless individuals who use that address for the delivery of public assistance checks and other mail, and that 922 of the 1,247 had registered as Democrats.[6]

Noting that "rules governing registration have eased over the years to increase voter registration," the authors stressed that "critics say the system has opened the door to voter fraud. Supporters of Republican Rudolph Giuliani, who lost by 47,080 votes to Dinkins in the close 1989 race and who is virtually neck and neck with Dinkins in current mayoral polls, are particularly concerned about the integrity of the registration rolls." Richard Schwartz, Giuliani's deputy campaign manager, stated that when the system makes it easier for people to vote, "you have to be a great deal more vigilant about defending it against fraud and abuse. We're concerned that's not being done at this point." Another important Giuliani supporter, Ray Harding, a Liberal Party leader, stated, "It sounds like someone's orchestration to increase Democratic Party enrollment."

The article highlighted that the "ability of 1,247 people to use the post office to register fuels concerns among some election law lawyers and experts that the operations at the Board of Elections are in disarray." Indeed, the journalists pointed out that the New York City Board of Elections was not even aware of the situation of the post office registrants, but that the board should have known because it employs several mechanisms to catch such instances.

The authors also noted that the two top administrators in the Manhattan office of the board—Bart Regazzi, the chief clerk and a Republican appointee, and William Perkins, the chief deputy clerk and a Democratic appointee—had been notified by the central board that they would be fired for poor management if they did not resign. The board ended up dismissing up to twenty of the over fifty staff at the Manhattan board because of significant mismanagement problems. The article noted that Perkins, the Democratic appointee, would join the Dinkins campaign, implying possible involvement by Democrats and the Dinkins campaign in the questionable activity.

Several voter registration organizations and advocates for the homeless presented an alternate viewpoint in various forums, including letters to the editor, meetings with elections officials, and public hearings.[7] They contended the charges of fraud were premature and implausible. In the first place, they pointed out, the area around the main post office is in reality home to thousands of homeless people because the area has countless soup kitchens, drop-in centers, and shelters. Moreover, they argued, it is likely, given the complexity of the voter registration form and procedures, especially for people with lower levels of education and for whom English is a second language, that many registrants misunderstood the rules and mistakenly listed their mailing address as their residence. In this regard, the advocates also noted that the board of elections does not always acknowledge a separate mailing address even when it is provided by registrants in the section of the application provided for that purpose. This may happen for several reasons, including mistakes made by the board's data entry clerks, and it potentially disenfranchises anyone who receives mail at a post office box or at work rather than at home. These errors occur frequently, especially during peak periods when the volume of registration applications increases and the board hires temporary data entry workers who are unfamiliar with the board's unique computerized registration system and procedures. Thus, the advocates argued, the "evidence" presented in the article proved neither that any fraud was intentionally committed nor that there were related partisan motives or involvements. Lastly, they contended that the fault may lie partly with the complexity of the registration system itself.

While it is theoretically possible that some of these registrations were fraudulent, no definitive evidence of fraud was ever produced. Nonetheless, the board's response to the article—and to intervention by party officials—was to summarily cancel the registrations in question, claiming that the applicants had illegally registered. By law, however, the board was required to first notify the registrants by mail of their need to reregister properly and that their registration would be canceled. These people were essentially disenfranchised. Advocates contended that the board's response was inappropriate and unnecessarily harsh.

A month later a second *Newsday* article reported that other "foul-ups and administrative mismanagement at the city Board of Elections have opened the door to potential voter fraud."[8] It said that a *Newsday* probe, including "a computer analysis of Board registration records, interviews and a review of internal Board of Election documents," showed more than 6,300 new voters appeared to have registered twice in 1992, including some who used the same address both times. The authors highlighted that duplicate registrations provide a basis for potential vote fraud—whether these registrants registered twice "by mistake or intentionally"—and that the system operated by the board of elections is "designed to catch such duplicate registrations" but suffers from mismanagement, especially in its Manhattan office. The article suggested that William Perkins, the top administrative Democratic appointee of the Manhattan board, was principally responsible for the duplicate registrations because he had not followed all board procedures designed to identify and eliminate potential duplicates, and it noted that Perkins was fired by the board and subsequently joined the Dinkins campaign.

The article also reported that during the year prior to the 1992 elections massive voter registration drives had taken place, largely sponsored by the Democrats and by Dinkins's allies, including Bill Lynch, who had left the Dinkins administration to head the Democratic Party's campaign in New York City. These registration drives reportedly produced 719,659 registrations in New York City, an exceptionally and, by implication, suspiciously high number. Indeed, the authors quoted two top board officials who contended that "none of us can believe there were 700,000 new voters," further casting a cloud over the Democrats' registration activity. However, board figures show that approximately 150,000 were reregistrations, so the number of new registrants was smaller than 700,000. Moreover, given that nearly 2 million eligible voters were unregistered in New York City in 1992 and that in other presidential races similarly large numbers of voters had been registered in massive drives, the number of registrants was not exceedingly high.

The authors highlighted that the central board had known about administrative problems in the Manhattan office, and they cited the inability to effectively process all the registrations received during September of 1992 when "virtual chaos reigned in the Manhattan borough office." The article reported that the Manhattan office had an 11 percent error rate, compared to a 1–2 percent rate in each of the other four boroughs. *Error rate* refers to mistakes in the board's computer records. These errors are detected by locating mismatches between the board's computer records, which, under the SCRIBE system, generate the poll lists, and the original information on paper registration records. Such "errors" can translate into fraud at the polls on election day or, more commonly, can cause confusion, delays, and disenfranchisement. The highest rates of error, 18 and 24 percent, respectively, were reportedly found in Central Harlem and Washington Heights/Inwood, both Dinkins strongholds. As a result, the board had hired an outside data processing firm for $80,000 to "clean up" Manhattan's voter rolls.[9]

The authors acknowledged the importance of the context within which this article appeared: "Voter registration issues are taking on added significance this year because the two candidates are running close in the polls and because of the relatively small number of votes by which Dinkins defeated Giuliani in 1989—47,080 out of 1,814,739." The article quoted Giuliani supporter Henry Stern, former president of the Citizens Union and subsequently Giuliani administration appointee as Parks Department commissioner, who stated, "people have every right to be concerned about fraudulent voting."

As with the first *Newsday* article, however, no alternative perspective was presented. No mention was made of the fact that the 6,300 registrations in question were actually only *potential* duplicates, or that duplicate registrations may occur without any intent to commit fraud or any occurrence of double voting. The article did not discuss the fact that when one changes residence one must also reregister. Nearly 20 percent of all Americans move each year, many of them low-income individuals who move within the same city, and elections experts and voter registration organizations routinely suggest reregistration to people unsure of when or where they registered last—a not uncommon circumstance. Moreover, numerous individuals in New York City have exactly the same name. It is possible that some of the potential duplicate registrations came from different individuals.

A third *Newsday* piece raised concerns about "lax" registration practices by the board of elections and about personnel in its Manhattan office.[10] "An ongoing look at alleged irregularities" the article claimed, had revealed that the Manhattan board "broke state rules" by allowing 11,000 voter registration applications to be processed even though they were unsigned. The signature is used to verify a person's identity on election day. The report quoted a board employee, Republican Rosanna Kostamoulas, who charged that William Perkins, the former Democratic chief clerk fired from the Manhattan board and subsequently hired by the Dinkins campaign, had authorized the processing of the registrations without signatures. Moreover, Kostamoulas charged that Perkins allowed unsigned buff cards to go to poll sites for the 1992 presidential election and for the 1993 Community School Board elections. (Buff cards are the actual buff-colored registration forms signed by registrants. They were transported to the polls each election day before the computerization of the registration rolls and digitization of signatures was fully implemented.) Perkins denied giving such an instruction and claimed that he was "being used as a scapegoat for problems that are not unique to the Manhattan office." The article suggested that these circumstances created possibilities for vote fraud and explicitly implicated the Democrats and the Dinkins campaign. Interestingly, Republican appointee Bart Regazzi, the chief clerk at the Manhattan board, who was also dismissed, was not mentioned in the article. The news report was accompanied by calls from the Republican ranks for the cancellation of the unsigned registrations.

A subsequent inquiry revealed, however, that most of the "unsigned" registration cards had not actually been submitted without signatures as the article suggested. Under pre-SCRIBE procedures, once a registrant's buff card is full, the signature is supposed to be copied and attached to a new buff card, which then goes into one of the binders that poll workers use on election day and that serve as the registration list. It appears that this procedure was not followed by the Manhattan board for some of the registrants in question. Yet these unsigned cards appeared to correspond to actual voters. Therefore, canceling these registrations would have illegitimately disenfranchised these individuals. Still, Republicans argued that it was possible for these cards to be fraudulent. Moreover, they contended that the board had violated state law, which it had. Responding to pressure from voting rights advocates and Democratic board members, the board canceled only some of the "unsigned" registrations.

The SCRIBE system that is now in use digitally scans the signature of the voter and reproduces it onto the list that poll workers use on election day to verify voters' registration. In 1992 a new problem developed in several boroughs: many of the signatures were not properly scanned, and over 20,000 registrations in Manhattan alone did not contain a signature. This could be the case for several reasons, just one of them being lack of a signature on the original application. The names lacking a signature were deleted from the poll list or marked "challenge." Election workers were instructed to challenge these registrants and to allow them to vote by affidavit ballot only; this is still the policy and practice of the board.

On election day in 1993 numerous legitimate voters, especially in Manhattan, either were told that there was no record of their registration or were challenged, sometimes by poll watchers sent by one of the campaigns. Although the precise number of such incidents is not known, anecdotal evidence suggests that hundreds of individuals experienced the problem. Many of them had lived in the same dwelling for many years, and they had voted in previous elections. In some of these cases poll workers offered voters an affidavit ballot or told them that they could obtain a court order by going to an administrative judge, usually located at the borough board of elections office. In such cases, the board is supposed to subsequently verify the voter's registration and count the vote. In other cases, whether because poll workers were poorly trained or because they were acting in a partisan or discriminatory manner, voters were not offered affidavit ballots unless they were knowledgeable of their voting rights and asserted them. Individuals whose names did not appear on the rolls were told, improperly, that they could not vote. Thus, in the episode of the unsigned registration cards, which was apparently a result of board mismanagement and technological failures of the SCRIBE system, a kind of fraud was perpetrated upon innocent voters, who were disenfranchised.

Following the publication of these *Newsday* articles, a *New York Post* editorial highlighted what it characterized as "funny stuff at the polls," claiming that "investigations of electoral fraud by both *The Post* and *Newsday* have revealed literally thousands of examples of voters who registered twice, or who failed to indicate whether they are American citizens. Some *are*, in fact, illegal aliens. And some New York City residents, it appears, have acknowledged that they were paid to register more than once." The *Post* editorial cited mismanagement at the board of elections, pointing out Perkins as the main culprit. Revealing its partisan bias, the *Post* stated that the Dinkins administration "found the whole business less troubling than might have been hoped." It had hired Perkins, reported the *Post*, "and his tasks include registering new voters." The editorial concluded that "it would be comforting to know that the Board of Elections is developing some sort of strategy to deal with the problem. For our part, we intend to keep our eyes trained [on] election fraud."[11] However, the *Post* did not ever produce any evidence that illegal aliens had registered or that people were being paid to register twice. The political motivation for such reportage is clear: the *Post* supported Giuliani throughout the year, as evidenced by its editorials, news reports, and formal endorsement.

While it remains theoretically possible that some registration and vote fraud was committed in the cases highlighted in these articles, to date no substantial fraud in 1993 has been documented or proven. Nor has any fraud been shown to have existed in the previous mayoral election, or in subsequent elections for that matter. Moreover, alternate explanations of the facts highlighted in these articles, as well as in the series of articles that followed and in the Senate investigation, can plausibly account for these circumstances. More importantly, alternative measures could have been taken to address these circumstances without resulting in the disenfranchisement that ultimately did occur.

While the articles highlighted important problems at the board of elections—particularly at its Manhattan office—the overwhelming effect was to sensationalize and distort the issues raised, implicate the Democrats and Dinkins operatives and supporters, and fuel Republican concerns about potential vote fraud in the 1993 elections. The articles provided fodder for the subsequent Republican-led activities, including the Senate investigation, the ballot-security operation, and the institution of restrictive practices by the board during the 1993 elections. The fact that the impetus for the focus on alleged fraud, and much of the information, originated from Republican operatives, including officials at the New York City Board of Elections, suggests partisan motivations. And the changes in practices at the board of elections that resulted from these events contributed to voter disenfranchisement and low voter turnout.

Republican-Led Antifraud Efforts

These initial news reports were followed by an investigation into voter fraud in New York City that was launched by Michael Nozzollio (R), chair of the New York State Senate Election Law Committee (hereafter referred to as Senate Committee). The announcement of the investigation, which came at the end of May, cited "numerous reports and allegations of widespread election fraud and abuse in New York City, . . . [which] have been widely reported in the media over the last few weeks."[12] Much of the subsequent public hearing, held on July 28, 1993, focused specifically on the registration practices and operations of the board of elections—particularly its Manhattan office—and upon registration activities by the Democratic Party, the Dinkins campaign, and their supporters.

The Senate Committee investigation was clearly Republican-led and focused on Democratic Party activity. The announcement stated, "'The rampant election fraud and abuse in New York City that has been reported indicates a growing trend of voter fraud for partisan advantages,' Nozzolio said. 'It would appear that New York's election laws are being abused in an effort to advance individual parties and candidates. . . . When thousands of people can register to vote more than once it is time to step back and demand some answers as to how this could have happened.'" The focus was sharply directed at the board of elections. Indeed, following the announcement, discussions took place between the Senate Committee and the board, and particular practices were instituted and changed as a result.

Nozzolio listed several of the alleged incidents reported in the media and explained that they "precipitated the need for an in-depth, . . . comprehensive investigation and analysis of possible voter fraud and registration efforts in New York City. This investigation is intended to alleviate continued voter fraud in this year's upcoming citywide elections." The Senate Committee seemed to have reached the conclusion that fraud was occurring even before the ostensible start of the investigation. Its list of alleged incidents included those reported in the news: 6,300 duplicate registrants in 1992; 1,247 Manhattan registrations claiming the main post office as a residence, 922 of whom registered as Democrats; a New York City lawyer who admitted voting four times in the 1989 mayoral election, each time for the Democratic candidate; and a "non-partisan" agency-based voter registration program of the New York City Housing Authority that was "organized" with assistance from members of the Dinkins campaign staff.

Agency-based voter registration represented an additional focus of the Senate Committee and is connected to another explicitly stated issue the investigation was intended to address: the matter of election law reform. According to the announcement, "Nozzolio noted that New York's election law has been relaxed in the last few years in an effort to increase voter registration. The State Assembly [dominated by the Democrats] has introduced numerous bills this year that would further liberalize New York's election law." Nozzolio concluded, "We cannot disregard the importance of protecting the integrity of the electoral system, the ideals of one person, one vote, in a symbolic rush to achieve election reform. This analysis will assist our efforts in trying to balance the integrity of the electoral process with increasing voter participation." In this regard, William Powers, New York State Republican Party chairman (and no relation to Peter Powers), repeatedly stressed to editorial boards and members of the legislature that a thorough and aggressive investigation into these allegations was critical to ensure that the upcoming New York City elections would be fair and free of fraud and contended that it would be premature to pass election law reform before the Senate Committee issued the findings of its investigation.

Assembly Democrats accused Republicans of using the fraud issue to undermine efforts to pass electoral reform: "The Senate has for years balked at making it easier for people to vote," said Eric Vitaliano (D), chair of the Assembly Election Law Committee. "The real problem in New York City is getting people to vote once."[13] Vitaliano contended that Republicans were also laying the groundwork for weakening the forthcoming implementation of the National Voter Registration Act.

The New York City Board of Elections responded to the announcement of the Senate's investigation by seeking to minimize the allegations and to focus attention solely on the Manhattan office and mismanagement by particular personnel, especially Perkins. In a press release the board stated that the "thrust of these allegations tend to include the entire board of elections and each of our offices in the five boroughs, when in reality the issues are centered exclusively in our borough office in Manhattan. It is the board of elections executive management that uncovered the laxity prevailing in that office and exercised immediate and appropriate action to remedy the situation. Our findings clearly lead to the conclusion that this is an issue of mismanagement. At no time was there ever evidence of intentional fraud." Republicans maintained otherwise throughout the 1993 elections, however. "It goes beyond mere housekeeping," said Nozzolio at a public hearing in New York City. "It leads to a clouding of election results, which in turn throws into question the integrity of the whole election process."[14]

Nozzolio and other Republicans, in the Senate and in the city, continued to play a prominent role in pressing the board to change its practices. According to one key election official, Nozzolio "kept track of what the Board was doing" to step up security measures, particularly by identifying duplicate registrations, eliminating deadwood, and removing registrants whose signatures were missing due to the transition to the SCRIBE system, particularly in Manhattan.[15] Nozzolio held another hearing in September and attended meetings of the commissioners and staff at the city board to both "monitor the Board's actions" and press for the imposition of further restrictive measures. Republicans did achieve many of these desired changes, which, in turn, "likely led to some legitimate registrants being knocked off the rolls."[16]

As the Republican-led state investigation proceeded, many news reports continued to cover allegations of registration fraud and the possibility of vote fraud in the coming elections. From the time of the Senate's public hearing right up through election day, the issues and circumstances that these reports highlighted were incorporated into the investigation's proceedings. The reports and related Republican activity continued to bring pressure to bear on the board to alter particular practices. Several of the allegations of fraud cited in subsequent articles reportedly also originated from Republican sources. The Republican ballot-security operation was instrumental in this regard.

During the months prior to the elections, Republican operatives organized this vigorous poll-watching/ballot-security operation, which was implemented on election day in New York City and contributed to disenfranchisement. The growing specter of fraud—which Republicans were largely responsible for generating—was used to justify the operation. Republicans reportedly compared updated address lists from various sources—they used phone listings, utility lists, lists from various mail-order houses and commercial vendors, and lists compiled by political consultants—to the official registration lists of the board of elections in order to ferret out false registrations or voters who might have moved. Registrants' whose addresses didn't match could then be challenged on election day.[17]

Some of the data obtained from the ballot-security operation was apparently provided to investigative journalists and served as a basis for their articles and analysis. According to the *New York Times,* William Powers, the state Republican Party chair, said shortly before the election that the party would deploy thousands of volunteer poll watchers to head off anticipated fraudulent activity.[18]

Both campaigns petitioned the board of elections and the police department for specific measures to prevent the election-day problems each believed the other would perpetrate. Indeed, shortly before the election Mayor Dinkins and candidate Giuliani engaged in what the *New York Times* called "bitter sparring" over what measures should be taken to ensure a fair election. "The Dinkins campaign expressed concern that off-duty police officers supporting Giuliani might intimidate Democratic voters, while the Giuliani campaign demanded extra police officers to make sure no fraud occurred in polling places where the Mayor's supporters outnumber the challengers." Peter Powers, Giuliani's campaign manager, had sent a letter to Raymond Kelly, the police commissioner, requesting that Kelly assign at least 2,700 officers to polling places to "help guard against illegal behavior." Kelly announced that a cadre of 52 captains would be created to supervise polling places, and that 3,500 police officers would be assigned to sites. In addition, in response to requests from both campaigns, the U.S. Department of Justice sent 113 observers to monitor 48 polling places in Manhattan, Brooklyn, and the Bronx for possible voter fraud.[19]

Between seven hundred and eight hundred poll watchers were reportedly hired by the Republican Party and deployed to selected sites, largely in low-income and minority neighborhoods. Most of these poll watchers were from the uniformed services; they included off-duty police, transit officers, and fire department personnel. Testimony of election-day observers subsequently revealed that these poll watchers challenged thousands of voters, intervening in poll workers' activity and creating "intimidating conditions, delays, and confusion."[20] Such incidents are cited in the reports of VAC and the New York State Democratic Party, and concern about them was raised at a public forum that voting rights advocates and Democratic Party operatives organized and conducted in Brooklyn soon after the election. The U.S. Department of Justice also investigated these allegations, but has issued no report to date.

One issue repeatedly highlighted in reports regarding fraud possibilities was noncitizen registration and voting, which became one focus of the Republicans' ballot-security effort: "Acting on concerns expressed by Rudolph Giuliani's mayoral campaign, the city Board of elections has invoked a little known section of election law in an attempt to determine if large numbers of non-citizens are improperly registered."[21] Peter Powers, manager of the Giuliani campaign, had pressured the board's executive director, Danny DeFrancesco, to exercise this option. DeFrancesco asked the state board of elections for a list of naturalized citizens from the Immigration and Naturalization Service (INS). This list would then be matched by computer against the applications of registrants whose forms indicated that they had been naturalized; those whose names were not on the INS list would be purged. The state board of elections indicated that such a request was unprecedented. For obvious reasons, at the time the request was made public, immigrants rights advocates expressed grave concerns over any such action being carried out. When the state board requested the list from the INS, however, the INS refused to produce it because federal law prohibits releasing such information for reasons of privacy and potential discrimination against immigrants.

Nonetheless, the board did institute measures to ensure greater scrutiny of registration applications for citizenship information and more vigorous checks in processing such applications. Immigrant rights advocates stated such activity and the news about it had a strong chilling effect on the registration and naturalization of immigrants, and on the efforts of community-based organizations that provide services to them. According to immigrant rights advocates, immigrant voters strongly supported Dinkins in 1989, and the Dinkins administration had inaugurated several programs aimed at aiding immigrants in New York.

In one instance, the intensive scrutiny of potential noncitizen registration and voting led to a probe by the city's Department of Investigation and the Manhattan district attorney's office. The probe focused on allegations of noncitizens registering in 1989 and voting for Dinkins, allegedly in exchange for false papers. The office of Councilman Guillermo Linares, a strong Dinkins supporter, was implicated in the probe. Linares denied involvement in such activity, and to date the investigation has not produced any evidence of illegal registration and voting or of involvement by Linares.

One *Newsday* article clearly expressed a long-standing Republican concern about "the many loopholes in the voter registration system. Currently, a prospective voter need only fill out a registration card and attest to the accuracy of the information provided in order to register by mail. The

Board of Elections conducts no identification checks or verification of citizenship."[22] State senator Guy Velella, (R-Bronx), who was the chair of Victory '93, the state Republican committee operation that sponsored the ballot-security program, announced that he would introduce an election law reform that would require a photo ID card for all new voters. Presumably, this new form of identification would provide increased security against potential registration and vote fraud by anyone, including noncitizens.

On July 28, 1993, the day of the Senate Committee's public hearing, *New York Newsday* reported that over 22,000 potential duplicate registrations existed and that "the numbers of double registrations far exceeds earlier estimates" by the board.[23] The initial *Newsday* article that revealed the existence of 6,300 potential duplicates, coupled with the Senate Committee's investigation, had led directly to the board's own intensive efforts to recheck all 3 million registrations for duplicates, which yielded the revised number. In the article and the public hearing, senior board officials stressed that the duplicate registrants would be stricken from the rolls before the end of August.

Other *Newsday* articles highlighted additional registration issues involving the board. Cases of potential registration fraud came to light in Queens, "indicating" that "the problem of voter fraud" was not confined to Manhattan. Three hundred dead New Yorkers were still listed as registered by the board, and "at least two dozen of them were dead before the 1989 mayoral election but still managed to vote." *Newsday* asserted that possibly a thousand voters were registered under phony names; that seven hundred registrants were naming the Addicts Rehabilitation Center in East Harlem as their residence even though only 434 can be housed there at any one time; and that sixty-eight registrants were naming St. Mary's Church in West Harlem as their residence.[24]

Nearly all these reports carried commentary questioning the integrity of the ballot and suggesting that the outcome of the election might be altered due to fraudulent voting. Almost every article was framed in such a way as to implicate the Democrats, the Dinkins campaign, and their supporters. Most contained explicit statements by Republicans and their supporters to this effect and urged that measures be taken to guarantee a fair election. For example, state Republican chairman William Powers accused Democrats backing Mayor Dinkins of planning "to stuff the ballot box in certain neighborhoods" and declared: "We have to stop them."

As the election drew nearer, the level of scrutiny and the charges and countercharges escalated. Both mayoral campaigns, as well as other electoral campaigns and voting rights organizations, petitioned and pressured the board to respond concretely to each of the concerns presented. The mayoral campaigns also sought action from the state board of elections and the U.S. Department of Justice. As a result of the "voter fraud furor," in two unprecedented actions both the executive director of the state board of elections and the chief criminal prosecutor from the U.S. Department of Justice appeared at the New York City Board of Elections on election day and observed several poll sites. The Department of Justice also sent approximately 120 observers to poll sites in boroughs covered by the Voting Rights Act. The supervision of poll sites by 52 police captains and 3,500 officers was also unprecedented.[25] As a crowning element to the chaos, the NAACP bused approximately a hundred "Reverse Freedom Riders" from the South into New York City for the week of the election in order to increase voter participation, especially of African Americans. Although they were there not to cast ballots but to serve as get-out-the-vote workers and election observers, Republicans objected to their presence.

Analysis

A distinct pattern of events contributed to low turnout during the 1993 elections—particularly in low-income neighborhoods—and has important implications for past and future electoral politics: information was "leaked" to the newspapers by Republicans; the news reports, in turn, generated what a *New York Post* front-page headline called "voter fraud furor"; a Republican-sponsored state investigation about the alleged fraud was launched, focusing on mismanagement and "lax" practices at the board of elections, and a public hearing on the matter was held; and further news reports and partisan scrutiny ensued. Several changes in the board's practices resulted from this public attention. Indeed, the board took what one senior official characterized as "extra-extraordinary" measures to ensure that the election was fair and free of fraud. As a result of changes in particular board practices and of the Republican ballot-security operation, disenfranchisement of legitimate voters occurred. Analysis of available data about the impacts of such activity indicates that those who were disenfranchised were primarily low-income individuals and minorities. The data include reports obtained from the board of elections, VAC, the Dinkins campaign, the New York state Democratic and Republican parties, the Senate Election Law Committee, and participants in a postelection public hearing in Brooklyn that was sponsored by Democratic politicians and activists. I also conducted interviews and discussions with several elections experts, including officials from the city and state boards of elections; voting rights advocates; political party members from the different campaigns; numerous election-day observers and some voters at VAC's public hearing; and poll watchers from the Dinkins campaign.[26]

Board Practices

The greater the number of restrictive administrative procedures elections officials employ to "secure" the vote, the greater the likelihood that administrative disenfranchisement will occur as a result. Measures designed to "secure the integrity of the ballot" involved specific procedures and special instructions to workers who handled registration applications, processed them, and maintained the data banks. Voter registration applications were increasingly and systematically held to strict compliance standards. For example, the board switched its computerized registration system (EASY) from a "straight" process of entering data from registration applications to a "smart" process, which required that additional data elements be examined to ensure that applications were signed and dated, included accurate address and citizenship information, and so on.

Intensive efforts to identify potential duplicates and "questionable" registrations were mandated, and other procedures were instituted to either verify the registrations or cancel them. This involved a redoubling of efforts and a detailed examination of registration files. It also involved hiring a consulting firm for $80,000 to specifically examine Manhattan's registration file. The company located approximately 100,000 errors in the Manhattan registration file of over 800,000 registrants. Most of these potential problem registrations were either canceled or placed on a challenge list, while in other cases the registrants were successfully contacted and their registrations updated. These procedures likely resulted in the cancellation of legitimate voters' registrations that only appeared to be duplicates or questionable.

Routine security measures and procedures were emphasized and reinforced. These included the procedures for completing affidavit ballots and the subsequent validation or invalidation of such ballots, the manner in which absentee ballot applications and absentee ballots were administered, the preparation of the voting machines and materials, the recruitment of a bipartisan staff of poll workers and interpreters, and so on. For example, some requests for absentee ballot applications by voters and registration organizations were scrutinized or went unfilled. In contrast, the Republican Party mailed absentee ballot applications to registered Republicans. A much larger proportion of votes were cast by absentee ballot in Queens and Staten Island, the two boroughs that Giuliani won handily, than in the other three.

A modified challenge process was adopted for election day following a series of meetings with both mayoral campaigns and the city and state boards. Under this new scheme, election inspectors were issued special instructions regarding when and how they were to challenge voters and when poll watchers could do so. Challenged voters would be required to sign a written oath. Other security measures were reinforced, creating what some characterized as intimidating and complex procedures at poll sites, which periodically resulted in substantial delays. As a result of these procedures, some voters were not permitted to cast ballots, and some frustrated voters left poll sites without doing so.

Although the above measures were ostensibly introduced to prevent fraud and to ensure that the integrity of the ballot, the result was inevitably disenfranchisement. No examples of what might be construed as real fraud were ever produced. Although more than 22,000 potential duplicate registrants were identified citywide—18,000 in Manhattan—as a result of the board's ballot-security measures, only twelve people appeared to have possibly voted twice. These twelve cases were forwarded to Manhattan district attorney Robert Morgenthau's office for investigation and possible prosecution. The district attorney, however, did not prosecute any of them.

Impacts on Registration and Participation

To analyze voter registration and participation, I have employed a similar methodology to the one I used to study performance measures of the board's work. Board practices clearly resulted in some disenfranchisement, but it is impossible to precisely determine the total number of citizens who were disenfranchised because insufficient mechanisms currently exist to document all such instances. Nonetheless, on the basis of analysis of specific documented incidences of disenfranchisement, we can identify the nature of each disenfranchising practice, and we can determine the frequency with which particular practices occurred. When these are taken together, we can arrive at an estimate of the number of people who were disenfranchised.

Numerous problems at poll sites throughout the city were documented that graphically illustrate the disenfranchising consequences of the changed administrative practices and the Republican ballot-security operation. VAC documented problems that occurred on election day in 1993 at a public hearing held just after the election. VAC then correlated these complaints with demographic data on the assembly districts and neighborhoods where such problems occurred and found that low-income and minority areas experienced the highest proportion of election-day problems.[27]

The largest percentage of complaints VAC received concerned poll-site and poll-worker problems. About one in every three reported polling incidents involved issues concerning worker performance, site operation and hours, site changes, staffing, and worker recruitment. Roughly 18 percent of the citizens informing VAC of election-related problems criticized the way in which poll sites operated. Voters complained that their poll sites had moved without proper notification (in many cases because schools had been closed for asbestos removal), and some poll sites had opened late, were inadequately staffed, or lacked sufficient supplies. There were also reports that machines had broken down. As VAC stated in its 1994 annual report, "Each of these problems represents the potential disenfranchisement of eligible voters. . . . These types of problems can lead to confusion, delays and disenfranchisement."

Over one-fifth of individuals notifying VAC of election mishaps cited problems with poll-worker performance. Election personnel committed administrative errors, misinformed voters, and mishandled affidavit ballots. One reported problem was that many voters' signatures did not appear on the SCRIBE poll list, and another was that poll lists arrived late to poll sites. In some cases poll workers offered voters an affidavit ballot or told them that they could obtain a court order by going to an administrative judge. In other cases poll workers did neither, but told the individuals, improperly, that they could not vote. Numerous individuals reported experiencing this particular problem on election day, including many who had been living in the same dwelling for many years and had voted in previous elections. Others reported that they had registered by the deadline and fulfilled other qualifying requirements but were not listed at their poll site as registered and eligible to vote. Voters reported that the information they had written on change-of-address forms in previous elections was still not reflected on registration lists at the poll site.

At some poll sites workers ran out of affidavit ballots either because the initial supply from the board of elections was insufficient or because problems with registration lists necessitated the overuse of affidavits. Additionally, there is a general public perception that affidavit ballots don't count. There were reports that election inspectors mistakenly allowed voters to cast affidavit ballots for the wrong election district, though at the correct polling site; under election law such ballots cannot be counted as valid. Some of the legitimate registrants who were not informed by poll inspectors of their right to cast an affidavit ballot when no record of their registration could be found left without voting.

Approximately 20 percent of poll inspectors who work the polls every election—the line staff of the board with whom voters interact—do not receive training. Even though this rate is lower than during previous periods, lack of effective training appears to contribute to the occurrence of election-day problems. Moreover, there are often shortages of inspectors on election day. Although the caliber of the training methods and materials used has improved, even if one fails the test at the end of the training, and has therefore been proved incompetent to perform necessary tasks, one can still serve as an election inspector on election day. Some people perceived poll workers as unresponsive or rude, and in many cases voters were given incorrect information. A few poll workers described the inhibiting atmosphere created by non–Chinese-speaking poll workers who did not trust Chinese interpreters. Poor assistance was reportedly received by Chinese-speaking voters, and bilingual interpreters were generally scarce at poll sites. As registration groups have attested, voters have cited such experiences as reasons for subsequent nonvoting.[28]

Before the election, Democrats and Republicans came into conflict about whether and how certain registrants should be removed from the voter rolls. Republicans—both on the board and at the state and city levels—successfully pressed the board to cancel the registrations thousands of voters who Democrats believed were illegitimately removed. Democrats, particularly board commissioners and allies of the Dinkins campaign, argued that at least 10,000 of the registrants who were removed should be reinstated before the general election, and they maintained that 5–10 percent of mail-check cancellations were erroneous.

To cancel registrations, the board sends a postcard to every registrant each year. If this nonforwardable postcard is returned to the board, a second card is sent that is forwardable, and the voter is required to respond within fourteen days. If the voter does not respond, the board changes the registrant's status from A (active) to M (moved). These registrants are designated as "challenge" on the SCRIBE poll lists that are sent to poll sites. Poll inspectors are instructed to challenge all such voters. The names of voters who do not go to the poll site to vote are then removed from the rolls.

Analysis by board Democrats of affidavit ballots cast in previous elections, particularly the 1992 election, indicated that a significant number of invalidated affidavit ballots were cast from the same address from which individuals were initially registered: the registrants had not moved after all. Their registrations had thus been wrongly canceled, and thereafter their affidavit ballots had been improperly rejected. Indeed, New York City Board of Elections commissioner Douglas Kellner stated that his analysis of affidavits cast in 1992 showed that 25–30 percent were erroneously invalidated by board clerks or inspectors because they did not properly locate the voter's registration record either at the board or at the poll site. He demonstrated that for the hotly contested Fourth City Council District election, clerks were instructed to do more thorough searches for registration records to verify affidavit ballots, and a much smaller number were invalidated.[29]

Republicans rejected the arguments made by Democrats, countering that the board's cancellation procedures were mandated by law and that they were necessary to protect against fraud, even while acknowledging that board clerks or the postal service could be in part responsible for improper cancellations. In a straight party vote, Democrats voted for reinstatement of the 10,000 canceled registrants before the general election, while Republicans voted against the measure. The deadlock prevented any action from being taken. According to the Democratic board commissioner, 35–40 percent of the canceled voters were Republicans, and the rest were largely Democratic, indicating that Dinkins was likely to be more negatively effected than Giuliani.

In an earlier episode, Republican state senator Nozzolio, who led the investigation into the board's operations and into the fraud allegations in New York City, requested that the board cancel up to 12,000 registrations of voters whose records were missing a signature, as indicated by an analysis that a Republican Party operative prepared for a public hearing. This time, however, the Democrats who held the executive staff positions at the board rebuffed Nozzolio by arguing that the signatures were missing from the poll lists because of the Manhattan board's mishandling of the transition to SCRIBE digitization and that the signatures could instead be photocopied onto the poll lists from the original registration forms. Nevertheless, the board instituted more stringent checks on such records, and a high proportion of cancellations did occur. The number of registrations that were canceled in 1993 for all reasons was disproportionately high in Manhattan:

62,545, or 4 percent, of the voting age population, compared with Brooklyn (38,595, or 3.5%), the Bronx (24,748, or 3%), Queens (29,246, or 2.3%), and Staten Island (4,374, or 1.5%).

In 1993, as result of pressure put on the board by Republicans to eliminate deadwood and to guard against fraud, the board altered its practices—particularly in Manhattan—and produced more challengeable voters, and it canceled a larger proportion of voters in Manhattan and Brooklyn than in the other three boroughs. A higher proportion of total registrations were canceled in 1993 compared to recent years, reversing the board's liberalizing trend: 208,703, or 6.3 percent of all registrations after additional registrants were purged for nonvoting, compared with 182,582 (or 5.4%) in 1992. While this shift is not exceptionally large, it does reflect the changes in the board's practices in 1993.

The second largest category of complaints received by VAC concerned incidents of intimidation, harassment, and misbehavior, primarily by groups of poll watchers. Such incidents contribute to an atmosphere that inhibits voting. Individuals reporting voter intimidation represented approximately 16 percent of the respondents. Evidently, the presence of groups of off-duty police and some poll watchers created a feeling of apprehension for a number of citizens. In addition, the "generally abrasive" manner in which poll watchers delayed the election process, as they called for counts and systematically challenged voters, did little to comfort citizens patiently waiting to cast their ballots. There were also accounts of signs alerting voters that they might be reported to or deported by the INS or other authorities. Some voters were asked to present passports, birth certificates, identification, and other types of citizenship documents. Eligible citizens attempting to cast their vote said they found these activities extremely disconcerting, and such activity is illegal. The U.S. Department of Justice investigated these and other allegations.[30] Conversely, despite the widespread concern around election fraud, a relatively low 3 percent of the people testifying at the VAC hearing reported incidents of voter misbehavior to the commission. One poll worker, for example, noticed when someone who was listed as already having voted presented himself to cast a vote.

Anticipating the potential negative impact of the Republican ballot-security operation, the New York State Democratic Party and the Dinkins campaign developed plans to minimize that impact. The Democrats deployed their own poll watchers on election day to monitor Republican activities and the operation of the polls, and they established an extensive phone bank, staffed by lawyers, to receive, document, and respond to complaints.

Soon after the election, the New York Democratic Committee announced establishment of its formal "investigation into allegations of voter intimidation and harassment at the polls in primarily minority communities on election day." On the basis of over 120 reports written by Democratic poll watchers involving several thousand incidents, the committee charged that "this intimidation and harassment was orchestrated by the New York State Republican Committee and may have violated the civil rights of scores of New York City voters."[31]

The incidents documented by the Democrats focus primarily on voter intimidation and harassment by between seven hundred and eight hundred Republican poll watchers and inspectors. Other incidents were also reported that involved board employees, whether inspectors or coordinators, in poor and minority neighborhoods in Manhattan, Brooklyn, and the Bronx. The kinds of incidents reported included "unnecessarily" and "excessively" challenging voters; denying voters access to affidavit ballots; shutting down voting machines; campaigning too close to a polling station; and the posting of signs on election day at or near polling sites in immigrant communities, particularly Haitian and Dominican neighborhoods, alleging that INS officials would be at polls and threatening voters with arrest and deportation for illegal voting.

Like those delivered at the VAC hearing, the Democratic poll watchers' reports revealed that numerous voters were involved in many of the incidents. For example, several reported incidents involved numerous voters being challenged by both Republican poll watchers and board employees to show proof of citizenship status. In other incidents poll watchers challenged dozens of voters over the course of several hours, with the result that some voters left without voting. At other sites machines were shut down, which caused delays and confusion, and some poll sites ran out of affidavit and emergency ballots so that voters left without voting.

A high percentage of affidavit ballots were used in the 1993 election, and the greater the use of affidavit ballots, the greater the possibility of administrative error that may result in disenfranchisement. Moreover, as a result of the intensive scrutiny of the Manhattan office of the board of elections and the changes in its practices, a disproportionately large number of the affidavit ballots were cast in Manhattan that year. In 1993, Manhattan had the most valid affidavits ballots—meaning that board error made the request of such a ballot necessary—(15,993 ballots cast, with 44% valid), followed by Brooklyn (18,267 cast, with 24% valid), Queens (8,858 cast, with 17.5% valid), Staten Island (1,426 cast, with 15% valid), and the Bronx (8,115 cast, with 12% valid).

One assembly district in Brooklyn, the 55th, experienced an unusually high proportion of problems, as reflected in reports from VAC's public hearing, the Democratic Party, and the board of elections. Numerous poll sites (including those at P.S. 5, P.S. 219, P.S. 335, and Atlantic Tower) did not receive the correct registration lists until late afternoon or early evening of election day (between 4 p.m. and 6:30 p.m.). This meant that all individuals who came to vote had to cast affidavit ballots because poll workers could not verify their registration. As the previous analyses of affidavit ballots indicate, increased use of such procedures tends to increase the number of administrative errors by board personnel and, thus, the number of duly registered voters who are disenfranchised. In addition, in several of these locations, lengthening lines due to delays produced by completion of the affidavit process reportedly led voters to leave without voting at all.

Analysis of affidavit ballots cast in the 1993 elections indicates that approximately 13,000 of the 38,608 affidavit ballots that were invalidated were cast in Brooklyn, with a high proportion originating from the 55th Assembly District. It appears that nearly 11,000 of these 13,000 invalidated ballots were cast by duly registered voters. Though the recorded turnout from the 55th Assembly District was approximately 3,000 votes lower than in 1989, suggesting that other factors also may have reduced turnout, it appears that such poll-site problems may well have been a factor.

The demography and voting history of the district suggests that political motives may account for this episode. The 55th District comprises predominantly African Americans and Latinos, with only a small white population. In 1989 the district had delivered the overwhelming majority of its votes to Dinkins, as it did again in 1993. Certainly, if there was one district that provided a ripe opportunity to suppress the Democratic vote, this one was it.

In September of 1993 hundreds of public schools were closed due to an asbestos crisis, necessitating the establishment of new poll sites for the primary and general elections. Changes like this one can easily lead to disenfranchisement. Even though most of the schools were reopened by the general election date, numerous poll sites were changed, and some voters were reportedly not notified. In some cases, voters were unable to find their poll sites or found it too inconvenient to go to their proper site.

Who Was Disenfranchised

Data presented in VAC's report, in the New York State Democratic Committee's report, and at VAC's Brooklyn forum indicate that those who were disenfranchised as a result of board practices and the Republican ballot-security operation were primarily low-income and minority citizens. Most of the incidents cited above occurred in neighborhoods where predominantly low-income and minority voters reside. Indeed, analysis of turnout in the 1993 election reveals that the areas that experienced the largest decreases in participation rates were inhabited predominately by low-income and minority residents; these communities were also targeted by a pattern of challenges and disruptions by Republican poll watchers.

Overall, turnout in 1993 declined by 0.6 percent, or 11,272 votes, from 1989.[32] Declines in turnout, however, varied by racial group: black turnout declined by about 2.4 percent in majority black assembly districts, or 8,524 votes (and by 3.9% in majority black election districts); in Latino districts turnout declined by about 5.6 percent, or 6,409 votes; in "mixed minority" districts it declined by 2 percent or 2,380 votes; and in white "liberal" areas it declined by 0.1 percent or 174 votes.[33] The effect on the outcome of this close election is clear. As John Hull Mollenkopf notes, "The fact that disproportionately fewer blacks turned out thus made a major contribution to Dinkins' defeat. . . . It is stunning that over half of the shift produced by the decline of black turnout occurred in Harlem, home ground. . . . As a result, the 1993 mayoral election was slightly more white and less black and Latino than in 1989 and its preferences were also slightly more racially polarized. The higher the percentage of registered voters who were white, the less likely an election district was to experience a vote decline between 1989 and 1993."[34]

Much of the decline in turnout occurred in Manhattan and particularly within its low-income and minority neighborhoods. Given that much of the focus on potential registration and vote fraud was in Manhattan, and that the board's efforts to eliminate such possibilities were greatest with regard to Manhattan's records, this finding is not unexpected. In the 1989 race Manhattan was decisively a Dinkins stronghold; it delivered the largest number of votes for Dinkins and the largest margin of victory. In 1993, however, it produced a significantly lower percentage of votes overall, and fewer votes for Dinkins. Similarly, parts of the other boroughs that had supported Dinkins in 1989 and that also reportedly had administrative problems associated with the Republican ballot-security operation also experienced declines in turnout. Thus it appears that distinct partisan, racial, and class impacts directly resulted from the security measures the board implemented and from routine board practices, as well as from the Republicans' ballot-security operation.

It would be wrong, however, to attribute the declines in turnout solely to those causes. Certainly other factors also may have contributed to demobilization of these constituencies. Still, though it is not possible to tease out the precise amount of demobilization or disenfranchisement each variable is responsible for, the evidence presented in this chapter suggests that administrative disenfranchisement is one factor. Aside from the Republicans' deliberate targeting of areas of likely Dinkins voters, in general cumbersome bureaucratic procedures disproportionately adversely affect such groups: poor people reside in neighborhoods that receive poorer services, they are less skilled at effectively maneuvering through bureaucratic processes and dealing with administrative agencies and officials, and they feel less empowered to do so. They experience greater barriers and costs, and they have less access to needed resources. Although the number of voters who are administratively disenfranchised is relatively small in relation to the total number of registrants, and although some disenfranchisement may result from voter ignorance and the workings of registration law, significant numbers of legitimate voters were disenfranchised by the board, and also by the Republican ballot-security operation.

Budget Cuts to the Board

After winning the 1993 election, Mayor Giuliani made successive cuts to the board of election's budget that produced a reduction in services precisely at the time when the board needed to gear up to implement the NVRA. These cuts exceeded the normal fluctuation in the board's budget, which depends on the number of elections within each year. More importantly, the cuts fell hardest on personnel, compromising the board's capacity to fulfill its statutory obligations and undermining some of the achievements of the previous decade's progress in the modernization of the board's operations. Moreover, because legally mandated requirements had to be met first, the budget reductions primarily limited the board's capacity to conduct its already minimal outreach and public information programs.

The proposed cuts for FY96 were even more substantial than those for FY95. The Giuliani administration proposed a cut of $3 million and fifty-four permanent staff positions, and the elimination of the board's temporary and overtime budget, the latter having been used to augment the board's staff during peak registration and election periods. This would have been on top of the previous reduction by fifty-one positions.[35] In part because advocates were able to get the U.S. Department of Justice to intervene and warn the Giuliani administration of the potential violations to the Voting Rights Act and the NVRA if such cuts were sustained, the Giuliani administration reversed itself and restored $2.5 million of the proposed $3 million cut. The board stated that the proposed cut would have had "a devastating effect on the services of the Board, the modernization program, and our ability to meet legally required mandates. . . . The Board cannot absorb these additional Personnel Services cuts and is deeply concerned that the quality of voter services will revert to the days prior to the modernization of the Board's administration of elections and operations and the potential disenfranchisement of the voting population."[36]

At the urging of advocates, the board detailed the estimated impact on the board's operations if the full cut was made, focusing primarily on how it would affect minority communities. The board noted that cuts would have a detrimental impact on the phone bank, which assists voters in the three languages mandated by the Voting Rights Act (English, Spanish, and Chinese) with information regarding voter registration, poll sites, absentee ballots, and the like; on the language assistance program, which, at the recommendation of the Department of Justice, translates materials and recruits and trains interpreters in Spanish and Chinese; on the training department, which trains the 22,000 poll workers and, due to improvements made over the years with the help of the New York City Elections Project (NYCEP), had increased the number of workers trained, decreased the use of affidavit ballots, and reduced administrative problems that produce disenfranchisement; and on registration processing, particularly during peak months prior to each election, which could lead to a failure to process applications in a timely manner and therefore to names being absent from poll lists.

Although the intervention of advocates—coupled with that of a favorably disposed U.S. Department of Justice under a Democratic administration—led the Giuliani administration to reduce the cut to the board's operating budget and services for FY96, staff was cut 15 percent from 1994 to 1996, from 363 to 312. These personnel cuts led to reductions in the number of deliveries of voter registration forms, so voter registration groups had to pick the forms up in bulk quantities; a slowdown in processing voter registration forms, producing a backlog; and a consolidation of election districts within single poll sites so as to reduce the number of poll workers required. Some argued that cuts to the board were essentially cuts to services. In the subsequent fiscal year, FY97, the board's funds were cut again—particularly for outreach and publicity to provide the public with election information.[37]

Political Implications

During the 1993 election the news reports, the state investigation and public hearing, the subsequent changes in election administration, and the ballot-security operation were coordinated efforts led by Republican Party officials that directly led to the disenfranchisement of thousands—perhaps tens of thousands—of primarily low-income and minority voters. As exit polls revealed, the electorate was even more sharply divided in 1993 than it had been 1989, especially in racial and class terms. Thus the evidence strongly suggests that the Dinkins administration and its supporters were hurt most by the loss of these voters.[38]

Conversely, Republican and Liberal party interests benefited from these events, as did factions of the Democratic Party that were temporarily subordinated by the ascendancy of the Dinkins/liberal faction. From the outset, these fusion political groups had expressly united to defeat the Dinkins administration by reconstructing the Koch coalition: the electoral and political constituencies that had elected Koch and kept him in office from 1977 to 1989, particularly "white, ethnic, middle-class voters, augmented by support from the more conservative, property-owning elements of the black population and from the poorer but more conservative Latino population."[39] The Giuliani campaign fundamentally strove to appeal to distinctly middle- and upper-class concerns, and it privileged particular racial and ethnic groups. According to several analysts, these fusion constituencies have been the primary beneficiaries in policy terms.[40]

There are certainly several factors that affected turnout in the areas of the city that experienced a decline, as well as in the areas that saw an increase, but the disenfranchisement of eligible voters documented in this study is one factor not well studied in the political science literature. Ballot-security measures and politically motivated administrative practices by boards of elections can significantly impact participation. Administrative practices and bodies such as boards of elections—like election law itself—

are sites of political struggle. Republicans successfully highlighted those aspects of the city board's procedures and of New York election law that might open the door to the perpetration of the kinds of fraud that would inflate turnout. They successfully pressed the city board to institute restrictive procedures and thus contributed to increased disenfranchisement.

In this way, Republicans succeeded in reversing the achievements of a decade of work by voting rights groups. These advocates had exposed restrictive procedures by New York's election boards and particular provisions in the election law that, according to them, constituted a different form of fraud: they produced disenfranchising effects and decreased turnout. Just as the success of advocates' efforts in favor of the liberalization of election law and board practices had produced modest increases in access to registration and participation, so the success of these Republican-led efforts illustrates that politically motivated activity can force the development of more restrictive laws and administrative practices that restrict access to registration and participation.

Republicans' desire for greater safeguards were once again firmly reflected in discussions about election law and practice in New York for the remainder of the decade. For example, Republicans in the statehouse and on state and local boards of elections have repeatedly raised concerns regarding noncitizens casting ballots, and they have pressed for measures to protect against illegal registration and voting; the site of these measures range from NVRA implementation to the processing of registration forms to the casting to votes. In addition, Republicans and some Democrats have continued to work to reduce "deadwood," which they believe "makes for greater opportunities for fraud."[41] While we might acknowledge that Republican concerns are not totally without basis—it is possible to commit fraud, and Democrats may possess the means to perpetrate it in some circumstances (for example, at poll sites that are overstaffed by Democrats due to a shortage of Republican workers)—these concerns appear unwarranted. Little fraud has ever been proven, and what has been uncovered does not approach the degree that is claimed and for which remedies are sought. Still, for several years after Giuliani's election in 1993, New York's boards of elections continued to reflect this shift in emphasis toward more restrictive practices to protect against fraud. According to some of its officials, the city board remained on "high alert."[42]

Republican efforts to change the board and liberal election practices, some argue, were intended to extend well beyond the 1993 municipal elections. Furthermore, sharp budget and staff cuts to the board have affected everything from voter registration to election-day operations, eroding some of the improvements made during the previous decade. Voting rights groups contend Republican maneuvering has been done with an eye toward affecting the 1994 gubernatorial and congressional races and the 1996 presidential race, and also toward shaping the implementation of the NVRA.[43] These episodes, therefore, suggest that competing political groups are capable of acting to alter the outcome of elections by shaping the manner in which those elections are conducted.

Florida's Wake

ELECTIONS AND REFORM SINCE 2000

Although there were some important improvements to election administration in New York City after 2000, largely due to the fallout of the debacle in Florida, we found even greater evidence that particular election problems were disenfranchising tens of thousands of eligible voters. New York City's 2001 elections were among the most intensely and extensively scrutinized after the 2000 presidential election, and a monitoring operation yielded an unprecedented amount of information. It revealed that election administration problems were pervasive and that they affected electoral participation and political outcomes.

Three main kinds of election administration problems were found to disenfranchise voters in the city's 2001 elections: those involving voting machines, poll workers and poll sites, and administrative procedures. Particular election practices produced these three kinds of election problems, and certain kinds of election problems disproportionately affected minority citizens while other election practices and problems affected whites and minorities equally. The patterns of disenfranchisement contributed to the outcomes of several close races.

Although the 2001 elections ran more smoothly than earlier ones—as did subsequent elections—voters still found many obstacles to their political participation. Ironically, it was the *Orlando Sentinel Tribune* that reported that aspects of New York City's 2001 elections rivaled some of the election follies in Florida's 2000 presidential election: "A candidate rescinds his election-concession speech, poll workers start recounting ballots, and political supporters threaten to sue over the election results."[1] Thankfully, though, the story is not all gloomy. In 2001, voting rights and civic organizations used the opening provided by the 2000 debacle in Florida to force several changes in New York City election administration.

The 2001 Elections in New York City: It Could Have Been Worse

The controversial 2000 election in Florida exposed flaws in election processes across the country and raised troubling questions about our democracy. This uncovering of the underbelly of election technologies and practices in the United States gave democracy reformers an opportunity to press for changes in election systems across the country. In New York, public scrutiny ran high from the outset of the 2001 elections. A host of key players mobilized to prevent a repeat performance of Florida's election debacle: the media, voting rights and civic organizations, the state's and city's highest elected officials, and election administrators all worried that Florida-like problems might manifest themselves in New York's 2001 elections.

This was a real possibility for several reasons. First, due to newly implemented term limits, more candidates were running for more open seats than at any time in nearly a century, creating the potential for close and contested races. More than six hundred people had announced their intention to run for office, with over four hundred eventually filing petitions with the board of elections for sixty-one open seats. If lower-level elected positions—such as judgeships and positions on county committees—are included, over a thousand candidates were on the ballot in the September primary elections. All the highest-level offices were up for grabs: mayor, public advocate, comptroller, four of the five borough presidents, and thirty-six out of the fifty-one City Council seats. In addition, many races were highly competitive because of a new campaign finance law that provides public funds on the basis of any contributions a candidate obtains by a four to one ratio, and thus enables many cash-poor candidates and political novices to run for office. In some council races, six or more candidates vied for the same seat. Thus, with so many candidates running for so few offices, it was inevitable that many races would be decided by a small number of votes, just as in Florida. Such scenarios did occur in over a dozen races.[2]

Before the primary election, candidates and elections officials in New York sparred over which standards to apply in cases of disputed ballots. Because there were no clear and agreed-upon guidelines for administering and counting paper ballots, these issues were paramount for the major candidates, and they were hotly debated at meetings of candidates and board personnel, at the board commissioners' meetings, and among members of the mayor's task force on election reform. For example, optical scanners were used to read some paper ballots. The scanners can read six pixels or more of a possible sixteen pixels in the oval where a voter marks a ballot, much as on standardized tests in educational institutions. However, as in Florida, in manual recounts in contested races officials use a broader more liberal standard to determine voter intent. Some of the liberal Democratic board of elections commissioners wanted a broader standard to determine the result in disputed cases, so that almost anything hitting the oval on a ballot, such as a check mark, would count. Several Republican commissioners wanted a stricter standard that would invalidate any ballot without at least six pixels marked in an oval, which is called for in the state's election law.

Given the tenuous situation in the wake of Florida's debacle, the majority of the commissioners on the New York City Board of Elections ruled in favor of a relatively liberal and more extensive standard than in previous races, although the courts would ultimately decide the fate of disputed ballots if push came to shove. Hence, some of the candidates in 2001 pushed for more uniform standards and practices to avoid costly disputes and delays in ballot counts. After numerous meetings to iron out such differences and to agree upon guidelines, the four major Democratic candidates for mayor filed a lawsuit three days before the scheduled primary election to call for a guarantee that uniform standards for counting disputed ballots would be established. Even Mayor Giuliani publicly supported the lawsuit, not wanting to be "the next Jeb Bush."[3]

Another point of contention revolved around exactly who would preside over the counting and have authority to determine final outcomes. There was also worry about finishing the counting in a timely manner, which could greatly impact the dynamics of electoral races. The lawyers for the candidates met with the Chief Administrative Judge Jonathan Lippman to request that the court ensure that the board use a uniform and more liberal standard to count votes. A spokesperson for Judge Lippman said, "We really want, to be honest, to avoid another situation like what happened in Florida in the last presidential election." The potential problem of counting disputed paper ballots would also impact the timely determination of winners, which many feared would also replicate the Florida dynamic. Indeed, in one New York City race in 2000—Kruger versus Goodman—the recount was finished eight weeks after election day, several weeks after the Supreme Court settled the disputed presidential election.[4]

The troubled past of the New York City Board of Elections made such concerns plausible. Worries ran high in nearly all quarters, including among state and city elected officials and election administrators. No one wanted another Florida, and no one wanted to be the next Katherine Harris or Jeb Bush. This—along with pressure form voting rights and civic groups and the microscope of the media's attention—led the state's and city's highest elected officials (the governor, the attorney general, state legislators, and the mayor of New York City) to establish task forces to avoid a repeat of past problems. This broad mobilization of such diverse players led to several important developments. The Election Law committees of the two houses of the New York state legislature established separate task forces following the November 2000 elections. Each task force held a series of public hearings across the state during the winter and spring and made recommendations for legislative action and administrative improvements.

State Attorney General Eliot Spitzer issued one of the earliest and most extensive reports. His report details obstacles voters encounter and challenges New York would face in the 2001 elections, noting the forty-year-old lever voting machines that malfunction frequently; long lines and inadequate voting hours; polling places that are not accessible to the disabled; voters who show up to poll sites only to be told their names are not on the registration rolls; election-day workers who lack adequate training and who provide insufficient and incorrect information to voters on various registration issues as well as about emergency and affidavit ballots; and absentee and military ballots that are not counted "even though the voter's intent is clear" because the envelop lacks postmarks or because the ballots have "marks or tears." The report states that because of such problems and its "tenuous record," the New York electoral system would face "unprecedented stress" in the 2001 elections, particularly because of term limits and the high number of competitive races expected, which could have "significant ramifications."[5] The report included a series of detailed short-term and long-term recommendations, some of which were implemented.

A week after Spitzer's report was published, the governor issued Executive Order 108, establishing a bipartisan task force on election modernization. The mission of the task force, according to the executive order, was "to examine the methods by which elections are conducted in New York State and to recommend ways to improve and modernize our electoral system so that every New Yorker's right to vote is honored, respected and upheld." The governor's task force held public hearings in the spring and issued an interim report in May 2001. The final report was published in May 2002.

Perhaps most telling are the worries of elections officials themselves. Their concerns about the 2001 elections ran high, as expressed in documents and statements issued by senior New York City Board of Elections personnel. One statement by a high ranking official summed up these anxieties: At a forum held in the winter of 2001, "Richard Wagner, the head of the union representing election workers, said that before every election, 'election workers all say the same prayer—please let it be a landslide.'"[6]

The Florida election fiasco gave the media additional reason to devote significant resources to scrutiny of the 2001 elections in New York City, which reached unparalleled levels. All the major dailies and local television stations carried stories on the potential pitfalls. It is hard to calculate the impact these reports had in producing pressure for changes, but equally hard to overestimate the media's role. Investigative journalists and other members of the media highlighted past and potential election problems in countless news articles, editorials, and reports and thus were pivotal in putting pressure on the city to make changes in election practices.

A broad coalition of over sixty nonpartisan voting rights and civic organizations, the Coalition for Voter Participation, which is similar to the coalitions that came together in the late 1980s and early 1990s, also mobilized a large monitoring operation. Although the member groups were not united on all issues, they generated dozens of joint letters in favor of both short-term and long-term solutions, and they provided information about past failures of New York's election administration to the media and elected officials. During public hearings held by elected officials and government bodies, including the New York City Council and the New York City Voter Assistance Commission, dozens of voting rights and civic organizations warned about the possibility of a repeat performance of the Florida fiasco. Many of the groups presented data about problems in the

2000 elections and expressed grave concerns about the potential for the New York City Board of Elections to mismanage the 2001 elections. These groups also provided information to the state and city boards of elections about election problems they uncovered, and they made recommendations for improvements.[7]

Thankfully, the coalition had some success in ensuring that another Florida would not happen in New York. Along with key elected officials and local election administrators, it successfully lobbied to obtain greatly needed new funding for the New York City Board of Elections. A three-member election task force established by Mayor Giuliani was also helpful in brokering an increase in funding. As a result of these efforts—and in the context of heightened awareness of potential pitfalls in the post-Florida media-hyped climate—approximately $8 million was appropriated by the City Council and mayor's office. Pay for poll workers was increased from $125 to $200 per sixteen-hour election-day shift, boosting recruitment and quality of poll workers—and costing approximately $5.2 million. Additional voting machines were purchased, as well as seven additional paper-ballot scanners, nearly doubling the board's capacity. The board's voter information services were reconfigured: instead of forty lines with live operators and forty with an automated system, there were now sixty lines with live operators. The city also placed $1 million into a reserve fund for technical upgrades and for the board to restore dollars previously cut by the Giuliani administration.

These groups also produced a second important change: critical reforms to the board's operations before and during the elections. These procedural and administrative changes helped the New York City Board of Elections conduct smoother-running elections in 2001. The board expanded efforts to recruit poll workers and multilingual translators, especially from outside regular party channels, with civic groups recruiting thousands of new poll workers and translators to fill vacant slots. Training materials, procedures, and instructions for poll workers were also improved, and additional voting machine technicians and maintenance workers were recruited and hired. In fact, many of the coalition's short-term recommendations were adopted by the New York City Board of Elections, City Council, and the mayor's office.

Despite these improvements, however, many election problems beset the New York City Board of Elections in 2001 and had significant impact on voters and candidates.

What Problems Did Voters Face? What Were the Consequences?

There were three main kinds of problems voters faced in the 2001 elections that were not dissimilar from those in previous and subsequent elections. The first were voting machine failures, including breakdowns, shortages of machines, failures of technicians, and, worst of all, undervotes, or "lost votes." The second were poll-site and poll-worker problems, including shortages of poll workers, poll-worker errors, inadequate service to language minorities, and delays and confusion. The third were administrative problems, including difficulties with paper ballots, problems due to the consolidation of election districts, failure to inform voters of poll-site changes, and problems with vote tabulation.[8]

I identified these election problems by analyzing three primary sources, which were combined into a single dataset for analysis: (1) responses to a citywide monitoring project's survey about poll-site conditions and poll-worker performance, which was completed by voters in the general election; (2) election data from the New York City Board of Elections, including data on undervotes in the general and Democratic primary runoff elections and on a broader range of election problems in the general election; and (3) a survey of nearly four thousand voters by the Asian American Legal Defense and Education Fund, primarily concentrated in Asian districts.[9]

Findings about the extent and distribution of election problems were then combined with census data and with election data on voter registration and turnout to determine which constituencies, by race, ethnicity, and income, were most affected by particular election problems and practices. The New York City Board of Elections and the New York City Planning Commission created a computer program file that allows census data to be matched to election data at the election-district level. This data file links election districts to census blocks, allowing determination of the race and ethnicity of registered voters in particular geographic areas. This larger, combined database also allows for examination of certain close races to assess how the documented election problems may have affected their outcomes. The findings are presented in both quantitative and in narrative formats.[10]

Additional sources of data include reports from voting rights and civic organizations, such as the Citizens Union, which surveyed hundreds of poll workers. I analyzed transcripts and reports from state and city election task forces, election agencies, and elected officials, including Attorney General Eliot Spitzer, the New York State Assembly 2001 Task Force, the New York City Council, VAC, Governor Pataki's and Mayor Giuliani's 2001 task forces, and recently published articles. Lastly, I conducted dozens of semistructured interviews with candidates, elected officials, election administrators, and other personnel in the these organizations and agencies.

For 2001 I have compiled information at the election-district (ED) level. The ED is the smallest political unit in New York, each containing approximately eight hundred registered voters, and it allows for more precise analysis of election problems, their administrative sources, and their effects on particular groups. Approximately one-quarter of all the EDs in the city were examined: 1,237 out of the total of 5,797, or 28 percent. The dataset is a large and representative sample covering nearly every neighborhood in New York City; overall the monitored EDs correlate with the racial and ethnic profile of all EDs in New York City. The greatest difference is that our sample includes about 7.4 percentage points more whites than the city at large. We characterize the racial and ethnic makeup of the monitored EDs on the basis of which racial or ethnic group has a majority or plurality in each district.

Many of Florida's problems appeared in New York City, albeit on a smaller scale and with less media attention. As one election watchdog group summarized it, "Thousands of New Yorkers were unable to vote in 2001, not because of any fault of their own, but because they are victims of an antiquated and under-funded election system."[11] In New York City, thousands of votes were "lost," thousands of other voters were wrongly turned away from poll sites or did not have their votes properly counted, hundreds of voting machines broke down, poll workers made errors, long lines deterred voters in some areas, and a host of other administrative failures and obstacles challenged would-be voters.

Frequently, for example, a voter's name did not appear on the voter rolls because the registration application was not properly processed or because it was not transmitted in an effective and timely manner to the election board by another government agency, such as the Department of Motor Vehicles, where the voter initially registered to vote. Sometimes a voter's name was improperly removed (or "purged") from the voter rolls. While some such instances occurred because a voter did not properly complete the application, all too often these outcomes were the result of failures of election administration. In addition, many would-be voters were discouraged by long lines at the polls caused by insufficient staffing, a paucity of working voting machines, or a lack of necessary voting materials, such as affidavit, or provisional, ballots. Poll workers frequently provided voters with incorrect information; illegally asked for identification, which is not required in New York; or otherwise intimidated eligible citizens. New York's forty-year-old mechanical voting machines undercounted votes and frequently broke down. Finally, poll workers lost ballots or misread or changed vote tally counts.

Significantly, a disproportionate number of minority voters were hurt by particular kinds of election problems, and in some neighborhoods they were disenfranchised at higher rates. Other kinds of election problems affected whites more. For example, while Asians experienced greater problems at poll sites and with poll workers than other groups, whites experienced other kinds of elections problems, such as machine failures, to a greater extent. A breakdown by income was not conducted because my dataset did not contain such information. Nevertheless, race and income are closely correlated in New York City as elsewhere, and thus can be rough proxy measures for each other. Equally important, disparate disenfranchisement patterns may have affected the outcomes of some electoral races.

What was the relationship between the three kinds of election problems—machine problems, poll-site problems, and administrative problems—and the total votes for the mayoral candidates? Statistically, poll-site and administrative problems together accounted for 2.3 percent of the variance in votes for the mayoral candidates, using a simple regression model.[12]

Table 2—Ethnicity of Election Districts

	Ethnicity of Monitored Election Districts (Majority or Plurality Ethnicity)		Ethnicity of All New York City Election Districts (Majority or Plurality Ethnicity)	
	Frequency	Percent	Frequency	Percent
White	894	54.7	2,743	47.3
Latino	278	17.0	1,245	21.5
Black	330	20.2	1,215	21.0
Asian	78	4.8	263	4.5
Subtotal	1,580	96.7	5,466	94.3
Missing [a]	54	3.3	331	5.7
Total	1,634	100.0	5,797	100.0

[a] No data were available for some election districts.

A number of races were that close. Michael Bloomberg defeated Mark Green in the general election by approximately 40,000 votes out of over 1.5 million cast, or 2.7 percent, for example, and Green defeated Fernando Ferrer in the Democratic Party primary runoff election by about 16,000 votes out of 790,000, or 2 percent. Therefore these two election problems could have determined the outcomes of these close elections if the problems were biased against the supporters of the losing candidate, and data on election problems and their impact do indicate that in many cases particular election practices disproportionately affected minority groups.

To find out the extent to which of these three types of problems were associated with one another, we ran correlation analyses and found significant correlations between poll-site problems and administration problems and between voting machine problems (excluding the specific problems with undervotes and breakdowns, which were part of a different data set) and administration problems. For all ethnicities combined these correlations were small but statistically significant. We also explored correlations for each ethnicity individually. For blacks, Latinos, and whites, there is a correlation between poll-site and administrative problems. There was no correlation between any of the three problem types in Asian districts.

Finally, the mean number of voting problems by type for racial and ethnic groups shows that whites and Latinos had a similar pattern— machine problems substantially outweighed poll-site problems, which slightly outweighed administrative ones. Blacks had fewer of all three problem types than the other groups, and Asians had more machine and poll-site problems than the others groups did, as well as far more of either type than administrative problems. However, when we include additional data on machine-related voting problems—such as the "lost votes" that are part of a separate data set—blacks and Latinos experienced a higher proportion of election problems. That is, data from all sources, when taken together, show that some election problems adversely affected minorities more than whites and vice versa. Overall, however, minorities were disenfranchised at higher rates.

Significantly, these disparate patterns of election problems and voter disenfranchisement may have affected the outcomes of some races, particularly certain City Council races, the Democratic primary runoff election for mayor and public advocate, and the mayoral race in the general election. These election problems were significant enough to raise serious questions about the integrity of the voting process and election outcomes in 2001, but it could have been much worse.

Indeed, the New York City Board of Elections must be commended for successfully carrying out these elections, particularly in light of the tragic events of September 11. New York's primary elections began at 6:00 a.m. that day but were aborted after the attack on the World Trade Center. Like many agencies in the area, the board of elections could barely function for days. Board personnel were locked out of their offices, and the computers did not work. The board had to hold four elections during the fall of 2001, partly due to these events. The city was originally scheduled to have two elections: a primary election to determine the candidates for each party for each office, and a general election. As it turned out, in addition to the rescheduled primary, two runoff elections were necessary for the Democratic Party candidates for mayor and public advocate because no single candidate won 40 percent or more of the vote, as required by law. The fact that elections officials and workers pulled their operation back together in time for any elections to take place at all is testimony to their hard work. The 2001 elections seriously tested New York's system, and while the board of elections was stretched to its limit, it did not break. This chapter focuses on election problems, but I would be remiss not to acknowledge the good work many board officials perform on a regular basis.

Voting Machine Problems

Thousands of votes are routinely "lost" in New York City elections. Lost votes, or undervotes, occur when voters go to the polls but do but do not cast a vote for the highest-level office, such as president or mayor, or when their votes for that office are not recorded properly. Although in some cases voters actively decide not to vote for any of these candidates, the vast majority of undervotes occur when voters cast ballots for the highest-level candidates but their votes are lost, often because of a failure of the voting technology or because of poor instruction by poll workers. This is especially evident in elections where only one or two offices are at stake, as was the case in the New York City 2001 Democratic primary runoff election.

In the 2000 elections New York City had a higher proportion of undervotes than Florida and the nation as a whole. Its average undervote rate was 3.9 percent, significantly higher than the national average of 2.8 percent and Florida's 2.9 percent. Moreover, New York state's votes had a pattern of racial and ethnic bias in the 2000 elections that was as bad as or worse than Florida's pattern. More affluent white suburban districts, such as Nassau and Suffolk counties, lost fewer votes, as did upstate regions as a whole, compared to New York City. Within the city, there were also disparities. The Bronx has the highest percentage of low-income and minority individuals, and 4.7 percent of all votes cast were lost there, compared to 1.6 percent in Staten Island. In the Greenpoint-Williamsburg section of Brooklyn, a largely poor and minority area, the rate of lost votes was three times the national average.[13] According to Stephanie Saul's analysis as reported in *New York Newsday,* the rate of lost votes by borough in 2000 was: Bronx, 4.7 percent; Manhattan, 4.3 percent; Brooklyn, 3.9 percent; Queens, 3.5 percent; and Staten Island, 1.2 percent. Nassau County's lost votes were 1.2 percent of the total, and Suffolk County's, 0.7 percent. Similar patterns were found in the 2001 elections.

Michael Bloomberg (R) defeated Mark Green (D) in the general election by approximately 40,000 votes out of almost 1.5 million cast, or a 2.7 percent margin. In that election, Latino election districts had the highest average percentage of lost votes, followed by African American and Asian districts. White districts had the lowest average percentage of lost votes.[14] Given these racial differences, it is likely that the margin of victory would have been smaller had it not been for the lost votes, even though Bloomberg still ultimately may have won.

The Democratic Party primary runoff election for mayor was a similarly close race, between Fernando Ferrer and Mark Green. In the end, Green won by 15,981 out of 790,019 total votes cast, a 2 percent margin. The lost votes in the runoff election were just as significant as and perhaps even more controversial than those in the general election because they are more likely to be "real" lost votes. That is, whereas people may choose not to cast a vote for mayor in an election with multiple races, they are unlikely to show up at the polls in an election that determines the result of one or two races if they are not planning to vote in the more important race. The only other race in this runoff election was for public advocate, and the vote total for that office was lower than the total for mayor. Mark Herman, a commissioner of the New York City Board of Elections from Staten Island, stated, "The truest numbers of an under vote you would get are in a runoff."[15]

In this election the proportion of lost votes was not distributed evenly. Voters in low-income and minority districts, who voted at a higher rate for Ferrer, lost more votes proportionally than higher-income and white voters, who were more likely to vote for Green.[16] For example, in the Bronx, which went for Ferrer, 144,342 votes were counted and there were 4,158 lost votes, or 2.8 percent of the total. The majority of voters in the Bronx are Latinos, who overwhelmingly voted for Ferrer according to exit polls. By comparison, in Manhattan, where Green won, 221,316 votes were counted altogether and 4,281 were lost, or 1.9 percent of the total. According to exit polls and census data, Manhattan voters for Green were predominantly white. Given the lower rate of lost votes in Manhattan than in the Bronx, Green lost fewer votes proportionally than Ferrer. Interestingly, Queens, the other borough for which data are available, had the lowest estimated lost vote rate of the three, 1.8 percent. Green received more total votes (94,342) than Ferrer (77,330) in that borough. This supports the contention that Ferrer lost a higher proportion of votes in his strongholds while Green lost a smaller proportion in his. Data were missing for the other two boroughs, Brooklyn and Staten Island, which account for about one-third of total voters.[17] These findings were determined by use of a one-way analysis of variance to examine whether there were differences in the average lost votes for each racial and ethnic group.

Had it not been for the lost votes, Green ultimately may have won the election, but the margin of victory would have been smaller—perhaps very close. A *New York Newsday* report claimed that "the number of uncounted or 'lost' votes citywide may have exceeded Green's 15,981-vote margin of victory." Ferrer's contention that the election results are questionable is plausible, yet, the *Newsday* report continues, "the lost votes presumably would have been split between Green and Ferrer, roughly along the lines of the counted votes in each district." We cannot draw a more definitive conclusion because election information for about one-third of the election districts is missing.[18]

Nevertheless, these findings raise troubling questions about the election results. Similar proportions of lost votes appeared in several close City Council races. The number of lost votes may not be enough to overturn any election (though no one knows for sure), but the undervote problem leaves too many voters disenfranchised and candidates and the public wondering about who the true winners are.[19]

A Disabled Latch: The Cause of Lost Votes

Lost votes in New York City often occur because a sensor latch—a locking device that prevents voters from inadvertently pulling the handle to end their voting session unless they have pulled down at least one lever to cast a vote—was disabled. In their attempt to cast a ballot, voters sometimes mistakenly move the big red handle that begins and ends the voting session, instead of pulling down levers to select candidates. If the sensor latch is disabled, they then exit the voting booth without casting a vote. Another way people lose votes is by pushing the levers back up after they move them down to select candidates, perhaps because they are in the process of making up their minds or are correcting errors, then ending the voting session by pulling the big red handle without casting votes for all their choices. According to Commissioner Herman, "People who've voted many times eventually get the message that they lose their votes when they put the buttons back up."[20] A functioning sensor latch device would prevent these occurrences because it ensures voters don't leave the voting booth without properly casting a ballot. Voters who intend not to cast a ballot after they enter the voting booth can push a special button marked "Vote for None of the Above" to leave the booth.[21]

While it is unclear why the New York City Board of Elections disabled the sensor latches, the harm to voters is all too clear. As late as 1976 inspector training materials contained information about how to set and use the device, according to Douglas Kellner (D), Manhattan commissioner of the board of elections. A review of the board's archives was ordered by the commissioners of the board in the spring of 2002 to determine who had disabled and removed the latches, when they had done so, and why. The resulting report, prepared by John Grady, does not answer these questions, but it does discuss why board staff is reluctant to reinstall the latch: if a voter misuses the device by pulling the handle with enough force to break a shear pin, the machine will be disabled. In addition, if a voter leaves the machine without completing the process, the machine will remain active. This situation could open the door to election fraud by a poll worker or another voter, who could then cast a vote if not noticed or caught by the poll inspectors. Voting rights groups counter that such problems could be addressed through proper instruction to voters and training materials for poll workers.[22]

In other parts of New York state, such as Albany, where similar machines are used but where the sensor latch is not disabled, the undervote is far less—only 1.3 percent in the 2000 elections. Similarly, Nassau and Suffolk counties, wealthier suburban areas on Long Island, also have functioning devices and fewer lost votes.[23] Nassau County's undervote was 1.2 percent, and Suffolk County's was only 0.7 percent in 2000. In fact, altogether New York counties outside of New York City had a 1.2 percent lost-vote rate, far less than the city's 3.9 percent rate. In Philadelphia, which uses the same kinds of voting machines but with the sensor device enabled, only 0.5 percent of the voters lost their vote during the 2000 elections.[24] These findings speak both to the effectiveness of the sensor latches and to how particular election technologies and practices can produce racial, income, and regional disparities in elections.

If enabled, the sensor latches would prevent many voters from improperly using a voting machine and thus losing their vote, but the board rejected the idea of replacing them in 2002, contending that it would be too costly and too time-consuming and that it would make the machines too vulnerable to fraud.[25] The board's own estimate, though, makes this change seem perfectly feasible: it would cost approximately $275,000 to $400,000 to replace the sensor latches, the necessary changes could be made within one year, and they could include mechanisms to reduce the chances of fraud. Fixing these devices would be a short-term solution; a middle-to-longer-term solution lies in new voting technology. These issues were priorities for voting rights organizations and some elected officials and election administrators. According to Commissioner Kellner, lost votes are "a serious problem that the Board of Elections must address."[26] Thankfully, because of a lawsuit brought by the Brennan Center for Justice, the New York City Board of Elections reversed itself and reinstalled the sensor devices for the 2004 elections.

Distribution of Additional Voting Machine Problems

The incidence and demographic distribution of additional machine problems reveal an uneven pattern for the general election. Some kinds of machine problems affected minorities more than whites and vice versa. We examined data for Manhattan, which was provided by the New York City Board of Elections. Data from the other boroughs were not available, but the results are likely to be comparable because each borough follows the same rules. The board records various kinds of machine problems as reported by poll workers, machine technicians, and other board personnel out in the field on election day. Data on machine breakdowns in Manhattan show that white and Latino election districts had a very similar pattern of machine problems and that there was a higher proportion of machine problems in black and Asian districts. The latter two more often had a single problem than white and Latino districts did, and Asian districts more often had three or more problems. Altogether 22.2 percent of the monitored EDs in Manhattan experienced machine problems. This suggests that a large number of voters were affected.

The second dataset we examined was generated by a general-election monitoring operation conducted by the Coalition for Voter Participation and led by the New York Public Interest Research Group (NYPIRG) and the Center for Excellence in New York City Governance, at New York University (NYU). The operation sent voters to survey poll-site conditions in all of New York's five boroughs. Altogether 853 surveyors visited 415 of New York City's 1,268 polling sites—one-third of all poll sites—to document election-day conditions and operations. Importantly, the survey covered every assembly district in the city—in other words, nearly every neighborhood was surveyed. The NYPIRG/NYU study found fewer machine problems than did the studies by the Manhattan Board of Elections. The NYPRIG/NYU study shows that only about 10 percent of all monitored EDs experienced poll-site problems and that the black districts that were monitored had fewer machine problems than other districts.

Had it not been for the tragedy on September 11—the original day of the primary election—the Coalition for Voter Participation would have monitored many more poll sites. The coalition had lined up over four thousand surveyors to monitor the primaries, but the tragedy overwhelmed more than just the coalition's monitoring operation. The primary was postponed for two weeks, and in those two weeks electoral politics took a backseat to questions of terrorism, war, and international politics. Voters had been evacuated from their homes, damaged polling sites had to be relocated, and the board's central office, which was only six blocks from the World Trade Center site, had unreliable telephone service and power for weeks. Similarly, NYPIRG, the lead organization in the coalition, lost its offices and the Web site that was to be used to submit survey results for over three weeks. It is testimony to their commitment that both the board and the coalition were able to reestablish themselves and carry out their respective operations.[27]

The discrepancy between the findings of the NYPIRG/NYU study and that of the Manhattan Board of Elections may be due to differences in the survey design. The NYPIRG/NYU study had voters fill out survey forms when they went to vote—the surveyors did not stay at a poll site for the entire day to observe conditions—whereas the board of elections data reflect information about problems from each poll site over the course of the entire election day. Moreover, the NYPIRG/NYU survey covered a slightly higher proportion of white EDs than the board survey did. Nevertheless, these differences in design are minor considerations because of the other sources of information contained in the database. These minimal differences do not skew results presented in the remainder of this study.

Lastly, the voting machine breakdowns in 2001 were not an anomaly. As Stephanie Saul, an investigative journalist, observed: "While the Board of Elections reports that these machines have become more reliable in recent years, over 6.5 percent of them still broke down last election day," in November 2000.[28] The reasons for such incidents are many, including poor maintenance and frequent use. Other reasons in 2001 had to do with the shortened time frame due to the postponement of the primary because of the September 11 attack, and the need for a runoff election.

Nearly half of the broken machines in 2000, and again in 2001, were in two assembly districts in Brooklyn. In 2000, two machine technicians responsible for these breakdowns were fired. The central office of the New York City Board of Elections wanted to fire them immediately after the elections, but several Republican commissioners, "at the behest of the Republican Party Leader" in Brooklyn, prevented this. The central board prevailed, however, in part because of bad press and pressure from voting rights organizations. The same thing happened in 2001, though in different Brooklyn assembly districts. The responsible parties—again technicians—were also fired.[29]

Lever machines like these have not been manufactured for over a decade, so replacement parts must be recycled from machines obtained from other jurisdictions. Furthermore, capable technicians are difficult to come by and hold on to. The board employs sixty full-time salaried voting machine technicians, but they ran short in 2001, even after contracting with outside machine technicians from other jurisdictions.[30]

New York maintains a fleet of roughly 6,400 mechanical voting machines, each weighing nearly seven hundred pounds and containing thousands of parts. They are "based on a machine first designed by Thomas Edison in 1869 to record votes in Congress (it was his first patent)."[31] This number of machines, however, is insufficient to meet the needs of all the registered voters in New York City: state law requires that each election district of eight hundred or more registered voters have two machines.[32]

But the board of elections has long been violating this law, and the law has not been enforced. In the 2000 elections, for example, the city board of elections used 641 fewer voting machines than required. In an attempt to correct the problem for the 2001 elections, the city purchased an additional 273 machines in 2001, which were used. Still, the city needed to purchase about 533 machines altogether to meet state law. (The total figure for 2001 is lower than the one for 2000, due to the consolidation of election districts and the decrease in the number of poll sites.) As a result, in 2001 Manhattan was about 113 machines short of the 1,659 it needed to fully comply with the law; Queens was about 111 short of the 1,908 it needed; and Brooklyn was about 143 short.[33]

The board does not deny it allocates fewer voting machines than required by law—largely because the manufacturer of the machines has long since ceased producing them—and it rightly claims that it needs more money to acquire machines from other jurisdictions where possible, as well as parts and technicians to maintain its dwindling fleet. The board also claims that it allocates fewer machines to those districts and boroughs, such as the Bronx, that have historically low voter turnout. Before 2001 the Bronx received no double machines in any election districts. However, because the number of registered voters has grown over the past decade, due in part to the influx of immigrants and their attainment of citizenship, the board has probably been discouraging voter turnout in such areas by creating longer lines at poll sites. Therefore, the board's failure to provide additional voting machines in certain districts as required by law may have discriminatory impacts.[34]

The repeated and frequent use of these aging machines strains their capacity and contributes to their breaking down. The city has attempted to replace its voting machines in the past. In the late 1980s it began a process of purchasing electronic voting machines, but the board of elections was unable to come to a consensus on the bidding process to select new machine technology, select a vendor, and proceed to purchase. Some contend this was partly due to partisan deadlock on the bipartisan board of elections. Others raised questions about security and safeguards. Some reform advocates and voting rights groups (such as NYPIRG) raised concerns about the relatively closed purchasing process.[35]

Obtaining new voting machines in the future is a primary concern for all stakeholders in New York. The city and state boards of elections have been actively looking into options, and the governor's task force explored several options and presented demonstrations of new technologies at several public sites, including some in New York City. Mayor Giuliani's task force recommended that the board of elections acquire new voting technology, and Mayor Bloomberg is on record in support of such an initiative, though he has done little on it to date. However, the passage of the Help America Vote Act has sped up this process.

Several factors thus combine to produce delays, long lines, and voter disenfranchisement: a high incidence of lost votes, broken voting machines, and shortages of voting machines and machine technicians—along with a decrease in the total number of poll sites, chronic shortages of poll workers, and poorly trained and poorly performing workers. Such conditions are particularly common during the crunch times before and after working hours when most individuals vote. At those times the wait can be over an hour in many busy jurisdictions. The data indicate that this was less of a problem in 2001 than in previous years, particularly compared to presidential elections and the 1993 mayoral election. Still, even Mayor Giuliani had to wait nearly thirty minutes to cast his vote. Several changes implemented by the board in 2001 led to improvements that, along with a decrease in voter turnout, reduced delays from 2000 to 2001.

Pressure brought to bear on the city and its board of elections by a coalition of voting rights groups, scrutiny by the media, and the state and city task forces led to an increase in funding to the board, which allowed it to purchase more voting machines and recruit and hire a larger number of technicians. These developments appeared to cut down on the number of machine breakdowns and delays. In the months leading up to the 2001 elections, however, the board had several vacancies on its staff of salaried voting machine technicians. According to Mayor Giuliani's election task force: "The Board of Elections, with the assistance of the Task Force, combed the country and recruited temporary" machine technicians. About thirty extra technicians were recruited from Suffolk, Duchess, Rockland, and Orange counties; from the City University of New York's work experience program; from the Central Labor Council; and from as far away as Chicago, which sent eight paid workers from its board of elections, in order to make sure the elections could be conducted, particularly following the September 11 tragedy. Although these improvements were helpful, there was still a shortage of technicians, which led to machine breakdowns and delays in repair.[36]

Poll-Worker and Poll-Site Problems

Although it is the job of the poll worker to facilitate voting, not to hamper it, poll workers' actions and inaction—as well as chaotic and confusing poll-site conditions—are some of the highest hurdles voters face. According to Commissioner Kellner, our "biggest single problem is inspector train-ing." When poll workers give improper information, voters may cast their ballot improperly and lose their vote. Similarly, when poll sites open late, are not fully staffed, lack sufficient materials, or are not set up properly, de-lays, long lines, and frustration for voters and poll workers alike are the re-sult, and all of this can discourage and disenfranchise eligible voters. Poll workers sometimes fail to explain how to use the machines or how to fill out paper ballots, and they often neglect to tell voters that they have a right to an affidavit, or provisional, ballot. In addition, poll workers must know how to correctly direct voters to their proper polling place. The board of elections recruits and trains thousands of part-time workers to staff polling sites during elections. The 312 full-time staff of the board are joined by nearly 25,000 workers on election day. Often, however, the board is short the number of poll workers needed.[37]

In 2001, the board of elections was short 3,371 poll inspectors, or 15 per-cent of the 22,410 needed, despite the extraordinarily successful efforts of the Citizens Union, CUNY, and several other schools and organizations that recruited over 2,500 new poll workers. By comparison, in 2000 the board was short over 4,000 poll workers. An additional number of other critical poll-worker positions went unfilled in 2001. According to the board of elections, it was short 99 (8%) out of a total of 1,198 poll-site coordina-tors needed; 207 (18%) out of a total of 1,146 information clerks; 3,092 (49%) out of a total of 6,276 poll clerks; 6 (1%) out of a total of 729 door clerks; 122 (25%) out of a total of 483 Chinese interpreters; 256 (33%) out of a total of 779 Spanish interpreters; and 19 (59%) out of a total of 32 Korean interpreters. Despite considerable effort and some progress, poll-worker problems thus continue to plague New York's elections.

Similarly, poll-site conditions can vary significantly and shape voter par-ticipation. First, the number of poll sites has been reduced over time. The board lost approximately two hundred poll sites over the past decade be-cause of higher real estate costs and accessibility requirements. There were approximately 1,500 poll sites in 1990 and about 1,312 in 2002. This causes two other problems: the location of poll sites is now more uneven in some communities, and there are a larger number of election districts per poll site, up from four on average to five.

For example, the Lower East Side of Manhattan contains some poll sites that are located inside apartment buildings where voters live, such as the Grand Street apartment complex, which houses mostly middle-income and Jewish voters. These residents vote conveniently, in their lobby. By con-trast, poll sites are not often located in housing projects—public housing complexes that contain a high proportion of low-income and minority people—so those voters must travel greater distances to their poll sites. Some have argued that these patterns reflect dominant politicians' influ-ence on the board of elections. In the case of the Lower East Side of Manhattan, Sheldon Silver, the State Assembly member for the district, is the Democratic majority leader of the Assembly and is currently one of New York's most powerful elected officials; he exerts greater influence over poll-site conditions than do other leaders or constituencies. This discrepancy may lead to lower turnout in some areas—the greater the distance the poll site is from a person's home, the greater the burden of traveling there.

The number of election districts in a poll site, and the number of voters per election district, can make the site more or less chaotic. The more EDs a poll site has and the more voters per ED, the more crowded the site can become, the longer the lines can be, and the more likely that confusion can develop. Smaller poll sites with fewer and less populous EDs are likely to have shorter lines and fewer problems. These results were borne out in the surveys.

A survey by the NYPIRG/NYU monitoring project found that many poll workers incorrectly answered questions posed by surveyors. One question asked whether a registered voter who moved within the city could still vote. ("If someone is registered and recently moved from one place within New York City to another, can they vote today even if they haven't reregistered?" The correct answer is yes.) Another question asked whether voters were allowed to bring another person with them into the voting booth for assistance. ("If a voter needs assistance, can someone come into the booth with them?" The correct answer is yes.) Although most poll workers correctly answered these two questions (83% and 89% respectively), the majority of poll workers gave false information to related follow-up questions. Asked whether voters who have moved should vote at their old poll site instead of their new one, 57 percent of the poll workers said incorrectly that the voter should vote at their old poll location. (The motor voter law made voting at the new location permissible.) Similarly, regarding voter assistance, 53 percent of the poll workers incorrectly stated that only poll workers could assist voters. The correct answer is that anyone except a voter's employer or union representative may accompany them. If voters acted on such incorrect information, they might not vote, or they might vote in the wrong location or without adequate assistance.

The NYPIRG/NYU study identified additional poll-worker and poll-site problems: more than half of the surveyors were not asked if they needed help using the voting machine, even though poll workers are required to ask every voter; more than a fifth of the surveyors did not see the required ballot poster displayed at their polling station; 17% of the surveyors were not provided a voter rights flyer as required when they requested one; 30% of poll workers did not wear the required name tags; and nearly half of the surveyors found the ballot "slightly" or "very confusing."

The NYPIRG/NYU survey found that these problems were not evenly distributed throughout the city. Manhattan scored worst on several fronts: poll workers in Manhattan were least likely to follow the proper procedure by asking voters if they needed assistance with voting machines (compared with poll workers in Staten Island, who scored the highest); Manhattan had the longest waiting times to vote (an average of 7.1 minutes); and poll workers in Manhattan were the least likely to be wearing the required name tags. On the other hand, Manhattan was best on visibility of ballot posters. The Bronx ranked the lowest on providing voter rights flyers but better than Manhattan on waiting times (an average of 3.2 minutes). The latter difference may be due to the Bronx's lower overall turnout in the general election, but Brooklyn's average wait time was 5.4 minutes even though it had roughly the same turnout rate as the Bronx (223 voters per election district compared with 216 voters per district for the Bronx). This was a marked improvement over the 2000 elections, when lines and waits were several times longer than these across the city, partially due to higher voter turnout. To poll workers' credit—and that of the board of elections more generally—the NYPIRG/NYU surveyors found the poll sites mostly "calm and quiet" or "busy but orderly" rather than "confusing or chaotic," and few sites suffered machine problems.

Still, findings and those of other monitoring projects—including the study by the Asian American Legal Defense and Education Fund (AALDEF), which surveyed nearly 4,000 Asian voters (over 1,500 in the primary elections and more than 2,300 in the general elections); and the Citizens Union's survey of the 225 poll workers it recruited to work the elections; as well as information from the New York City Board of Elections itself—all show that many significant poll-worker and poll-site problems persisted in the 2001 elections. Data from these surveys corroborate the contention that problems in all three areas of focus of this chapter (machine failures, poll-worker and poll-site problems, and administrative foul-ups) pose significant obstacles to thousands of voters in New York elections.

AALDEF placed attorneys and volunteers as monitors in polling sites throughout New York City with a large number of Asian American voters for the September 25th primary elections, the October 11 runoff elections, and the November 6th general elections in 2001. Their purpose was simple: to ensure that the New York City Board of Elections complied with Section 203 of the federal Voting Rights Act, which mandates that Chinese bilingual ballots and assistance are available to the voters. In addition, they sought to record any problems that Asian Americans, including Korean Americans, encountered during voting.[38] While their surveys documented all three general kinds of problems, they primarily revealed problems with poll workers and poll sites.

In the primary and runoff elections, AALDEF observed thirty-one polling sites and surveyed more than 1,500 Asian American voters, one-quarter of whom were voting for the first time. More than three hundred voters complained of some kind of problem. During the general election, AALDEF monitored thirty polling sites. Twenty-seven of the sites were required to provide Chinese language assistance, and at six sites Korean interpreters were provided. AALDEF reported surveying more than 2,300 Asian American voters, over seven hundred of whom reported having some type of problem.

AALDEF's surveys revealed a number of problems that occurred in both elections; many registered voters' names were omitted from the registration lists, and at times those voters were turned away without being given the option of casting an affidavit ballot—in other words, they were not permitted to vote; poll workers were inconsistently notified of training sessions, and trainers gave improper information to Chinese interpreters; poll workers did not provide Chinese-language materials, and some interfered with the voters who were receiving language assistance; poll workers did not follow election procedures, and they were hostile toward voters—both violations of election law; there was confusion over poll-site changes; and poll inspectors did not seem to understand the rules regarding the use of affidavit ballots.

Voters reported problems suggesting that poll workers provided misinformation or conflicting information. For example, some voters were told to go to another polling site only to be told at the second site that they could not vote there; then they were sent back to the original site or to a third site. During the primary elections approximately 250 of the Asian voters surveyed were asked to show identification even though it is not required, and in the general election 375 were asked to do so. Other voters reported rude treatment by poll workers. All of these problems have the potential to disenfranchise voters. Similar problems have been documented in previous elections.[39]

There are several reasons voters in New York experience problems with poll workers. Poor working conditions and the patronage system of appointing workers are at the root. The leaders of the political parties—county chairs, district leaders, and election commissioners—maintain control over the recruitment and training process. Democratic and Republican officials select most of the poll inspectors, clerks, translators, and supervisors on the basis of party loyalty rather than competence, as is true of almost all the staff of the board. In New York City poll workers who fail the test administered at the end of a training session can be assigned to work on election day. Some are functionally illiterate, so it is difficult for them to find a name on a voter registration roll, while others are not sure when to use affidavit ballots versus emergency ballots or how to direct a voter to the correct voting table.[40]

Only a month before the primary elections in 2001, Mayor Giuliani announced that the city would provide funding for an increase in pay for poll workers: the stipend for a sixteen-hour day to work the polls had been $125, and the Coalition for Voter Participation, the board of elections, and Mayor Giuliani's election task force were successful in increasing the pay to $200. While the board of elections has been calling for a pay increase for years, pressure from the City Council, voting rights organizations, and the media also helped make the case to the city.[41] Obviously poor pay makes working the polls less appealing to more competent individuals, and it creates little incentive for enrolling to work an election, let alone for working efficiently. The increased stipend and recruitment efforts by several groups helped the board of elections recruit and hire more poll workers in 2001.

In 2001, the Citizens Union Foundation (CUF) teamed up with the City University of New York (CUNY) and other schools to recruit over 2,500 poll workers for the board. A follow-up survey of 252 recruits revealed that only "49 (19%) of respondents were assigned to a training session and 195 or (77%) were not, 183 or (73%) of survey respondents were never assigned to work, and 62 or (25%) of respondents were assigned to work at a poll site." The CUF received phone calls and emails expressing frustration "because they were not notified one way or the other by the Board of Elections. In fact, for many applicants the only notice they received after they submitted their application form was our survey."[42]

The board's data on poll-site conditions indicate that Asian districts experienced the greatest incidence of problems, followed by white, Latino, and black districts. Asian districts were the most likely to have three or more problems than the other districts. Moreover, the overwhelming majority of monitored EDs in Manhattan experienced poll-site problems, nearly three out of four. According to NYPIRG/NYU's data, however, white districts had the most poll-site problems and black districts the fewest, but a high proportion of monitored EDs experienced poll-site problems, almost one out of four. However, the NYPIRG/NYU results may reflect the fact that their surveyors were concentrated in predominantly white areas. The board, which reported a considerably higher incidence of problems, monitored sites throughout election day, whereas NYPIRG/NYU surveyors observed sites only for a very short time.

Administrative Problems

The consolidation of election districts in the 2001 elections led to the disenfranchisement of eligible voters. In some areas the board of elections combined more than one election district onto a single voting machine in order to save time and money, causing problems particularly in the Democratic primary runoff election.[43] It was cheaper to use fewer voting machines, and due to the attack on September 11, which postponed the primary election, the board had only twenty-six days instead forty-five between the runoff and the general election, and there is a significant amount of work involved in resetting all the voting machines for each election.

Consolidation of election districts contributed to greater confusion at poll sites and an increase in the kinds of scenarios that can disenfranchise eligible voters: Disenfranchisement can occur when a voter enters the correct polling place but ends up at the table for the wrong election district, and voters often are not directed to the correct table. As one voting rights advocate put it, "it's like being in the right church but wrong pew."[44] If a voter's name does not appear on the poll list, the voter should be offered an affidavit ballot, but often voters are incorrectly told that they are not registered and that they are therefore ineligible to vote. In some of these instances, poll workers wrongfully send voters out of the poll site even though they have not cast a vote or filled out an affidavit ballot. Even when a voter is offered an affidavit ballot it may be voided because it was not completed properly or because election workers did not process it properly. In addition, delays and long lines may develop because of some of these problems, and voters may leave without voting, whether out of frustration or because they must to get to work or attend to children or personal needs.

Controversy around the effect of combining EDs led one Ferrer supporter, Reverend Al Sharpton, to file a complaint with the U.S. Department of Justice. Sharpton contended that the consolidation of EDs might have affected the outcome of the Democratic Party runoff election because fewer voting machines were available per registered voter in minority EDs, which forced minorities to fill out a disproportionately higher number of paper ballots. The board of elections had used only 58 percent of its machines for the runoff because it had combined elections districts. Sharpton argued that the consolidation should have received the approval of the Department of Justice under the federal Voting Rights Act, which requires federal approval for voting changes in the Bronx, Brooklyn, and Manhattan. The board of elections countered that it had combined election districts because it had no choice, given high costs and the truncated time frame due to the loss of the two weeks following September 11. Consolidation also allowed the board to keep some voting machines in warehouses for the general election in November, which would give their technicians and mechanics time to prepare the machines properly. According to Commissioner Kellner, district consolidation is common and does not require Department of Justice approval,[45] but the Department of Justice did notify the board of elections that it would investigate whether the its decisions had had a disproportionate impact on minority voters.[46] At the time of this writing, the outcome of the Department of Justice investigation remains pending.

As has occurred in previous elections, the use of a large number of paper ballots in the 2001 elections appears to have led to the disenfranchisement of a significant number of eligible voters, particularly in the Democratic Party's runoff election. There are three kinds of paper ballots used in New York elections: affidavit ballots are used when a voters name does not appear on the registration rolls, emergency ballots are used when a voting machine breaks down, and absentee and military ballots are used by voters who are unable to vote in person on election day. Such paper ballots can be invalidated for a number of reasons. A voter may not have registered to begin with or may not have registered in a party, which is required for voting in a party's primary election, and some people fail to update their address after they have moved. In other cases, a voter's registration application may not have been properly processed, or the voter rolls have not been updated and are missing names or digitized signatures. Sometimes poll workers don't issue paper ballots to voters who are eligible to cast them, or they make mistakes in processing the paper ballots. Similarly, voters themselves may make mistakes in completing paper ballots. Regardless, the greater the use of manual, paper-intensive procedures, the greater the likelihood and degree of error and thus voter disenfranchisement.

For example, Fernando Ferrer believes the outcome of the Democratic primary runoff election was far from certain because of the thousands of paper ballots that had to be counted. Altogether, 51,245 emergency and affidavit ballots were filed by people who had trouble with their machines or were not listed as registered voters. The board had to deem each of these valid or invalid. They also had 5,764 absentee ballots to count. For days the outcome of the election was in question. As time went on, board officials and campaign aides on both sides who were monitoring the counting process and challenging questionable ballots said that many paper ballots were ruled invalid. In the end, over 40,000 were invalidated, among them a disproportionate number of Ferrer's ballots. While some affected voters may not have properly been registered in the first place, Ferrer claimed that many voters were disenfranchised in the runoff election; not only were ballots invalidated, but voters were "turned away in droves" from the polls. Ferrer supporters claimed there were two main problems in the runoff election. First, there was a large number of lost votes, especially in districts favoring Ferrer. Second, they accused Green's advisers of pressuring the board of elections to invalidate paper ballots.[47] Representatives from Green's campaign deny these allegations.[48] A representative from the board said both campaigns challenged voters in the other's strongholds, which produced a higher number of invalid paper ballots.[49]

In the 2001 general election, the rate of paper ballot use varied among the boroughs, raising questions about why such differences existed and suggesting possible disparate impacts and outcomes. Brooklyn experienced the highest use of emergency ballots, indicating a greater number of machine breakdowns, especially in a few Assembly districts.

The New York City Board of Elections claims that the large number of affidavit ballots that are regularly cast in each election does not necessarily indicate an equally large number of errors on the board's part. The board's current perspective regarding affidavit ballots is that valid ballots indicate that the board committed administrative errors, and invalid ballots suggest that individual voters or provisions of the election law are responsible. While it is true that the large number of affidavit ballots cast does not necessarily indicate an equally large number of errors on the board's part, other actions or inactions by the board may cause legitimate voters' ballots to be invalidated. As documented by this study and in the 2001 monitoring projects—as well as by voting rights advocates' analyses of past elections, investigations by the New York State Assembly Election Law Committee, and the board's self-study described in chapter five—board errors have led to a significant number of affidavit ballots being incorrectly invalidated. As for valid affidavit ballots, the largest number were cast by voters who were at the right polling place but at the table for the wrong election district. If poll workers had directed these voters to their correct table, they would have been able to cast their vote on a machine instead. Such poll worker lapses increase the use of paper ballots, and the greater the use of paper ballots, the greater the likelihood of errors and invalidation of votes.

To be sure, many, if not most, of the affidavit ballots were properly invalidated. Both the Ferrer and Green campaigns carefully scrutinized such ballots. Ferrer apparently had generated enthusiasm and turnout among people who do not often vote and may never have voted, and perhaps this contributed to a higher overall number of paper ballots and a higher proportion of invalidated affidavit ballots. This is a clear example of how reforms such as election-day registration would solve such problems and increase voter turnout. Election-day registration allows all qualified voters who show up at their poll site to cast a ballot and to have their vote counted. There are no affidavit ballots that can be invalidated, and legitimate voters are not turned away. The six states that have election-day registration consistently have the highest turnout in the United States. Critics of election-day registration have charged that it opens the door to fraud, but the experiences of these six states do not show their concerns to be warranted. Where computerized statewide registration systems are continually updated, duplicate registrations are prevented, and the enactment of election-day registration can be coupled with increases in the penalty for fraud.[50]

Voters and poll workers alike face additional hurdles. Voter information is often missing from poll books or is wrongly listed because administrative problems at the board of elections led to voter registration forms being lost or misprocessed. In still other cases, voters' names appear but without the digitized signatures, which forces them to vote with affidavit ballots. Some voters do not receive timely notice regarding the location of their poll site—particularly important if it has changed. This happens often, and it was an even greater problem in 2001 because of the World Trade Center disaster. Registered voters who move within the city are permitted by law to vote at their new polling place. Thus it is necessary for poll workers to know where voters are supposed to vote and how to redirect voters if they show up at a wrong location. All too often, poll workers do not give voters the correct information, and this can lead to their disenfranchisement. As the NYPIRG survey shows, this was a significant problem in the 2001 elections. The board has an insufficient number of telephone lines for answering questions from voters and poll workers on election day. Voters call to find out where their poll sites are, to ask any one of dozens of other possible questions, and to report problems they are facing on election day; poll workers call to report broken machines, inadequate staffing, lack of critical materials, electioneering, and so on. In 2001 the board's Web site provided neither this useful voter information nor the capacity to report problems. All of these factors frustrate voters and render poll workers unable to provide needed assistance to voters.

On the evening of the Democratic primary runoff election, Green appeared to have won handily—by 40,000 votes, according to initial reports—and Ferrer conceded defeat. However, the police and the media based this count upon flawed and unofficial reports from poll workers. Roughly 42,000 votes had been counted twice. After these revelations surfaced, Ferrer rescinded his concession and stated, "We don't know who won." He called for a "fair, complete, and accurate final count." As further reports came in from the board of elections, Green's margin narrowed, from 40,000 to 21,056 to 18,000, and then ultimately down to 15,981. We learned from Florida that reporting unofficial tallies on election night can reek havoc. The confusion in New York occurred particularly because the media had rushed to report unofficial results, which are produced by means of a complicated and error-prone system. Poll workers who have already worked a sixteen-hour day read numbers off the voting machines to police officials, who write down totals and bring the results to police headquarters. There the tallies are entered into a computer system and relayed to the media. At each juncture errors can easily be made.[51] Apparently, after polls closed on the night of the runoff election, the police misreported the results, a discovery that led to the drop in margin from 40,000 to 21,056. The drop to 18,000 occurred when the board of elections recanvassed the machines for the official vote totals, and the drop to 15,981 came with the final tallies of all the paper ballots, indicating that Ferrer had received more paper votes than Green.

The 2002 Elections

On November 5, 2002, New York held elections for statewide offices—governor, comptroller, attorney general, and state legislator. Despite efforts by the New York City Board of Elections to address several of the deficiencies found in the 2001 elections, similar patterns of election problems manifested themselves again in 2002.

For the second year in a row, the coalition of voting rights and civic groups conducted a citywide survey of poll-site conditions, again "to gauge how voters were treated at the polls in New York City." The lead organization, NYPIRG, published a report of the survey of voters, titled "Report from the Polls II." The 2002 survey found similar and significant election problems. Indeed, the results were almost identical to the results of the 2001 survey. "City election officials made little progress in improving city elections between 2001 and 2002: Despite new training initiatives, many poll workers still failed to correctly answer key questions about the rights of voters. Poll workers did not improve their performance in meeting key requirements to ask voters if they know how to use the lever voting machine."[52]

The kinds of obstacles voters faced in obtaining basic information were as bad or worse in some cases. For example, 59 percent of voters surveyed in 2002 were told by poll workers that registrants who have moved should vote at their old polling place rather than their new polling place. This is 5 percent higher than in 2001. Such incorrect information could lead to eligible voters being disenfranchised. Given the findings in the 2002 survey, particularly regarding poll workers failing to provide voters with sufficient information about how to properly use voting machines, coupled with the fact that the same voting machines were used in the 2002 elections, the total amount and proportion of lost votes were presumably comparable to the figures for 2000 and 2001.[53] In addition, AALDEF conducted a survey of over 3,000 Asian American voters at sixteen sites in Manhattan, Brooklyn, and Queens. The survey also produced findings similar to those of the 2001 elections—a large number of Asian American voters experienced various problems that led to their disenfranchisement.

On the brighter side, The New York City Board of Elections did not experience a shortage of voting machines in the 2002 elections. This was due in part to the fact that other jurisdictions had purchased electronic voting machines and sold their lever machines to the New York City board. In fact, nearly every election district that needed a machine had one, and most of the larger districts had two, as required. In addition, there were fewer poll-worker shortages. Several factors produced this outcome, including the fact that the board was able to maintain the increased pay for poll workers and that it worked more closely with civic groups to recruit workers and upgrade training.

Internally, the board instituted a new computer program called Maptitude. This program, which is used to draw EDs for redistricting purposes, also allows workers to visualize where registrants are in relationship to particular kinds of buildings and to determine if people are registered to vote improperly—from a work address, for instance. Five people were found to be registered at Macy's in Manhattan; others were registered at Rockefeller Plaza.[54] This program also permits the board to identify and correct data entry errors. In cases of questionable registrations, the board sends a letter to applicants notifying them that their registration will be canceled and giving them an opportunity to correct their registration status.

The 2004 Elections in New York: The Saga Continues

The 2004 elections in New York were business as usual. A familiar pattern of election problems beset voters across the state, with the largest number and most severe incidents in New York City. Although voter turnout was slightly higher in 2004 than in 2000, essentially the same provisions, election machinery, and personnel were in place. With the exception of new rules imposed by HAVA—especially the identification requirements for first-time voters who registered by mail—New York's election administration proceeded according to standard operating procedure. It was no surprise, then, that in New York City: "voters were once again faced with broken voting machines, long lines, poorly trained poll workers and chaos at too many polling sites." NYPIRG and Common Cause jointly established an Election Day telephone help line—which received over 3,000 calls on Election Day, nearly double the 1,800 calls they had received in 2000—and sent more than 150 poll-site monitors into the field. "Unfortunately, we received a steady stream of complaints about late poll site openings; broken voting machines; long lines; chaotic conditions at poll sites; voters being wrongly asked for IDs by clearly poorly trained poll workers; and bizarre poll worker improvisations, like voters being divided into lines of Republicans and Democrats. . . . The high turnout and intense interest in this year's election has highlighted some of the ongoing problems faced by voters in New York City. Simply put, too many voters faced too many problems trying to vote. The City and Board of Elections can and must do better."[55]

Similar problems were found in New York City by several other voting rights and civic organizations that mounted monitoring operations, including the Center for Independence of the Disabled, the League of Women Voters, the Women's City Club, and AALDEF. The groups' surveys of voters and election observers revealed the usual range of problems: poll-site access for disabled residents was limited, absentee ballots were never mailed to some eligible voters, names were missing from voter registration rolls, people were confused about the newly enacted HAVA law, language interpreters were lacking, and poll workers were requiring longtime voters to show identification and were deeming invalid many forms of identification that were considered acceptable under board of elections policy.[56]

AALDEF, which sent over six hundred volunteer attorneys, students, and community workers to over 175 poll sites in eight states, reported that Asian American voters faced significant obstacles in exercising their right to vote. Concentrating on New York, the group documented a variety of problems: racist remarks were made to Asian voters, election workers were misdirecting voters to incorrect poll stations, poll workers were improperly asking for ID and failing to give voters affidavit ballots, and fewer than the legally required number of bilingual poll workers and interpreters were available.[57]

Investigative journalists echoed such reports: "Many voters who went to the polls in New York City on Tuesday were met with long lines, broken voting machines and poorly trained poll workers despite a federal law designed to upgrade the voting system," reported *New York Newsday*.[58] Another typical report, from the *New York Times*, focused on deficiencies of the New York City Board of Elections: "Its Web site and phone lines, where thousands went looking for information about where to vote, failed. Tens of thousands of voters stood for hours at polls, where they frequently found befuddled workers who could not locate basic paperwork and gave incomprehensible directives, including, in one case, telling voters to segregate themselves by party affiliation. Antiquated mechanical voting machines at times broke down, and there were not enough mechanics on hand to fix them."[59]

These widespread complaints prompted Mayor Michael Bloomberg, who faces reelection in 2005, to announce plans to reconvene a special task force "to improve the Board's operations, increase its productivity, and hold it publicly accountable for its performance."[60] Bloomberg criticized the board's aging technology and its patronage system, which "dictates hiring decisions based on party connections, or family connections, not merit."[61]

Elections officials reacted by trying to minimize the extent and scope of the problems. Chris Riley, a spokesperson for the New York City Board of Elections, acknowledged that the board's telephone lines, overwhelmed by the large number of callers, had failed and that the board's Web site had crashed on the eve and the day of the election. Still, Riley said: "We believe things went well. No poll site had to be closed."[62]

Douglas Kellner, a commissioner of the New York City Board of Elections who has been a leader of effort to reform the board, pointed out that there have been improvements to the board's operations: "An objective comparison of election administration in New York City between 2004 and 2000 shows that there have been substantial improvements on a number of fronts. We have better poll workers. Our voting machines, although 40 years old, worked better this time than four years ago. Electronic ballot scanning of the absentee, affidavit and emergency ballots has become second nature." He concluded, however, that "we could still do an even better job."[63]

In the case of poll workers, for example, Kellner contended that there had been improvements, but that they were insufficient: "Although the Board could be more selective" because of the increased stipend, he explained, "it has not geared up a system of evaluating poll workers so that only those who are qualified are assigned. There are still a substantial number of poll workers who do not attend training classes. I am also troubled by that fact that when I travel to poll sites I observe poll workers who appear to be unqualified even though they have attained passing scores on the 'test' that is given after training."[64]

Advocates also acknowledge that there have been improvements, and they support the board's efforts, but their assessment of the board's performance yielded a sharper critique: "While many poll workers are hard working and dedicated, it's clear that too many don't know the rules or should be replaced." Similarly, regarding machine malfunctions advocates are less forbearing: "There were 485 official 'trouble calls' identifying nonfunctioning voting machines on Election Day, that's just too many."[65] Because of such malfunctions—5 percent of the machines in the fleet broke down—voters were forced to use 14,000 emergency ballots on election day, making the likelihood of error and thus voter disenfranchisement greater. Although advocates acknowledge the challenging circumstances elections officials operate under, they demand greater accountability and better performance. "They are poorly paid, underresourced and they have a fleet of jalopies to deal with," advocates charged. "But that doesn't excuse 5 percent of machines breaking on Election Day."[66] The board did, however, replace the machines' sensor latches, which likely reduced the number of lost votes.

Regarding the board's telephone bank and Web site, which were overwhelmed by high demand in the days leading up to the election and on election day itself, advocates have consistently been critical: "It's an embarrassment the Board of Elections web site crashed the day before the election. Unfortunately it's more embarrassing when a voter can make it on to the site. It's time that the Board's web site should be able to tell voters if they're registered, where their poll site is located and give them a look at a sample ballot for their district. NYPIRG has raised these problems year after year and there has been little if any improvement in this area."[67]

Although no thorough analyses of the extent and impact of election problems have yet been completed at the time of this writing, they will likely show similar patterns of voter disenfranchisement as in previous recent New York City elections. In addition, these and other kinds of voting problems, such as singling out students for special scrutiny, reappeared in various counties in the state. Elections officials told a student at Hamilton College in Clinton, for example, that he was not a permanent resident and therefore had to vote from his parents' home in another state.[68]

New York also witnessed partisan wrangling over election practices in several close races, including one hotly contested race that remain unsettled even after the new year began. In that election, incumbent Nicholas A. Spano (R) had a five-hundred-vote lead over challenger Andrea Stewart-Cousins (D) in the race for the Senate seat in Westchester County on election night, but after a court-ordered recount began, his lead dwindled to less than a hundred votes out of over 113,000 cast. Lawyers for both sides sparred over standards and procedures for counting over 5,200 absentee ballots, about 3,500 affidavit ballots, and hundreds of disputed votes that one side or the other contended were ineligible or fraudulent, including votes cast by students, residents in a homeless shelter, and election workers themselves. In each instance the standards employed and the interpretation of the election law used to determine whether contested ballots were valid or invalid were sharply debated, precisely because they could shape the outcome.

For example, over forty-five absentee ballots were cast by poll workers who could not vote in person at the poll site of their residence because they were working at a different polling station. Because almost all of these absentee ballots were cast by registered Democrats, lawyers for Mr. Spano sought to have them invalidated by arguing that the judge assigned to the case should strictly adhere to election law, which technically requires poll workers to vote by special ballot and those who will be out of the county on election day to vote by absentee ballot. Interestingly, Westchester County election commissioners from both parties said they did not know about that part of the election law, and that they have always directed elections workers to vote by absentee ballot if they are working a station not their own. Moreover, the Westchester poll-worker handbook instructs workers to use absentee ballots, not special ballots. "Lawyers for Ms.

Stewart-Cousins argued that it was unfair to disenfranchise registered voters because of errors made by elections officials, while lawyers for Mr. Spano countered that the law must be enforced, however harsh the penalty."[69] Each side maneuvered during the months-long recount to have these and other kinds of ballots either thrown out or counted, depending on how they believed it would affect the outcome of the recount. In the end Spano retained his seat, winning by eighteen votes.

Legislatively the continued stalemate between the Democratically controlled Assembly and Republican-controlled Senate left New York at the close of 2004 as one out of only five states in the country that had not received federal funds provided by HAVA.[70] As of early 2005, New York stood to lose up to $200 million, primarily to replace its lever voting machines, because the state had not yet certified its compliance with federal mandates, which included enacting requisite legislation, appropriating 5 percent matching funds, and establishing an administrative complaint procedure. Some election reform advocates worried that New York might fail to meet federal requirements in time to obtain the funding.[71] Even after the legislation is adopted and state funds are allocated, bids will need to be evaluated and new voting machines purchased, election workers will need to be trained to use the new equipment, and voters will need to be educated.[72]

Conclusion

Despite improvements to the operations of the New York City Board of Elections over the past two decades and particularly after the 2000 elections, many election problems continue to beset the board. Moreover, the range of election problems had significant impacts on voters and candidates. Particular practices and election problems contributed to voter disenfranchisement. In several instances, minority constituencies were disproportionately affected. These patterns of problems and voter disenfranchisement contributed to the outcomes of several elections, particularly for mayor and public advocate. The state has a long way to go to create an election system that efficiently and effectively serves all New Yorkers.

Implications for Policy

E. E. Schattschneider has said: "The most legitimate question to be asked in a democracy is:—how can people get control of the government."[1] Elections are one of the most acceptable political means to achieve this end. One way in which democracy has been thwarted, however, is by restrictions on access to the franchise. Election administration has played a role in constricting democracy so that the people cannot "get control of the government," in part because a considerable number of them have been stymied and disenfranchised by the way in which elections are administered.

The social and historical dimensions of nonvoting in the United States suggest that electorates are shaped by and are the result of politics. The stunted development of the American electorate is partially a product of politics. This is particularly the case for urban, poor, and minority communities whose marginalization from the democratic process is further reflected in government policies that slight them. In a political democracy such disparities raise troubling questions about the legitimacy of public policy and governance.

But the news is not all bad. The project of democracy is ongoing, and we have seen that electoral processes can be improved. My hope is that this book will contribute to knowledge about causes of nonvoting and methods to improve electoral participation. I have tried to show that formal electoral arrangements are not neutral in their impact on voter participation and that, instead, electoral rules and institutions are sites of political struggle and are shaped by these struggles. The outcomes of such conflicts have important consequences for electoral politics. Such has been the case in New York.

This book shows that election practices matter: particular practices of boards of elections can decrease or increase voter registration and participation by decreasing or increasing the likelihood that eligible voters can vote and that their votes will be counted. Moreover, we found that distinct political actors and interests are associated with the different electoral procedures and administrative practices that can facilitate such decreases or increases, producing differential impacts on particular constituencies. In short, election administration acts as a gatekeeper, blocking or facilitating access to the franchise. In New York, this gatekeeping function has contributed to several critical electoral outcomes, and such outcomes, in turn, have had important impacts on politics and policy. These findings point to a set of best practices and to reform measures that can improve elections.

If nothing else, this book is a cautionary tale that has implications for the debate about voting behavior. While there is little dispute among scholars about who the voters and the nonvoters are, disagreement centers on questions about why such disparities exist and, occasionally, about the consequences of these patterns of participation, and especially about what might remedy these circumstances. I suggest that the relationships social scientists have found between nonvoting and social variables such as education, income, age, and race may result, in part, from particular election laws and practices. Although several factors certainly contribute to their low voter participation, the implementation of electoral rules and administrative practices also matters. In short, the gatekeeping capacity of election administrators is significant and is a piece of the puzzle of participation. Scholars have not adequately recognized that the implementation of election law and the practices of institutions of election administration can affect both patterns of voter participation and electoral outcomes. Nor have they sufficiently acknowledged and analyzed the political environments and relations associated with such institutions and practices.

Countless eligible citizens have been deprived of their voting rights in New York—hundreds of thousands in New York City alone during the past two decades. Voter disenfranchisement occurred because of a broad variety of problems in the administration of the elections. The patterns of voter disenfranchisement in New York—with the problems disproportionately affecting urban, low-income, and minority constituents—are consistent with the findings of research on the impact of election administration on voter participation in other jurisdictions. The conclusion that voter disenfranchisement was widespread in New York elections is inescapable when the findings of studies of election practices in other cities and states are also considered; disenfranchising election administration practices are not unique to New York, as documented in studies conducted by national and state voting rights and civic organizations, election experts, and academics, as well as congressional and government agency staff.[2]

This assessment is further corroborated in the dozens of interviews and discussions I have had with election administrators and experts on elections in New York, in other states, and nationally. Throughout the country poor election administration performance—whether a matter of poor planning, inadequate training, insufficient staffing, overcrowded and confusing poll-site conditions, lack of effective means for poll workers and voters to communicate with elections officials, prejudicial treatment, or political machinations—has led to a significant number of eligible voters being disenfranchised. Similarly, documents from court cases also show how election administration produces voter disenfranchisement.[3]

Suppression of Registration and Turnout in Other Jurisdictions

Partisan struggles at the turn of the twentieth century over voter registration procedures and the establishment of bipartisan election administration revealed the stakes involved for the political actors and constituencies engaged in and affected by these conflicts. The victorious political actors who shaped these election laws, institutions, and practices contributed to the marked decline in voter participation during the twentieth century. Today's restrictive registration procedures and election administration practices are the legacy of these historical developments; despite some liberalization they are still used by contemporary political actors, particularly Republicans and conservative Democrats, to maintain low registration and turnout, especially for low-income and minority voters. The suppression of registration and turnout produced by these election practices has had important electoral and policy consequences, particularly at the state and local levels. These findings suggest that investigation of other jurisdictions may shed further light on these issues.

For example, Secretary of State Katherine Harris (R) of Florida hired a private firm to identify suspected felons so their names could be removed from the registration rolls, then she ordered the removal of 94,000 suspected felons from the registries. However, many of the registrants purged in Florida were not actual felons but instead were legitimate voters with names similar to those of felons in the state, and most of the people affected were members of racial minorities and likely Democratic voters. Studies have estimated that tens of thousands of eligible voters showed up to vote in Florida on November 7, 2000, but were wrongfully turned away, at least in part due to this purge. Whether by design or default, this kind of voter disenfranchisement alone contributed to the outcome of the 2000 presidential election and therefore to the policies successfully pursued by the Bush administration.[4]

In 1993 Republicans similarly brought pressure to bear on the New York City Board of Elections to eliminate allegedly fraudulent registrations, and a significant number of minority voters were purged from the rolls. Another part of the Republicans' ballot-security operation entailed hiring over seven hundred off-duty police and fire personnel and deploying them to predominantly minority districts. While these "poll watchers" ostensibly were there to monitor the polls and ensure the integrity of the voting process, in many instances they capriciously challenged the credentials of registered voters—particularly minority voters—creating disruptions, delays, and confusion that led to hundreds of additional voters being intimidated and disenfranchised. These developments had a negative impact on the participation of members of minority constituencies, contributing to the defeat of Mayor Dinkins and the election of Mayor Giuliani, and to subsequent public policy changes. Unfortunately, there are other such examples in New York and across the country.

In fact, Republican-sponsored ballot-security measures have been "used to keep minorities from voting" in many states. In 2004 various voter suppression and intimidation tactics were employed in Texas, Kentucky, Ohio, Illinois, Florida, Arizona, and Pennsylvania; in 2002 they were used in South Dakota, Arkansas, Michigan, and South Carolina; and earlier episodes occurred in New Jersey, North Carolina, Louisiana, Georgia, Missouri, Michigan, and Indiana.[5]

In the name of protecting the integrity of the ballot from fraud, elected officials and elections administrators of both major parties instead perpetrated a worse and more insidious form of fraud: bureaucratic disenfranchisement of eligible voters, particularly low-income voters and members of racial and ethnic minorities. Such disenfranchising election practices have disproportionately harmed Democrats, especially particular factions and candidates within the Democratic Party, and minor-party candidates for decades. Vote fraud is minimal in the United States. "Disenfranchisement of voters through antiquated voting systems, system error, and improper management of registration databases, as occurred in Florida in the 2000 election, is a far bigger problem than traditional forms of election fraud."[6]

The political implications of measures aimed at shaping election practices—agency-based voter registration programs, the NVRA, and HAVA—have been lost on neither Republicans nor Democrats. In New York we saw how Republicans sought to limit expansion of the electorate in general and among likely Democratic voters in particular by thwarting full and fair implementation of such measures. The relatively poor performance of the NVRA early on in New York compared with other states, and particularly in New York City, suggests that Republicans were mindful of this and that they were successful to a significant degree. Yet pressure by voting rights advocates and liberal Democrats who sought to ensure effective implementation of the NVRA—especially for low-income and minority voters and those in New York City—apparently not only limited the extent of Republicans' attempts to thwart the NVRA but also forced improvements in implementation in 1996 and beyond. Full implementation of the NVRA, coupled with well-designed and implemented HAVA measures, could further boost voter participation.

Such developments have the potential to alter the balance of political power. In New York this potential is evident if one considers the number of clients served by agencies mandated to provide voter registration under the NVRA. The Department of Motor Vehicles, for example, has more than 4 million transactions yearly, and all driver's license holders interact with the DMV at least once every four years. Two additional agencies, the Department of Social Services and the Department of Labor, which see over a million clients per year, reached another significant sector of the unregistered eligible population. Other mandated agencies—such as those that serve the aged and people with disabilities—reach another million people. In addition, New York City's Pro-Voter law, enacted in 2000 after years of inactivity by the New York City Voter Assistance Commission (VAC), mandates an additional thirty New York City agencies to provide voter registration opportunities to their clients, reaching yet another million city residents. Therefore, if these laws were fully implemented, the several million eligible but unregistered New Yorkers—almost 2 million in New York City—would have the opportunity to register to vote. Depending on other developments, a surge in voter participation by low-income and minority voters could have a decisive impact in municipal elections in New York City, in statewide races, and in federal elections. If, instead, the Republicans who control the administrations at the state and city levels continue to blunt the impact of Pro-Voter, VAC, the NVRA, and HAVA, their dominance may be sustained.

Such political maneuvering is not unique to New York; it is also evident in other states. Take Missouri, for example. In 2004 Missouri's chief election official, Secretary of State Matt Blunt (R), ran for governor against incumbent Bob Holden (D). Blunt, who was active in the Bush-Cheney campaign in one of the biggest political battleground states in 2004, presided over Missouri's election apparatus. In 2004 Blunt tried to stop St. Louis from holding early voting so voters could cast ballots before election day. St. Louis, which is home to a large black population and votes overwhelmingly Democratic, sought to implement early voting to avoid the kinds of problems that occurred in 2000 when elections officials wrongly prevented many voters from casting ballots by closing poll sites early and not allowing voters in line to cast ballots. Even though the Missouri state legislature passed a law allowing St. Louis to implement early voting, Blunt issued a decree stating the law did not authorize early voting to occur in 2004, even though the bipartisan sponsors of the law held the opposite interpretation. Tellingly, Blunt went out of his way to help a group that usually votes Republican to cast ballots—soldiers in combat zones. Blunt allowed soldiers to vote by fax, which other voters are not allowed to do because faxed ballots are not secret. Blunt went on to defeat Holden in 2004.[7]

Similar dynamics were evident in how HAVA measures were being designed and implemented at the state level. For example, in 2000 millions of voters' names were not on the rolls on election day. Under HAVA, voters who experience this problem must be given the option of voting on a provisional ballot. Some states and elections officials have interpreted this new HAVA requirement narrowly, disqualifying ballots cast by registered voters who show up at the wrong polling place; others have interpreted it broadly, allowing such ballots to be counted, at least for statewide and federal offices. Florida, Missouri, Ohio, and Colorado have either laws or rules promulgated by the state's chief election official—all Republicans in these battleground states—that disqualify ballots cast by duly registered voters who do not get to their correct polling place. In many such instances, however, the fault often lies not with voters who go to the wrong site, but with poll workers who do not direct them to the proper poll site, or with elections officials who sent out voter notification cards late or with incorrect information. A larger number of voters experienced these problems in 2004 because polling places were moved due to redistricting that occurred in 2002 and because of the influx of millions of new registrants late in the campaign season, which delayed voter notification mailings.

In one particularly revealing case, Secretary of State Donetta Davidson (R) of Colorado issued a ruling allowing provisional ballots cast in the wrong polling place to count, but only for president, not for U.S. Senate. It was expected that the Senate race in Colorado, which was predicted to be one of the closest in the nation, could determine which party would control the Senate. Thus the consequences and motives of such rule making are clear: more voters would be disenfranchised—particularly movers, who disproportionately are low-income and minority individuals, who tend to vote Democratic. As a recent a *New York Times* editorial pointedly characterized the situation: "The wrong-precinct rule serves no legitimate purpose, and it denies eligible voters the right to vote."[8] On the other hand, states that employ a more liberal rule on provisional ballots ensure that more votes cast are actually counted, which embodies the original idea behind this provision of HAVA.

The 2004 Election

Contrary to popular belief, election problems were more abundant in 2004 than in 2000. A wide range of voting rights organizations, civic groups, and partisan campaigns mounted monitoring operations and documented election problems before, during, and after the election that led to the disenfranchisement of hundreds of thousands—perhaps millions—of eligible voters. In many instances restrictive and slipshod election practices were the cause of such problems. All too often, the hand of partisan officials was evident.[9]

Restrictive voter registration procedures revealed such partisan underpinnings. Florida's secretary of state, Republican Glenda Hood, for example, presided over the planning of a purge of over forty thousand suspected felons from the registration lists. The plan was reminiscent of one facet of the 2000 debacle, but this time voting rights advocates prevailed. Their litigation and ensuing scrutiny by media outlets showed the list of felons to be flawed and forced Hood to scrap the plan to use it. In some jurisdictions—including Florida and Iowa—elections officials routinely rejected applications by registrants who failed to check a box indicating that they are a citizen, even though they were required to sign an attestation swearing, under penalty of perjury (a felony), that they are a citizen and qualified to vote. Although voting rights advocates sued Florida's Hood over this and similar restrictive registration requirements, the suit was dismissed on procedural grounds before the election.[10] Thousands of otherwise eligible would-be voters were disenfranchised because of these restrictive election practices.

In Ohio, Republican secretary of state Kenneth Blackwell ordered that registration forms must be submitted on eighty-pound or heavier paper stock, which meant that anyone who downloaded a voter registration form from an elections Web site and printed it out on normal twenty-pound paper stock, filled it out, and submitted it would be disenfranchised: the application would be rejected. Although this rule was rescinded after intense criticism and pressure, including the threat of a lawsuit, no one knows for sure what happened to the applications submitted that did not meet the specification while the rule was in effect. Presumably such applications were rejected, and an unknown number of voters were therefore disenfranchised.[11]

Elections officials in some jurisdictions, including Florida and North Carolina, required registrants who submitted applications before the registration deadline to also make any necessary corrections to their forms before that deadline, which led to thousands of such applications being rejected and these would-be voters being disenfranchised.[12] Such practices particularly affected people of color. A *Washington Post* analysis of Miami-Dade County showed that 35 percent of these rejected registration applications were filled out by African Americans and 25 percent by Latinos.[13] In Ohio, Republicans challenged 35,000 new registrants, disproportionately minority and low-income voters, when information packets mailed to them at the residence listed on their applications were returned as undeliverable. Elections officials called some registrants in before election day, requiring them to testify in person that they were who they claimed to be and resided at the address on the form. This practice was eventually stopped but not before many such registrants were disqualified or intimidated.[14] In New Hampshire students were told that they would lose financial aid if they did not complete a questionnaire prior to registering to vote.[15] Similar problems occurred in state after state, all in the name of safeguarding the ballot from election fraud.

There were also the all-too-common cases of elections officials and staff at government agencies such as social service offices and the Department of Motor Vehicles "losing" voter registration forms or committing administrative errors, failing to process forms in a timely manner, and so on. Given that over a million voters experienced registration problems of this sort in the 2000 election, it is likely that a comparable number of people were thus disenfranchised in 2004.[16]

Ironically, some of provisions of HAVA were manipulated by state elections officials, leading to voter disenfranchisement. This was particularly the case with provisional balloting, or fail-safe voting, a reform intended to provide duly registered voters a means to cast a ballot in the event that their name does not appear on the voter rolls—an omission that can happen for many reasons, including errors by elections officials. More than 1.2 million provisional ballots were cast in 2004. Congress did not specify how they would be used and counted: these decisions were left up to the states, many of which adopted overly restrictive rules that undermined the intent of the remedy. Provisional ballots were to the 2004 election what butterfly ballots and hanging chads had been to the 2000 contest.

Two-thirds of the states had already been using some form of fail-safe voting before the 2000 elections, and two types of systems had emerged— one that is more restrictive and disenfranchises eligible voters, and another that is more lenient and allows more votes to be counted. In 2004, twenty-eight states considered provisional ballots valid only if they were cast in the correct voting precinct or polling place.[17] The problem with this rule is many voters end up in the wrong polling place because elections officials misdirect them, change poll sites without notifying them, or never tell them were to go in the first place. A typical example involved a voter in Missouri who was sent to four different polling places by election workers. Each time the workers told him that he was at the wrong polling place, but they could not tell him where his correct polling station was. At the fourth poll site he cast a provisional ballot, which was thrown out because he was supposed to have voted at a fifth polling station.[18] Unfortunately such examples were numerous, as documented by the election monitoring projects and in postelection analyses.[19]

The more lenient rule, which existed in seventeen states, allowed ballots cast in the correct jurisdiction—usually the county, township, or city—to be valid.[20] The NVRA defined a registered voter's jurisdiction as their county, and HAVA is to be read in conformity with the NVRA, but over half of the states enacted contrary legislation or had elections officials who treated such ballots more strictly.

Given the prediction that the election would be close—and thus the probability that such rules that could swing the election one way or another—Democrats and Republicans sought to shape how states and localities would treat provisional ballots. Democrats sued several states, including the battleground states of Ohio, Florida, Michigan, and Missouri, to expand the scope of the "place" in which such ballots would be considered valid, which would have the effect of increasing the number of votes counted. By contrast, Republicans moved to have provisional ballots counted as valid only at the narrow voter precinct level, as in Iowa. The Republican-controlled Department of Justice intervened in Michigan and argued that provisional ballots cast outside the voter's precinct must be thrown out. In every case, the courts (often with Republican-nominated judges presiding) ruled against the plaintiffs and with the restrictionists.[21]

Voter identification was another problem area in which partisan wrangling was evident. HAVA requires first-time voters whose applications will be delivered to the board of elections by mail to present identification to an elections official either at the time they register or when they vote. The acceptable list of identification is vague, but it does indicate that voters may present a current valid photo ID, a government document that shows the voter's name and address, a utility bill, or a bank statement. Young people, low-income individuals, minorities, newly naturalized citizens, and people with disabilities are much less likely than others to posses the identification the law requires. Many members of these groups do not own a vehicle, posses a driver's license, or live in a household with bills in their name. Importantly, these voters tend to disproportionately register Democrat and vote for Democrats. Thus when seventeen states require *all* voters to show identification at the polls—six of them having enacted such a law in 2003 alone[22]—it raises questions about the political motivations behind establishing these requirements.

In Ohio Secretary of State Blackwell issued a directive stating that if a first-time registrant whose application was submitted by mail did not present identification at the polls the provisional ballot would not count unless the voter produced ID by the end of election day. But HAVA clearly states that provisional ballots are to be verified and counted after the election, and Ohio law does not require identification. Although Blackwell's directive was challenged in court by the League of Women voters, the lawsuit lost, and many first-time registrants lost their vote.[23] Two other states refused to give provisional ballots to voters who did not have identification, and another ten states automatically threw out provisional ballots of all voters who could not present identification by the end of election day.[24] By contrast, fifteen states validated provisional ballots as long as voters were properly registered and, if they couldn't produce identification on the day of the election, presented ID to elections officials shortly after election day.[25]

As we have seen throughout this study, in the name of safeguarding the ballot from fraud, by implementing such rules elections officials perpetrated another, more insidious form of fraud against the voters themselves—politically motivated administrative disenfranchisement. The number of voters disenfranchised by these practices is unknown, but the tens of thousands of complaints received by the monitoring projects indicate that the number was significant. These state actions "eviscerated the better parts of HAVA; made them into false promises."[26]

Machine failures were again an obstacle to voting in 2004. Although questions about the integrity of new electronic machines dominated the news, another factor produced serious problems for voters: the insufficient number of machines. There were too few machines in too many places across the country, so voters had to wait for hours in long lines.[27] Given the long-held expectations of higher turnout, the insufficient number of voting machines raises disturbing questions: Were elections officials merely unprepared (whether due to incompetence or lack of resources)? Or were these circumstances an intentional means to suppress voter turnout? In the November election Ohio had fewer voting machines in cities with large minority populations than it had in previous elections, including the March 2004 presidential primary.[28] Franklin County, Ohio, where a large number of African Americans reside, experienced significant delays, as did the campus of Kenyon College, where only two voting machines were deployed. Some voters reported waiting eight to ten hours in line. Because the wait times were so bad, a federal judge ordered that the polls be kept open past the closing time and that paper ballots be distributed to voters in line.[29] Although the monitoring projects documented cases of people simply leaving the lines and not voting, no one knows how many did so. Whether these conditions were created by design or default, widespread voter disenfranchisement was the result.

Old machine problems persisted while new ones arose. Tens of millions voted on faulty punch-card systems and error-prone lever machines, and 29 percent of the electorate used new electronic voting machines.[30] Aside from the plethora of voting machine breakdowns and other, now familiar problems—including over 92,000 ballots in Ohio that did not record a vote for president, 76,000 of them from punch-card machines—there were mysterious incidents of vote totals changing, and without a voter-verifiable paper trail there was no way to ensure that votes were recorded as voters intended to cast them.[31] Many observers and analysts marvel that the world's richest country relegates different voters, depending on where they live, to the use voting technologies that vary widely in efficiency and accuracy, particularly in light of the *Bush* v. *Gore,* ruling, which calls for a single standard for the casting and counting of ballots.[32]

As usual, there were myriad poll-worker-related problems: workers did not give voters provisional ballots even though they were supposed to, some machine malfunctions were due to poor poll-worker training and poll-worker errors, some workers gave out misinformation, and so on.[33] Most disturbingly, there were serious efforts to suppress the vote, primarily by partisan poll watchers and groups associated with party operatives. In a manner reminiscent of the episodes in New York City in 1993 and at the turn of the twentieth century, just days before the election, the Republican Party in several states announced plans to "challenge" preselected voters whom they suspected of being improperly registered or unqualified to vote. In Ohio Republican poll watchers planned to challenge the 35,000 first-time voters whose information packets had been returned as undeliverable. The Republican Party had agreed to end a similar practice in 1982 as part of a settlement to a lawsuit brought by Democrats in New Jersey. Tactics like this had not been used in Ohio in many years.[34] Voting rights groups responded by challenging the use of this practice, claiming it was being deployed to intimidate and disenfranchise primarily minorities and voters in Democratic strongholds. Initially a court ruled in favor of the voting rights groups, but upon appeal the practice was deemed valid. On election day voters were challenged in mostly minority neighborhoods, which apparently led to eligible voters being required to vote on provisional ballots or turned away.[35]

In Florida, Republicans compiled a database of thousands of voters they believed to be felons or to have falsely registered. Officers from the Florida state Department of Law Enforcement entered the homes of elderly black voters in Orlando to interrogate them, stating that they were looking for potential vote fraud. Some of the individuals questioned were volunteers in get-out-the-vote campaigns.[36] In Wisconsin the GOP tried to challenge registrants they considered suspect in Milwaukee, a Democratic stronghold. Similar efforts were mounted in Nevada and Colorado.[37] In Detroit, Michigan, where more than 80 percent of the population is black, John Pappageorge, a Republican state legislator, said: "If we do not suppress the Detroit vote . . . we're going to have a tough time in this election."[38]

Under Attorney General John Ashcroft, the U.S. Department of Justice shifted its focus from ensuring voter access by identifying and prosecuting civil rights violations to "voter integrity," a pursuit of potentially fraudulent voters that often results in restrictive practices that disenfranchise eligible voters and suppress especially the minority vote.[39] "Justice Department challenges of racially discriminatory voting cases have virtually halted," contends one expert. Its prosecution of alleged civil rights violations dropped from 159 cases in 1999 to 84 in 2003.[40]

Determination of a winner in several close and contested races continued well past election day and in some cases even extended into the new year. In the governor's race in Washington state, Republican Dino Rossi, who early on led Democrat Christine O. Gregoire by 261 votes out of over 2.9 million cast, saw his lead slip to 42 votes, and then watched his opponent come out in front after court battles and hand and machine recounts.[41] In the course of the weeks and months, both sides maneuvered to exclude or include ballots and tried to influence how different counties used varying standards to validate or invalidate disputed votes—all with the obvious intent of shaping the outcome.

These sorts of issues led to a variety of lawsuits, most of which flew under the public radar screen. In Ohio, where a margin of 136,000 votes (out of 5.5 million cast, or about 2.5%) gave George W. Bush the electoral college majority he needed to win the presidency, the National Voting Rights Institute and Michael Badnarik and David Cobb of the Libertarian and Green parties, respectively, filed a lawsuit, seeking a review of 155,000 provisional ballots and a recount of all ballots. Calls to investigate voting problems in Ohio—including overly long lines, voting machine malfunctions, uneven allocation of machines, vote suppression tactics, and lack of uniform policies on provisional ballots—became the subject of a rare formal challenge of the electoral votes in Congress, led by Democratic senator Barbara Boxer of California and Stephanie Tubbs Jones, a representative from Ohio.[42]

Although no one expected the outcome of the election to change, the lawsuits, recounts, and investigations by federal agencies and voting rights groups will not be the end of calls to improve America's voting systems. Doug Chapin, director of electionline.org, a nonpartisan group that monitors reform efforts, said: "This is not a fringe issue, because a sizable group is interested in pursuing this as a policy issue going forward. There's now a critical mass of people involved who want to address the problems that occurred in 2004. This issue is not going to go away."[43] These episodes fly in the face of the view that the 2004 elections ran smoothly, and they do not inspire confidence in our election system.

The gatekeeping role of election administration—the role of either blocking or facilitating voting—is evident in each of these cases, as are partisan political considerations, interests, and consequences. In New York the policy impacts of Republican electoral gains in the state and city have been significant. Analysts have noted that cuts to state and city government expenditures for social services, public education, and housing fall disproportionately on low-income and minority individuals. At the same time, Republicans have offered a mix of tax cuts and subsidies that predominately benefit businesses and upper-income groups. According to one critic, Republicans are "energetically engaged in redistributing income upward." Fiscal analysts have echoed this sentiment about current state and city fiscal policy.[44]

Competing Explanations for Election Practices and Problems

Three explanations are generally offered to explain the kinds of disenfranchising practices this book documents. Each explanation comes from a different set of groups involved in elections: elected officials and election administrators; election experts, academics, and investigative journalists; and voting rights groups and reform advocates. While some overlap exists between these groups' explanations of board practices, each group presents a particular perspective on why election boards operate the way they do and why voter disenfranchisement occurs. When the first group, elected officials and election administrators, acknowledges that these disenfranchising practices of election administration occur at all, it tends to attribute the practices primarily to necessities created by legal requirements for ballot security, budgetary limitations, or voter ignorance. The second group, election experts and journalists, generally ascribes disenfranchisement to election administration's bureaucratic inertia, inefficiency, and incompetence. The third group, advocates, focuses on dominant political relationships, which, it argues, shape election practices and outcomes.

Although I emphasize the political-relations explanation, each of these explanations has merit. Indeed, a more comprehensive approach seems to lie in delineating the connections between the three, which are not mutually exclusive but rather complementary.

Legal Constraints, Security Concerns, and Budgetary Limitations

Some elected officials and election administrators maintain that legal strictures, security requirements, and budgetary constraints best account for registration procedures and board practices that may hinder voter participation. They contend that election boards generally operate satisfactorily and in line with reasonable expectations, given their legal requirements and budgetary limitations. To be sure, legal and budgetary limitations are many and real. States' constitutions and election law do assign mandates, delimit activity, set time frames, and set the parameters within which elections officials operate. My examination of New York's constitutional provisions, election statutes, and court rulings reveals a long history of preoccupation with the particulars of voter registration and election administration. The specific data elements required on voter registration forms, the language and layout of such forms and ballots, the means of distributing and processing forms, the appointment of board staff and recruitment of poll workers, the selection of poll sites, and the conduct of election-day operations are detailed in such rules. In the case of the New York City Board of Elections, although it is funded wholly by the city, it is a creature of the state and is subject to state oversight.

Regarding the question of possible disenfranchisement, elections officials contend that if anyone is turned away on election day or casts an affidavit ballot that is invalidated, the individual is ineligible to vote as defined in the election law, and the person's inability to vote does not reflect practices of the board of elections. For example, as a safeguard against fraud, New York law requires individuals to register twenty-five days or more prior to an election, and in a prescribed manner. If a person attempts to vote without registering in a proper and timely way, the board of elections is required to disallow the ballot. Another example of a legal safeguard against fraud is the nonvoting purge, which was in effect until a 1990 court injunction halted it in New York. Election boards were required to remove from the rolls the names of registrants who had not voted within a four-year period in order to reduce "deadwood." And until 1992 election law required a citizen to register sixty days in advance of a party's primary election in order to vote. Elections officials contend that such registration safeguards are necessary to protect the integrity of the ballot.

Even when boards acknowledge that some administrative errors occur, they contend that such errors are unintentional and few in number, and that they do not affect electoral outcomes. Furthermore, they argue that low rates of registration and participation are primarily due to other factors, such as voter ignorance, apathy, disaffection, and so on.

In addition, elections officials contend that boards have traditionally been underfunded, particularly for programs that might expand the franchise. Elections officials consider themselves to be the stepchildren of government. For example, R. Doug Lewis, executive director of the Election Center, an international service association of election and registration officials, wrote in a memo to elections officials in 1995: "We are continually asked to do more with less. And, because of what I call the 1776 Syndrome ('We've had elections since 1776 and never had to spend any real money on them but we keep having them'), we are almost always the red-headed step-children of the budgetary process at almost all levels of government." Independent observers similarly characterize election administration. The National Municipal League, for example, said: "Election administration is an orphan of state government, underfinanced and relegated to an obscure position."[45]

It is true that boards generally occupy poor facilities, lack effective technology, and underpay their staff. Board employees contend that they are typically paid less than most comparable government employees. Having come from working- or middle-class backgrounds for the most part, elections officials resent being scapegoated unjustly by critics they consider to be elitist and ill-informed, such as advocates, journalists, scholars, and some elected officials. Indeed, in many respects boards are the whipping boys of such critics, especially elected officials. Governors Cuomo and Pataki, Assembly Democrats and Senate Republicans, Mayors Koch, Dinkins, Giuliani, and Bloomberg, and many City Council members have blamed elections officials for failures of election systems under their regimes. Elections officials counter that their operations are underfunded by state and county officials, who then turn around and unjustly blame the boards for inadequate registration and participation. Nevertheless, while boards have periodically made requests for budget increases, they have rarely made requests for funding for outreach programs.

Clearly legal and budgetary restrictions and the requirement that election boards safeguard the ballot are real, and clearly they negatively impact the state and city boards' capacity to carry out their mandate. Yet elections officials themselves are increasingly acknowledging that administrative problems exist.[46]

While we can acknowledge that the legal and budgetary straightjackets that elections officials find themselves in contribute to restrictions on access to registration and voting, we have also seen how election boards retain broad discretionary powers to shape the implementation of election law, the use of funds, the activities and deployment of personnel, the kinds of equipment used, election procedures, and so on. While to some extent election law is specific about a host of restrictive practices related to the distribution and processing of voter registration forms, the adjudication of affidavit ballots, the recruitment and training of board employees and poll workers, the deployment of voting machines, and election-day operations, the law allows for vast discretion on the part of election boards and produces differential outcomes.

Justification of such policies in terms of budgetary constraints and security concerns might be more properly viewed as a reflection of historical developments and the interests of dominant politicians. For example, New York City's 1984 election debacle highlighted numerous election problems that gave greater force to the lobbying efforts of a coalition of reform advocates who successfully pressed the Koch administration to increase funding and institute changes to modernize the New York City Board of Elections. Unfortunately, some of these gains were reversed, largely due to pressure brought to bear on the board by state and city Republicans associated with the Giuliani campaign of 1993. Budget cuts and security measures further curtailed the board's progress. The advent of the NVRA and the intense pressure from voting rights groups and the media in the wake of Florida's 2000 election helped restore funding to the state and city boards of elections in New York and also prompted important improvements. Thus legal constraints, security concerns, and budget limitations have political considerations at their root.

To be sure, the blame for voter disenfranchisement does not lie solely with election administration. Yet in most of the cases analyzed in this book, boards of elections have largely been responsible for disenfranchising outcomes. Moreover, in many instances distinct partisan and political interests have been involved in such election practices and outcomes. As advocates have long maintained: "State and local governments allot only a tiny fraction of their budgets to election matters. We recognize there is a tendency among many public officials to give the election process low funding priority once they take office. Yet, elections are fundamental to government. They dictate its composition and, to a great extent, its decisions. . . . The costs of the changes we've discussed are small in the general scheme of things and well worth it."[47] And advocates have come to the conclusion that such underfunding is not accidental: "Why would elected officials want to allot significant funds to expand the franchise when they were elected by a smaller electorate? It's not in their interest."[48]

Bureaucratic Inertia, Inefficiency, and Incompetence

Some election experts, scholars, and investigative journalists, as well as some civic groups, maintain that faulty election administration is one more example of government ineptitude and incrementalism. They attribute many of the election problems that depress registration and turnout to the way bureaucracies work—or do not work. Similarly, the initial failure of attempts in New York to expand the franchise through agency-based registration initiatives is also attributed to bureaucracies' characteristic inefficiency and slowness to change. Scholars of public administration and policy processes have produced numerous studies analyzing examples of inefficient and ineffective government agencies and policies, and organizational theory also offers explanations for bureaucracies' continued resistance to change.[49]

The episodes related to agency-based voter registration initiatives in New York lend credence to these claims. Poor implementation of the state and city agency programs resulted in little increase in voter registration, and it was only because of the federal and state mandates of the NVRA and pressure from advocates that implementation improved. However, the different political actors and interests associated with different patterns of implementation reflect more than mere bureaucratic inertia and inefficiency. Politicians and party organizations play an important role in influencing election practices, and the disenfranchisement that results from inefficiency and incompetency generally functions to serve their political interests. Thus, such conditions and outcomes might be better viewed as a reflection of the dominant political interests that have historically shaped the institutional environment of election boards and continue to influence the political context in which they operate.

Political Relationships

A third explanation, then, involves the political makeup of election administration and the political environment within which it operates. Voting rights organizations and reform advocates characterize disenfranchising election administration practices as reflective of entrenched political interests. They argue that the dominant party organizations and leaders who appoint board commissioners and employees directly infuse the policies and practices of election boards with their political interests and motivations. They contend that what might appear to result from legal and budgetary limitations, security concerns, or bureaucratic inefficiency really reflects the imprint of dominant politicians who have historically forged disenfranchising rules and practices and continue to do so because they have incumbency and patronage interests in maintaining a constricted electorate. Insurgent candidates and new and unpredictable voters pose a threat to such politicians' power. Therefore, it is logical for them to keep in place a dysfunctional system that they can dominate and benefit from. Although the formal authority to appoint commissioners to boards of elections rests with legislative bodies, such as the City Council in New York City, it is extremely rare for recommendations by county party leaders to be rejected. Since the turn of the twentieth century there have been only a few instances of such rejections in New York City.

In New York, election boards are staffed by political appointees who have used outmoded equipment and have followed routine procedures developed decades ago. Critics argue that the prominent role that political party leaders play in the selection of personnel contributes to the generally low caliber of the staff, and that election administration has generally sung to a nineteenth-century tune.[50] Pressure to reform election administration in the mid- to late 1980s was met with stiff opposition by board officials and the regular party organizations, particularly in New York City. Although parties have declined and their role has been transformed, they continue to be important, and the disenfranchisement that results from inefficiency and incompetence generally functions to serve their interests by maintaining a stable and constricted electorate and party system.[51] To the extent that party organizations share interests and personnel with the politicians who dominate state and local government, they play an important role in influencing election practices. This is true of jurisdictions in most other states and localities as well.

Election administration in New York, as in many other places, is a partisan operation. Party leaders hire and fire board staff, from commissioners to poll workers, and partisan differences are evident in an array of areas: from the establishment of standards and practices for processing registration applications and absentee ballots, to the recruitment and training of poll workers, to the selection of poll sites and the counting of ballots. Despite the bipartisan structure, each party can dominate critical areas of election administration. Until the recent revival of the Republican Party and a change to Republican leadership on the New York City Board of Elections—John Ravitz (R) replaced Danny DeFrancesco (D) as executive director in 2003—Democrats had the upper hand. Through their pride of place in the administrative apparatus, they were able to exert greater influence on some processes—including selection of poll sites, decisions about hiring and firing, and assignment of service contracts. Similarly, Thomas Wilkey (D) was able to exert a disproportionate amount of influence on the day-to-day operations of the state board of elections before he was replaced by Peter Kosinski (R). Nevertheless, each party can shape particular election practices, and partisan gridlock is all too often the operating principle for New York's bipartisan boards of elections, in which one party can cancel out another party's wishes. Such conditions and outcomes might be best viewed as reflecting the stamp of dominant political interests that initially created bipartisan election boards and continue to influence and to benefit from their practices.

I have argued that historical political biases set the trajectory for the development of New York's electoral system in the twentieth century. The actors involved in past struggles over rules and practices believed the stakes were high, and the developments they set in motion have proven significant for subsequent developments in New York. Contemporary political actors use the rules and institutions they created to perpetuate such arrangements and their own incumbency.

State Senator Bogues once asked Alan Rothstein of the Citizens Union:

> I'm curious, in view of the poor registration, poor voter participation in this state and certainly in the city, I'm curious in terms of the Citizens Union's evaluation and assessment of how this all came about and what is it really all about? You know, historically, years of elections throughout the state have been run, for the most part, by people who have been appointed to these jobs through the political process. . . . There is also a perception which is very very poor I think in politics that there are many incumbent politicos who would prefer that there not be extensive voter registration. Hence, if there is an enlarged voter registration, it might affect their incumbency or whatever. In your judgment, that is, in the judgment of the Citizens Union, do you feel that there is any evidence to support this allegation or perception that prevails?"

Rothstein replied, "I think I share your perceptions, I most definitely do. . . . There is a concern that they've got to stay in office, and one way is that you don't change the rules of the game when you know the game and how it's been played."[52]

My research corroborates the claim made by some scholars that important aspects of machine politics have persisted in New York. It is true that a cash-intensive, candidate-centered politics comprising campaign consultants and an apparatus tied to candidates and incumbents has largely displaced local party organizations. Such candidate and incumbent organizations primarily engage in fund-raising activities, advance campaign strategies, and control potential candidates' access to the ballot. Yet elements of more traditional machine politics, such as control of patronage resources and selective voter mobilization and demobilization, remain part and parcel of their activities. The stakes of local elections remain significantly tied to patronage resources and relationships, including control of important municipal agencies, commissions, and judgeships. Old-style political patronage is evident in patterns of personnel appointments and in the dispensing of contracts to political allies for the provision of ballot printing and voting machines, and for the service, storage, and transportation of the machines.[53]

Although scholars of New York politics have noted that electoral challenges from advocates have periodically been successful, elite political groupings and regular party organizations continue to be adept at dominating or recapturing control of the electoral process in New York City. My findings suggest that dominant politicians and groups may have survived such insurgent efforts or made comebacks because of their capacity to limit voting through their continued control of the state and city boards of elections. In addition, regular parties raise critical campaign funds and continue to control candidates' access to the ballot, and also select judges to run for election who will make the desired rulings on ballot access challenges. Lastly, their ties to election administration appear to foster weak enforcement of campaign finance reporting requirements and lax prosecution of incumbent or party candidates who violate such requirements.[54]

Party leaders and elections officials generally defend the bipartisan structure of election administration and the patronage system of appointments. "I happen to believe in the patronage system very much because it has proven to work. It works in the selection of judges, truckers and board employees."[55] Elections officials claim that patronage works because party workers are loyal, are more motivated, and work hard for little pay under poor conditions. Regarding poor voter turnout, elections officials and party leaders generally maintain that plenty of opportunities currently exist for people to register and vote and that people do not vote primarily because of ignorance or disaffection, not because of election practices.

This study, however, has shown that the greater the number of stringent procedures to safeguard the ballot, the greater the likelihood that eligible voters will be barred from exercising their voting rights. To the extent that election boards have employed restrictive procedures in response to the explicit or implicit wishes of dominant political actors, they have commensurately disenfranchised voters. Moreover, such restrictive election practices disproportionately affect urban, low-income, and minority citizens. Such practices not only have reduced the size of the electorate and increased the bias in favor of middle- and upper-income groups but also have contributed toward the reduction of party competition, producing more oligarchic parties. It hardly needs saying that practices that have contributed to Republican electoral advantage in New York have also translated into distinct policy consequences.

However, this study also shows that New York's voter registration procedures and election administration practices can vary depending upon the specific constellation of political forces that influence boards of elections. For example, successful lobbying by voter registration advocates convinced Governor Cuomo to issue two executive orders requiring agency-based registration to expand the franchise, even though Republicans effectively thwarted that effort; and with effective implementation of the NVRA, voter registration rates in New York have increased. Efforts by advocates in New York City, coupled with a series of damaging political scandals, successfully prodded Mayor Koch to support programs to improve the operations of the New York City Board of Elections, despite opposition from the board and the county party organizations. In the wake of Florida's 2000 elections, further improvements have come to the New York City Board of Elections, and the advent of HAVA holds promise for greater improvements for both the state and the city if the law is fairly and effectively implemented. My findings indicate that changes in board practices that tended to enhance access and reduce disenfranchisement were associated with one of three factors: (1) increased strength and specificity of federal, state, or city mandates; (2) a chief executive or dominant political party that perceived that increased participation of nonvoters might benefit that official or party; or (3) pressure from outside groups that was sufficient to force reform of election practices.

Future Research and Reform

If partisanship in election administration has contributed to election problems and voter disenfranchisement, then reducing the influence of politics on how election managers do their work as much as possible should make a significant and positive difference. In most states and locales, however, elections officials are either elected or appointed, in the latter case most often by an elected partisan official. In both cases partisanship is typically evident in the everyday operations of election administration. In most states the secretary of state holds primary authority for the conduct of elections. Over thirty secretaries of state are elected in partisan elections; a few are appointed by the governor or state legislature. Several states have bipartisan boards of elections whose members are also appointed by partisan elected officials. Thus, as a National Municipal League publication of three decades ago states, "any method of selecting [election] officials will have political overtones."[56] This is as true today as it was then. Some state election systems are more centralized than others, but because implementation of election procedures occurs at the local level, elections officials wield broad discretionary capacities in every system, even those rare ones with substantial state oversight. To the extent that elections officials are tied to the interests of political parties and elected officials, whether directly or indirectly, they are prone to manifest some degree of partisan leaning or political loyalty. According to election experts, this still accurately describes the current state of affairs.

But it need not. Reform is possible. Indeed, improving election administration, which will decrease voter disenfranchisement and increase registration and voting, is feasible if structural reform is instituted. HAVA—among other models—provides a means to realize such potential.

To better insulate boards of elections from dominant political groups and to produce improvements, two principle changes are critical. First, to the extent possible, a nonpartisan (not bipartisan) and professional election administration with clear lines of authority and accountability must be created. Second, specific standards or indicators must be established that can readily measure the performance of election board operations.[57] This latter change will give the public, independent outside monitors, and all stakeholders the capacity to evaluate the operations of election administrators. It also has the potential to make elections more service oriented and voter friendly. This approach may hold the greatest potential for improvement. Indeed, with greater public input into how elections are functioning, adjustments could be made to address problems.

Election reform advocates have proposed various schemes for modifying the political structure of election boards. For example, the New York Public Interest Research Group (NYPIRG), which has lobbied for nearly twenty years for political reform of New York state's election administration, proposed in 1987 the creation of a citizens advisory committee for the New York City Board of Elections that would be modeled on the Permanent Citizens Advisory Committee to the Metropolitan Transit Authority. The committee would "study, investigate, monitor and make recommendations with respect to the operations of the New York City Board of Elections."[58] In addition, NYPIRG and members of the Statewide Coalition for Voter Participation proposed several options for changes to the state board of elections, from the addition of a fifth, nonpartisan commissioner to elimination of the board altogether. Finally, NYPIRG promoted legislation that would require election administrators to report to the public a broad range of information that would allow for evaluation and intervention. Detailed written standards and procedures, strong oversight mechanisms, and enforcement agencies hold potential to improve performance, regardless of political and managerial structure. HAVA has the potential to establish standards nationally—at least in some areas, such as voting technologies—if the newly established Election Assistance Commission (EAC) undertakes such tasks effectively.[59]

The Citizens Union Foundation (CUF) launched an initiative in 2002 to restructure election administration in New York. Specifically, it aims to eliminate the partisan structure of New York's election boards. The foundation commissioned studies and held forums on the prospect of such reform, and interestingly it found support for reform of election administration not just among advocacy organizations but also among state legislators and candidates for the legislature, whom they surveyed in 2002 to ascertain their position on election reform issues, including reform of the New York City Board of Elections. Of those who returned the survey questionnaires, 86 percent of the candidates for the New York State Assembly favored reforming the board, as did 85 percent of candidates running for State Senate.[60]

The work of these groups harks back to that of earlier reformers, such as Joseph Harris, who called for the wholesale restructuring of election administration: "No substantial improvement in elections can be made without improving the character of the election officers, without divorcing the machinery from politics."[61] But resistance to such change remains strong. Harris's statement of seventy years ago accurately describes most election administrators today: "Election boards and officers in charge of elections resist any change in their status, and the political organizations actively oppose any measure which would reduce their patronage."[62] For example, when Governor Pataki established the New York State Task Force on Election Modernization in 2001, following the 2000 presidential election fiasco in Florida, it dodged the issue of the bipartisan structure of election administration: "The ramifications and advisability of changing the current bipartisan system requires in depth study and consideration that is beyond the mandate of this task force."[63] As Gerald Benjamin writes, "No surprise here. In this, as in so many other areas in which our governmental system in New York is structurally flawed, we cannot expect the major beneficiaries of the system, or those who are accountable to them, to change it in any fundamental way."[64]

Further research into the politics of election administration in other jurisdictions would be fruitful. In particular, examination of existing nonpartisan electoral systems at the local and state levels in the United States, as well as in other countries, might yield information that would allow better assessment of policy prescriptions. Skeptics may argue that because political power generally flows down from hierarchically organized structures, whatever their makeup, nonpartisan systems may reflect dynamics similar to those in partisan or bipartisan systems. Further research in other jurisdictions might help settle such disputes. There are a number of potential problems, however, in doing this kind of research. For example, researchers will need to grapple with the lack of mechanisms available to gather accurate and comprehensive data on the performance of election administration.

Comprehension of the historical evolution and contemporary practice of election administration is important for a full understanding of election systems and voting behavior. Further research by social scientists into election administration may shed light on the debate in the political science literature concerning the causes of low levels of electoral participation and may provide additional evidence suggesting directions for contemporary electoral reform policy. It is my hope that future research on voting behavior will benefit from the present study.

Florida provided an opportunity to devise a model election administration and to enact and implement it. The flaws in our electoral system exposed by the 2000 election debacle in Florida made the most technologically advanced and richest nation in human history the laughing stock of the world and gave democracy reform advocates an opening to press for electoral changes. Not surprisingly, a plethora of reform measures have been proposed at the federal, state, and local levels, although only a fraction of the over 3,000 bills have actually passed.[65]

Some of these bills propose that bipartisan commissions study potential reforms. These commissions primarily focus on improving the efficiency of election administration and machinery by increasing federal or state funding. Other proposals aim to establish uniform standards and procedures in election administration that ensure the integrity of the processes of casting and counting ballots. Professional organizations that represent elections officials—including the National Association of State Election Directors (NASED), the National Association of Secretaries of State (NASS), the National Conference of State Legislatures (NCSL), and the National Association of County Recorders, Election Officials, and Clerks (NACRC)—have also established task forces to examine potential reforms. A number of private organizations have set up prestigious commissions to examine elections and recommend reforms, including the National Commission on Federal Election Reform, headed by former Presidents Carter and Ford and managed by the Century Foundation, and the Constitution Project's Forum on Election Reform. Academic institutions, such as CalTech and MIT, and a broad range of voting rights and civic groups, including the NAACP and Demos, also issued reports and recommendations.

The reform proposals that are percolating vary, particularly at the state level. Many reforms involve upgrading election machinery and developing uniform voting standards. HAVA provides further means for upgrading election administration and for evaluating the changes to election systems across the country that will be implemented in the coming years. HAVA also established a new federal office, the Election Assistance Commission, which, among other responsibilities, is mandated to report to Congress on election reform issues.[66] But change has been slow, incremental, and cosmetic at best.

Unless substantial reform is instituted, we can expect more of the same. If real change is to be achieved, stronger national standards are needed and greater oversight of and accountability for election systems at the state and local levels is vital. Political manipulation of election practices for partisan ends must be reduced, with the aim of creating truly nonpartisan and professional election administration. To achieve the establishment of uniform standards, reform of HAVA is necessary. As one leading election reform advocate sums it up:

HAVA must be revisited and amended. In essence, Congress did not address the larger problem of the decentralized nature of our entire election system. By design, HAVA was a weak piece of legislation, failing to clarify how computerized voting lists and provisional ballots were to be implemented and limiting the authority of the Election Assistance Commission (EAC), the agency created to implement the act. . . . Congress should address the need for both national standards and a more robust enforcing authority. If not, more decision making will fall to the states. Until HAVA is amended, individual state election officials and legislatures must decide what machinery to use; how to implement the mandated computerization of registration lists; how to deal with list purges; how to implement voting-rights restoration laws, provisional ballot counting, and identification requirements for new and existing voters.[67]

We lack uniform standards because we have devolved power to the lowest level of government and the one with the least resources at its disposal.[68] Currently, the EAC only can make guidelines; it might be better if it could make rules. However, if the prevailing bipartisan structure allows the two major parties to dominate the EAC and the process, such changes may prove merely cosmetic. Real reform will be brought about only with more fundamental structural change that reduces the role of partisan control and provides mechanisms to make the electoral system more responsive and accountable to the voting public.

Recommendations

The findings of this study—and of other studies of election systems in the United States—point to a common set of recommendations to improve election administration. Some are particular to New York; others are applicable to most jurisdictions. For example, in 2001 the U.S. General Accounting Office (GAO) published a report that put forth a set of recommendations for improving election administration. The issue of highest concern in the report was funding. In addition, a host of other changes were recommended, including adding telephone lines, providing electronic poll lists, allowing state and county employees to work at the polls, instituting student poll-worker programs, improving poll-worker training, consolidating precincts, and purchasing new voting machine technology and other equipment to automate election operations. The GAO also called for mechanisms for capturing information with which to properly assess the performance of election administration, which is all too often lacking.[69]

Similarly, Richard Soudriette, president of the International Foundation for Election Systems (IFES), a Washington-based nonprofit organization that assists in monitoring, supporting, and strengthening electoral systems and processes worldwide, argues that "long-term advances in U.S. election administration will require more resources, informational as well as financial." This is a prerequisite to improved elections in the United States.

Fortunately, some of this funding will come from the federal government. The Help America Vote Act, which was passed by Congress on October 29, 2002 and signed by the president in November, provided for $3.9 billion of these sorely needed funds. Additional spending from state and local treasuries should follow, hopefully in amounts sufficient for full and fair implementation of the law. Furthermore, a host of specific recommendations and best practices have been identified and promoted by national studies and commissions.[70]

My recommendations, some specific to New York, some for election administration nationwide, are as follows:

Increase funding to New York's boards of elections.

The increase in funds to New York City Board of Elections begun in 2001 should be maintained or increased. The increase in the stipend for poll workers has helped to attract more and better qualified workers. Similarly, the extra expenditures on machine technicians helped reduce machine breakdowns. The expanded phone lines improved voters' access to critical election information on and around election day. These resources should be expanded even further. Greater logistical support for election boards, including transportation of workers and mechanics, has also improved election-day operations. The city board's staff, which was cut by 15 percent during the Giuliani administration, should be restored to previous levels. Many critical positions remain unfilled, so remaining workers are overburdened and dissatisfied.

Professionalize election administration.

States should establish outside monitoring programs to help professionalize boards of elections, similar to the New York City Elections Project (NYCEP) of the mid-1980s. These could be modeled on the Permanent Citizens Advisory Committee to New York's Metropolitan Transit Authority. New management techniques and client-centered practices should be adopted, along with performance standards for service-based evaluations.

Establish nationwide uniform standards and procedures.

Uniform standards and procedures can help settle some of the problems and disputes highlighted in this book. For example, clear and uniform standards regarding the handling of absentee, provisional or affidavit, and emergency ballots would reduce poll-site problems and decrease the likelihood of disputed elections. Similarly, uniform criteria for allocating voting machines and workers, for combining election districts, for providing language assistance, and for designating poll sites would reduce poll-site problems and allegations of disparate treatment. Finally, uniform standards in recanvassing would help settle disputed elections and ballots.

Expand recruitment of election personnel outside political party organizations.

As an interim step toward nonpartisan, professionalized election administration, election personnel should be recruited from sources other than political party organizations. If staff positions were filled on the basis of nonpartisan and civil service mechanisms, hiring and firing could be based on technical expertise and job skills rather than party loyalty. These basic features are so integral to most other governmental agencies that the current partisan arrangements in electoral administration are strikingly anachronistic. One way to recruit new workers is to allow people to substitute working the polls for jury duty, as Nebraska does. College students could also be recruited and provided with incentives, such as service learning credit.

Improve training, materials, and working conditions for poll workers.

Election administrators should adopt new standards and materials to ensure that workers are adequately prepared to serve the voting public, and they should improve election-day working conditions. Split shifts should be created so workers do not have to work for over sixteen hours at the polls. This will enlarge the pool of workers, improve the quality of applicants, and increase workers' attentiveness. Boards should improve mechanisms for processing applications from poll workers and multilingual translators and for communicating with applicants, and they should increase the length of training classes and the quality of trainers. Class sizes should be reduced and locations should be expanded. More hands-on training should be provided. Workers should practice opening and closing machines and following affidavit ballot procedures, and they should learn all critical facets of election law and voters' rights. The training sessions should use role plays to focus on special situations, such as when machines break down and emergency ballots are needed. Training manuals need to be rewritten in clearer language and should cover more procedures and situations, and the manuals should be posted on the boards' Web sites. Communication technologies, such as training videos, could also be used more effectively. The New York City Board of Elections did produce a training video in 2002 for under $300,000. This is an effective and a cost-efficient way of ensuring that poll workers get critical information. Web-based training methods could be developed and implemented. Finally, the standards for the poll-worker examination should be raised, and examinees must be required to pass the examination in order to work an election.

Establish a process and structure to purchase new voting technology with broad input by voting rights and civic organizations.

New York needs to replace its outdated lever voting machines, but how will it move to obtain new voting technology? New York should adopt a process to ensure that voter's concerns and needs are central. This can happen only if representatives from voting rights and civic groups are intimately involved in the process from the start. The acquisition of new voting machines should not be contracted out to private vendors without public input. New voting machines should be accessible to New York's diverse population, including people with disabilities and foreign-language speakers. They must be able to handle a variety of election systems, including proportional voting and write-in balloting, and future options such as instant runoff voting. New voting machines must also be secure. Independent experts should review the possibilities of tampering, whether by computer programmers, elections personnel, or voters. The potential for technological failures should be considered, and backup plans integrated into the planning. It is critical that a means for audits—whether by a verifiable paper trail or otherwise—be built in. Finally, machines should be able to produce receipts for voters; this would allow them to verify that their vote was properly counted or to rectify the problem if it was not.

Improve and expand voter educational materials and outreach programs.

Voter education needs to be vastly expanded. Critical information about who is running for office, what the responsibilities of the offices are, how to register to vote, and how to cast a ballot should be widely disseminated. Voter guides and pamphlets should be printed and mailed to every household; materials should be available at government offices and access to them should be integrated into existing procedures, much like voter registration forms in the motor voter program; all media—print, radio, television, and the Internet—should be used more extensively to convey critical voting information.

Adopt election-day registration and other vote-enhancing practices.

Once New York establishes a statewide registration system as required under HAVA, this will provide the basis for moving toward election-day registration, which would be the best way to eliminate a host of election problems—from trouble with affidavit and emergency ballots to racial and income disparities in turnout. Where election-day registration has been adopted, it has proven to be the most effective system for facilitating voter participation and reducing racial and class disparities. The other election innovations with which some states are experimenting have also been used effectively, such as early voting, mail voting, and Internet voting—all of which New York should explore.

Expanding Democracy

Democracy reform advocates call for measures that would not only improve the operations of election administration, but would go much further in expanding voter participation and invigorating democracy in the

United States. Some, for example, call for establishing a holiday for election day, extending voting over a two-day period (possibly a weekend, or a weekday and part of a weekend) or over a two-week period, and allowing people to vote by mail and over the Internet.

Still others call for expanding the franchise to ex-felons or noncitizens. These reformers point out that currently 4 four million people, disproportionately African Americans and other people of color, are denied voting rights even after having served their sentences, and that almost 20 million noncitizens, 12 million of whom are legal permanent residents, are similarly without the vote, though they are subject to all laws and taxation. These reformers believe democracy is diminished not just by poor voter turnout, but also by the exclusion of these individuals. They argue that far-reaching reforms such as allowing ex-felons or noncitizens to vote could increase electoral competition, make the parties more responsive and accountable to the electorate, and invigorate our democracy.[71]

Many reformers point to a wide range of innovative election laws and programs that already exist in several states and have proven successful in expanding voter participation and democracy. Election-day registration exists in six states: Maine, New Hampshire, Wisconsin, Minnesota, Idaho, and Wyoming; voting by mail is used effectively in Oregon and Washington; early voting programs have been used in several states; expanded use of absentee voting has been implemented in over thirty states; and Internet voting has been used effectively in Arizona.

Such electoral reforms provide easier access to the franchise and thus enhance possibilities for marginal voters to participate, which, in turn, encourages challengers to run and stimulates competition and effective appeals that further draw voters into the active electorate, and so on. States with election-day registration, for example, have the highest turnout; states that permit voting by mail and early voting also show an increase in voter participation. Not surprisingly, many of these states have progressive social policies reflecting the demands of newly included minorities and the previously disenfranchised.[72]

Dominant and incumbent politicians of all political stripes who were elected by a constricted electorate are cool to such reforms, particularly the broader reforms. They often see new voters as a threat. Elected officials and election administrators often resist changes not just because of incumbency interests but also due to bureaucratic inertia. These officials and members of other conservative groups point to potential voter fraud to justify the status quo,[73] and some not only oppose easing registration and voting processes but also propose reforms that call for greater safeguards to the ballot. The requirement that all voters present identification at poll sites, which several states enacted in 2003 and 2004, is one example of such restrictive measures.[74]

The United States is the richest, most technologically advanced society in human history. We use automated banking machines, check in at electronic airport kiosks, and trade stocks and transfer billions of dollars electronically; we have created systems that allow people to engage in such activities with convenience, confidence, and accountability, and they are almost completely free of fraud. We do not lack the technological capacity to conduct elections in similar fashion. What is lacking is the political will to do so.

The political will to provide funding and make necessary changes to improve elections is critical for any viable reform strategy. Moreover, proposed election reforms "will be impossible to implement without the involvement and support of more than 22,000 elections officials across the United States, as well as the organizations such as the National Association of Secretaries of State (NASS), the National Association of State Election Directors (NASED), the International Association of Clerks, Recorders, Election Officials, and Treasurers (IACREOT), the National Association of County Officials (NACO), and the Election Center."[75] And there is the rub. Elections officials are the linchpin for making elections work better in the United States. Members of these associations and others are beholden to elected officials (if they are not themselves elected) and to their affiliate party organizations. Most elected officials and election administrators are loath to change election systems because generally it is not in their interests to do so. Unless sufficient pressure is brought to bear, as happens during times of crises such as the periods following New York's problematic 1984 elections and Florida's 2000 fiasco, change will not be forthcoming.

Thus far most change has been at best incremental and minimal. Even after the fiasco in Florida elections officials and experts are reluctant to acknowledge that significant problems exist: "Only a minute percentage of elections in the United States are unsatisfactory, whether because the law or administrative rule failed to meet the need, or because election workers failed in the performance of their duties. In brief, the U.S. election system is basically sound."[76] Elections officials and their organizations essentially asked Congress for funds and requested that standards for everything from voting systems to election management systems be voluntary. Importantly, they also strove to maintain state and local control over the implementation of any reforms. Their point is clear: Problems are minimal. Provide elections officials with money and let them decide how they will spend it. Guidelines are welcome, but please, no requirements. The post-2000 federal legislation, HAVA, essentially provided just what they asked for.

The events in Florida in 2000 changed things. The democracy renewal movement got a shot in the arm and grew in size and strength so that it is now larger and more diverse than at any time since the civil rights era. Predominantly white civic organizations, such as the League of Women Voters, People for the American Way, and Common Cause are teaming up with organizations of African Americans, Latinos, Asians, and other communities of color, and together they are working to monitor elections and win broad reforms. Together these groups provide hope for real change beyond simply the upgrading of voting machines. Many groups, including labor unions, are developing a broader democracy agenda that links electoral reforms to issues of economic and social justice. This mobilization could prove enormously powerful and significant if it can expand over the next several years.

On February 17, 2005, Senators Hillary Clinton of New York and Barbara Boxer of California and Representative Stephanie Tubbs Jones of Ohio introduced a comprehensive election reform bill that, if passed, promises to dramatically improve our election system. Entitled the Count Every Vote Act, it calls for a "voter verified paper ballot" for electronic voting machines and "ensures access" for all citizens. Uniform standards would be set for provisional ballots, and the Federal Election Assistance Commission would be required to issue standards so election personnel are properly trained in every community. The law would increase voter participation by making election day a federal holiday, requiring all states to permit early voting, allowing for "no-excuse" absentee balloting, providing for "fair and uniform voter registration and identification," reducing wait times at polling places, restoring voting rights to felons who have served their time, and requiring states to allow election-day registration. The Count Every Vote Act also contains measures that would protect voters from deceptive practices that suppress voting and would restrict "the ability of chief state election officials as well as owners and senior managers of voting machine manufacturers to engage in certain kinds of political activity." The bill was endorsed by an array of civil rights organizations and voting rights advocates, including People for the American Way, Lawyers Committee for Civil Rights Under the Law, the NAACP, Common Cause, the National Voting Rights Institute, Demos, and the National Asian Pacific American Legal Consortium.[77]

Although there is a broad mobilization to expand the franchise and further democratize America's electoral system, other forces are working to thwart such reform efforts. The tragic events of September 11, 2001, shifted much of the focus that had been on election reform to issues of war and peace. But election problems persist and election reform made its way back onto the political agenda at the national and state levels in 2004. Florida created an opening to expand democracy in the United States; it remains to be seen if it will usher in democracy's moment.[78]

Notes

Introduction: The 2000 Election

1. National Task Force on Election Reform (NTFER) 2001; Cox 2001.

2. Six states have bipartisan boards of elections (Illinois, Maryland, New York, North Carolina, Virginia, and Wisconsin), five states have more than one state entity with overall election management responsibility (Oklahoma, Rhode Island, South Carolina, South Dakota, and Tennessee), and the remaining thirty-nine states have a single appointed or elected official in charge. In thirty-four states the secretary of state is the chief elections official. In all cases, partisan actors and dynamics are involved. The same is true for local election boards and officials. Federal Elections Commission 2004.

3. Caltech/MIT Voting Technology Project 2001 and 2002; a joint project of the American Political Science Association (APSA), the American Psychological Association (APA), and the Consortium of Social Science Associations, which commissioned a number of studies, including Roth 2001, Traugott 2001, Woods and Hancock 2001; Constitution Project 2001 and 2002; National Commission on Federal Election Reform 2001; U.S. House of Representatives Committee on the Judiciary, Democratic Investigative Staff 2001; U.S. House of Representatives Committee on Government Reform, Minority Office 2001; U.S. Commission on Civil Rights 2001; Advancement Project 2001; Lichtman 2001; Merzer and staff 2001; Keyssar 2001; Election Center, National Task Force on Election Reform 2001; National Association of Secretaries of State 2001; National Conference of State Legislators 2001; Congressional Research Service 2001; U.S. General Accounting Office 2001; Rakove 2001; Alverez, Sinclair, and Wilson 2002; Knack and Kropf 2002; Palast 2003; Crigler, Just, and McCaffery 2004. Two comprehensive Web sites that contain studies on elections, voter participation, and election administration are www.electionline.org and the bibliography section of Working Paper Sites of Political Science at www.workingpapers.org, which includes an election 2000 bibliography.

4. U.S. House of Representatives Committee on the Judiciary, Democratic Investigative Staff 2001; U.S. House of Representatives Committee on Government Reform, Minority Office 2001; U.S. Commission on Civil Rights 2001; Advancement Project 2001; Lichtman 2001; Alverez, Sinclair, and Wilson 2002; Palast 2003.

5. Election Reform Information Project 2004, 1. Forty-three lawsuits were filed between June and election day, and a number of postelection suits were filed as well. Many alleged that eligible voters would be or were disenfranchised in Ohio, Florida, Washington, Nevada, Missouri, North Carolina, and other states (Election Reform Information Project 2004, 9). If Kerry and Edwards had not conceded the day after the election, states with close margins of victory would likely have been the subject of further scrutiny and litigation, including Michigan, Iowa, Pennsylvania, and New Mexico.

6. Election Protection Coalition 2004; Common Cause 2004; Demos 2004a; Election Reform Information Project 2004. The Election Protection Coalition, a consortium of dozens of national, state, and local organizations that was launched by the People for the American Way Foundation, documented more than 39,000 complaints and established a database of voting problems using an electronic incident-report system. A comprehensive report of the data will be published in 2005. Common Cause and its affiliates fielded more than 210,000 calls from voters. Altogether these and other groups, partisan campaigns, the Department of Justice, and international observers sent tens of thousands of monitors into the field in about half the states.

7. Election Protection Coalition 2004; Common Cause 2004; Demos 2004a; Election Reform Information Project 2004; Carbo 2005; Pastor 2005; Wang 2005; House Judiciary Committee Democratic Staff 2005; and over one hundred news articles from around the country, many of which are summarized and cited in Election Protection Coalition 2004, in the other above-cited reports, and on the Web sites of their respective authors' organizations.

8. Brian C. Mooney, "Voting Errors Tallied Nationwide," *Boston Globe,* December 1, 2004.

9. Wang 2005, A-4.

10. Harris 1934.

11. U.S. General Accounting Office 2001.

12. Harris 1934, 1974; Converse 1972, 1974; Rusk 1974; Goldberg 1987.

13. Burnham 1974a, 1974b; Argersinger 1985–86; Allen and Allen 1981; Minnite and Callahan 2003.

14. Keyssar 2000; Piven and Cloward 2000.

15. This question was dubbed the "puzzle of participation" by Richard Brody (1978).

16. Palast 2003.

17. Harris 1934, 1.

1: Election Administration

1. Schumpeter 1943; Pateman 1970; Putnam 2000; Schlozman 2002. Some who do not view nonvoting as a problem include Berelson, Lazarsfeld, and McPhee 1954; Will 1983; Ranney 1983.

2. Rosenstone and Hansen 1993, 57; International Institute for Democracy and Electoral Assistance 2003; Lowenstein and Hasen 2001, 45; Powell 1986; Jackman 1987. Regarding the class and race skew in the electorate, see Rosenstone and Hansen 1993; Teixeira 1992; Verba, Scholzman, and Brady 1995; and Piven and Cloward 2000. On partisan implications of low turnout, see Lijphart 1997; Erickson 1995; Piven and Cloward 2000; Issacharoff, Karlan, and Pildes 2001; Citrin, Schickler, and Sides 2003; Wolfinger and Rosenstone 1980; Bennett and Resnick 1990; Nagel and McNulty 1996; and Denardo 1980. Regarding turnout declines in urban areas, see Karnig and Walter 1989; Sauerzopf and Swanstrom 1993; and Hajnal and Lewis 2003. On voter eligibility issues, see M. McDonald 2002; and McDonald and Popkin 2001. Michael McDonald maintains a useful Web site, elections.gmu.edu/voter_turnout.htm.

3. Burnham 1965; Wolfinger and Rosenstone 1980; Piven and Cloward 2000; Lowenstein and Hasen 2001, 46; Nardulli, Dlager, and Greco 1996.

4. Hill and Leighley 1992; Martin 2003; Key 1949, 527, quoted in Martin 2003, 110; Piven and Cloward 1979; Verba, Schlozman, and Brady 1995.

5. Dalton and Wattenberg 1993; Rosenstone and Hansen 1993; Piven and Cloward 2000; Schlozman 2002.

6. Campbell et al. 1960; Verba and Nie 1972; Downs 1957; Reiter 1979; Wolfinger and Rosenstone 1980; Schaffer 1981; Abramson and Aldrich 1982; Uhlaner 1989; Teixera 1992; Nie et al. 1996; Putnam 2000; Blais 2000.

7. Schattschneider 1960; Burnham 1970; Kleppner and Baker 1980; Avey 1989; Piven and Cloward 2000. Regarding new campaign technologies and the decline of parties, see Ware 1985; and Wattenberg 1990. On the media, see McChesney 1999. Proponents of the legal-institutional model include Kelly, Ayers, and Bowen 1967; Converse 1972, 1974; Rusk 1974; Wolfinger and Rosenstone 1980; Kleppner 1982; Glass, Squire, and Wolfinger 1984; Powell 1986; and Jackman 1987. Regarding election practices, see Merriam and Gosnell 1924; Harris 1934, 1974; League of Women Voters Education Fund 1972b; Carlson 1974; Oliver 1996; Franklin 1999; Lijphart 1997; and Southwell and Burchett 2000.

8. Harris 1929, 65.

9. Converse 1972, 285–86.

10. Burnham 1974a.

11. Harris 1929, 65.

12. Converse 1974.

13. Harris 1929, 309.

14. Allen and Allen 1981.

15. Kleppner and Baker 1980, 207.

16. Piven and Cloward 1988, 108.

17. McCreary 1887, 59.

18. Michael and Mack 1904.

19. Converse 1972, 286.

20. Burnham 1970, 79 and 83.

21. Kleppner and Baker 1980, 207.

22. Harris 1934, 19.

23. Piven and Cloward 1988, 6–7.

24. Minnite and Callahan 2003; Sabato and Simpson 1996.

25. Converse 1972, 1974; Rusk 1970, 1974; Campbell et al. 1960, 1965; Kelly, Ayers, and Bowen 1967.

26. Carlson 1976.

27. Converse 1972, 1974; King 1994; Heckelman 1998, 2000.

28. Kleppner 1982, 59–60; Burnham 1970, 1974a, 1974b; Piven and Cloward 2000; Erie 1988; Argersinger 1985–86; Cox and Kousser 1981; Allen and Allen 1981.

29. Kleppner 1982; Gienapp 1982; R. L. McCormick 1981; Cox and Kousser 1981; Argersinger 1985–86; Allen and Allen 1981; Erie 1988; Heckelman 1998, 2000.

30. Kleppner 1982; Allen and Allen 1981; Burnham 1974a, 1974b; Piven and Cloward 2000.

31. Scholars who examine definitions of fraud include Ostrogorski 1902/1964, 1910; Evans 1917; Bryce 1921; Harris 1929, 1934; Allen and Allen 1981; Cox and Kousser 1981; R. L. McCormick 1981; Argersinger 1985–86; and Heckelman 1998, 2000.

32. Harris 1934, 4 and 6; Riis 1890/1971.

33. Allen and Allen 1981, 171.

34. Allen and Allen 1981, 172–74.

35. Allen and Allen 1981; Argersinger 1985–86; Kleppner 1987, 168.

36. Schiesl 1977; Erie 1988; Argersinger 1985–86; Hays 1964.

37. Burnham 1970, 1974a and 1974b; Kleppner and Baker 1980; Kleppner 1982; Piven and Cloward 2000; Erie 1988; Avey 1989; McGerr 1986; Argersinger 1985–86; Hammack 1982; Gienapp 1982; R. L. McCormick 1981; Cox and Kousser 1981; Allen and Allen 1981.

38. Piven and Cloward 2000, chapter 2.

39. Erie 1988; DiGaetano 1988; Shefter 1984, 1994.

40. Wolfinger 1972; Mayhew 1986; Erie 1988; Mollenkopf 1994; Shefter 1994.

41. Key 1949.

42. McGerr 1986; Piven and Cloward 2000.

43. Piven and Cloward 2000; Schattschneider 1960.

44. Minnite and Callahan 2003.

45. Goldberg 1987; Sabato and Simpson 1996.

46. Sabato and Simpson 1996; Minnite and Callahan 2003; Cunningham 1991; Keyssar 2001.

47. Goldberg 1987; Sabato and Simpson 1996; Minnite and Callahan 2003. This view is held by top city, state, and federal elections officials, as indicated in interviews and meetings with author.

48. Piven and Cloward 1988, 215, quoting a 1984 Harvard/ABC News Symposium.

49. Crotty 1980, 101–2.

50. Merriam and Gosnell 1924, 3–4, 78–108.

51. Ibid., 96–98 and 107–8.

52. Gosnell and Smolka 1973, 118–22; National Municipal League 1973; Smolka 1973; Carlson 1974; League of Women Voters Education Fund 1972b.

53. League of Women Voters Education Fund 1972b.

54. Caltech/MIT Voting Technology Project 2001 and 2003; joint project of the American Political Science Association (APSA), the American Psychological Association (APA), and the Consortium of Social Science Associations, which commissioned a number of studies, including Roth 2001, Traugott 2001, and Woods and Hancock 2001; Constitution Project 2001 and 2002; National Commission on Federal Election Reform 2001; U.S. House of Representatives Committee on the Judiciary, Democratic Investigative Staff 2001; U.S. House of Representatives Committee on Government Reform, Minority Office 2001; U.S. Commission on Civil Rights 2001; Advancement Project 2001; Lichtman 2001; Merzer 2001; Keyssar 2001; Election Center 2001; National Association of Secretaries of State 2001; National Conference of State Legislators 2001; Congressional Research Service 2001; U.S. General Accounting Office 2001; Rakove 2001; Knack and Kropf 2002; Palast 2003; Crigler, Just, and McCaffery 2004.

55. U.S. General Accounting Office 2001.

56. Caltech/MIT Voting Technology Project 2001, 2003.

57. Election Center 2001.

58. Soudriette 2001, 134.

59. Cox 2001, 2.

60. The national associations of elections officials are the National Association of State Election Directors (NASED); the National Association of Secretaries of State (NASS); the National Association of County Recorders, Election Officials, and Clerks (NACRC); the National Association of Counties; the National Conference of State Legislatures (NCSL); and the International Foundation for Election Systems (IFES).

61. Doug Chapin, "Election Update" (September 11, 2002), www.electionline.org.

62. Doug Chapin, "Election Update" (September 13, 2002) www.electionline.org.

63. Drinkard, Jim, and Peter Eisler. "Weakest Part of Any Voting Machine: People." *USA Today,* March 1, 2001.

64. Analysis of the different experiences of Florida and Georgia in 2002—and recommendations for improvement—can be found in a report published by the Century Foundation, "The Help America Vote Act: Impact and Potential for New York" (Abrams et al. 2003). I am one of the authors of the report. This section is based on research conducted by Jason Tarricone.

65. Dugger 2004.

66. U.S. General Accounting Office 2001; Election Center 2001; Election Administration Reports.

67. Federal Elections Commission 2004; U.S. General Accounting Office 2001.

68. Shefter 1994; Groarke 2000.

69. On the African American experience, see Lewis 1974; on youth, see Roe and Maurer 1974; on people with disabilities, see National Center for Policy Alternatives 1988. On the contemporary period, see People for the American Way and NAACP 2004; Common Cause 2004; Carbo 2005; Wang 2005.

70. Smolka 1974; Election Administration Reports.

71. Rapoport 2005.

72. "Professional Education Programs, Certified Elections/Registration Administrator (CERA)." Available at www.electioncenter.org.

2: Historical Roots of Election Rules and Practices in New York

1. Keyssar 2000; Piven and Cloward 2000; Burnham 1974a, 1054; Lincoln 1906.

2. Harris 1929, 2; 1934.

3. R. L. McCormick 1981, 252–63.

4. R. P. McCormick 1953; Tolman 1895; Ivins 1887; Lincoln 1906; Myers 1917; Smith 1922; Werner 1928; Flick 1935; Bass 1961; Lowi 1964; Muccigrosso 1968; Cerillo 1973; McSeveney 1972; R. L. McCormick 1981; Hammack 1982; Shefter 1985; McGerr 1986.

5. Alexander 1909/1969.

6. Felt 1973; Dorsett 1972; Schiesl 1977; Hays 1964; Weinstein 1968; Erie 1988.

7. Harris 1929; R. L. McCormick 1981, 163.

8. Harris 1929, 7; Shefter 1985, 1994.

9. Shefter 1985, 22–23; Lowi 1964, 182–83.

10. Merton 1957/1968; Dahl 1961; Rosenbaum 1973; Erie 1988; Shefter 1978.

11. Lincoln 1906, 4:825–26.

12. Ibid., 5:92.

13. Harris 1929, 73–74.

14. Lincoln 1909, 6:388–89.

15. Myers 1917; Ivins 1887; Smith 1922; Werner 1928; Flick 1935; Alexander 1909/1969.

16. Griffith 1974, 69.

17. Alexander 1909/1969, 214.

18. U.S. House of Representatives 1869, 4.

19. Ibid.

20. Ibid., 101, 111, 108.

21. Alexander 1909/1969, 240.

22. Gienapp 1982, 31.

23. Hershkowitz 1978, 13, preface, and 18–19; see also Hammack 1982.

24. Tilden 1873, appendix, and 18–19.

25. Piven and Cloward 1988, 86; McGerr 1986, 49–50.

26. Harris 1929; R. L. McCormick 1981; Bass 1961; Muccigrosso 1968; Cerillo 1973.

27. Lincoln 1909, 7:719–20.

28. Ibid., 9:34, 180.

29. This section draws heavily upon R. L. McCormick 1981; McSeveney 1972; McGerr 1986; Cerillo 1973; and Hammack 1982.

30. R. L. McCormick 1981, 43–51.

31. R. L. McCormick 1981, 44–46; Lowi 1964; Hammack 1982; McGerr 1986; Piven and Cloward 1988; Shefter 1994.

32. Tolman 1895, 81–82; R. L. McCormick 1981, 46.

33. R. L. McCormick 1981, 46; Tolman 1895, 72.

34. R. L. McCormick 1981, 47.

35. Cerillo 1973, 54; Hammack 1982; Muccigrosso 1968.

36. Quoted in R. L. McCormick 1981, 52.

37. White 1994.

38. R. L. McCormick 1981, 53–55.

39. Piven and Cloward 1988, 109.

40. This section draws upon G. Benjamin 1995, 1997; and Lincoln 1906, 3:114–16.

41. Lincoln 1906, 3:114–17.

42. G. Benjamin 1995, 122.

43. R. L. McCormick 1981.

44. G. Benjamin 1995, 122; Lincoln 1906, 3:123–24; New York State Code, Laws of 1880, Chapter 528, and Laws of 1882, Chapter 410.

45. G. Benjamin 1995, 122, quoted from New York State Governor's Office, *Messages From the Governor* (1892), 103.

46. New York State Code, Laws of 1894.

47. R. L. McCormick 1981, 52.

48. Revised Record of the 1894 Constitutional Convention, 3:111 and 3:244, cited in G. Benjamin 1995, 123.

49. Revised Record of the 1894 Constitutional Convention, 3:248 and 3:270, quoted in G. Benjamin 1995, 123–24.

50. Lincoln 1906, 3:129.

51. Revised Record of the 1894 Constitutional Convention, 3:245 and 3:254, quoted in G. Benjamin 1995, 124.

52. Gosnell 1924/1969, 146, quoted in G. Benjamin 1995, 123.

53. R. L. McCormick 1981, 89.

54. Harris 1934, 103; Harris 1929, 76.

55. City of New York, Annual Report of the Commissioner of Accounts, 1910, 23–24, and Annual Report of the Commissioner of Accounts, 1911, 11, cited in Seidman 1941.

56. Fosdick 1912.

57. City of New York, Annual Report of the Commissioner of Accounts, 1917, available at the Municipal Archives.

58. Herlands 1940.
59. Thomas and Blanshard 1932.
60. Sayre and Kaufman 1965.
61. R. L. McCormick 1981, 262.
62. Ibid., 252–53.
63. Scarrow 1983, 83.
64. Stonecash 1994b.

3: The Impact of Election Rules and Practices in New York State, 1984–2004

1. Scarrow 1983; data are from U.S. Census, "Voting and Registration," Current Population Surveys, CPS P-20 and CPS 2002, available at www.census.gov/population/www/socdemo/voting.html.

2. Fuchs and Thompson 1994, 32–33; Schneier and Murtaugh 2001; U.S. Census Bureau statistics available at www.census.gov/population/www/socdemo/voting.html (Internet release date: February 27, 2002).

3. Judd and Swanstrom 2004, 194; Sauerzopf and Swanstrom 1993; Affigne and Tate 1993; Mollenkopf 1994; New York City Voter Assistance Commission 1994; New York City Department of Planning Web site, at www.nyc.gov/html/dcp/home.html.

4. Judd and Swanstrom 2004; Fuchs and Thompson 1994; Sauerzopf and Swanstrom 1993; Schneier and Murtaugh 2001.

5. Schneier and Murtaugh 2001; Stonecash 1994s; Blair Horner, New York Public Interest Research Group (NYPIRG), interview with author.; Richard Winger, Ballot Access News, interview with author.

6. Piven and Cloward, *The Nation,* November 2, 1985. The following section draws on the analysis and data in Piven and Cloward 1988 and 2000.

7. Thompson 1990.

8. Piven and Cloward 1988.

9. Ibid.; Raskin 2003.

10. *New York Times,* March 13, 1996.

11. New York Election Law, Article 5-210 (2); testimony of NYPIRG and others (including NYCLU) at public hearing of the Joint Committee on Election Law of the New York State Assembly and Senate, March 13, 1984, and in subsequent interviews with author in 1994–1995.

12. New York Election Law, Section 6-134; Piven and Cloward 1988; interviews with election officials.

13. Quote from William Gerling, Monroe County Outreach Voter Registration Committee, March 13, 1993.

14. Jerome Koenig, interview with author.

15. Interviews with state and national elections officials, experts, and key lobbyists.

16. Tom Wathen, executive director of NYPIRG, press release, October 9, 1984, NYPIRG files and on file with author; testimony of Hulbert James, executive director of Human SERVE, at public hearing of the Joint Committee on Election Law of the New York State Assembly and Senate, March 13, 1984, on file at the New York State Archives and with author; Thompson 1990.

17. Crocker 1992.

18. Thompson 1990, 10, 57–58; Mollenkopf 1987.

19. Public hearing of the Joint Committee on Election Law of the New York State Assembly and Senate, March 13, 1984.

20. Interviews with legislators and their staff, election experts and officials, and advocates.

21. While most of the public hearings focused on the New York City Board of Elections, the state's county boards of elections, as well as the state board, were also the focus of scrutiny. Advocates believed the greatest improvements were made to the New York City board.

22. March 1984 Joint Committee hearing; author interviews with Laura Alschuler of the League of Women Voters and with leaders from ACORN and the Community Service Society.

23. March 1984 Joint Committee hearing. This procedure validates a person's registration, thus reducing the number of registrations lost. Jerome Koenig served as chief of staff of the Elections Committee from 1975 until he retired in 2000. He is widely regarded as one of the most knowledgeable experts in election law and procedures in New York state. Koenig has drafted and written large portions of what has been adopted as the state's election law since 1975.

24. March 1984 Joint Committee hearing.

25. March 1984 Joint Committee hearing, Hope Geisler's testimony, 157–58.

26. Ibid. Several other elections experts I interviewed concurred with these assessments.

27. Ibid. A lawsuit in the northern district, *Auerback* v. *Kinley,* produced an injunction against Albany County that extended to Oswego, Tompkins, and Ulster counties. In the southern district, *Williams* v. *Salerno* covered Westchester County.

28. U.S. District Court, Southern District of New York, October 23, 1984.

29. March 1984 Joint Committee hearing, Alan Rothstein's testimony, 60, 83, and passim.

30. Ibid.

31. Data from the state and city boards of elections.

32. New York State Board of Elections, press release, May 15, 1995.

33. Piven and Cloward 1988, chapter seven; Piven and Cloward 2000, chapters ten and eleven. See also Knack 1995; and Rhine 1995.

34. *Washington Post,* May 6, 1994.

35. Piven and Cloward 1988, 227. Prior to 1984, five states (Maine, Ohio, Michigan, Arizona, and Oregon) allowed people to register to vote at motor vehicle bureaus (220).

36. *Clark* v. *Cuomo* (1984). The lower court accepted Republican claims that their party would be "irreparably harmed" because state employees would administer registration in a biased manner and influence registrants to enroll as Democrats and that the governor had overstepped into the legislature's constitutional power over voter registration.

37. Piven and Cloward 1988, 235.

38. Office of Governor Mario Cuomo, press release on establishment of New York State Task Force on Encouraging Electoral Participation, November 1987.

39. The Statewide Coalition for Voter Participation, cochaired by Human SERVE and NYPIRG, had actively lobbied the governor, the legislature, the state board of elections, and newspaper editorial boards, stating that "successful implementation of this Executive Order is one of our top priorities for the coming year,"

1990 (author interviews with NYPIRG and Human SERVE staff). The groups in the coalition "had been among those who persuaded Governor Mario Cuomo to implement an agency voter registration program" (Election Administration Reports, October 15, 1990). "The Governor issued the Executive Order at the urging of the Statewide Coalition for Voter Participation" (NYPIRG briefing packet on the executive order, NYPIRG files).

40. New York State Election Law, Section 3-102.

41. Laws of 1974, Chapter 607. The Assembly Committee on Election Law published a scathing report titled *Is Anybody in Charge Here?* (March 24, 1988).

42. The discussion in the next few paragraphs on the constitutional and statutory basis of the boards draws on G. Benjamin 1995. I also rely on information from an address Benjamin delivered at the New York City Bar Association meeting on November 18, 2002 (transcription was provided to the author by the sponsoring organization, the Citizens Union; on file at the Citizens Union). In the main, I draw upon New York state's Constitution and election law themselves, and on interviews with top elections officials in the state, election law committee staff, and election lawyers in the state and city of New York. New York State Election Law 3-100.1.

43. Celia Wexler, interview with author. G. Benjamin 1995, 118. Richard Winger, publisher of Ballot Access News, corroborated this claim (in interview with author and at www.ballot-access.org).

44. Benjamin address, New York City Bar Association, November 18, 2002; interviews with election experts, election administrators, and elections officials.

45. Minutes of the state board of elections meeting of June 27, 1990 (approved July 18, 1990). The two Republicans voted against the Democratic plan, and the two Democrats voted against the two Republican plans.

46. *The Sunday Observer-Dispatch* (Utica), July 8, 1990.

47. *New York Times,* October 4, 1990. Aquila said she suspected that Republicans especially feared—legitimately—that people in social service agencies would be more likely to register as Democrats.

48. *Newsday,* October 5, 1990.

49. Quote from Stout in an Associated Press article written by David Bauder (July 19, 1990); quote from Donohue in a *Democrat and Chronicle* article by Read Kingsbury; the quote is from notes taken by Celia Wexler at the June state board of elections meeting, on file at Common Cause and with author.

50. Quote from Plunkett, in the *Democrat and Chronicle* article by Read Kingsbury; Susan Schwardt, president of the League of Women Voters, to Helena Donohue, Republican commissioner of the state board of elections, June 22, 1990, on file at League of Women Voters and with author; "Fact Sheet and Action Alert" of the Statewide Coalition for Voter Participation, NYPIRG files.

51. Helena Donohue, quoted in the *Times Union* (Albany), February 26, 1991. She added that she also wanted a script written that state workers involved in voter registration would have to follow so they would avoid letting their own political views affect registrants. The second quote appeared two days later in the *Times Union,* February 28, 1991. This daily newspaper has the largest circulation in the Albany area.

52. *The Sunday Observer-Dispatch* (Utica), July 8, 1990.

53. Quote from Plunkett in *The Record* (Albany) October 4, 1990; quote from the lawsuit in the *New York Times,* October 4, 1990; press release from NYPIRG,

October 3, 1990. The lawsuit, *100 Percent Vote/Human SERVE et al.* v. *New York State Board of Elections,* was filed in October 1990. The plaintiffs were members of the Statewide Coalition for Voter Participation, which included Common Cause, NYPIRG, the Community Service Society (CSS), District Council 37, and the National Congress for Puerto Rican Rights.

54. Court order of Judge Irma Santealla, February 22, 1991.

55. Editorial, *New York Times,* October 15, 1990.

56. Court order of Judge Irma Santealla, February 22, 1991.

57. According to advocates, the board limited the sites to fewer than half of the five hundred identified in 1990. They claimed that during the month of March alone, when the board rejected New York City's offer of postage-paid forms, its supply fell short of agency need by more than a hundred thousand. Shirley Traylor, counsel for CSS, letter to Thomas Wallace, executive director of the state board, March 20, 1991, on file at CSS.

58. Judith Ritter, counsel for CSS, letter to Michael Losinger, deputy executive director of the state board of elections, June 7, 1991, on file at CSS.

59. *Times Union* (Albany), May 24, 1991.

60. *Times Union* (Albany), February 28, 1991.

61. *New York Times,* May 2, 1992. The *Times* blamed Republican opposition and the "timidity" of Governor Cuomo, who had indicated that he would veto the legislature's reapportionment plans unless they were accompanied by serious election reform. The *New York Times* said that "the main anger should be reserved for the Republicans who fight real reform," but that "Cuomo, who raised hopes, never rallied support for reform and fudged on his standards."

62. They are the Office of Mental Health, Office of Mental Retardation and Developmental Disabilities, and Office of Vocational Education Services for Individuals with Disabilities. This brought the number of sites to more than four hundred statewide for all agencies covered by the law. The agencies did not actually begin implementing the program, however, until 1994. New York State Board of Elections 1991 and 1992 Annual Reports.

63. In keeping with the bipartisan structure within the board, the deputy executive director is a member of the opposite political party. Thus, the new deputy executive director at the time, Thomas Zolezzi, was a Republican. (Today the Republican deputy director is Peter Kosinski).

64. Interviews with author.

65. Michael Losinger, interview with author.

66. New York State Board of Elections Annual Reports and memoranda.

67. Figures are based on the total number of registration forms returned to the state board of elections and a generous estimate of a 25 percent rate of return on all forms acquired at agency sites. There is no way to determine precisely how many forms were actually returned. Some clients probably declined to register—or took forms and did not return them—for various reasons, including already being registered, fear, and lack of interest. New York State Board of Elections, 1992 Annual Report.

68. New York State Board of Elections, 1992 Annual Report.

69. Statistics on file at NYPIRG and reported in testimony at public hearing of New York City Voter Assistance Commission, December 1994. In 2000, 52.1 percent of New York City residents of voting age held a driver's license, compared with 93.3 percent in the rest of the state. The data sources are as follows: New York State DMV

Internet Office; New York State Licenses on File 2000; U.S. Bureau of the Census, Profile of General Demographic Characteristics for New York: 2000; and New York City Department of City Planning, Population Division—Demographic Profile. Racial and age figures are currently unavailable. The data on racial disparities in New York City came from the Institute for Puerto Rican Policy and are based on the 1990 Census STF3 file.

70. New York State Board of Elections, press release, May 15, 1995.

71. New York State Board of Elections, data provided to author.

72. Wilkey and Jerome Koenig, the former chief of staff of the Assembly Election Law Committee, carefully crafted the enabling legislation for a proposed amendment to the state constitution that was ratified by voters in 1994. The amendment would have changed constitutional language regarding voter registration. New York also used the occasion to eliminate certain outdated provisions in the state constitution, including literacy tests, a voting age set at twenty-one, and a requirement that voters register one year before a primary election.

73. Human SERVE 1995 report on the first year of the NVRA. See also Piven and Cloward 2000.

74. *New York Times,* April 4, 1995.

75. Ibid. Several memos from Jackson to the executive chamber, dated January 17, 1995, and February 6, 1995, outline this strategy. When these memos were made public in March, voting rights advocates and liberal Democrats—including New York City's five Democratic county chairs—held several press conferences condemning this move by the Pataki administration (New York State Archives; office of the governor; Department of Motor Vehicles).

76. Editorial, *New York Times,* April 4, 1995.

77. Jerome Keonig, interview with author.

78. These data, based on the U.S. Census of 1990 and DMV data, were compiled by NYPIRG and were widely circulated. Elected officials and election administrators routinely incorporated the data into their own memos and reports at the time.

79. Jerome Koenig, interview with author, April 24, 2003.

80. Advocates successfully pressed Wilkey for my appointment to the task force as a representative of the Voter Assistance Commission, of which I was the coordinator from 1993 to 1996. I served on the State Task Force Subcommittee on Agency-Based Registration.

81. Data from the State Board of Elections, compiled by Human SERVE; M. Green 1995.

82. Implementation of Nassau County's motor voter programs was delayed for much of 1995 due to opposition by local officials, according to state board officials.

83. One was then–public advocate Mark Green in New York City, and a second was then–state comptroller Carl McCall.

84. M. Green 1995. Green's study also showed that eighteen of every twenty people eligible for registration materials received them in the public assistance office in Staten Island, and nine of the ten did so at the Kingsbridge and Melrose Centers in the Bronx. These centers are located in better-off areas that overwhelmingly voted for Giuliani over Dinkins in 1993.

85. *New York Times,* October 2, 1995.

86. Office of the New York State Comptroller 1996. McCall did this report in

lieu of a more complete audit, more typical of the comptroller's office, because audits generally take much more time to complete.

87. Assembly Election Law Committee notice of the public hearing.

88. In a court settlement signed January 19, 1996, the Department of Labor dropped its opposition to implementing the state NVRA law. Advocates even got the department to consent to using a combined form, a major victory for advocates. *New York Times,* January 20, 1996. In 220,000 transactions from February to June 1996, only 13,000 people were registered to vote. Most of the remainder of the transactions produced declinations or blank forms (either a client declined to register or the worker never offered the client the opportunity to register), according to data provided by the state board of elections to Human SERVE and CSS.

89. New York City Board of Elections. Data include all registrations, from NVRA agencies and elsewhere.

90. At the time of this writing the lawsuits are not fully settled. The state has only made agreements and changes regarding some of the affected agencies.

91. New York State Board of Elections.

92. HAVA, passed on October 29, 2002, is the first major federal election reform legislation since the National Voter Registration Act of 1993 and the Voting Rights Act of 1965.

93. Rapoport 2003.

94. The groups represented included the NAACP Legal Defense and Education Fund, NYPIRG, the League of Women Voters, the Puerto Rican Legal Defense and Education Fund, and several organizations of people with disabilities. Wilkey also appointed other election officials and administrators of affected state agencies, such as the DMV.

95. E. Benjamin 2003.

96. Editorial, *New York Times,* March 17, 2003.

97. E. Benjamin 2003.

98. The New York State Citizens' Coalition's testimony on implementation of the Help America Vote Act at public hearing of Joint Committees on Election Law and Government Operations of the New York State Assembly and Senate, April 14, 2003. See also Abrams et al. 2003; Demos 2003 and 2004b; NYPIRG's HAVA Web pages at www.nypirg.org; Brennan Center for Justice Web pages at www.brennancenter.org; L. McDonald 2002; and Rapoport 2003.

99. Brennan Center for Justice 2004.

100. New York Public Interest Research Group 2004b.

101. Yancey 2003. Pataki hired Buley during the fall 2002 primary season.

102. New York State Citizens' Coalition's testimony on implementation of the Help America Vote Act at public hearing of Joint Committees on Election Law and Government Operations of the New York State Assembly and Senate, April 14, 2003. See also Abrams et al. 2003 and Demos 2004b.

103. "Statement of Neal Rosenstein, Government Reform Coordinator, NYPIRG, on Stopgap Legislative Implementation of the Help America Vote Act, August 12, 2004," NYPIRG files.

104. Abrams et al. 2003; New York State Citizens' Coalition's testimony on implementation of the Help America Vote Act at public hearing of Joint Committees on Election Law and Government Operations of the New York State Assembly and Senate, April 14, 2003.

105. Editorial, *New York Times,* August 10, 2004.

4. The New York City Board of Elections

1. Quotes from George Friedman, former Bronx County Democratic leader and a commissioner of the New York City Board of Elections, and Franz Leichter, former New York state senator from Manhattan, a vocal critic of the city board, who testified at a public hearing of the New York State Assembly Election Law Committee, October 19, 1988.

2. Robert Elliot, partner of Peat, Marwick, Mitchell & Co., member of the New York City Partnership Task Force, and chairman of the oversight board of the New York City Elections Project, interview with author, September 17, 1992.

3. These New York–based advocacy groups include the organizations referred to in the previous chapter. For a list of current reform groups, see www.nycelectionwatch.org/coalition.html.

4. Loughlin 1974; Gottlieb and Baquet 1990.

5. Lowi 1964; Wolfinger 1972; Erie 1988; Mayhew 1986; Mollenkopf 1994.

6. Mollenkopf 1991.

7. Lowi 1964; Shefter 1994; Hammack 1982; R. L. McCormick 1981.

8. Shefter 1994.

9. Shefter 1985, 1994; Erie 1988; McNickle 1993. About political clubs, see Peel 1935; Adler and Blank 1975; Gerson 1990; and Kraus 1988. About elite interests, see Lowi 1964; Newfield and DuBrul 1977; Newfield and Barrett 1988; Thompson 1990; Shefter 1994; and Mollenkopf 1994.

10. Mollenkopf 1987, 494; Thompson 1990; Mollenkopf 1994.

11. Mollenkopf 1992, 97; Shefter 1994; Mayhew 1986.

12. Shefter 1985, 102–3; Mollenkopf 1992, 127, 122; Schneier and Murtaugh 2001.

13. Peel 1935; Adler and Blank 1975; Gerson 1990.

14. Ken Fireman, *Newsday,* 1988; Gottlieb and Baquet 1990.

15. Newfield and Barrett 1988; New York State Commission on Government Integrity, 1990 report; Mollenkopf 1992.

16. Mollenkopf 1992, 236; Thompson 1990.

17. Tom Wathen, executive director of NYPIRG, press release, October 9, 1984, on file with author; testimony of Hulbert James, executive director Human SERVE, at public hearing of Joint Committee on Election Law of the New York State Assembly and Senate, March 13, 1984; Thompson 1990.

18. Thompson 1990, 6, 57–58; Mollenkopf 1987, 1994; Roberts, *New York Times,* April 1, 1984.

19. Trinkl 1984, 3.

20. Editorials, *New York Times,* November 2 and 12, 1984; Schanberg, *New York Times,* October 2, 1984.

21. Editorial, *New York Times,* November 12, 1984; Gene Russianoff, NYPIRG, testimony before the Citizens Commission on Civil Rights, New York City, November 8 and 26, 1984, and before a public hearing of the Assembly Election Law Committee, October 22, 1987.

22. Editorial *New York Times,* August 14, 1985.

23. NYPIRG Press release quoting Tom Wathen, October 9, 1984; Sydney Schanberg, *New York Times,* October 2, 1984.

24. Gene Russianoff, staff attorney for NYPIRG, to Carol Bellamy, New York City Council president, October 15, 1984.

25. Bea Dolen is quoted in the *New York Times,* October 4, 1984; Alair Townsend is quoted in the *New York Times,* October 4 and 12, 1984.

26. Barbanel 1984.

27. Ibid.

28. Bea Dolen, in *New York Times,* November 12, 1984.

29. Shefter 1985; Fitch 1993; Mollenkopf 1994; Newfield and Barrett 1988.

30. Shefter 1985, 176–77.

31. Assembly Election Law Committee 1987 Annual Report; Assembly Election Law Committee Notice of Public Hearing for its hearing of October 19, 1988.

32. B. Green 1991.

33. Interviews with members of the Cuomo administration and the Assembly, including Jerome Koenig, chief of staff of the Assembly Election Law Committee, and Michael Losinger, former deputy director of the Department of Motor Vehicles and prior to that deputy director of the state board of elections; also interviews with activists and officials at the city level: Linda Davidoff, executive director of Human SERVE, and Gene Russianoff, staff attorney for NYPIRG; elections officials on the city board of elections and with the New York City Elections Project (NYCEP); and officials from the Koch administration.

34. *New York Times,* September 7, 1985; October 19, 1985; November 5, 1985.

35. Author interviews of NYPIRG staff and elected officials.

36. Gene Russianoff, staff attorney of NYPIRG, *New York Times,* November 12, 1984, and in testimony at public hearing of New York State Assembly Election Law Committee, October 22, 1987; Franz Leichter, testimony at public hearing of New York State Assembly Election Law Committee, October 19, 1988; Wade 1994.

37. Testimony of advocates to state legislators, the Koch administration, the City Council, and the board of elections; correspondence between advocates and author.

38. Gene Russianoff, program coordinator of NYPIRG, letter to David Moskovitz, director of NYCEP, May 27, 1986, NYPIRG files and on file with author.

39. Editorial, *New York Times,* August 14, 1985.

40. Frank J. Macchiarola to Mayor Koch, August 13, 1985, in New York City Partnership 1985.

41. Jon Del Giorno, former administrative manager of the New York City Board of Elections, interview with author, December 1992.

42. David Moskovitz, executive director of NYCEP, interview with author, October 2, 1992.

43. New York City Partnership 1985 and interviews with author.

44. Summary report of the first oversight board meeting, held on October 21, 1985, in New York City Municipal Archives and on file with author.

45. Quote from testimony of David Moskovitz, director of NYCEP, at public hearing of the New York State Assembly Election Law Committee, October 19, 1988; Maureen Walsh, director of NYCEP, interview with author, 1992.

46. David Moskovitz, interview with author, October 2, 1992.

47. Stephanie Dawson, interview with author, October 22, 1992.

48. David Moskovitz, interview with author, October 2, 1992.

49. NYCEP Report and interviews with author.

50. New York City Elections Project 1986.

51. New York City Elections Project Oversight Board 1986, 2; David Moskovitz and Stephanie Dawson, interviews with author in 1986 and 1992, respectively.

52. NYCEP Status Report, July 13, 1987.

53. David Moskovitz, interview with author, 1992.

54. Board staff including Naomi Bernstein, William Cro, and Danny DeFrancesco, interviews with author; Gene Russianoff, interview with author, 1992.

55. Interviews with board commissioners, executive staff, clerks, and Partnership task force staff.

56. Ferdinand Marchi and Richard Wagner, testimony at public hearing of the New York State Assembly Election Law Committee, October 19, 1988.

57. Quote from NYCEP briefing document, at New York City Municipal Archives and on file with author.

58. *New York Times,* November 12, 1984.

59. Daniel DeFrancesco, executive director of the New York City Board of Elections, speech at the Conference of the New York State Election Commissioners Association, September 7, 1990.

60. New York City Elections Project 1987.

61. Stephen Louis, memo to Stuart Osnow, January 7, 1986, in New York City Municipal Archives and on file with author.

62. Jerome Koenig, interview with author, April 2003.

63. Robert Black and George Friedman, at public hearing of the New York State Assembly Election Law Committee, October 19, 1988; Adler and Blank 1975.

64. Bea Dolen and Fred Panteleone, former executive director and deputy executive director, respectively, of the New York City Board of Elections, testimony at hearing of New York State Assembly Election Law Committee, October 19, 1988.

65. Vincent Montalbano, director of political action for District Council 37, testimony at public hearing of the New York State Assembly Election Law Committee, October 19, 1988.

66. Alan Rothstein, representing the Citizens Union, and Gene Russianoff, NYPIRG, testimony at public hearing of the New York State Assembly Election Law Committee, October 19, 1988.

67. Interviews with members of the Partnership's task force, NYCEP, and advocacy organizations. Regarding the situation in 1986, David Moskovitz testified before the Assembly Election Law Committee on October 19, 1988. Regarding the 1990 episode, Daniel DeFrancesco testified before a meeting of the Government Operations Committee of the City Council in 1990.

68. New York City Elections Project 1986.

69. A similar revealing struggle ensued in 2003 when Republican John Ravitz became the executive director.

70. *Newsday,* April 21, 1988.

71. Press release, August 17, 1988, on file with author.

72. Coalition for Voter Participation, draft letter to Robert Black, president of the Board of Elections, September 1988, on file with author; *Newsday,* September 8, 1988.

73. *New York Times,* September 8, 1988.

74. *Newsday,* September 5, 1988.

75. Draft letter dated September 6, 1988, in NYPIRG files and on file with author. Other signatories included David Dinkins, Charles Rangel, and Stanley Hill. *New York Times,* September 8, 1988.

76. *New York Times,* September 8, 1988.

77. *New York Times,* September 9, 1988; reference to riots was made by Ferdinand Marchi, commissioner and president of the Board of Elections, in testimony at a public hearing of the New York State Assembly Election Law Committee, October 19, 1988; last quotes are from the *New York Times,* September 15, 1988.

78. Fireman, *Newsday* 1988; Gottlieb and Baquet 1990.

79. Gottlieb and Baquet 1990.

80. Ibid.

81. Maria Laurino, *The Village Voice,* April 1990.

82. New York City Partnership 1986; New York City Partnership and New York City Elections Project Oversight Board 1990.

83. This was an addition to the original plans for modernization, one for which advocates had effectively lobbied.

84. David Moskovitz, testimony at public hearing of the New York State Assembly Election Law Committee, October 19, 1988.

85. NYCEP Status Report, July 13, 1987. Other improvements to election-day materials were made in 1988.

86. NYCEP Status Report, January 1989.

87. Daniel DeFrancesco, memo to Louise Altman, March 14, 1995, in NYPIRG files and on file with author.

88. David Moskovitz, interview with author.

89. Jerome Koenig, interview with author, 1992.

90. NYCEP Status Report, June 1990.

91. Horner 1990.

92. Gene Russianoff, interview with the author.

93. Horner 1990.

94. Smolka 1974; Election Center, at www.electioncenter.org.

95. NYCEP report, July 15, 1988.

96. "Affidavit Ballots" 1986.

97. Board Commissioner Douglas Kellner, Democrat from Manhattan, an appointee of Denny Farrell, the Manhattan County Chair, interview with author.

98. Board memorandum to the Law Department of Corporation Counsel, December 1992, at New York City Board of Elections, New York City Law Department of Corporation Council, and on file with author.

99. Interviews with officials at the New York City Board of Elections and other election experts.

100. New York City Board of Elections, memorandum to NYPIRG, November 30, 1993, at New York City Board of Elections, NYPIRG, and on file with author.

101. *New York Times,* December 19, 1993.

102. Jerome Koenig, interview with author, April 2003.

103. New York City Board of Elections, Electronic Voting Systems Project Operations Review, September 1993, Deloitte & Touche, at New York City Board of Elections and on file with author.

104. Testimony of Norman Adler and Jerome Koenig at public hearing of Joint Committee on Election Law of the New York State Assembly and Senate, March 13, 1984. See p. 16 of the transcript.

105. *Newsday,* May 1993.

106. Interviews with Jerome Koenig, Douglas Kellner, and other board staff.

107. New York City Board of Elections Annual Reports, 1988–1993.

108. Interviews with board administrators and employees.

109. New York State Election Law, Section 5-210 (8).

110. New York State Election Law, Section 8-302 (3) (a).

111. The Community Service Society, ACORN, and the Asian American Legal and Defense Fund (AALDEF), in interviews with author.

112. Jerome Koenig, interview with author, April 2003.

113. New York State Election Law, Section 4-117 (1).

114. New York State Board of Elections Annual Reports and interview with board personnel; various reports of the *Times Union* (Albany) newspaper; Web site of the Citizens Union's *Gotham Gazette* www.gothamgazette.com; and New York Wired Group Web site www.newyorkwired.com.

115. Arian et al. 1991, 23.

116. White 1994.

117. Brewer and Stonecash 2001; Schneier and Murtaugh 2001.

5. The Specter of Vote Fraud

1. Testimony of Suzanne Israel Tufts at public hearing of the New York State Senate Election Law Committee, July 28, 1993. Tufts headed both ballot-security operations.

2. Congressional Record, U.S. Senate, March 16, 1993, 2906.

3. Press release / public announcement of NYS Senate Election Law Committee Public Hearing.

4. Interviews with Thomas Wilkey, executive director of the New York State Board of Elections; Emmit Femeau, executive director of the Washington, D.C., Board of Ethics and Elections; William Kimberling of the Federal Elections Commission.

5. *Daily News,* March 15, 1994.

6. *Newsday,* April 4, 1993, p. 27.

7. Three such advocates, Will Daniel, director of Homeless Voter; Donna James, director of the voter registration for the Coalition for the Homeless; and Shakoor Aljuwani, director of the Manhattan Voter Participation Project of the Community Service Society, responded to the *Newsday* article in a letter to the editor dated April 5, 1993. This letter, however, was not published. It is on file with the author.

8. Joe Calderone and Russ Buettner, *Newsday,* May 12, 1993.

9. *New York Post,* May 29, 1993.

10. *Newsday,* May 27, 1993.

11. Editorial, *New York Post,* May 28, 1993.

12. Press release / public announcement of NYS Senate Election Law Committee Public Hearing.

13. *Newsday,* May 28, 1993.

14. *New York Post,* July 29, 1993.

15. Jon Del Giorno, administrative manager of the city board or elections, interview with author, 1994.

16. Interview with officials of New York City Board of Elections.

17. Interviews with and publications of officials of the city board of elections, NYPIRG, New York State Democratic Party, Richard Schwartz, and Victory '93 (the Republican statewide committee); People for the American Way and NAACP 2004.

18. I interviewed and had meetings with several individuals who made this claim about Republican links to news media, including journalists in both print and television media, a Giuliani administration official who worked on the campaign, a Democratic official who claimed to have been told about it by a Republican official, and a board of elections official. *New York Times,* November 1993.

19. *New York Times,* November 1993.

20. Interviews with Jerome Koenig and Gene Russianoff, 1993 and 1994.

21. *Newsday,* July 8, 1993.

22. *Newsday,* October 18, 1993.

23. *Newsday,* July 28, 1993.

24. See, in particular, *Newsday,* June 30, 1993; *New York Post,* July 28 and October 26, 1993.

25. *New York Times,* November 1, 1993.

26. I was the coordinator of the Voter Assistance Commission (VAC).

27. Data analysis was conducted by the staff of VAC, particularly Jocelyn Sargent and Dirk Slater, and involved 163 complaints made by nearly one hundred people.

28. Such groups include the Community Service Society, NYPIRG, ACORN, and the Coalition for the Homeless.

29. Douglas Kellner, communication with author.

30. Richard Jerome at the Voting Rights Section of the Civil Rights Division of the U.S. Department of Justice handled this investigation. The city board of elections forwarded allegations of voting irregularities to the district attorney's office and the state board of elections. No one was ever prosecuted; nor was any report made public.

31. Al Gordon, chair of the New York State Democratic Party, letter to the U.S. Department of Justice, November 30, 1993, at U.S. Department of Justice and on file with author.

32. These data are drawn from Mollenkopf 1994.

33. Ibid., 210–11.

34. Ibid., 210–12.

35. Board memos, March 5 and 14, 1995.

36. Ibid; Daniel DeFrancesco, executive director of the city board of elections, letter to Louise Altman of Human SERVE, at New York City Board of Elections and on file with author.

37. Jon del Giorno, administrative manager of the city board of elections, and Joseph Gentilli, former deputy executive director of the city board, interviews with author and testimony in meetings and at a public hearing of the New York City Council Committee on Governmental Operations, October 1993.

38. Voter Research Surveys exit polling, 1993, available at Voter News Service; *New York Times,* November 9, 1993.

39. Mollenkopf 1992, 4.

40. Ibid.; Fitch 1995; Conason 1995; various reports by the City Project, the Fiscal Policy Institute, and the Community Service Society, published between 1994 and 1998 and available on their respective Web sites.

41. Jerome Koenig, interview with author, 2003.

42. Jon del Giorno, administrative manager of the city board, interview with author, May 30, 1996.

43. Ibid.

6. Florida's Wake

1. "Election Follies: As a New York City Primary Election Shows, Chaos Isn't Exclusive to Florida," *Orlando Sentinel Tribune,* October 17, 2001.

2. Hicks 2001.

3. This quote is from a board of elections official who wished to remain anonymous. Several elected officials, investigative journalists, and members of voting rights organizations also echoed this sentiment.

4. Quote from *Newsday,* September 4, 2001; *New York Times,* September 8, 2001.

5. Office of Attorney General Eliot Spitzer, i–ii.

6. The quote is from testimony given by Robert Abrams, president of the board of the Citizens Union Foundation and former attorney general of the state of New York, at public hearing of New York City Council Committee on Governmental Operations, February 8, 2001. The forum where Richard Wagner made the statement was held by the Center for Excellence in New York City Governance at New York University; it was called "Pulling the Lever: Is New York City Ready for the 2001 Election?"

7. At the Coalition for Voter Participation Web site are a mission statement, a list of member organizations, and a number of reports. See www.nycelectionwatch.org/coalition.html.

8. Portions of this section were originally published by the Century Foundation as "The 2001 Elections in New York City" (Hayduk 2002).

9. The monitoring operation was principally organized by the New York Public Interest Research Group (NYPIRG) and the New York University Center For Excellence in Governance, which developed the survey instrument and recruited surveyors primarily through the Citywide Coalition for Voter Participation. I am a member of the coalition and participated in the development of the survey.

10. Research assistance in data gathering and analysis was provided by, in alphabetical order, Jennifer Heettner, Jillian Jonas, Josh Klein, John Mollenkopf, Troy Wass, and Cindy Young. I wish to especially thank John Mollenkopf, who provided me with data that linked census information with election data, allowing for analysis of the impact of election problems on particular constituents and neighborhoods; and Josh Klein, who lent invaluable assistance by leading the analysis of the data. Of course, I take responsibility for any errors.

11. Russianoff and Palmer 2001.

12. We used a regression model to see if the voting problem type (independent variable) influenced the votes for mayoral candidates (dependent variable) for the monitored EDs. We found that voting problems explained over 2 percent of the variance in those mayoral votes. The R Square, .023, indicates that 2.3 percent of the variance in mayoral votes is explained by the incidence of two of our three large categories of voting problems. This is a statistically robust finding—the significance probability is better than .01 for both poll-site and administrative problems. Machine problems were not found to be statistically significant in this analysis, but were significant regarding the undervote.

13. Caltech/MIT 2001; U.S. House of Representatives Committee on Government Reform, Minority Office 2001; Advancement Project 2001; Stephanie Saul 2001b; Russianoff and Palmer 2001.

14. These findings were determined by use of a one-way analysis of variance to examine whether there were differences in the average lost votes for each racial and ethnic

group. Data from the New York City Board of Elections contains all cases for every election district in the city.

15. Saul 2001d.

16. Saul 2001c.

17. Saul 2001e. Saul's method for calculating lost votes in 2001 elections was as follows: "We looked at all the election night reports of canvass from the three boroughs mentioned. Those reports list the total public counter. We calculated the difference between the total public counter and the total vote, then divided the total vote into that number. The resulting number is a percentage undervote." Email correspondence with author, January 22, 2002.

18. Saul 2001c, 2001d.

19. Cooper and Cardwell 2001.

20. Saul 2001d. See also Cooper and Cardwell 2001.

21. John Grady, Report to the New York City Board of Elections Commissioners, 2–3, undated, at New York City Board of Elections.

22. Douglas Kellner, interview with author; John Grady, Report to the New York City Board of Elections Commissioners, 2–3, undated, at New York City Board of Elections.

23. According to Jon del Giorno, administrative manager of the New York City Board of Elections, Nassau and Suffolk counties use slightly different but comparable voting machines (interview with author, 2002).

24. Saul 2001d. See also Cooper and Cardwell 2001.

25. Saul 2001d; Cooper and Cardwell 2001; New York City Board of Elections Staff, 2002 Report to Commissioners of the New York City Board of Elections.

26. Douglas Kellner, interview with author, 2002.

27. Researchers removed incomplete forms and duplicate surveys from the same election districts from the study in order to employ scientifically sound methods, which left a total of 559 completed surveys. Assembly districts are made up of hundreds of election districts. They roughly correspond to neighborhoods, and therefore contain tens of thousands of registered voters.

28. Saul 2001d; Cooper and Cardwell 2001.

29. Regarding the episode in 2000, the source is Jerome Koenig, former chief of staff of the Assembly Election Law Committee, interview with author. Regarding the episode in 2001, Jon del Giorno, interview with author, September 3, 2002.

30. Mayor's Task Force on Election Modernization 2001, 7.

31. Testimony of Arthur J. Fried, executive director of the Center for Excellence in New York City Governance, Robert F. Wagner Graduate School for Public Service, New York University, at public hearing of New York City Council Committee on Governmental Operations, February 8, 2001.

32. New York State Election Law, Section 7-203(2), 2000.

33. Saul 2001a.

34. Saul 2001g. See also a memo to the board of elections and to the U.S. Department of Justice from the Puerto Rican Legal Defense and Education Fund (PRLDEF), October 2001, on file with author.

35. Linda Stone Davidoff, "NYC Issues 2001: The Voting Process," available at www.Gothamgazette.com. One commissioner in particular, Douglas Kellner, was primarily responsible for holding up the purchase of new voting machines due to security concerns. Other experts who raised concerns include Ronnie Dugger. See 1988, 1995.

36. Mayor's Task Force on Election Modernization 2001, 7–8; Saul 2001f.

37. Saul 2001d.

38. These communities studied include Chinatown, Flushing, Elmhurst, Floral Park, Richmond Hill, Sunset Park, and Homecrest.

39. Earlier documentation of problems was presented at hearings of the New York City Voter Assistance Commission, the New York State Assembly Election Law Committee, and the New York City Council Committee on Governmental Operations; in Office of Attorney General Eliot Spitzer 2001; in the Governor's Task Force on Election Modernization 2002; in the Mayor's Task Force on Election Modernization 2001; and in AALDEF exit poll reports.

40. Linda Stone Davidoff, "NYC Issues 2001: Polling Places," available at www.gothamgazette.com. Jerome Keonig said that "some trainers are not up to the job" (interview with author).

41. Mayor Mayor's Task Force on Election Modernization 2001, 10. In July 2001, in testimony before City Council, the board estimated that it might be short up to 4,000 poll workers if pay was not increased.

42. Citizens Union Foundation Election Reform Project 2002.

43. Mayor's Task Force on Election Modernization 2001, 22; Cooper and Cardwell 2001; Jon del Giorno, interview with author, September 3, 2002.

44. Neal Rosenstein, NYPIRG, interview with author, 2002.

45. Saul and Rayman 2001.

46. Saul 2001c.

47. Saul 2001c, 2001d; Cooper and Cardwell 2001; Katz and Blood 2001.

48. Jerry Goldfedder, election lawyer for Mark Green, interview with author, 2002.

49. Jon del Giorno, interview with author, September 3, 2002. Jerome Koenig corroborated this view in our 2003 interview.

50. Minnite and Callahan 2003. Other Demos reports on election-day registration are available at www.demos-usa.org.

51. A similar situation occurred in 1997 during the Democratic primary election between Ruth Messinger and Reverend Sharpton, in which the initial numbers changed. Initially the results showed that Messinger had won, but then Sharpton gained votes in the counting of paper ballots, which left the outcome uncertain and the possibility of a runoff election open while ballots were counted over many days. Ultimately Messinger gained the most votes, but she lost valuable time and momentum in the process, and the situation provoked doubt on the part of some minority voters, all of which affected the dynamics of the general election. These episodes show that such electoral problems and dynamics are neither new to New York nor particular to Florida.

52. New York Public Interest Research Group 2002, 1.

53. Analysis of lost votes, or undervotes, in the 2002 elections was not conducted because data were not available.

54. Jerome Koenig, interview with author, 2003.

55. Quotes from Neal Rosenstein, in testimony before the Voter Assistance Commission's annual hearing on the status of the electoral process in the city of New York, December 7, 2004. In 2004, about 7.4 million voters cast ballots in New York State compared with 6.8 million in 2000; in New York City, about 2.4 million voters turned out compared with 2 million in 2000, according to the New York State Board of Elections Web site (www.elections.state.ny.us).

56. New York Public Interest Research Group 2004a.

57. AALDEF, press release, "Asian American Civil Rights Group Reports Widespread Voter Problems on Election Day," November 2, 2004, at AALDEF.

58. Williams 2004.

59. Steinhaur 2004.

60. Bloomberg announced his intent to form a task force on November 11, 2004, during his weekly radio address. Bloomberg 2004. The task force replicates Giuliani's Mayor's Task Force on Election Modernization, formed after the debacle in Florida and just prior to the 2001 municipal elections in New York City.

61. Bloomberg 2004. Also cited in McIntire 2004.

62. Williams 2004.

63. Douglas Kellner, testimony at the public hearing of the New York City Voter Assistance Commission, December 7, 2004.

64. Douglas Kellner, testimony at the public hearing of the New York City Voter Assistance Commission, December 7, 2004.

65. Neal Rosenstein, testimony at the public hearing of the New York City Voter Assistance Commission, December 7, 2004.

66. Gene Russianoff, quoted in Steinhauer 2004.

67. Neal Rosenstein, testimony at the public hearing of the New York City Voter Assistance Commission, December 7, 2004.

68. Rock the Vote 2004.

69. Foderaro 2004.

70. "Electionline Weekly," December 2, 2004, available at www.electionline.org.

71. Tova Wang, senior program officer and democracy fellow at the Century Foundation, interview with the author, December 2004.

72. Editorial, "New York's Electoral Mess," *New York Times*. December 8, 2004.

7. Implications for Policy

1. Schattschneider 1960, xi. My thanks to Joel Lefkowitz for pointing out Schattschneider's observation.

2. Caltech/MIT Voting Technology Project 2001; The National Commission on Federal Election Reform 2001; Constitution Project 2001; National Conference of State Legislators 2001; U.S. General Accounting Office 2001; Congressional Research Service 2001; U.S. Commission on Civil Rights 2001; Lichtman 2001; U.S. House of Representatives Committee on Government Reform, Minority Office 2001; U.S. House of Representatives Committee on the Judiciary, Democratic Investigative Staff 2001; Merzer and staff 2001; Rakove 2001; Roth 2001; Keyssar 2001; Palast 2003; Election Protection Coalition 2004; Common Cause 2004; Demos 2004a; Election Reform Information Project 2004.

3. One example is *NAACP v. Harris*. I was one of the expert witnesses in the case and produced a report that focused on voter disenfranchisement caused by election administration in seven Florida counties.

4. The company hired, Choice Point, settled a lawsuit brought by the NAACP in 2002. See the settlement agreement in *NAACP v. Harris*. Palast 2003; Keyssar 2001, 87–88.

5. M. McDonald 2002; People for the American Way and NAACP 2004; Common Cause 2004.

6. Minnite and Callahan 2003, 10.

7. Editorial, "An Umpire Taking Sides," Making Votes Count series, *New York Times,* July 9, 2004. Holden won his seat in 2000 by a very slim margin: roughly 21,000 votes out of 2.3 million cast.

8. Editorial, "The New Hanging Chads," *New York Times,* August 19, 2004.

9. The Election Protection Coalition 2004; Common Cause 2004; Demos 2004a; electionline.org, 2004, Election Reform Information Project 2004; Carbo 2005; Pastor 2005; Wang 2005; House Judiciary Committee Democratic Staff 2005; over one hundred news articles from around the country, many of which are cited and summarized in Election Reform Information Project 2004; and the other reports cited earlier in this volume and the Web sites of their respective authors' organizations. See Introduction, note 6, for details about the 2004 monitoring efforts of the Election Protection Coalition and other groups.

10. Election Protection Coalition 2004, 4.

11. Wang 2005; Election Protection Coalition 2004, 4.

12. Wang 2005.

13. Cited in Wang 2005.

14. Tova Wang, interview with author, December 2004; Election Protection Coalition 2004; House Judiciary Committee Democratic Staff 2005.

15. Rock the Vote Web site at www.rockthevote.com.

16. A 2001 Caltech/MIT study showed that over 1 million voters experienced such registration problems in the 2000 elections. Caltech/MIT Voting Technology Project 2001.

17. Election Reform Information Project 2004, 5.

18. Editorial, "Improving Provisional Ballots." *New York Times,* November 21, 2004.

19. Demos 2004a.

20. Election Reform Information Project 2004, 5; Demos 2004a, 2004c.

21. Election Reform Information Project 2004.

22. Wang 2005.

23. Wang 2005.

24. Demos 2004a, 2004c.

25. These states included Washington, Nevada, Alaska, New Jersey, Maryland, Montana, Wyoming, Wisconsin, North Carolina, Alabama, West Virginia, Iowa, Illinois, Michigan and Georgia. Election Reform Information Project 2004.

26. Tova Wang, interview with the author, December 2004; Demos 2004a, 2004c.

27. Wang 2005; Election Protection Coalition 2004; Rosenfeld 2004.

28. Rosenfeld 2004.

29. Wang 2005; Rosenfeld 2004.

30. Election Data Services Web site, www.electiondataservices.com.

31. Wang 2005.

32. Pastor 2005; Wang 2005.

33. A preliminary study of provisional ballots by Demos shows that nearly half of the hundreds of recorded provisional ballot problems were due to poll workers' failure to provide voters with such ballots as required. Demos 2004a. See also Election Protection Coalition 2004 and House Judiciary Committee Democratic Staff 2005.

34. In 1981 Republicans had sent postcards, predominantly to minority voters, warning of criminal penalties for voting illegally. Hundreds of thousands of cards returned as undeliverable were used to compile a list of voters to be challenged at the polls. On election day in 1981, hundreds of armed guards were stationed at

minority poll sites. In that election Democrat Jim Florio lost to Republican Tom Kean by about two thousand votes in the closest election in New Jersey history. After the Democrats filed a lawsuit charging the Republicans with intimidation of black and Latino voters, an agreement was reached in 1982 in which Republicans agreed never to target minority voters, even though they insisted that that had never been their goal and that instead they were trying to ensure that the election would be free of fraud. Schwaneberg 2004.

35. House Judiciary Committee Democratic Staff 2005.

36. Herbert 2004.

37. Wang 2005; Carbo 2005; Election Protection Coalition 2004; Common Cause 2004.

38. Britt 2004.

39. Carbo 2005.

40. Carbo, 2005. Data on the number of Department of Justice prosecutions is from the Transactional Records Access Clearinghouse at Syracuse University, cited in Carbo 2005.

41. Tizon 2004; Sanders 2005.

42. Stohlberg and Dao 2005.

43. Mooney 2004.

44. Fitch 1995; Schneier and Murtaugh 2001; Stonecash 2001 (particularly part 3). See also annual reports published by the Fiscal Policy Institute and the Community Service Society over the past ten years, which detail impacts of the budgets proposed by the Pataki administration and enacted by the state legislature, as well as budget policy in New York City under the Giuliani and Bloomberg administrations. Available at www.fiscalpolicy.org and www.cssny.org, respectively.

45. R. Doug Lewis, memo on file with author; quote from National Municipal League 1973, 10; Election Center 2001; U.S. General Accounting Office 2001.

46. Merzer and staff 2001, 8.

47. Alan Rothstein, Citizens Union, testimony at public hearing of Joint Committee on Election Law of the New York State Assembly and Senate, March 13, 1984.

48. Gene Russianoff, New York Public Interest Research Group, interview with author, 1994.

49. Wildavsky and Pressman 1973; Sabatier and Mazmanian 1983.

50. Loughlin 1974; Gottlieb and Baquet 1990.

51. Green and Farmer 2003.

52. Public hearing of the Joint Committee on Election Law of the New York State Assembly and Senate, March 13, 1984.

53. Wolfinger 1972; Mayhew 1986; Erie 1988; Thompson 1990; Mollenkopf 1992; Shefter 1994; Ken Fireman's four-part *Newsday* series on elections, 1988; Gottlieb and Baquet 1990.

54. Mollenkopf 1992; Thompson 1990; Shefter 1987, 1994.

55. George Friedman, Bronx Democratic Party Leader, quoted in Gottlieb and Baquet 1990.

56. National Municipal League 1973, 11.

57. Minnite and Callahan 2003; Wade 1994; Plunkett 1992; Smolka 1974; Rapoport 2005; Gene Russianoff, testimony before public hearing of the Assembly Election Law Committee, October 19, 1988.

58. NYPIRG proposed an amendment to the election law, Section 3-204. Gene Russianoff, testimony at public hearing of the New York State Assembly Election Law Committee, October 22, 1987.

59. Rapoport 2005; Wang 2005.

60. The question read: "Do you favor restructuring the Board of Elections to broaden Board membership beyond the two major parties and structure staff to be more professional and less party-based?" The number of respondents was relatively small in relation to the number of candidates running. No breakdown of the number of incumbents versus the number of challengers was available. Linda Stone Davidoff, Executive Director of CUF, memo, August 29, 2002, on file at CUF and with author.

61. Harris 1934, 95.

62. Ibid., 27.

63. Press release of task force on file in governor's office and with author.

64. Gerald Benjamin, address to the New York City Bar Association meeting on November 18, 2002, p. 5 (transcription was provided to the author by the sponsoring organization, the Citizens Union; on file at the Citizens Union).

65. See electionline.org; Center for Policy Alternatives Web site at www.cfpa.org; National Conference of State Legislators www.ncsl.org/programs/legman/elect/taskfc/database.htm.

66. Help America Vote Act, Section 201-210.

67. Rapoport 2005.

68. Pastor 2005.

69. U.S. General Accounting Office 2001.

70. Soudriette 2001, 137; People for the American Way 2004; Common Cause 2004; Demos 2004a; Rapoport 2005; Hayduk and Mattson 2002.

71. Electionline.org. Regarding restoring voting rights to ex-felons, see the Demos Web site at www.demos-usa.org; about efforts to restore or expand voting rights to noncitizens, see www.immigrantvoting.org.

72. Hill and Leighley 1992.

73. Voting Integrity Project at www.votingintegrity.org.

74. Demos 2003.

75. Soudriette 2001, 137.

76. Smolka 2001, 146–51.

77. Office of Senator Hillary Clinton 2005.

78. Hayduk and Mattson 2002.

Selected Bibliography

Books, Articles, and Individual Reports

Abrams, Robert, Arthur J. Fried, Ronald Hayduk, Adam Ross, Paul Melendres, and Jason Tarricone. 2003. *The Help America Vote Act: Impact and Potential for New York*. New York: The Century Foundation. Available at www.reformelections.org /data/reports/help_america_vote.pdf.

Abramson, Paul R., and John H. Aldrich. 1982. "The Decline of Electoral Participation in America." *American Political Science Review* 76:502–21.

Adler, Norman M., and Blanche Davis Blank. 1975. *Political Clubs in New York*. New York: Praeger.

Advancement Project. 2001. "America's Modern Poll Tax: How Structural Disenfranchisement Erodes Democracy." Available at www.advancementproject.org.

Affigne, Anthony DeSales, and Katherine Tate. 1993. "The Limits of Urban Democracy: Voter Turnout, Politics and Race in U.S. Cities." Paper presented at the 1993 Annual Meeting of the American Political Science Association, Washington, D.C.

Alexander, Dealva S. 1909/1969. *A Political History of the State of New York*. 4 vols. New York: Ira J. Friedman.

Allen, Howard W., and Kay Warren Allen. 1981. "Voter Fraud and Data Validity." In *Analyzing Electoral History*, ed. Jerome Clubb, William H. Flanigan, and Nancy Zingale. Beverly Hills, Calif.: Sage.

Alverez, Michael, D. E. Betsy Sinclair, and Catherine H. Wilson. 2002. "Counting Ballots and the 2000 Election: What Went Wrong?" Paper delivered at the Annual Meeting of the Midwest Political Science Association, Chicago, April 26–28.

Argersinger, Peter H. 1985–86. "New Perspectives on Electoral Fraud in the Gilded Age." *Political Science Quarterly* 4 (Winter).

Arian, Asher, Arthur S. Goldberg, John H. Mollenkopf, and Edward T. Rogowsky. 1991. *Changing New York City Politics*. New York: Routledge.

Avey, Michael. 1989. *The Demobilization of American Voters: A Comprehensive Theory of Voter Turnout*. New York: Greenwood.

Barbanel, Josh. 1984. "Voting Board Struggles with Registration Load." *New York Times*, October 4.

Bass, Herbert J. 1961. "The Politics of Ballot Reform in New York State, 1888–1890." *New York History* 42 (no. 3).

Benjamin, Elizabeth. 2003. "Election Reform Process Under Fire." *Times Union* (Albany), April 15, 2003.

Benjamin, Gerald. 1995. "Reforming New York's Constitutional System of Election Administration." In *Effective Government Now for the New Century: The Final Report of the Temporary New York State Commission on Constitutional Revision*. New Paltz: Nelson Rockefeller Institute of Government, State University of New York.

————. 1997. "Reforming New York's Constitutional System of Election Administration." In *Decision 1997: Constitutional Change in New York,* ed. Gerald Benjamin and Henrik N. Dullea. Albany N.Y.: Rockefeller Institute Press.

Bennett, Stephen Earl, and David Resnick. 1990. "The Implications of Nonvoting for Democracy." *American Journal of Political Science* 34:771–802.

Berelson, Bernard R., Paul F. Lazarsfeld, and William N. McPhee. 1954. *Voting: A Study of Opinion-Formation in a Presidential Campaign.* Chicago: University of Chicago Press.

Blais, Andre. 2000. *To Vote or Not to Vote: The Merits and Limits of Rational Choice Theory.* Pittsburgh: University of Pittsburgh Press.

Bloomberg, Michael. 2004. "Mayor Michael Bloomberg's Address on Election Reform." November 10. Available at www.gothamgazette.com.

Brennan Center for Justice. 2004. "Telephone Survey on New York State's Implementation of the Voter Identification Provisions of the Help America Vote Act (HAVA)." Conducted in January and February 2004. Available at www.brennancenter.org/programs/downloads/hava/HAVAID_4-13_04.pdf.

Brewer, Mark David, and Jeffrey Stonecash. 2001. "Political Parties and Elections." In *Governing New York State,* 3rd edition, ed. Jeffrey Stonecash, John Kenneth White, and Peter Colby. Albany: State University of New York Press.

Britt, Donna. 2004. "Ensuring that Voting's Sanctity Wins Out." *Washington Post,* October 1.

Brody, Richard A. 1978. "The Puzzle of Political Participation in America." In *The New American Political System,* ed. Anthony King. Washington, D.C.: American Enterprise Institute.

Bryce, James. 1921. *Modern Democracies.* New York: MacMillan.

Burnham, Walter Dean. 1965. "The Changing Shape of the American Political Universe." *American Political Science Review* 65 (March): 1.

————. 1970. *Critical Elections and the Mainsprings of American Politics.* New York: W. W. Norton.

————. 1974a. "Rejoinder to Comments by Philip Converse and Jerold Rusk." *American Political Science Review* 68 (September).

————. 1974b. "Theory and Voting Research: Some Comments On Converse' 'Change in the American Electorate.'" *American Political Science Review* 68 (September).

Caltech/MIT Voting Technology Project. 2001. "Voting: What Is, What Could Be." Available at www.vote.caltech.edu.

————. 2003. "Update: Where We Have Been, Where We Are Going." January. Available at www.vote.caltech.edu.

Campbell, Angus, Philip E. Converse, Warren Miller, and Donald Stokes. 1960. *The American Voter.* New York: John Wiley.

————. 1965. *Elections and the Political Order.* New York: John Wiley.

Carbo, Steven. 2005. "Color it Wrong." In "Democracy at Risk: A Special Report." *The American Prospect* (January).

Carlson, Richard J., ed. 1974. *Issues of Electoral Reform.* New York: National Municipal League.

————. 1976. *The Effect of Voter Registration Systems on Presidential Election Turnout in Non-Southern States: 1912–1924.* Ann Arbor, Mich.: University Microfilms International.

Cerillo, Augustus, Jr. 1973. "The Reform of Municipal Government in New York City." *The New York Historical Society Quarterly* 57 (no. 1).

Citizens Union Foundation Election Reform Project. 2002. "Making Votes Count." February 2. Available at Citizens Union Foundation of New York.

Citrin, Jack, Eric Schickler, and John Sides. 2003. "What If Everyone Voted? Simulating the Impact of Increased Turnout in Senate Elections." *American Journal of Political Science* 47 (January): 75–90.

Common Cause. 2004. "A Report to Voters: A First Look at the 2004 Election Data." Available at www.commoncause.org.

Conason, Joe. 1995. "Guiliani Does New York: Police Mayor in FIRE City." *The Nation* (December 18).

Congressional Research Service. 2001. "Voting Technologies in the United States," by E. A. Fischer. CRS Report for Congress (RL30773). Available at cnie.org/ NLE/CRSreports/Risk/rsk-55.cfm.

Constitution Project. 2001. "Building Consensus for Election Reform." Available at www.constitutionproject.org.

———. 2002. "Florida Not Alone in Struggle to Balance State and Local Authority over Elections." Joint project with Election Reform Information Project. Available at www.constitutionproject.org.

Converse, Philip E. 1972. "Change in the American Electorate." In *The Human Meaning of Social Change,* ed. Angus Campbell and Philip Converse. New York: Russell Sage Foundation.

———. 1974. "Comment on Burnham's 'Theory and Voting Research'" *American Political Science Review* 68 (September).

Cooper, Michael, and Diane Cardwell. 2001. "Ferrer Doubts Green Victory after Miscount." *New York Times,* October 15.

Cox, Cathy. 2001. "The 2000 Election: A Wake-Up Call for Reform and Change." Atlanta: State of Georgia. February. Available at www.sos.state.ga.us/pressrel /2000_election_report.htm.

Cox, Gary W., and J. Morgan Kousser. 1981. "Turnout and Rural Corruption: New York as a Test Case." *American Journal of Political Science* 25 (November).

Crigler, Ann N., Marion R. Just, and Edward J. McCaffery. 2004. *Rethinking the Vote: The Politics and Prospects of American Election Reform.* New York: Oxford University Press.

Crocker, Royce. 1992. "Voter Registration and Turnout: 1948–1990." Congressional Research Service, Library of Congress, August 11.

Crotty, William J., ed. 1980. *Paths to Political Reform.* Lexington, Mass.: Lexington Books.

Cunningham, Dayna. 1991. "Who Are to Be Electors? A Reflection on the History of Voter Registration in the U.S." *Yale Law and Policy Review* 9 (no. 2).

Dahl, Robert. 1961. *Who Governs? Democracy and Power in an American City.* New Haven: Yale University Press.

Dalton, R. J., and M. P. Wattenberg. 1993. "The Not-So-Simple Act of Voting." In *Political Science: The State of the Discipline II.* Washington, D.C.: American Political Science Association.

Demos: A Network for Ideas and Action. 2003. "Democracy Dispatches" 33. May 14. Available at www.demos-usa.org.

———. 2004a. "Continuing Failures in Fail-Safe Voting." December 6. Available at www.demos-usa.org.

———. 2004b. "Expanding the List of Acceptable ID's." Available at www.demos-usa.org/ HAVA.

———. 2004c. "Placebo Ballots." October 28. Available at www.demos-usa.org.

Denardo, James. 1980. "Turnout and the Vote: The Joke's on the Democrats." *American Political Science Review* 74:406–20.

DiGaetano, Alan. 1988. "The Rise and Development of Urban Political Machines." *Urban Affairs Quarterly* 24 (December).

Dorsett, Lyle W. 1972. "The City Boss and the Reformer: A Reappraisal." *Pacific Northwest Quarterly* 63 (no. 4).

Downs, Anthony. 1957. *An Economic Theory of Democracy.* New York: Harper and Row.

Dugger, Ronnie. 1988. "Counting Votes." *The New Yorker* 64 (November 7): 40.

———. 1995. "Boss Tweed, Hacker." *New York Times,* January 23.

———. 2004. "How They Could Steal the Election This Time." *The Nation,* August 16/23.

Election Center. 2001. "Election 2000: Review and Recommendations by the Nation's Elections Administrators." Available at www.electioncenter.org.

Election Protection Coalition. 2004. "Shattering the Myth: An Initial Snapshot of Voter Disenfranchisement in the 2004 Elections." Available www.pfaw.org.

Election Reform Information Project. 2004. "The 2004 Election." Election Reform Briefing 9. Available at www.electionline.org.

Erickson, Robert S. 1995. "State Turnout and Presidential Voting: A Closer Look." *American Politics Quarterly* 23:387–96.

Erie, Steven P. 1988. *Rainbow's End: Irish Americans and the Dilemmas of Urban Machine Politics, 1840-1985.* Berkeley: University of California Press.

Evans, Eldon Cobb. 1917. *A History of the Australian Ballot System in the U.S.* New York: Columbia University Press.

Federal Elections Commission. 2004. "The Administrative Structure of State Election Offices." Available at www.fec.gov.

Felt, Jeremy P. 1973. "Vice Reform as a Political Technique: The Committee of Fifteen in New York, 1900–1901." *New York History* 54 (no. 1).

Fitch, Robert. 1993. *The Assassination of New York.* New York: Verso.

———. 1995. "'Spread the Pain'? Tax the Gain!" *The Nation* (May 8).

Flick, Alexander C., ed. 1935. *History of the State of New York.* 10 vols. New York: Columbia University Press.

Foderaro, Lisa. 2004. "Judge Hears Testimony of Improper Voting by Poll Workers in a Westchester Race." *New York Times,* December 10.

Fosdick, Raymond B. 1912. "A Report on a Special Examination of the Activities of the Board of Elections in Relation to the Primary Election of March 26, 1912." By the Commissioner of Accounts. Available at the New York City Municipal Archives.

Franklin, Mark N. 1999. "Electoral Engineering and Cross-National Turnout Differences: What Role for Compulsory Voting." *British Journal of Political Science* 29:205–24.

Fuchs, Esther R., and J. Phillip Thompson. 1994. "Racial Politics in New York State." In *Governing New York State,* 3rd edition, ed. Jeffrey Stonecash, John Kenneth White, and Peter Colby. New York: State University of New York Press.

Gerson, Jeffrey. 1990. "Building the Brooklyn Machine: Jewish and Black Succession in the Brooklyn Democratic Party Organization, 1919–1964." Ph.D. diss., CUNY Graduate Center.

Gienapp, William E. 1982. "Politics Seem to Enter into Everything: Political Culture in the North, 1840-1860." In *Essays on American Antebellum Politics, 1840–1860,* ed. Stephen E. Maizlesh. College Station: Texas A&M University Press.

Glass, David, Peverill Squire, and Raymond Wolfinger. 1984. "Voter Turnout: An International Comparison." *Public Opinion* 6:49–55.

Goldberg, Robert. 1987. "Election Fraud: An American Vice." In *Elections American Style,* ed. James A. Reichley. Washington D.C.: Brookings Institution.

Gosnell, Harold G. 1924/1969. *Boss Platt and His New York Machine.* New York: Russell and Russell.

Gottlieb, Martin, and Dean Baquet. 1990. "A Perennial Maze: New York's Election System." *New York Times,* October 18–21.

Governor's Task Force on Election Modernization. 2002. Report on Election Modernization. Office of the Governor of New York and New York State Archives.

Green, Bruce, ed. 1991. *Government Ethics Reform for the 1990s.* New York: Fordham University Press.

Green, John, and Rick Farmer. 2003. *The State of the Parties.* Latham, MD: Rowman and Littlefield.

Green, Mark. 1995. "A Vote of No Confidence: How NYC Is Violating the 'Motor Voter Law.'" October 1. Office of the Public Advocate of New York City.

Griffith, Ernest S. 1974. *A History of American City Government: The Conspicuous Failure, 1870–1900.* New York: Praeger.

Groarke, Margaret. 2000. *Expanding Access to the Vote: An Analysis of Voter Registration Reform in the United States, 1970–1993.* Ph.D. diss., City University of New York.

Hajnal, Zoltan L., and Paul G. Lewis. 2003. "Municipal Institutions and Voter Turnout in Local Elections." *Urban Affairs Review* 38 (May): 645–68.

Hammack, David C. 1982. *Power and Society: Greater New York at the Turn of the Century.* New York: Russell Sage Foundation.

Harris, Joseph P. 1929. *Registration of Voters in the United States.* Baltimore: Lord Baltimore Press.

———. 1934. *Election Administration in the United States.* Washington D.C.: Brookings Institution.

———. 1974. "Election Reform: The Perspective of Forty Years." In *Issues of Electoral Reform,* ed. Richard J. Carlson. New York: National Municipal League.

Hayduk, Ronald. 2002. "The 2001 Elections in New York City." New York: The Century Foundation. Available at www.tcf.org/Publications/ElectionReform/nyc-hayduk.pdf.

Hayduk, Ronald, and Kevin Mattson, eds. 2002. *Democracy's Moment: Reforming the American Political System in the 21st Century.* Lanham, Maryland: Rowman and Littlefield.

Hays, Samuel P. 1964. "The Politics of Reform in Municipal Government in the Progressive Era." *Pacific Northwest Quarterly* 55 (no. 4): 157–69.

Heckelman, Jac C. 1998. "Bribing Voters without Verification." *The Social Science Journal* 35 (no. 3): 435–43.

———. 2000. "Revisiting the Relationship between Secret Ballots and Turnout: A Test of Two Legal-Institutional Theories." *American Politics Quarterly* 28 (April): 194–215.

Herbert, Bob. 2004. "A Chill in Florida." *New York Times,* August 23.

Herlands, William B. 1940. "Administration of the Election Law in New York City." By the Commissioner of Investigations. Available at the New York City Municipal Archives.

Hershkowitz, Leo. 1978. *Tweed's New York: Another Look.* New York: Anchor.

Hicks, Jonathan. 2001. "What Term Limits Have Wrought: A Multitude of Candidates." *New York Times,* September 9.

Hill, Kim Quaile, and Jan E. Leighley. 1992. "The Policy Consequences of Class Bias in State Electorates." *American Journal of Political Science* 36 (May).

Horner, Larry. 1990. "New York City Board of Elections: Accountability Safeguards." NYCEP Oversight Board discussion paper. In New York City Municipal Archives and on file with author.

House Judiciary Committee Democratic Staff. 2005. "Preserving Democracy: What Went Wrong in Ohio." January 5. Available at www.house.gov/judiciary_democrats.

International Institute for Democracy and Electoral Assistance. 2003. "Voter Turnout from 1945 to Date." Available at www.idea.int/vt/survey/ voter_turnout_pop2.cfm.

Issacharoff, Samuel, Pamela S. Karlan, and Richard H. Pildes. 2001. *When Elections Go Bad: The Law of Democracy and the Presidential Election of 2000.* New York: Foundation Press.

Ivins, William. 1887. *Machine Politics and Money in Elections in New York City.* New York: Harper & Brothers.

Jackman, Robert W. 1987. "Political Institutions and Voter Turnout in the Industrial Democracies." *American Political Science Review* 81 (no. 2): 405–23.

Judd, Dennis, and Todd Swanstrom. 2004. *City Politics: Private Power and Public Policy.* New York: Pearson Education.

Karnig, Albert K., and B. Oliver Walter. 1989. "Municipal Voter Turnout during the 1980s: The Case of Continued Decline." Paper delivered at the Annual Meeting of the Midwest Political Science Association, Chicago.

Katz, Celeste, and Michael R. Blood. 2001. "Green Leads by 18,000 Votes in Runoff Count." *Daily News,* October 18.

Kelly, Stanley, Jr., Richard Ayers, and William C. Bowen. 1967. "Registration and Voting: Putting First Things First." *American Political Science Review* 61 (June).

Key, V. O., Jr. 1949. *Southern Politics.* New York: Vintage.

Keyssar, Alexander. 2000. *The Right to Vote: The Contested History of Democracy in the United States.* New York: Basic Books.

———. 2001. "The Right to Vote and Election 2000." In *The Unfinished Election of 2000,* ed. J. N. Rakove. New York: Basic Books.

King, James D. 1994. "Registration Laws and Voter Turnout among the American States." *Publius, The Journal of Federalism* 24 (1994).

Kleppner, Paul. 1982. *Who Voted? The Dynamics of Electoral Turnout.* New York: Praeger.

———. 1987. *Continuity and Change in Electoral Politics, 1893–1928.* Westport, Conn.: Greenwood.

Kleppner, Paul, and Stephen C. Baker. 1980. "The Impact of Voter Registration Requirements on Electoral Turnout, 1900–1916." *Journal of Political and Military Sociology* 8 (Fall).

Knack, Stephen. 1995. "Does 'Motor Voter' Work? Evidence from State-Level Data." *Journal of Politics* 57.

Knack, Stephen, and M. Kropf. 2002. "Who Uses Inferior Voting Technologies?" *Political Science and Politics* 35.

Kraus, Jeffrey. 1988. "The New Bosses: Machines and Electoral Systems in Urban America." Ph.D. diss., CUNY Graduate School.

League of Women Voters Education Fund. 1972a. "Administrative Obstacles to Voting." Monograph. Washington, D.C.: League of Women Voters.

———. 1972b. "Removing Administrative Obstacles to Voting: Before the Election and Beyond." Monograph. Washington, D.C.: League of Women Voters.

Lewis, John. 1974. "Black Voter Registration in the South." In *Issues of Electoral Reform*, ed. Richard J. Carlson. New York: National Municipal League.

Lichtman, A. J. 2001. "Report on the Racial Impact of the Rejection of Ballots Cast in the 2000 Presidential Election in the State of Florida." Washington D.C.: U.S. Commission on Civil Rights. Available at www.usccr.gov.

Lijphart, Arend. 1997. "Unequal Protection: Democracy's Unresolved Dilemma." *American Political Science Review* 91 (March).

Lincoln, Charles Z. 1906. *The Constitutional History of New York*. 5 vols. Rochester, N.Y.: Lawyers Co-Operative Publishing.

———, ed. 1909. *Messages from the Governors*. 9 vols. Albany, N.Y.: J. B. Lyon.

Loughlin, W. P. 1974. "Election Administration in New York City: Pruning the Political Thicket." *Yale Law Review Journal* 84 (no. 1): 61–85.

Lowenstein, Daniel Hays, and Richard L. Hasen. 2001. *Election Law: Cases and Materials*. Durham, NC: Carolina Academic Press.

Lowi, Theodore. 1964. *At the Pleasure of the Mayor*. New York: Free Press.

Martin, Paul S. 2003. "Voting's Rewards: Voter Turnout, Attentive Publics, and Congressional Allocation of Federal Money." *American Journal of Political Science* 47 (no. 1): 110–27.

Mayhew, David. 1986. *Placing Parties in American Politics*. Princeton, N.J.: Princeton University Press.

Mayor's Task Force on Election Modernization. 2001. Report on the New York City Board of Elections. December 21. Office of the Mayor of the City of New York.

McChesney, Robert W. 1999. *Rich Media, Poor Democracy: Communication Politics in Dubious Times*. Chicago: University of Illinois Press.

McCormick, Richard L. 1981. *From Realignment to Reform: Political Change in New York State, 1893–1910*. Ithaca, N.Y.: Cornell University Press.

McCormick, Richard P. 1953. *The History of Voting in New Jersey: A Study of the Development of Election Machinery, 1664–1911*. New Brunswick, N.J.: Rutgers University Press.

McCreary, George W. 1887. *A Treatise on the American Law of Elections*, 3rd ed. Chicago: Callaghan & Co.

McDonald, Laughlin. 2002. "The New Poll Tax: Republican-Sponsored Ballot-Security Measures Are Being Used to Keep Minorities from Voting." *The American Prospect* (December 30).

McDonald, Michael P. 2002. "The Turnout Rate among Eligible Voters for U.S. States, 1980–2000." *State Politics and Policy Quarterly* 2 (no. 2).

McDonald, Michael P., and Samuel Popkin. 2001. "The Myth of the Vanishing Voter." *American Political Science Review* 95 (no. 4): 963–74.

McGerr, Michael E. 1986. *The Decline of Popular Politics: The American North, 1868–1928*. New York: Oxford University Press.

McIntire, Mike. 2004. "Citing Election Problems, Bloomberg Creates Task Force." *New York Times*, November 11.

McNickle, Chris. 1993. *To be Mayor of New York: Ethnic Politics in the City.* New York: Columbia University Press.

McSeveney, Samuel T. 1972. *The Politics of Depression: Political Behavior in the Northeast, 1893–1896.* New York: Oxford University Press.

Merriam, Charles E., and Harold Gosnell. 1924. *Non-Voting: Causes and Methods of Control.* Chicago: University of Chicago Press.

Merton, Robert. 1957/1968. *Social Structure and Social Theory.* New York: Free Press.

Merzer, M., and staff. 2001. *Report of The Miami Herald: Democracy Held Hostage.* New York: St. Martin's Press.

Michael, William H., and William Mack. 1904. *Encyclopedia of Forms and Precedents for Pleading and Practice.* Northport, N.Y.: Cockeroft.

Minnite, Lori, and David Callahan. 2003. "Securing the Vote: An Analysis of Election Fraud." (April). Available at www.demos-usa.org.

Mollenkopf, John Hull. 1987. "The Decay of Reform: One-Party Politics New York Style." *Dissent.*

———. 1991. "Political Inequality." In *Dual City: Restructuring New York,* ed. John Mollenkopf and Manuel Castells.

———. 1992. *A Phoenix in the Ashes: The Rise and Fall of the Koch Coalition in New York City Politics.* Princeton, N.J.: Princeton University Press.

———. 1994. *A Phoenix in the Ashes: The Rise and Fall of the Koch Coalition in New York City Politics,* reprint edition with afterword. Princeton, N.J.: Princeton University Press.

Montjoy, Robert S. 1993. "Implementation and Impact of Voter Registration Outreach Systems in the United States." Paper presented at the Annual Meeting of the Southern Political Science Association, Savannah, Georgia.

Mooney, Brian C. 2004. "Voting Errors Tallied Nationwide." *Boston Globe,* December 1.

Muccigrosso, Robert. 1968. "The City Reform Club: A Study in Late Nineteenth Century Reform." *The New York Historical Society Quarterly* 7 (no. 3).

Myers, Gustavus. 1917. *The History of Tammany Hall.* New York: Boni & Liveright.

Nagel, Jack H., and John E. McNulty. 1996. "Partisan Effects of Voter Turnout in Senatorial and Gubernatorial Elections." *American Political Science Review* 90:780–93.

Nardulli, Peter F., Jon K. Dlager, and Donald E. Greco. 1996. "Voter Turnout in U.S. Presidential Elections: An Historical View and Some Speculation." *Political Science and Politics* 29:480–90.

National Association of Secretaries of State. 2001. "NASS Election Reform Resolution." Available at www.nass.org.

National Center for Policy Alternatives. 1988. "Barriers to Registration and Voting." Mimeo. On file with author.

National Commission on Federal Election Reform. 2001. "To Assure Pride and Confidence in the Electoral Process." Jimmy Carter and Gerald Ford, chairs. New York: The Century Foundation and Miller Center for Public Affairs. Available at www.reformelections.org.

National Conference of State Legislatures. 2001. "Voting in America: Final Report of the NCSL Elections Reform Task Force." Available at www.ncsl.org.

National Municipal League. 1973. *Model Election System.* New York: National Municipal League.

National Task Force on Election Reform. 2001. "Election 2000: Review and Recommendations by the Nation's Elections Administrators." Houston, Tex.: The Election Center, July. Available at www.electioncenter.org.

Newfield, Jack, and Wayne Barrett. 1988. *City for Sale: Ed Koch and the Betrayal of New York*. New York: Harper & Row.

Newfield, Jack, and Paul DuBrul. 1977. *The Abuse of Power: The Permanent Government and the Fall of New York*. New York: Viking.

New York City Elections Project. 1986. "A Vote for Better Service: NYCEP's Proposals to Improve Election Day Operations." April 28. New York City Board of Elections and New York City Municipal Archives.

———. 1987. "A Proposal for a Uniform, Decentralized Election Day Training Program." April 2. New York City Municipal Archives and on file with author.

New York City Elections Project Oversight Board. 1986. "December Status Report to the Oversight Board of the Elections Project." New York City Municipal Archives and on file with author.

New York City Partnership. 1985. *Agenda for Reform of the New York City Board of Elections*. New York: New York City Partnership.

———. 1986. *Status Report of the Agenda for Reform of the New York City Board of Elections, October 1986*. New York: New York City Partnership.

New York City Partnership and New York City Elections Project Oversight Board. 1990. *Modernizing New York's Election System: A Status Report to the Honorable David N. Dinkins, Mayor of the City of New York*. New York: New York City Partnership and New York City Elections Project Oversight Board.

New York Public Interest Research Group. 2002. "Report from the Polls II: A City-Wide Election Survey by Voters, New York City General Election, November 5, 2002." Available at www.nycelectionwatch.org/pollreport02.

———. 2004a. "Heard It at the Board: A Report of the December 7, 2004, New York City Board of Elections Commissioner's Meeting." Available at www.nypirg.org.

———. 2004b. "Right Number, but the Wrong Answer: A Survey of New York's Local Boards of Elections' Answers about New Identification Requirements for Voters." Conducted in March 2004. Available at www.nypirg.org/goodgov/boesurvey/default.html.

New York State Assembly Committee on Election Law. 1988. *Is Anybody in Charge Here?* Albany: New York State Assembly.

Nie, Norman H., Jane Junn, and Kenneth Stehlik-Barry. 1996. *Education and Democratic Citizenship in America*. Chicago: University of Chicago Press.

Office of Attorney General Eliot Spitzer. 2001. "Voting Matters in New York: Participation, Choice, Action, Integrity." Available at www.oag.state.ny.us/press/reports/voting.pdf.

Office of Senator Hillary Clinton. 2005. "Senators Clinton and Boxer, Representative Tubbs Jones, and Others to Unveil Major Election Reform Bill." Press release. February 17.

Office of the New York State Comptroller. 1995. *Report on the New York State Board of Elections*. Albany: Office of the New York State Comptroller.

———. 1996. "Staff Study on New York State's Implementation of and Compliance with the National Voter Registration Act of 1993." Report 95-D-42.

Oliver, J. Eric. 1996. "The Effects of Eligibility Restrictions and Party Activity on Absentee Voting and Overall Turnout." *American Journal of Political Science* 40: 498–513.

Ostrogorski, Moisei. 1902/1964. *Democracy and the Organization of Political Parties*. 2 vols. Garden City, N.Y.: Doubleday.

Palast, Greg. 2003. *The Best Democracy Money Can Buy*. London: Plume/Penguin.

Pastor, Robert A. 2005. "America Observed." In "Democracy at Risk: A Special Report." *The American Prospect* (January).

Pateman, Carole. 1970. *Participation and Democratic Theory.* Cambridge: Cambridge University Press.

Patterson, Thomas E. 2002. *The Vanishing Voter.* New York: Knopf.

Peel, Roy. 1935. *Political Clubs of New York City.* New York: Praeger.

People for the American Way and NAACP. 2004. "The Long Shadow of Jim Crow: Voter Intimidation and Suppression in America Today." August. Available at www.pfaw.org.

Piven, Frances Fox, and Richard A. Cloward. 1979. *Poor People's Movements: Why They Succeed and How They Fail.* New York: Vintage.

———. 1988. *Why Americans Don't Vote.* New York: Pantheon.

———. 2000. *Why Americans Still Don't Vote: And Why Politicians Want It That Way.* Boston: Beacon.

Plunkett, Travis. 1992. "The Case against the State Board of Elections." *Empire State Report* (November).

Powell, G. Bingham, Jr. 1986. "Voter Turnout in Comparative Perspective." *American Political Science Review* 80 (no. 1): 17–43.

Pressman, Jeffrey, and Aaron Wildavsky. 1973. *Implementation.* Berkeley: University of California Press.

Putnam, Robert. 2000. *Bowling Alone: The Collapse and Revival of American Community.* New York: Simon and Schuster.

Rakove, J. N., ed. 2001. *The Unfinished Election of 2000.* New York: Basic Books.

Ranney, Austin. 1983. "Nonvoting Is Not a Social Disease." *Public Opinion* 6, no. 5 (October/November).

Rapoport, Miles. 2003. "Ballot Boxing: Round 1 of Election Reform Took Place in Washington. Now, Round 2 Is Playing Out in the States." *The American Prospect* (May 1).

———. 2005. "The Democracy We Deserve." In "Democracy at Risk: A Special Report." *The American Prospect* (January).

Raskin, Jamin. 2003. *Overruling Democracy: The Supreme Court vs. The American People.* New York: Taylor and Francis.

Reiter, Howard L. 1979. "Why Is Turnout Down?" *Public Opinion Quarterly* 43:297–311.

Riis, Jacob. 1890/1971. *How the Other Half Lives.* New York: Dover.

Rock the Vote. 2004. "Black Student Voter Suppression at Prairie View A&M University: A New Generation Fights Back Against Minority and Student Voter Suppression." Rock the Vote Campus Campaign Prairie View Report, February 23. Available at www.rockthevote.com/rtv_campuscamp_pvreport.php.

Roe, Charlotte, and Henry Maurer. 1974. "The Youth Vote: Difficulties of Extending the Franchise." In *Issues of Electoral Reform,* ed. Richard J. Carlson. New York: National Municipal League.

Rosenbaum, Allan. 1973. "Machine Politics, Class Interest, and the Urban Poor." Paper presented at the Annual Meeting of the American Political Science Association. On file with author.

Rosenfeld, Steven. 2004. "The Perfect Election Day Crime." November 12. Available at www.TomPaine.com.

Rosenstone, Steven J., and John Mark Hansen. 1993. *Mobilization, Participation, and Democracy in America.* New York: Macmillan.

Roth, S. K. 2001. *Disenfranchised by Design: Voting Systems and the Election Process.* Report of a joint project of the American Political Science Association, the

American Psychological Association and the Consortium of Social Science Associations. Available at www.apsanet.org.

Rusk, Jerold G. 1970. "Effect of the Australian Ballot Reform on Split-Ticket Voting, 1896–1908." *American Political Science Review* 64 (December).

———. 1974. "Comment." *American Political Science Review* 68 (September): 3.

Russianoff, G., and D. Palmer. 2001. "Don't Mourn, Monitor." *Gotham Gazette*, September 4. Available at www.gothamgazette.com

Sabatier, Paul A., and Daniel A. Mazmanian. 1983. "Policy Implementation." In *Encyclopedia of Policy Studies*, ed. Stuart S. Nagel. New York: Marcel Dekker.

Sabato, Larry J., and Glenn R. Simpson. 1996. *Dirty Little Secrets: The Persistence of Corruption in American Politics*. New York: Random House.

Sanders, Eli. 2005. "Washington Lawsuit Disputes Results of Race for Governor." *New York Times*, January 8.

Sauerzopf, Richard, and Todd Swanstrom. 1993. "The Urban Electorate in Presidential Elections, 1920–1992: Challenging the Conventional Wisdom." Paper delivered at the Urban Affairs Association Annual Convention, Indianapolis. April.

Saul, Stephanie. 2001a. "City Comes Up Short on Voting Machines." *Newsday*, August 2.

———. 2001b. "Disabled Latch Causes Loss of Some City Prez Votes." *Newsday*, July 22.

———. 2001c. "Ferrer: Voting Rights Act Violated." *Newsday*, November 18.

———. 2001d. "Many Ballots Not Counted in Runoff." *Newsday*, November 18.

———. 2001e. "Runoff's Lost Votes." *Newsday*, November 18.

———. 2001f. "Suffolk Lends a Hand in Election." *Newsday*, October 24.

———. 2001g. "Vote Machine Shortage Left Long Lines at Polls." *Newsday*, April 2.

Saul, Stephanie, and Graham Rayman. 2001. "Mayoral Voting Machine Tally Begins; Sharpton Files Complaint." *Newsday*, October 17.

Sayre, Wallace, and Herbert Kaufman. 1965. *Governing New York City*. New York: W. W. Norton.

Scarrow, Howard A. 1983. *Parties, Elections, and Representation in the State of New York*. New York: New York University Press.

Schaffer, Stephen D. 1981. "A Multivariate Explanation of Decreasing Turnout in Presidential Elections, 1960–1976." *American Journal of Political Science* 25:68–95.

Schattschneider, E. E. 1960. *The Semisovereign People*. New York: Holt, Reinhart & Winston.

Schiesl, Martin. 1977. *The Politics of Efficiency: Municipal Administration and Reform in America, 1800–1920*. Berkeley: University of California Press.

Schlozman, Kay Lehman. 2002. "Citizen Participation in America: What Do We Know? Why Do We Care?" In *Political Science: State of the Discipline*, ed. I. Katznelson and H. Milner. American Political Science Association. New York: W. W. Norton & Company.

Schneier, Edward, and J. Brian Murtaugh. 2001. *New York Politics: A Tale of Two States*. Armonk, N.Y.: M. E. Sharpe.

Schumpeter, Joseph A. 1943. *Capitalism, Socialism, and Democracy*. New York: Harper & Row.

Schwaneberg, Robert. 2004. "Voting Suit Revisits Intimidation Claims: Letters Targeting Ohio Minorities Said to Violate Settlement after Kean-Florio Race in '81." *Newark Star Ledger*, November 1.

Seidman, Harold. 1941. *Investigating Municipal Administration: A Study of the New York City Department of Investigation*. New York: Columbia University, Institute of Public Administration.

Shefter, Martin. 1978. "The Electoral Foundations of the Political Machine: New York City, 1884–1897." In *The History of American Electoral Behavior*, ed. Joel Silbey et al. Princeton, N.J.: Princeton University Press.

———. 1984. "Political Parties, Political Mobilization, and Political Demobilization." In *The Political Economy*, ed. Thomas Ferguson and Joel Rogers. Armonk, N.Y.: M.E. Sharpe.

———. 1985. *Political Crisis/Fiscal Crisis: The Collapse and Revival of New York City.* New York: Basic Books, 1985.

———. 1994. *Political Parties and the State: The American Historical Experience.* Princeton, N.J.: Princeton University Press.

Smith, Ray B., ed. 1922. *History of the State of New York: Political and Governmental,* vol. 3. New York: Syracuse Press.

Smolka, Richard. 1973. *Costs of Administering American Elections.* New York: National Municipal League.

———. 1974. "Need for Performance Standards in Election Administration." In *Issues of Electoral Reform.* New York: National Municipal League.

———. 2001. "Recommendations for Reform." *Journal of Democracy* 12 (no. 2): 146–51.

Soudriette, Richard. 2001. "Promoting Democracy at Home." *Journal of Democracy* 12 (no. 2).

Southwell, Pricilla L., and Justin I. Burchett. 2000. "The Effect of All-Mail Elections on Voter Turnout." *American Politics Quarterly* 28:72–79.

Steinhauer, Jennifer. 2004. "Warning for 2006 Is Seen in Failures at Polls in the City." *New York Times.* November 5.

Stohlberg, Sheryl Gay, and James Dao. 2005. "Congress Ratifies Bush Victory after a Rare Challenge." *New York Times,* January 7

Stonecash, Jeffrey, M. 1994a. "Introduction: Political Conflicts and Their Representation." In *Governing New York State,* 3rd edition, ed. Jeffrey Stonecash, John Kenneth White, and Peter Colby. New York: State University of New York Press.

———. 1994b. "Political Parties and Partisan Conflict." In *Governing New York State,* 3rd edition, ed. Jeffrey Stonecash, John Kenneth White, and Peter Colby. New York: State University of New York Press.

———, ed. 2001. *Governing New York State,* 4th ed. New York: State University of New York Press.

Teixeira, Ruy, A. 1992. *The Disappearing American Voter.* Washington, D.C.: Brookings Institution, 1992.

Thomas, Norman, and Paul Blanshard. 1932. *What's the Matter with New York: A National Problem.* New York: Macmillan.

Thompson, J. Phillip. 1990. "The Impact of the Jackson Campaigns on Black Politics in New York, Atlanta, and Oakland." Ph.D. diss., Political Science Program, CUNY Graduate Center.

Tilden, Samuel J. 1873. *The New York City Ring: Its Origin, Maturity, and Fall.* New York: T. Polhemus.

Tizon, Tomas Alex. 2004. "Lead Shifts in Washington Gubernatorial Vote." *Los Angeles Times,* December 23.

Tolman, William. 1895. *Municipal Reform Movements.* New York: Fleming H. Revell.

Traugott, M. 2004. *Why Electoral Reform Has Failed: If You Build It, Will They Come?* Report of the joint project of the American Political Science Association, the American Psychological Association, and the Consortium of Social Science Associations. Available at www.apsanet.org. Republished in Crigler, Just, and McCaffery 2004.

Trinkl, John. 1984. "Not a Million More Oct. 4, But Still New Voters." *Guardian*, October 17.

Uhlaner, Carole J. 1989. "Rational Turnout: The Neglected Role of Groups." *American Journal of Political Science* 33.

U.S. Commission on Civil Rights. 2001. "The 2000 Presidential Election." Available at www.usccr.gov.

U.S. General Accounting Office. 2001. *Elections: Perspectives on Activities and Challenges across the Nation.* GAO-02-3. October. Available at www.gao.gov/new.items/d023.pdf.

U.S. House of Representatives. 1869. 40th Congress, 3rd Session, Report #41.

U.S. House of Representatives Committee on Government Reform, Minority Office. 2001. "Income and Racial Disparities in the Undercount in the 2000 Presidential Election." August 20. On file with author.

U.S. House of Representatives Committee on the Judiciary, Democratic Investigative Staff. 2001. "How to Make over One Million Votes Disappear: Electoral Sleight of Hand in the 2000 Presidential Election." August 20. Available at www.house.gov/judiciary_democrats/electionreport.pdf.

Verba, Sidney, and Norman H. Nie. 1972. *Participation in America: Political Democracy and Social Equality.* Chicago: University of Chicago Press.

Verba, Sidney, Kay Lehman Schlozman, and Henry E. Brady. 1995. *Voice and Equity: Civic Voluntarism in American Politics.* Cambridge, Mass.: Harvard University Press.

Wade, Richard. 1994. "End the Party at the Board of Elections." *Daily News,* February 20.

Wang, Tova. 2005. "2004: A Report Card." In "Democracy at Risk: A Special Report." *The American Prospect* (January).

Ware, Alan. 1985. *The Breakdown of Democratic Party Organization, 1940–1980.* New York: Oxford University Press.

Wattenberg, Martin P. 1990. *The Decline of American Political Parties: 1952–1988.* Cambridge, Mass.: Harvard University Press.

Weinstein, James. 1968. *The Corporate Ideal in the Liberal State: 1900–1918.* Boston: Beacon.

Werner, M. R. 1928. *Tammany Hall.* Garden City, N.Y.: Doubleday, Doran, and Company.

White, John K. 1994. "Political Conflict in New York State." In *Governing New York State*, 3rd edition, ed. Jeffrey Stonecash, John Kenneth White, and Peter Colby. Albany: State University of New York Press.

Wildavsky, Aaron, and Jeffrey L. Pressman. 1973. *Implementation.* Berkeley: University of California Press.

Will, George. 1983. "In Defense of Nonvoting." *Newsweek* (October 10), 96.

Williams, Timothy. 2004. "New York Election Officials Say Voting Problems Could Persist Next Year." *Newsday,* November 3.

Wolfinger, Raymond. 1972. "Why Political Machines Have Not Withered Away and Other Revisionist Thoughts." *The Journal of Politics* 34.

Wolfinger, Raymond, and Steven Rosenstone. 1980. *Who Votes?* New Haven, Conn.: Yale University Press.

Woods, D., and Hancock, P. *Ballot Disaster Reveals Machines Do Not Accurately Recognize and Tabulate Our Votes.* 2001. Report of the joint project of the American Political Science Association, the American Psychological Association, and the Consortium of Social Science Associations. Available at www.apsanet.org.

Yancey, Roy. 2003. "Voting Machine Maker Hires Top Albany Lobbyist." Gannett News Service, April 24.

Collections of Reports

Asian American Legal Defense and Education Fund. Exit Poll Reports. 1989–2004. AALDEF

City of New York. Annual Reports of the Commissioner of Accounts. New York City Municipal Archives.

Election Administration Reports. 1988–2004. Edited by Richard Smolka.

Election Reform Information Project. "Election Update." Series available at www.electionline.org.

New York City Board of Elections. Memoranda and Annual Reports. 1901–2002. New York City Archives.

New York City Board of Elections Staff. Reports to Commissioners of the Board. 1985–2004. New York City Board of Elections.

New York City Elections Project. Status Reports on the Modernization of the New York City Board of Elections. 1986–1992. New York City Board of Elections and New York City Municipal Archives.

New York City Elections Project Oversight Board. Status Reports. 1985–1995. New York City Municipal Archives and on file with author.

New York City Partnership. Updates and Status Reports on the Modernization of the New York City Board of Elections. 1986–1992. New York City Municipal Archives.

New York City Voter Assistance Commission. Annual Reports. 1993–1994.

New York State Board of Elections. Memoranda and Annual Reports. 1974–2002. New York State Archives.

New York State Commission on Government Integrity. Reports on Elections, Campaign Finance, Ethics, and Government Accountability. 1988–1992.

New York State Legislature, Election Law Committees of the Assembly and Senate. Public Hearings and Reports, 1984 to 2003. New York State Archives.

U.S. Bureau of the Census. Data available at www.census.gov.

Hearings

Joint Committee on Election Law of the New York State Assembly and Senate, March 13, 1984.

Joint Committees on Election Law and Government Operations of the New York State Assembly and Senate, April 14, 2003.

New York City Council Committee on Governmental Operations, October 1993 and February 8, 2001.

New York City Voter Assistance Commission, December 1994 and December 2004.

New York State Assembly Election Law Committee, October 22, 1987; October 19, 1988; and July 28, 1993.

New York State Senate Election Law Committee, July 28, 1993.

Index